THE ELEMENTS OF
SOUL

THE ELEMENTS OF SOUL

A COMPLETE INTRODUCTION TO THE ULTIMATE
BUILDING BLOCKS OF BODY, MIND,
AND CONSCIOUSNESS

A GUIDE TO HIGHER INTELLIGENCE AND LOVE

SAM ADETTIWAR

S.R.I. Publications International
Colorado Springs, CO

Copyright © 2010 by Sam Adettiwar. All rights reserved. No part of this book may reproduced by any mechanical, photographic, or electronic process, or in the form of a phonographic recording; nor may it be stored in a retrieval system, transmitted, or otherwise be copied for public or private use—other than "fair use" as brief quotations embodied in articles and reviews—without prior written permission of the publisher.

The author of this book does not dispense medical advice or prescribe the use of any technique as treatment for physical or medical problems without the advice of a physician, either directly or indirectly. The intent of the author is to offer information of a general nature to help you in your quest for emotional and spiritual well-being. In the event you use any of the information in this book for yourself, which is a constitutional right, the author and the publisher assume no responsibility for your actions.

S.R.I. Publications International

2663 Cinnabar Rd

Colorado Springs, CO. 80921

For information about special discounts for bulk purposes, please contact S.R.I. Publications International at 719-488-0548 or www.soulresearchinstitute.org/publications.html.

Interior design by Booksurge

Cover design by Booksurge

ISBN: 0-9824113-0-8

ISBN-13: 9780982411308

To enlightened masters of the
past, present, and future—you!

Contents

List of Illustrations	*xv*
List of Tables	*xvii*
Acknowledgements	*1*
Preface	*3*

PART I SOUL INTRODUCTION

Chapter 1 What Is Soul?	**11**
Soul	12
Why It Is Important to Understand Soul	14
Consciousness, the First Element of Soul	14
Consciousness, the Ultimate Reality	17
Types of Consciousness	19
Mind, the Second Element of Soul	21
Mental Elements: The Ultimate Building Blocks of Mind	21

Classification of Mental Elements	24
Universal Mental Elements	28
Matter, the Third Element of Soul	30
The Brain	33
Material Elements, the Ultimate Building Blocks of Matter	33

Chapter 2 What Is Not Soul? 39

Reality	39
Non-reality	41
Maya: A Network of Non-reality	43
The Ego: A Non-reality	47
Time: A Non-reality	48
The Non-reality of Ultimate Beginning and End	48
God: A Reality or a Non-reality?	49
The Importance of Understanding Non-reality	50

Chapter 3 What Is Beyond Soul? 53

Enlightenment	53
If You Are Seeking Enlightenment	55

Chapter 4 How Soul Works: A Journey Beyond Quantum Mechanics 57

Soul Mechanics: A New Scientific Frontier	58
Volitional Action: Karma	59
Volitional Force	60
Volitional Energy	62
The First Law of Soul Mechanics: Accountability of Mental Action	65

The Second Law of Soul Mechanics: Mental Action-reaction	66
The Third Law of Soul Mechanics: Perfect Action	68
The Fourth Law of Soul Mechanics: Emptiness and Timelessness	70
What about Choice?	72
What about Desire?	74
What about Chance, Fate, Destiny, and Luck?	78

Chapter 5 Soul Intelligence: A Journey Beyond Emotional and Spiritual Intelligence   81

What Is Intelligence? A Mainstream Perspective	82
Why Soul Intelligence?	84
Redefining Intelligence	85
What about Artificial Intelligence?	87
Levels of Intelligence.	88

Chapter 6 Soul Meditation: A Vehicle for the Journey Beyond   97

What Meditation Really Is	98
Soul Meditation: A Vehicle for Developing Higher Intelligence	99
How to Develop a Lifestyle of Meditation	104
Developing Breath Awareness: A Daily Practice of Soul Meditation	108

PART II   SOUL EXPLORATION

Chapter 7 Exploring the Ultimate Building Blocks of Matter   119

Material Elements	120
Material Elements: A Historic Background	123

The Soul-atom: The Smallest Recognizable Unit of Matter	124
The Soul-atom and String Theory	126
The Soul-atom and the Sound Element	129
I-atom: The Smallest Recognizable Unit of Living Matter	130
Origin of Matter	133
Space and Abstract Elements of Matter	136
So What?	138

Chapter 8 Exploring Consciousness   141

Types of Consciousness	141
The Subconscious	146
Dynamics of Consciousness: The Cognitive Process of Soul	148

Chapter 9   Exploring the Ultimate Building Blocks of Mind   153

Chapter 10 The Universal Mind   157

Sensation	157
Feeling	159
Going Beyond Sensual/Physical Pleasures	162
Going Beyond Pain	163
Feeling vs. Emotion	165
Perception	167
Volition	168
Attention	169
Mental Life	170
How the Universal Mind Works	170

Chapter 11 The Special Mind 173

Thinking 173

Thoughtfulness 174

Rapture (Happiness/Bliss) 176

Concentration 177

Resolution 178

Vigor 179

Bare Desire (Intention/Inclination) 181

How the Special Mind Works 183

Chapter 12 The Unwholesome Mind 187

Greed 187

Hatred 190

Delusion 191

Restlessness 193

Shamelessness 195

Moral Recklessness 195

Conceit 195

Envy 198

Remorse 198

Superstitiousness 199

Suspicion 202

Sloth and Torpor 203

Avarice 205

How Unwholesome Mind Works 206

Chapter 13 The Wholesome Mind 209

Non-greed 209

Non-hatred	212
Mindfulness	213
Mindfulness vs. Concentration	218
Mindfulness: The Foundation for Developing Mental Powers and Eradicating Mental Weaknesses	219
Conscience and Shame	222
Faith	223
Tranquility	227
Lightness	227
Flexibility	228
Pliability	228
Skillfulness	228
Rectitude	229
Equanimity	229
Types of Equanimity	233
How Wholesome Mind Works	236

Chapter 14 The Divine Mind — 239

Loving-kindness	239
Compassion	243
Gladness	245

Chapter 15 The Noble Mind — 247

Noble Action	249
Noble Speech	251
Noble Vocation	252

Chapter 16 The Wise Mind — 255

Non-delusion	255

PART III SOUL REALIZATION
THE ATTAINMENT OF PERFECT INTELLIGENCE

Chapter 17 Developing an Intelligent Attitude — 265

The Virtue of Non-violence — 267
The Virtue of Truthfulness — 268
The Virtue of Non-stealing — 269
The Virtue of Sexual Piety — 271
The Virtue of Non-indulgence — 272
The Virtue of Physical Purity — 274
The Virtue of Contentment — 276
The Virtue of Austerity — 278
The Virtue of Self-study — 280
The Virtue of Surrender — 282
Is It Really Practical? — 284

Chapter 18 Developing Intelligent Senses — 287

Intelligent Eating — 288
Intelligent Touching — 290
Intelligent Smelling — 292
Intelligent Hearing — 293
Intelligent Seeing — 296

Chapter 19 Developing an Intelligent Body — 303

Intelligent Work Habits — 304
Intelligent Exercising — 307
Intelligent Pain Management — 310
Intelligent Management of Emotions and Addictions — 312

Intelligent Breathing	315
A Word of Encouragement	319

Chapter 20 Developing Intelligent Mind — 321

Transcending	321
Concentrating Mind: Experiencing "Zero"	325
Expanding Mind: Experiencing Infinity and Soul	330
Contemplating: Seeing Things as They Are	334

Chapter 21 Developing an Intelligent Heart — 341

Cultivating Loving-kindness	342
Cultivating Compassion	353
Cultivating Gladness	356
Cultivating Oneness	357
The Evolution of Love	359

Epilogue: Enlightened? Now What? — 363

Is It the End of Knowing?	364

Appendix A	Material Elements in Terms of Their Characteristics, Functions, Manifestations, and Proximate Causes	367
Appendix B	The 121 Types of Consciousness	371
Appendix C	Mental Elements in Terms of Their Characteristics, Functions, Manifestations, and Proximate Causes	383
Notes		*393*
Bibliography		*411*
Index		*419*
About the Author		*437*

LIST OF ILLUSTRATIONS

1.1	The elements of soul.	13
1.2	Human experience is the result of consciousness, mind, and body (matter).	16
1.3	Types of consciousness.	20
1.4	The ultimate building blocks of mind: The Chart of Mental Elements.	26 & 27
1.5	The physical support for consciousness includes five sense organs, the heart, and the brain.	32
1.6	The ultimate building blocks of matter: The Chart of Material Elements.	36 & 37
2.1	Types of reality and non-reality.	41
2.2	Tests for identifying reality and non-reality.	43
2.3	Layers of non-reality (maya).	46
4.1	Soul mechanics: volitional force and the karmic phenomena.	60
4.2	Soul mechanics: an analogy.	63
4.3	The four laws of soul mechanics.	72
4.4	Chance, fate, destiny, and luck.	79
5.1	The levels of intelligence.	91
6.1	Soul meditation combines four practices: mindfulness, non-reaction, wise attention, and concentration.	100
7.1	The ultimate reality of matter.	122
7.2	The soul-atom consists of an inseparable bundle of eight material elements.	126
7.3	The smallest "realizable" or "recognizable" unit of water (or any matter) is the soul-atom.	128
7.4	The smallest "realizable" or "recognizable" unit of living matter is the I-atom.	131

7.5	The origin of matter.	135
8.1	Interrelations between functional consciousness and all other types.	145
8.2	The dynamics of consciousness: the cognitive processes of soul.	151
10.1	The universal mind.	158
10.2	Types of feeling. Any human experience can be classified as one of six types.	160
10.3	How emotions occur.	166
11.1	The special mind.	174
11.2	The difference between bare desire, desire, and will.	182
12.1	The unwholesome mind.	188
12.2	The formation of ego.	192
13.1	The wholesome mind.	210
13.2	Seven mental powers and seven mental weaknesses.	221
14.1	The divine mind.	240
15.1	The noble mind.	249
16.1	The wise mind.	256
17.1	Five specific virtues for developing an intelligent attitude towards others.	274
17.2	Five specific virtues for developing an intelligent attitude towards oneself.	284
18.1	Five practices for developing intelligent senses.	300
19.1	Five practices for developing an intelligent body.	320
20.1	Daily practices for experiencing transcendence.	324
20.2	A meditative practice for concentrating the mind.	329
20.3	A meditative practice for expanding the mind.	333
21.1	The four elements of love.	342

LIST OF TABLES

4.1	Unwholesome Actions (To Be Minimized)	75
4.2	Wholesome Actions (To Be Maximized)	76
13.1	Stages of Development of Mindfulness	216
13.2	Mindfulness vs. Concentration	218
13.3	Faith vs. Belief	224
13.4	Levels of Equanimity	233
14.1	Loving-kindness vs. Compassion	244

Acknowledgements

To Babita, Gauri, and Krishna, my best friends and family. Thank you for allowing me to pursue a spiritual path and for providing warmth and encouragement while I was writing this book.

Babita, your sacrifices are huge. Despite being my wife (officially), you have allowed me the freedom to live a monk's life so that I could focus my energies on rigorous spiritual practice and the hobby of spontaneous writing. Your kind acceptance of a simple lifestyle, which has been challenging at times, has made all the difference. It allowed me to close down my companies and to renounce the professional world. Without your unconditional love and support I could not have devoted myself entirely to the spiritual quest that ultimately led to the making of this book.

Gauri, more of a friend than a teenage daughter, your young mind is a miracle of nature. You surprised me with many insights that helped simplify the text, especially while I was writing the Epilogue and designing the book cover. Krishna, more of a buddy than a young son, you continue to impress me with your computer skills. I can never forget how one day you came unexpectedly from nowhere, sat on my lap, and within minutes fixed the digital images I was working on and helped me finalize the book cover.

Dear Father, your English tutoring while I was growing up finally paid off. It was you who planted the seed of writing in me many years ago. Without your support, I never could have become the editor of my school magazine, I never could have won those essay competitions, and most likely I could not have written this book. Also, thank you for setting an example for me by publishing your own book and making inspirational movies. It must have given me the confidence to write and complete my work.

Father, without your courage and risk taking, I could not have left a small Indian town in search of a big dream. It was you who made it possible for me to study science and engineering at the top Indian institutes, which led to my graduate research work in the Untied States. This background has been instrumental in the development of my analytical abilities and a scientific perspective, which came in handy while writing many chapters of this book. I can never thank you enough for tirelessly working for many years and creating the most beautiful place on Earth—our farmhouse in India—out of a barren mountainside. It was here that I spent countless days meditating, contemplating, and confirming the spiritual insights that led to the formation of the core matter of this book.

Dear Brother, although being a national director of a software company, you spent your valuable time with me probing spiritual matters. Those discussions led to the polishing of quite a few passages in this book. Also, I give you full credit for coming up with the book title.

To my editor, Stephanie Gunning: Thank you for helping me transform a lengthy and complicated manuscript into a spiritual literary masterpiece (as I think of it now). You not only edited the book, but also indirectly taught me how to write! Much appreciation. Your spiritual background, combined with honed editorial skills is a blessing for writers like me.

* * *

Preface

Just as you are beginning to read this book in search of the truth, several years ago I began my search, which led to a long journey of self-study and intense spiritual practice that continues to date. On this journey, I was fortunate to experience something extraordinary that I feel is worth sharing with you.

A Personal Story of Awakening

June 21-22, 2005, was the night of the full moon, the last night of a seven-day retreat on the banks of the Indrayani River near Alandi, India. The air was unusually silent except for the soft sound of gentle breezes coursing outside the meditation area, which was flooded with clear, cool moonlight. In the midst of this environment, I was sitting still in deep and prolonged meditation. Then my body was pervaded by bliss. It was an experience of incredible grandeur.

At that moment, I realized that the gentle breezes had transformed into strong winds and were now making whirling sounds. I did not know why the winds had become so strong, but it felt as if there were only those winds and nothing else. There was no sensation of heaviness in my body. There was no feeling of physical presence. No me. There was just awareness of wind.

Suddenly a delightful shiver pierced through me, awakening me to my physical presence. Even though I sensed the body again, it felt weightless and empty. This was peaceful, liberating. As I was experiencing it, I began smiling spontaneously. The smile remained for a long time and simply would not go away. In fact, even though I tried to relax my face, the expression persisted. It was the most pure and natural gesture I had ever been aware of experiencing. It came from the realization that the ultimate mystery of the soul had been solved.

What followed afterwards was amazing. As I was experiencing the peacefulness of liberation, somehow I dropped into a contemplative mode. Questions sped like a blazing inferno through my mind along with literal flashes of answers. Many years of contemplation and meditative effort were rewarded in those moments. Most interesting to me was the wonderful sequencing and rhythmic pace that the questions and answers took.

A question would arise in my mind and immediately an answer would appear for it, as if there was nothing separating them. It felt like countless mental knots were opening up and then the ropes were vanishing, one after the other. It actually felt as if the heaviness of mind was being evaporated as these tangled concepts were releasing and dissolving.

Sitting amidst the whirling winds in the meditation room by the banks of the Indrayani on that auspicious moonlit night, I knew for sure that all the answers to my questions about the soul, the self, and the world had been delivered to me in a single rush. I knew with absolute certainty what I knew. I also felt that what I knew in that moment must be true beyond doubt. I had never felt such confidence and certainty about anything before. It was the peak moment of my life.

I was awakened!

Call it what you want. No matter what, words don't fit the bill. Moments of realization cannot actually be labeled. Nor is it important to do so.

How This Book Came to Be

Since the night of my awakening, I have never forgotten the answers that were revealed to me. I soon discovered that I had developed the ability to pose any spiritual question and have the answer revealed instantly in my mind. For certain, my transformation occurred due to years of persistence in practicing the highly influential teachings of the Buddha, an ancient enlightened master (living roughly around 500 B.C.E.) who was the source of teachings contained in the Tipitaka, and Patanjali, an Indian sage (living roughly around 300 B.C.E.), known for being the compiler of the Yoga Sutras.[1]

Having reached the level of purified intellect, I subsequently developed intense compassion and a desire to help guide the spiritual journey of others. I began writing down everything about that initial flood of questions and answers. Often when I was writing, it felt as if I was not able to stop. Writing simply went on for quite some time, as I recorded on paper whatever came to mind. On occasions when the flow of information did not spontaneously occur, I would ask a question or two and it would start again. Like that, I wrote several modules of question-answers at different times on various topics. Later, I added sub-topics to simplify and make the concepts more easily graspable by a larger number of people. I then removed the question-answer format to make it sound more like a discussion, and re-edited it so that it would encompass a gradual process through a practical series of meditations. What resulted from these efforts is this book, which I now present to you.

Based on the most purified and perfected spiritual knowledge available to me, I hope many readers will appreciate this book as a definitive guide on how to awaken to the ultimate reality of the soul and apply this ultimate knowledge to generate real happiness and peace for themselves and for others. My intention is also to provide the non-religious, non-spiritual community of health care practitioners, personal growth experts, philosophers, psychologists, life coaches, scientists, and modern evolutionary thinkers an authoritative source for understanding the ultimate building blocks of the soul, so that the ultimate human power—*perfect intelligence*—is awakened. Perfect intelligence is the highest level of intelligence, which arises through soul realization. Otherwise known as *soul intelligence*, it ranks higher than IQ, emotional intelligence (popularly known as EQ), and spiritual intelligence (SQ). Perfect intelligence is synonymous with mental perfection, pure awareness, enlightenment, nirvana, and so on. As such, these terms are used varyingly throughout the book to mean the same thing.

This book is the outcome of years of ardent and consistent spiritual practice on my part. You may find the ideas I am sharing with you frustrating, exhausting, intimidating, or even frightening at times. No matter how you feel about them, I guarantee that if you take whatever you need from my spiritual discoveries and continue to practice these techniques wisely until you make them your own, you will come closer to awakening and the attainment of perfect intelligence. How close you get and whether or not you ever arrive depends upon you.

It is the process of living our lives in search of perfection that matters, not whether or not we can call ourselves enlightened masters. Fortunately, we now have a tool (this book) not just to live happily, but also to live perfectly.

* * *

Part I
Soul Introduction

Let us now begin a journey of self-purification and perfection—a journey I am confident that you will find most rewarding. This journey begins with an introduction to the phenomenon of soul.

Any subject matter is not understood thoroughly unless we understand what it is as well as what it is *not* and what is *beyond* it. In chapter 1, you will come to understand what soul is in terms of its three key elements: consciousness, mind, and body.

In chapter 2, you will be introduced to how these three key elements constitute a reality and how everything else (concepts and mental constructs) constitutes non-reality. You will learn that what is not real is not soul. Also you will learn why it is so important to understand what is not soul.

Then, in chapter 3, you will be invited to comprehend the phenomenon of enlightenment—that which lies beyond soul.

Having been introduced to the nature of soul in the first three chapters, in chapter 4 you will discover how soul works. Concepts explored there will take you on a journey beyond quantum mechanics. These include the mechanics of soul, volitional energy, the phenomenon of karma, free will, choice, fate, destiny, luck, and so on.

You will study the phenomenon of intelligence and learn what soul intelligence is in chapter 5. In addition, I will explain why the development of soul intelligence is crucial for attaining perfection.

In chapter 6, you will learn a unique meditation technique called *soul meditation*, which serves as a vehicle for the development of the state of higher intelligence known as *meditativity*. Once you have developed meditativity, you will be ready to further explore the phenomenon of soul in Part II.

* * *

Chapter 1

What Is Soul?

Have you ever wondered who you are? When you look in the mirror, do you ever ask who the person reflected there is? If you do, and if you begin to contemplate your true nature, you'll go through a process of realization that will eventually lead you to the deepest possible answer to the question "Who am I?" First, you'll realize that you have a body (a material structure that sees, hears, tastes, smells, and feels). Second, you'll realize that you have a mind that feels the body, perceives the world, and thinks. If you are persistent and lucky, you may also realize that you are actually *experiencing* the body and the mind. This third, experiential aspect is consciousness.

Next, the following three realities will dawn upon you:
1. Body, mind, and consciousness are not separate. Your body cannot function without your mind. Your mind cannot function without your body. And you cannot have an experience

without possessing a body-mind, which means there is no consciousness without the body and mind. In other words, body-mind-consciousness is a single bundle composed of three interconnected and mutually-functioning components.
2. Body, mind, and consciousness are not fixed components, but constantly changing. The body grows and then ages. The mind fluctuates between happiness and sadness, from attentiveness to distraction, and so on. Whatever can be experienced through body and mind doesn't last forever. No matter what you do, your experiences change. None remains the same.
3. Because body, mind, and consciousness are observable *and* experiential, they are a phenomenon or a process, or—if you like—a group of phenomena or processes. Body is a material phenomenon. Mind and consciousness are non-material (mental) phenomena.

So far so good!

Then will come the tricky part. Because the experience of body-mind-consciousness is so intimate, it is easy—almost natural—to perceive the body as *your* body, mind as *your* mind, and consciousness as *your* consciousness. If you're like everyone else, with the rare exception of sages, you have ended up attaching yourself to the phenomena of body-mind-consciousness.

Soul

There is no such thing as your body, your mind, or your consciousness. There is only body-mind-consciousness, a unified phenomenon. This unified phenomenon is what *soul* really is. I humbly invite you to consider this possibility as I present my case in this book. In doing so, I promise you will eventually experience immense spiritual joy, a rapturous feeling of deep understanding.

Soul is simply a term used to denote an impermanent, impersonal phenomenon arising from the interaction of body (matter), mind, and

CHAPTER 1 WHAT IS SOUL?

consciousness. Soul is not something that belongs to any one person. It does not to you or me, or to anyone else.

Figuratively speaking, just as the elements of hydrogen and oxygen interact with each other to generate water ($h_2 0$), matter, mind, and consciousness interact with one other to generate the soul. While soul is obviously not a substance like water, its presence is dependent on matter, mind, and consciousness in the same way that water is dependent on the elements hydrogen and oxygen for its existence. To be precise, the existence of soul, as you will soon discover, is dependent on 28 elements of matter, 52 elements of mind, and 121 types of consciousness (see figure 1.1).[1]

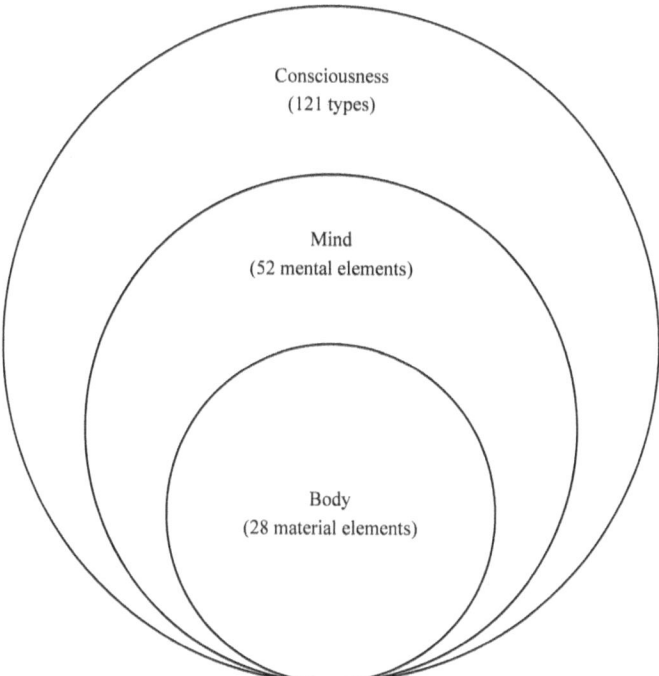

Figure 1.1. The elements of soul: body (matter), mind, and consciousness.

As a reality that continuously and rapidly arises and subsides, the phenomenon of body-mind-consciousness creates an illusion of a separate individual if its unified nature is not understood as soul. This illusion is the "ego" —the source of attachment.

Ego is the perception, "I am . . . some person separate from others," "I am an individual apart from others," "I am a separate *self* who *own*s this particular body, mind, and consciousness," and so forth.

Why It Is Important to Understand Soul

The ego separates us by hiding the reality of soul. It makes us ignorant. It keeps us from experiencing the world in its full, unified grandeur. It imprisons us by deluding and delimiting our intellect, thereby generating attachment, stress, pain, and a sense of imperfection and dissatisfaction. When we understand soul, our intelligence is purified and perfected, and ignorance is eradicated. When ignorance is eradicated, the ego dissolves and what arises naturally is everlasting happiness and peace. Understanding soul solves the problem of human suffering thoroughly and perfectly, because it eradicates the *root cause*: ignorance, the ego.

Right now, you may have a strong point of view about the concept of perfection and intelligence. Throughout this book I hope to guide you to expand your perspective and crack open the door to your ultimate potential, which is the attainment of *perfect intelligence.*

With that in mind, let us now embark upon the journey of understanding the soul—our soul journey—starting with an introduction of its elements.

Consciousness, the First Element of Soul

Fundamentally, consciousness can be defined as the phenomenon of knowing, cognizing, or experiencing.

Consciousness is that activity which knows or becomes aware of an object. It is the act of knowing. At the level of pure consciousness, there is no knower behind knowing. In other words, there is no knower separate from knowing. Knowing knows. Similarly, there is no seer behind seeing. Seeing sees. In this way, consciousness should be understood strictly as a phenomenon without any doer, actor, or agent performing it.

When we see an object, no person is seeing an object. Seeing is simply a phenomenon that can be understood as *eye consciousness.*

CHAPTER 1 WHAT IS SOUL?

When we hear sound, there is no person hearing. Hearing is simply a phenomenon that can be understood as *ear consciousness*. In an ultimate sense, all types of sensing and experiencing (encompassing seeing, hearing, smelling, touching, tasting, and thinking/knowing) can be understood as the phenomena of consciousness.

Consciousness cannot exist or arise by itself. It always arises alongside and is conditioned by mind and matter. This is a profound law of the universe.

Eye consciousness cannot occur without the presence of a physical eye (the matter) and the volition to see (the mind). Consciousness cannot see by itself. Otherwise you would be able to see through the walls of your home, since consciousness is distinct from both the senses and material resistance.

Just as consciousness cannot see without the physical eye, the physical eye cannot see without consciousness. An eye has no thought, no volition, and no desire to see. Nor does a physical eye have any way of knowing. When consciousness arises with the support of our physical eye and volition, we are able to see. Three distinct phenomena of consciousness, mind, and matter must arise together to constitute an experience of seeing, hearing, touching, tasting, smelling, or thinking. Consciousness, however, is the forerunner of all of these activities.

From the realm of matter, the physical eye consists primarily of two types of matter: non-organic matter and organic matter. Non-organic matter (not to be confused with *inorganic* matter) is known as *eye sensitivity*. Organic matter is known as the biological eye (all its components, including the eyeball, retina, nerves, and so on). Eye sensitivity is not something that can be detected under a microscope. It is *subtle* eye matter. Without it, a physical eye cannot function even if the eye is perfectly healthy, as in the case of a blind person by birth.

From the realm of mind, volition consists of a will or a desire to see. In order to see—to have the human experience of seeing—eye consciousness, eye sensitivity, at least one biological eye, and volition must arise together and be united. In short, there is no consciousness without mind-matter, no mind without consciousness-matter, and no matter without consciousness-mind.

Here is an analogy. An electric light bulb is made of a filament, a glass enclosure, and an inert gas contained within the enclosure. It glows when someone turns on a switch that provides it with electricity. It would fail to glow if there were no electric current, no filament, no inert gas, or no glass enclosure. All four of these components must be present for the phenomenon of an electric light bulb to be lit. In this analogy, consciousness is like the electric current, the mind is the volition or desire to turn on the switch, the non-organic or subtle matter is like the inert gas, and the organic matter is like the filament and glass enclosure.

Of the three elements of soul, consciousness resembles a head of state, for instance the president of a country, and mind and matter are like that president's cabinet member and soldier, respectively. Just as the president could not function without cabinet members and soldiers, consciousness does not function without mind and matter (see figure 1.2).

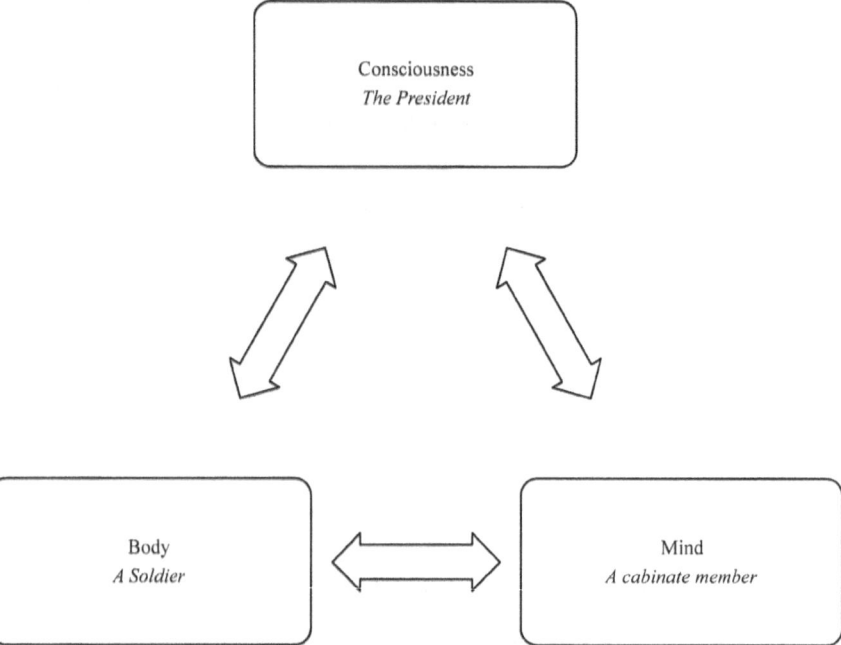

Figure 1.2. In the domain of human experience, consciousness serves as the president, mind as a cabinet member, and the body as a soldier. All human experiences occur when the elements of soul arise together and act interdependently.

CHAPTER 1 WHAT IS SOUL?

The phenomenon of consciousness is in a continuous state of flux. However, it is arising and ceasing with such immense rapidity that it creates a false impression of continuity and permanence. When "seeing" occurs, we feel that we are seeing because of our ignorance and this false impression. This illusion emerges with everything that we experience.

The flow of consciousness is similar to the flow of a river. The continuity of flowing water creates an illusion of one entity, a river moving from one location to another. We give this illusion an identity, such as the Mississippi River, the Nile, or the Ganges. The underlying reality is not the Nile, Mississippi, or Ganges, but the flow of water, a phenomenon of coming and going of water.

The flow of consciousness is also analogous to a lit candle. When a candle is burning, light energy arises and ceases at such rapid rate that it looks as if the candle is a giver of light. But in fact, it is the phenomenon of arising and ceasing energy that is responsible for the experience of light. While the flux in this analogy is consciousness, the candle represents the material reality that is present and the flammability represents the mental reality that is present.

Consciousness, the Ultimate Reality

Analytically, consciousness is the ultimate component of human experience. Our experience cannot be reduced further into any subtler reality. Whatever reality exists beyond consciousness cannot be experienced in the normal sense (meaning with the body or with the mind), as it is *beyond experience*. Thus, the phenomenon of consciousness is the ultimate essential component or reality of the soul. It is, however, a non-absolute ultimate reality because without the presence of mind and matter it does not arise in the realm of human existence.

As the ultimate reality of soul, consciousness is the ultimate object of both experience and knowledge. Beyond consciousness, nothing remains to be known. Consciousness is the *supreme* object of knowledge in an investigation. And although it is inseparable from mind and matter, it also exists by reason of its own intrinsic nature, which is distinct from mind and matter. That is why it is possible to know consciousness directly through experience. Hence, consciousness is the *correct* object of knowledge in an investigation.

Knowing consciousness directly through experience means experiencing it as *it is* and not knowing it through reading, studying, or thinking. There is nothing superior to experiencing consciousness as it is. Everything else falls into the realm of thought.

Here's an example. If you were investigating the taste of mango, the experience of mango taste would be the supreme object of knowledge in that investigation. Reading a book about the taste of mango, referring to an encyclopedia, or discussing the flavor with others and finding out that it is sweet cannot bring you the experience of the mango flavor. When you actually eat a mango and experience its sweetness, you'll have no confusion about what mango is.

Experiential knowledge is beyond thought because it is simply an experience. Sweetness is a name—a verbal construction—used to communicate the experience. Once the actual taste, the ultimate reality, is experienced, nothing remains to be investigated. That's pure knowledge. In writing *The Elements of Soul* I am attempting to guide you to have pure knowledge of who you are.

You could call the experiential knowledge of mango *taste consciousness* or something else. The point I am making is this: Any knowing, knowledge, cognition, or experience is essentially a phenomenon of consciousness and it is the ultimate reality.

Is it possible that there is an experiencer behind the experience? No. Experience is the arising and ceasing of consciousness in extreme rapidity. If you feel that *you* are someone tasting mango, then you are creating an "I" (the ego) out of the perception of continuity. The feeling of "I-ness" simply occurs because of not knowing that the experiencing of taste is taste consciousness.

When the feeling of "I-ness" occurs many times over, it becomes a mental pattern, a deep mental impression, or a memory. These types of mental construction influence or condition the consciousness unwholesomely and unprofitably, as will be shown later in this chapter. Genuine spiritual practices primarily focus on processes for

CHAPTER 1 WHAT IS SOUL?

the removal of this sense of I-ness or ego, as purification of mind ultimately leads to understanding and experiencing soul.

Around now you could be wondering if it is possible that consciousness itself is a universal being, a fixed entity that experiences or knows everything. No. Consciousness is not a being that performs the act of knowing. It is not a universal intelligence or an almighty figure in the conventional sense. It is a simply a *phenomenon* of cognition, an experience of awareness.

If you contemplated the examples of a light bulb, a river, and a candle, you would realize that if consciousness were a fixed entity, then you would never get an electric bill, there would never be changing water levels in the river, and the candle could never be exhausted.

Throughout this book, we will always approach consciousness as a phenomenon, as a flow, like the flow of a river, rather than as a fixed entity.

Types of Consciousness

Foremost, consciousness is a phenomenon of experience. However, depending upon the uniqueness, the utility, the manifestation, and the immediate cause of a given experience we could say that there are many kinds of consciousness we are capable of experiencing. As we have discussed, eye consciousness is the experience of seeing. This experience is functional and manifests as vision when the physical visual apparatus of a human body is sufficiently close to an object of vision. Depending upon the nature of the mind that arises with it, many types of consciousness can arise along with eye consciousness.

If the nature of your mind were hateful, then the consciousness that arises in you would be unwholesome consciousness. If the nature of your mind were compassionate, then the consciousness that arises in you would be wholesome consciousness. The ethical quality of the mind that arises gives us our two primary types of consciousness: wholesome and unwholesome. The fruit or consequence of these two ethically-variable consciousnesses gives us a third primary type of consciousness: resultant consciousness. Then there is an ethically-neutral type of consciousness: functional consciousness.

THE ELEMENTS OF SOUL

Right now we're laying groundwork. Although we will use this classification system to understand the technicalities or the mechanics of soul, remember that it is a basic system. Unwholesome, wholesome, resultant, and functional consciousness cannot be strictly defined in separate categories. For example, wholesome consciousness can also be wholesome-resultant or wholesome-functional consciousness, and so on. Thus, considering all the various possible combinations of the four primary types of consciousness, up to 121 kinds of consciousness can be derived.[2] The only exception is that wholesome and unwholesome consciousness cannot be combined (see figure 1.3).

The fact that there are 121 types of consciousness does not mean that we have only 121 types of experience. If you combine various types of mental and material elements with various types of consciousness *and* numerous conditions that exist between the three phenomena of soul you will find that our experiences can be numbered in the hundreds of thousands.[3]

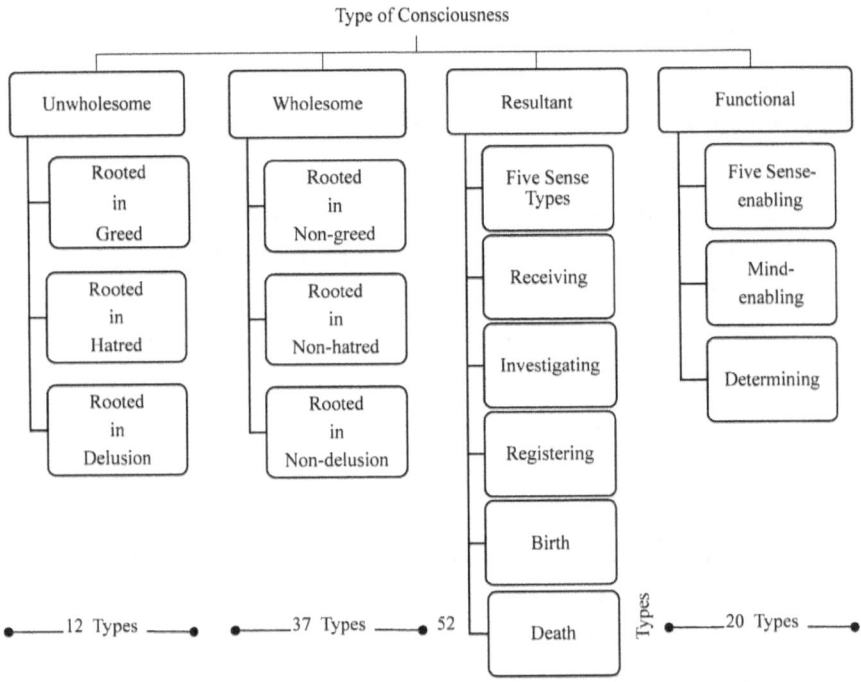

Figure 1.3. Types of consciousness: Four primary types and 15 subtypes give rise to a total of 121 sub-subtypes of consciousness. All partake in the phenomenon of cognition.

Whatever classification system you use, it's important to understand that there is no single consciousness behind all the others. No permanent, universal consciousness, almighty-father consciousness, universal-mother consciousness, or eternal consciousness exists. Many different types of consciousness are rapidly arising and passing away, thereby creating the phenomena of continuous existence. Note that all types arise and pass away.

Mind, the Second Element of Soul

If we look at a beautiful flower and then feel pleasant, we might exclaim, "That flower is so beautiful!"

The element of soul that sees the flower is consciousness. The element of soul that feels, perceives, thinks, judges, or qualifies the flower as "pleasant" and "beautiful" is mind.

Principally, mind can be defined as a non-material phenomenon made up of various *mental elements* that assist consciousness in the process of cognition by imparting qualities to the consciousness that is present. Feeling, perceiving, and thinking are some of the mental elements that make it possible for consciousness to know the flower as a flower that is beautiful and pleasant. The same is true for knowing anything else in the world.

Mind always arises and ceases together with consciousness. Mind always experiences the same object as consciousness. Just as the President of the United States could not manage the affairs of the nation without a cabinet, consciousness cannot rule its domain without mind. Consciousness cannot perform the function of cognition without mind.

Mental Elements: The Ultimate Building Blocks of Mind

Mind is really nothing other than a bundle of mental elements. Each mental element is a distinct mental phenomenon, a process or a flow. Feeling is a distinct mental phenomenon. Perception is a distinct mental phenomenon. Thinking is a distinct mental phenomenon. Other examples of mental elements are attention, greed, hatred, delusion, faith, compassion, loving-kindness, and so on. These combine with various types of consciousness to produce different human experiences.

Mental elements, such as feeling, perception, and attention, assist consciousness in essential cognitive functions such as feeling objects, perceiving objects, and attending to objects in order that they can be known through cognition. Mental elements, such as greed, hatred, and compassion, assist consciousness in ethical cognitive functions such as liking or disliking an object. When mental elements arise together (for example, hatred arising along with perception) the resulting cognition becomes hateful. When compassion arises together with perception, it assists consciousness in compassionately knowing the object of perception. In this manner, mind conditions or colors consciousness through various combinations of mental elements, which give rise to a variety of wholesome (good), unwholesome (bad) experiences, and neutral experiences.

Imagine you are in a flea market and spot a wallet lying abandoned on the ground. If greed arises at the moment you see the wallet, you will consider it an easy source of money. Here, a simple act—seeing a wallet—is colored by the mental element of greed and becomes a desire for easy money. If compassion and non-greed arise instead of greed, then the wallet becomes known as a cause of concern for its owner. It does not give rise to a desire for easy money.

In the first example, consciousness is conditioned into an unwholesome state. In the second example, consciousness is conditioned into a wholesome state.

Note that the two states cannot coexist. Either consciousness is wholesome or it is unwholesome. You may experience wanting to keep the money and you may also experience wanting to give it back to the owner. But this does not mean that the wholesome and unwholesome states are coexisting. It simply means that the wholesome state is rapidly arising and passing away followed by the unwholesome state rapidly arising and passing away. The wholesome and unwholesome states are alternating.

Depending upon the strength or potency of mental elements (greed versus non-greed) that are arising in consciousness, you will either take the wallet or give it back to its rightful owner.

CHAPTER 1 WHAT IS SOUL?

Your current state of consciousness depends upon your mental activity—the nature of mental elements that are arising in consciousness. If you saw a dirty, destitute person begging at a railway station, you might consider his appearance "disgusting" if the mental element of hatred arose in consciousness. But if the mental element of loving-kindness arose instead, your cognition would be different. Because of the element of loving-kindness, most likely you would consider the beggar as a lovable individual in desperate need of assistance.

Of course, the preceding examples are highly simplified versions of what happens. In reality, whenever consciousness arises, numerous mental elements arise with it. Several mental elements would arise with eye consciousness at the moment of seeing a wallet. Greed does not arise by itself. It always arises with elements of sensation, feeling, perception, volition, attention, delusion, restlessness, shamelessness, moral recklessness, and so on. Out of these numerous mental elements, greed and delusion act as the most prominent elements. While assisting consciousness in the process of cognition, each of these prominent elements is like a chief cabinet member of the president. All other mental elements function like lower level cabinet members.

Mental elements are distinct realities with their own intrinsic natures. Just as fire is intrinsically hot and water intrinsically wet, a mental element of hatred is intrinsically unwholesome and a mental element of non-hatred (or loving-kindness) is intrinsically wholesome. However, mental elements are not matter and do not have physical natures. They also are not energy modules, electromagnetic fields, or anything like that. They are without identity, and being non-physical they are without boundary. In addition, they are impersonal. They do not belong to any individual or entity. In fact, mental elements are ultimate realities, meaning they cannot be evaluated further than their own intrinsic natures. Because they are ultimate and impersonal we use the word "element" to denote their phenomenal nature.

As we saw earlier, because consciousness has its own intrinsic nature it is considered an ultimate reality. Similarly, because mental elements have their own intrinsic natures, they are considered ultimate realities.

Through investigation, it is possible to discover and know the mental elements as distinct in the same way that chemists and physicists can reduce matter to the elements of the periodic table (hydrogen, oxygen, carbon, iron, and so on). All of the elements appearing on the periodic table (material substances) have their own intrinsic nature.[4]

The elements of the periodic table can be studied and known through external observation. However, that is not the case with mental elements since no matter is involved in mind. The only way to discover and know mental elements directly and thoroughly is through experience. So, if you want to understand mind, meditation is necessary, as it facilitates experience. External observation does not suffice. That is why meditation is explored as a primary tool for understanding mind in this book.

Classification of Mental Elements

Just as chemical scientists have discovered a total of 118 elements of matter (as noted on the periodic table), ancient "spiritual scientists" —the enlightened masters Buddha and his foremost disciples—discovered a total of 52 elements of mind.[5]

Mental elements are subtle and the differences between them can be even subtler. Therefore, they are delimited using the following criteria.[6]

- *Characteristics*: The most unique and prominent qualities of the element
- *Functions*: The performance of specific tasks by the element
- *Manifestations*: The ways that the element is experienced
- *Proximate causes*: The main conditions leading to the occurrence of the element

Depending upon the four preceding criteria, I have classified the 52 mental elements into seven categories of mind, as shown on The Chart of Mental Elements (see figure 1.4 on page 26 and 27).

CHAPTER 1   WHAT IS SOUL?

- *Group I*: The universal mind (elements 1–6)
- *Group II*: The special mind (elements 7–13)
- *Group III*: The unwholesome mind (elements 14–27)
- *Group IV*: The wholesome mind (elements 28–45)
- *Group V*: The divine mind (elements 46–48)
- *Group VI*: The noble mind (elements 49–51)
- *Group VII*: The wise mind (element 52)

It is utterly impossible to thoroughly understand mind without experiencing all 52 of these mental elements, which are the ultimate building blocks of mind. But for now, as an example, let us briefly look at the universal mental elements to get a taste of how we are going to prepare the ground for understanding mind.

THE ELEMENTS OF SOUL

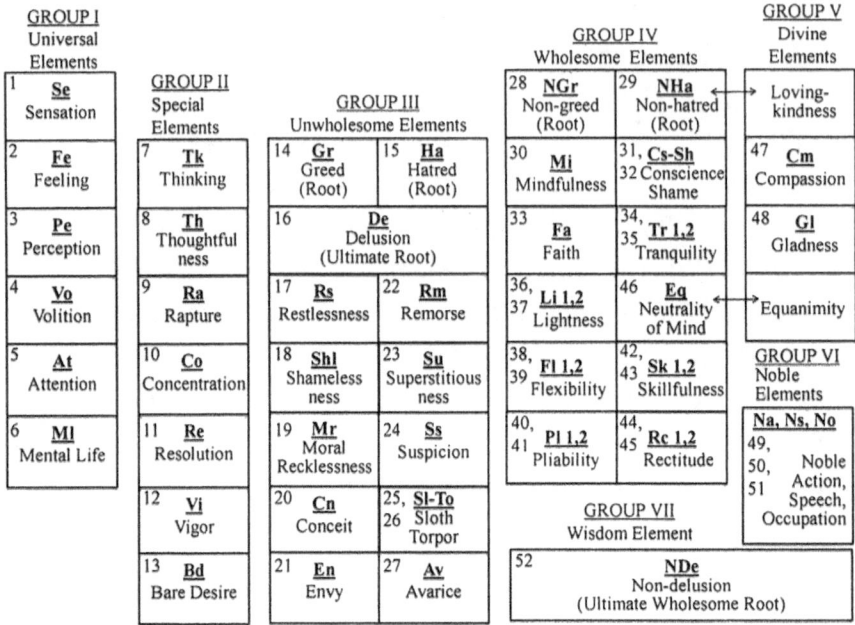

i. Six universal elements always arise together as a group (1-6). They are present in all mental activities.
ii. Special elements (7-13) are ethically neutral. When they arise along with greed (14) or hatred (15), they become unwholesome. When they arise along with Non-greed (28) or Non-hatred (29), they become wholesome.
iii. Four unwholesome elements always arise together as a group (16-19).
iv. Greed (14) or Hatred (15) can not arise by itself. It is always accompanied by elements 16-19.
v. Delusion (16) is ultimately responsible for all unwholesome mental activities.
vi. Sloth and Torpor (25-26) are twin elements. Conscience and Shame (31-32) are pair elements.
vii. In varying degrees of intensity, nineteen wholesome elements (28-46) always arise together as a group. They are present in all wholesome mental activities.
viii. Tranquility (34, 35) are pair elements. Tr1 primarily refers to tranquility of the mind. Tr2 primarily refers to tranquility as a distinct element present within that mind. So is the case with other five pairs (36-45).
ix. Loving-kindness is a highly evolved form of Non-hatred (29). Therefore, element number is not assigned.
x. Equanimity is a highly evolved form of neutrality of mind (46). Therefore, element number is not assigned.
xi. Non-delusion (52) is ultimately responsible for the occurrence of all wholesome, divine, and noble mental activities. Therefore, it is shown as their base.
xii. Just as a chemical substance is made of various elements of the periodic table, a mental activity (such as a thought or an emotion) is made of various mental elements of the chart above. Some examples:

Craving, Lust = 14 + (16-19) + (1-6) + some of special elements (7-13)
Anger, Fear = 15 + (16-19) + (1-6) + some of special elements (7-13)
Happiness = 9 + (1-6) + some of special elements (7, 8, 10-13)
Generosity = 28 + (1-6) + (29-46) + some of special elements (7-13)
Empathy = 47 + (1-6) + (28-46) + some of special elements (7-13)
Awakening = 52 + (1-6) + (10-13) + (28-46)

Figure 1.4: The Chart of Mental Elements illustrating the ultimate building blocks of mind. These elements arise in groups giving rise to various mental activities.

THE ELEMENTS OF SOUL

1	Se	**Sensation:** That which facilitates contact (touch) between senses and object.
2	Fe	**Feeling:** That which feels the sensed object as unpleasant, pleasant, or neutral.
3	Pe	**Perception:** That which interprets, recognizes, and identifies the felt object.
4	Vo	**Volition:** That which provides direction and gives ethical quality to perceived object.
5	At	**Attention:** That which takes on the direction provided by volition and guides the mind.
6	Ml	**Mental Life:** That which provides sustenance and maintenance to the mind.
7	Tk	**Thinking:** That which builds on attention to unfold and unravel the object.
8	Th	**Thoughtfulness:** That which examines the object more thoroughly.
9	Ra	**Rapture:** That which gives rise to delightful interest in the object.
10	Co	**Concentration:** That which unifies and fixes the mind on an object.
11	Re	**Resolution:** That which settles the mind on an object.
12	Vi	**Vigor:** That which provides reinforcement and energy to mind.
13	Bd	**Bare Desire:** That which intends or inclines the mind towards an object.
14	Gr	**Greed:** That which grasps or bonds or attaches the mind to an object.
15	Ha	**Hatred:** That which pushes away the object from the mind.
16	De	**Delusion:** That which hides the reality of object and thereby blinds and eludes the mind.
17	Rs	**Restlessness:** That which agitates and distracts the mind.
18	Shl	**Shamelessness:** That which makes the mind non-apprehensive about immorality.
19	Mr	**Moral Recklessness:** That which makes the mind apathetic about immorality.
20	Cn	**Conceit:** That which corrupts the mind by generating pride and vanity.
21	En	**Envy:** That which makes the mind resentful and jealous of other's successes.
22	Rm	**Remorse:** That which generates worry and repentance.
23	Su	**Superstitiousness:** That which interprets the object unjustifiably, wrongly, and unwisely.
24	Ss	**Suspicion:** That which generates distrust and negativity.
25	Sl	**Sloth:** That which makes the mind stiff and sluggish.
26	To	**Torpor:** That which makes the mind lethargic and clumsy, generating boredom.
27	Av	**Avarice:** That which makes the mind covetous and mean, making it hard to share.
28	NGr	**Non-greed:** That which makes the mind generous. It is the absence and the opposite of greed.
29	NHa	**Non-hatred:** That which generates loving-kindness. It is the absence and the opposite of hatred.
30	Mi	**Mindfulness:** That which makes the mind aware of phenomenon by bringing it to present moment.
31	Cs	**Conscience:** That which generates disgust for immorality out of self-respect and honor.
32	Sh	**Shame:** That which generates apprehension for immorality out of respect and honor for others.
33	Fa	**Faith:** That which clarifies the mind and illuminates it about an object. It trusts.
34	Trl	**Tranquility of mind:** That which makes the mind calm and still by crushing restlessness.
35	Tr2	**Tranquility as a distinct element:** That which has the quality of making the mind calm and still.
36	Lil	**Lightness of mind:** That which makes the mind non-sluggish, free of heaviness, sloth, and torpor.
37	Li2	**Lightness as a distinct element:** That which has the quality of making the mind non-sluggish.
38	Fll	**Flexibility of mind:** That which crushes rigidity and makes the mind free of superstition, conceit.
39	Fl2	**Flexibility as a distinct element:** That which has the quality of crushing mental rigidity.
40	Pll	**Pliability of mind:** That which facilitates crushing hindrances and makes the mind workable.
41	Pl2	**Pliability as a distinct element:** That which has the quality of making the mind workable.
42	Sk1	**Skillfulness of mind:** That which crushes disability and makes the mind proficient.
43	Sk2	**Skillfulness as a distinct element:** That which has the quality of making the mind proficient.
44	Rc1	**Rectitude of mind:** That which crushes mental tortuousness and generates straightforwardness.
45	Rc2	**Rectitude as a distinct element:** That which has the quality of mental straightforwardness.
46	Eq	**Neutrality of mind:** That which makes the mind balanced and impartial, freeing it from craving.
47	Cm	**Compassion:** That which makes it possible to see suffering and promotes eradication of suffering.
48	Gl	**Gladness:** That which removes envy and jealousy and promotes appreciation of other's successes.
49	Na	**Noble Action:** The quality of unconditional and deliberate refrain from unwholesome action.
50	Ns	**Noble Speech:** The quality of unconditional and deliberate refrain from unwholesome speech.
51	No	**Noble Occupation:** The quality of unconditional and deliberate refrain from unwholesome work.
52	NDe	**Non-delusion:** That which eradicates delusion or ignorance and generates wisdom.

Figure 1.4 (Continued): List of 52 mental elements. A unique symbol is designated for each. For example, Fe represents the element of feeling.

Universal Mental Elements

Sensation, feeling, perception, volition, attention, and mental life—these six elements perform universal or essential mental functions. They are present in every type of mental activity and in all types of consciousness. Without their presence, consciousness cannot perform the act of cognition. Without their presence, there is no mind, no consciousness, and no experience. Universal mental elements are neither inherently wholesome nor unwholesome. Rather they acquire the ethical qualities of other prominent mental elements that arise with them. For example, the element of *feeling* simply performs the function of directly experiencing an object. However, it becomes unwholesome when it arises with the mental element of hatred, at which point it manifests as a hateful-unpleasant feeling. If we see an enemy, for instance, we might feel hatefully unpleasant because hatred coexists with feeling. When we see our children, we might feel joyfully pleasant because loving-kindness coexists with feeling.

Similarly, the element of *perception* performs the function of interpreting, recognizing, or identifying the quality of objects. However, it becomes unwholesome when it arises with the element of greed, as in the case we previously discussed of perceiving someone else's lost wallet as a possible source of easy money.

Here's how the universal mental elements could arise and function in a typical cognitive process. Let us go back to the example of spotting a lost wallet in a flea market. When you notice the wallet, you decide either to keep the cash or to find the wallet's owner. In this cognitive process, the universal mental elements assist consciousness as follows.

The moment you see the wallet, eye consciousness arises along with the six universal mental elements. *Sensation* makes eye consciousness *touch* the object, because of which consciousness (the internal world) impinges upon the object (the external world). The process of cognition begins at the moment of contact between the internal and the external world.

Once contact is established through sensation, a feeling arises and consciousness feels the sensations, resulting in the appearance of the object.

CHAPTER 1 WHAT IS SOUL?

Perception then assists consciousness in interpreting the object based on the sensations and feelings. The object is thus understood as a wallet, based on its appearance (the sensation and the feeling). If it is not the first time you have seen it, then the object is interpreted as a wallet based on your memories of previous experiences.

Volition then kicks in and decides whether to have easy money or to find the owner. Through coordination among all other mental elements, volition determines your further course of action about the wallet. Volition thus gives rise to wholesome or unwholesome mental action depending upon whether it combines with wholesome (non-greed) or unwholesome (greed) mental elements, respectively.

Attention, which is present along with all the other mental elements the entire time you are engaged in this episode, bonds all the other elements to the object so that consciousness will remain in contact with the wallet throughout the cognitive process. Attention thus assists in constantly turning consciousness towards the object to carry out its volition.

The sixth element, *mental life*, maintains and sustains all the other mental elements during the process of cognition. Without mental life, consciousness cannot conclude the process of cognition. While considering the wallet, if you were to suddenly go into coma or die due to a fatal heart attack, you would not be able to take any mental action.

In the above example, eye consciousness rules a visual experience, such as seeing a wallet. Mental elements are always subservient to consciousness.

The six universal mental elements are always present in all cognitive processes. They combine with the remaining 46 elements in different permutations and combinations to give rise to a variety of experiences. How that happens and how such knowledge can be used to minimize unwholesome experiences and maximize wholesome experiences, increase happiness and peace, awaken higher levels of intelligence, and so on will be discussed in later chapters.

Having articulated the elements, I am going to add that the exact number does not really matter much. If you looked long and hard at the phenomena of mind you might come up with more elements, such as sub-elements and super-elements. The range or spectrum of mental elements would remain the same as we have discussed. This is akin to the spectrum of colors. There are only six basic colors even though there are many shades of those colors.

Whatever names or number we use to describe the elements, we are just labeling various unique mental phenomena. In developing your understanding of mind, the key is never to let go of the thought of it as a phenomenon. The key is to never make "something" out of names and numbers. Names and numbers do not have much significance in comparison to the intrinsic and phenomenal (impersonal) nature of mental elements.

From this brief discussion, I hope you now have at least an intellectual understanding that mind is not a single fixed entity, a unified field, an exotic energy field, or a unified super-intelligence, but simply a bundle of various unique mental phenomena (mental elements) that arise and pass away with consciousness.

As you'll discover for yourself, when understanding of the elemental and phenomenal nature of mind comes through actual meditative experience, mind is not clung to as *my* mind. It is simply looked upon as an impersonal phenomenon. Such spiritual vision makes it possible to experience soul.

Matter, the Third Element of Soul

As we have discussed, human experience involves a combination of matter, mind, and consciousness. The most tangible component of this equation is matter. Like mind and consciousness, matter is phenomenological. It is also elemental, although not necessarily in the way that you may be anticipating. Let us return to using the example of observing a flower to demonstrate the elemental nature of matter, specifically as it arises in the human body.

You have already learned that consciousness sees a flower and mind feels, perceives, thinks, judges, or qualifies the flower as "beautiful" or "pleasant." You also have learned that consciousness and mind

CHAPTER 1 WHAT IS SOUL?

cannot see without both organic and non-organic matter being present. The consciousness that sees a flower (eye consciousness) can function only when it arises using eye sensitivity (non-organic or subtle matter) and a biological eye (organic matter). In this case, both types of matter are situated in the eye socket of a live body, however subtle matter cannot be seen under a microscope or detected by mechanical devices. Similarly, ear consciousness hears sounds only when it occurs using ear sensitivity and the ear. Taste consciousness tastes flavors only when it occurs using tongue sensitivity and the tongue. Smell consciousness smells odors only when it occurs using nose sensitivity and the nose. Touch consciousness feels touch only when it occurs using body sensitivity and the skin.

When we talk about subtle matter (the five sensitivities) we are not referring to nerve centers, biochemicals, genes, or atoms, but rather to a phenomenon called the *material base*.[7] It is called a material base because consciousness arises using it as a material support. These material bases can be envisioned as the five invisible antennas situated in the five sense organs of a live body. These five invisible antennae detect five types of respective sense consciousness, and channel them through the five respective sense organs.

However, that is not still enough for the occurrence of a sensual experience. For example, eye consciousness cannot see unless a unique type of functional consciousness known as sense-enabling consciousness arises simultaneously with it. This functional consciousness cannot arise strictly using the five material bases that we have discussed so far. It takes support of another material base called *mind sensitivity*, which is the sixth material base (or we could call it the sixth invisible antenna). The sixth material base is situated within the cavity of the heart of a live body. It is also known as the subtle heart matter.[8]

Just as the antenna of an AM/FM receiver in your car detects radio waves from a radio station, our six invisible antennae (eye sensitivity, ear sensitivity, nose sensitivity, tongue sensitivity, body sensitivity, and mind sensitivity) detect various types of consciousness and channel them through our six physical organs (the eyes, ears, nose, tongue, body, and heart, respectively). And just as the receiver in your car decodes and converts radio waves it has detected into sounds, the *brain* decodes and converts the arisen consciousness into experiences.

In short, I propose that the six material bases and the six physical organs work together with the brain to facilitate cognition. We cannot hear sound in our car without an antenna *and* a receiver. Similarly, we cannot experience anything without the six material bases, the six physical organs, *and* the brain (see figure 1.5).

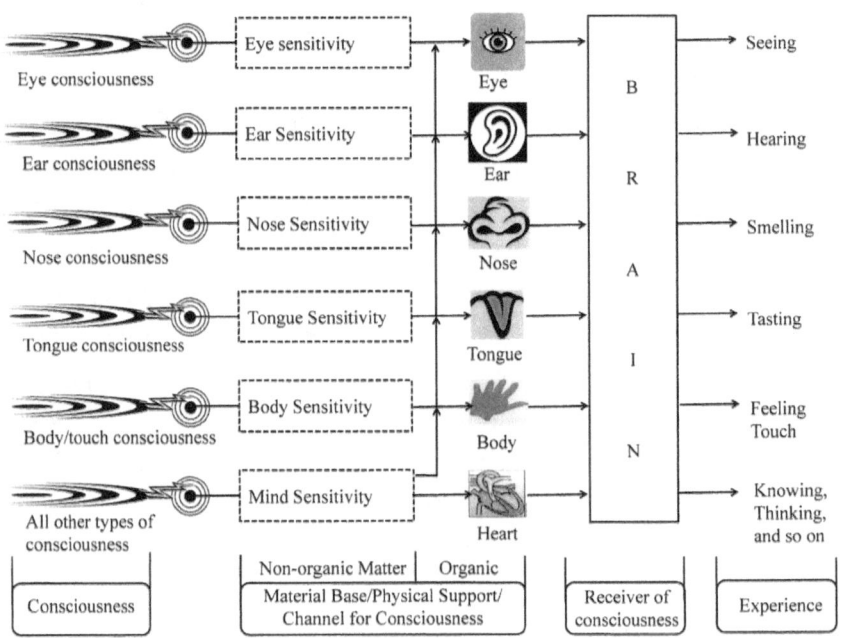

Figure 1.5. *Matter is the physical support for consciousness. In addition to five sensual organs, consciousness needs the support of the heart and the assistance of the brain.*

All six material bases form at conception. As the fetus grows, the six organs take shape around their respective bases. The heart is the first organ to fully form and function. This might be because it is associated with mind sensitivity, the sixth material base, which is the most important material base when it comes to having an experience. Note that mind sensitivity is not situated in the heart organ *per se*, rather in the blood-filled cavities inside the live heart.

This is a simplified version of how consciousness arises with the support of matter.

The Brain

Let's go back to the analogy of a radio. It is a scientific fact that radio waves are made of sine frequencies loaded with information, such as the voice of a DJ or music. The process of loading information is known as AM or FM modulation. We hear the DJ in our car because our car's receiver is capable of receiving the information through its antenna, demodulating (unloading) the information, and converting it into sound.

Mind (or a group of mental elements) is like the information that has been loaded onto consciousness. Similar to an AM/FM receiver, the brain unloads this information, which results in various neural activities. However, there is a huge difference between an AM/FM receiver and the brain. While the AM/FM receiver receives, it cannot transmit. The brain not only is a receiver, it is also a transmitter. Moreover, the brain is not just an electrical device or a computer. It is also a learning device—and much more than that.

Although the brain is essential to cognition, it is only a receiver and not a *source* of consciousness, as many neurologists and psychologists believe. But although the brain is not its prime material component, cognition cannot happen without the brain. Some spiritual scientists and thinkers tend to neglect the brain. The wise ones among us neither give the brain too much importance, nor do they overlook it.

Material Elements, the Ultimate Building Blocks of Matter

What are the five sense organs, the heart, and the brain (or any other organ in the body for that matter) made of at the ultimate level? Four primary material elements.

Think about them in light of the body. A physical organ has some softness and some hardness, and it is supported on something without which it cannot stand. Where do the softness, hardness, and support come from? If, for a moment, we could set aside our materialistic viewpoint and look at the *experiential* qualities of softness, hardness, and support as phenomena, rather than as some*thing* arising out of some*thing* else, then we are obviously reaching the ultimate reality of matter. As we have discussed, experiential knowledge equals ultimate reality.

Let's call these phenomena characteristics of the element of *earth*. Why call it "earth"? Softness, hardness, and support are recognizable qualities of soil mass.

A physical organ has fluidity and cohesion, qualities without which the organ would fall apart. Let us call these phenomena characteristics of the element of *water*.

A physical organ has a certain temperature. It grows and matures. Let us call these phenomena characteristics of the element of *fire*.

Finally, all organs have some motion, distention, and pressure without which there would not be any conveyance of fluids, movement of breath, or any movement of muscles, bones, limbs, stomach, and so on. Let us call these phenomena characteristics of the element of *air*.

If you were to contemplate these phenomena, you would eventually realize that there are no other experiential qualities of matter. In other words, the elements of earth, water, fire, and air are the ultimate realities of matter. In the human body, these are the foundation of the sense organs, the heart, and the brain. They are the essence of everything we experience as matter.

The elements of which I am speaking are not visible subatomic particles, such as electrons, protons, and neutrons, or objects that have size, shape, weight, or mass. Material elements are not mysterious or invisible primordial substances, nor are they particles or packets of energy. Rather they are fundamental material *phenomena of experience* manifested in form as visible or invisible matter.

The words "phenomenon" and "experience" have great significance in coming to understand matter as the element of soul, since they help

CHAPTER 1 WHAT IS SOUL?

us to remove our ignorance related to physical notions of matter as being a fixed, solid substance that is separate from us.

Perhaps you are wondering how all the organs and the brain (which seem to be incredibly complex) can be made of earth, water, fire, and air. Well, there is a caveat. Earth, water, fire, and air cannot produce complex material phenomena unless they combine with four causal factors and give rise to a total of 28 material elements (see figure 1.6, on page 36 and 37).[9] We shall discuss causal factors and material elements in future chapters.

THE ELEMENTS OF SOUL

GROUP I Essential Elements	GROUP IIA Derived Essential Elements	GROUP IIB Derived Sensual Elements	GROUP IIC Derived Sexual Elements	GROUP IID Derived Life Element	GROUP IIE Derived Subtle-Heart Element	GROUP IIF Derived Sound Element
1 **Ea** Earth	5 **Nu** Nutriment	9 **EySe** Eye Sensitivity	14 **MaSx** Male Sexuality	16 **Mal** Material Life	17 **MiSe** Mind Sensitivity	18 **So** Sound
2 **Wa** Water	6 **Ta** Taste	10 **EaSe** Ear Sensitivity	15 **FeSx** Female Sexuality			
3 **Fi** Fire	7 **Fo/Co** Form/Color	11 **NoSe** Nose Sensitivity				
4 **Ai** Air	8 **Sm** Smell	12 **ToSe** Tongue Sensitivity				
		13 **BoSe** Body Sensitivity				

GROUP III
Abstract Elements
(Attributes of Real Matter)

19 **BoIn** Bodily Intimation	20 **VoIn** Vocal Intimation	21 **Cn** Continuity
22 **Lt** Lightness	23 **Fl** Flexibility	24 **Pl** Pliability
25 **Pr** Production	26 **De** Decay	27 **Im** Impermanence
28 **Sp** Space		

i. Material elements are experiential (and not experimental) in nature.
ii. Elements 1-4 are the most fundamental and essential building blocks of matter. They are inseparable.
iii. Elements 5-28 are dependent upon the elements 1-4 and cannot arise by themselves.
iv. Elements 1-8 always arise together as a group. This group is known as the soul-atom. It is present in all material phenomena.
v. Element 9-28 cling to soul-atoms to form new groups. These groups of elements give rise to various material phenomena occurring in human body.
vi. In general, all material elements always arise in distinct groups forming matter due to four causes:
   Consciousness
   Volitional Force (Karma)
   Temperature
   Nutriment

Essential matter = 1 + 2 + 3 + 4 = (1-4), forms due to all four causes
Soul-atom = (1-4) + (5-8) = (1-8), forms due to consciousness
Sound = (1-8) + 18, forms due to consciousness and temperature
Life matter = (1-8) + 16, forms due to karma
Eye matter = (1-8) + 9 + 16, forms due to karma
Ear matter = (1-8) + 10 + 16, forms due to karma
Nose matter = (1-8) + 11 + 16, forms due to karma
Tongue matter = (1-8) + 12 + 16, forms due to karma
Body matter = (1-8) + 13 + 16, forms due to karma
Sexuality matter = (1-8) + 14 or 15 + 16, forms due to karma
Heart matter = (1-8) + 16 + 17, forms due to karma

Figure 1.6: The Chart of Material Elements illustrating the ultimate building blocks of matter. These elements arise in groups giving rise to various types of matter. A unique symbol is designated for each. For example: Ea for the element of earth.

THE ELEMENTS OF SOUL

1	Ea	**Earth:** That which characterizes hard or soft, and provides foundation to matter.
2	Wa	**Water:** That which characterizes fluidity, cohesion, and holds matter together.
3	Fi	**Fire:** That which characterizes heat and cold, and digests, ripens or matures material states.
4	Ai	**Air:** That which characterizes distention, causes movement and pressure, and conveys matter.
5	Nu	**Nutriment:** That which characterizes nutritive essence, upholds, fortifies, and consolidates matter.
6	Ta	**Taste:** That which impinges upon the tongue and becomes an object of taste consciousness.
7	Fo/Co	**Form/Color:** That which impinges upon the eye and becomes an object of eye consciousness.
8	Sm	**Smell:** That which impinges upon the nose and becomes an object of nose consciousness.
9	EySe	**Eye Sensitivity:** That which springs from desire to see and picks up visible datum as an object.
10	EaSe	**Ear Sensitivity:** That which springs from desire to hear and picks up audible datum as an object.
11	NoSe	**Nose Sensitivity:** That which springs from desire to smell and picks up odor as an object.
12	ToSe	**Tongue Sensitivity:** That which springs from desire to taste and picks up flavor as an object.
13	BoSe	**Body Sensitivity:** That which springs from desire to touch and picks up tactile sensations.
14	MaSx	**Male Sexuality:** That which springs from desire to propagate species and shows masculinity.
15	FeSx	**Female Sexuality:** That which springs from desire to propagate species and shows femininity.
16	Mal	**Material Life:** That which springs from desire to live and maintains and sustains matter.
17	MiSe	**Mind Sensitivity:** That which springs from desire to know and provides material base for mind.
18	So	**Sound:** That which springs from consciousness and temperature and becomes a sense object.
19	BoIn	**Bodily Intimation:** That which communicates ideas and feelings, and causes bodily movements.
20	VoIn	**Vocal Intimation:** That which communicates ideas and feelings, and causes voice.
21	Cn	**Continuity:** That which characterizes the occurrence, and anchors the continuous arising of matter.
22	Li	**Lightness:** That which characterizes non-sluggishness of body and crushes heaviness in matter.
23	Fl	**Flexibility:** That which characterizes non-rigidity of body and crushes rigidity in matter.
24	Pl	**Pliability:** That which characterizes workability of body and crushes physical unwieldiness.
25	Pr	**Production:** That which characterizes launching of matter and makes it arise for the first time.
26	De	**Decay:** That which characterizes aging of matter and leads it towards termination.
27	Im	**Impermanence:** That which characterizes breaking up of matter, makes it subside and cease.
28	Sp	**Space:** That which characterizes voidness, delimiting of matter, and enables distinctness in matter.

Figure 1.6 (continued): List of 28 material elements. A unique symbol is designated for each. For example, Ea represents the element of earth.

THE ELEMENTS OF SOUL

Having read this far, you have a basic theoretical understanding of the three key elements of soulful phenomena: consciousness, mind, and matter. There is a good deal more to be said about each. However, if you grasped their phenomenological nature in the context of human experience, you have received a complete sketch of the terrain we're going to explore together in the pursuit of understanding soul and thereby attaining perfect intelligence.

* * *

Chapter 2

What Is Not Soul?

When we study any subject, it is important that we understand not only what it is but also what it is *not*. Since it leaves no stone unturned, such knowledge facilitates mental perfection.

Having explored what soul is, let us now explore what it is not. In order to do this, we must understand the nature of reality as well as non-reality.

Reality

Reality is that which is universal and which exists as a distinct phenomenon possessing its own intrinsic nature. It is not something that is conceptual, mentally constructed, or conceived. It is the object of real experience, meaning, it is that which is not imagined but experienced.

Hydrogen and oxygen are real because they are universal and possess unique characteristics that make them two distinct elements of the periodic table. They are experienced universally as gases and as water when combined. Similarly, the elements of soul (matter, mind, and consciousness, as we discussed in the previous chapter) are real because they can be experienced and they are universal. They are the same for all beings. However, the elements of soul have an important distinction. Since these three elements consist of the *subtlest* phenomena that underlie all other phenomena (experiences and things), they are not simply a reality but an *ultimate* reality.

When you see something, eye consciousness is the subtlest reality in the experience of seeing. In fact, eye consciousness, which has the intrinsic nature of seeing an object, is itself experienced as "seeing." In other words, nothing subtler than eye consciousness can be experienced in the phenomenon of "seeing." Similarly, nothing subtler than the element of hatred (the mind) can be experienced in the phenomenon of anger. And nothing subtler than the element of fire (the matter) can be experienced in the phenomenon of temperature.

The elements of consciousness, mind, and matter do not perform their functions for any living being yet they are distinct, experiential, *and* universal. Eye consciousness will perform the function of only seeing (and not hearing). The element of hatred will perform the function of generating only anger (and not love). The element of fire will perform the function of generating only the experience of heat and cold (and never the experience of hard or soft, wet or dry).

If one does not understand the nature of reality as experiential, universal, and intrinsic, then one starts imagining that it is he (or she) who sees, who hates or loves, who feels hot or cold. The sense of separate self (the ego) is formed out of the ignorance about reality and non-reality.

The ultimate reality of consciousness, mind, and matter is *conditional* because all three are conditioned by each other and occur interdependently, as we discussed in the previous chapter. Then there is a fourth ultimate reality: enlightenment, which is *unconditional* and beyond soul, as we shall soon discuss.

There are only four ultimate realities in the universe.[1] In the ultimate sense, everything else is a non-reality, not soul (see figure 2.1).

CHAPTER 2 WHAT IS NOT SOUL?

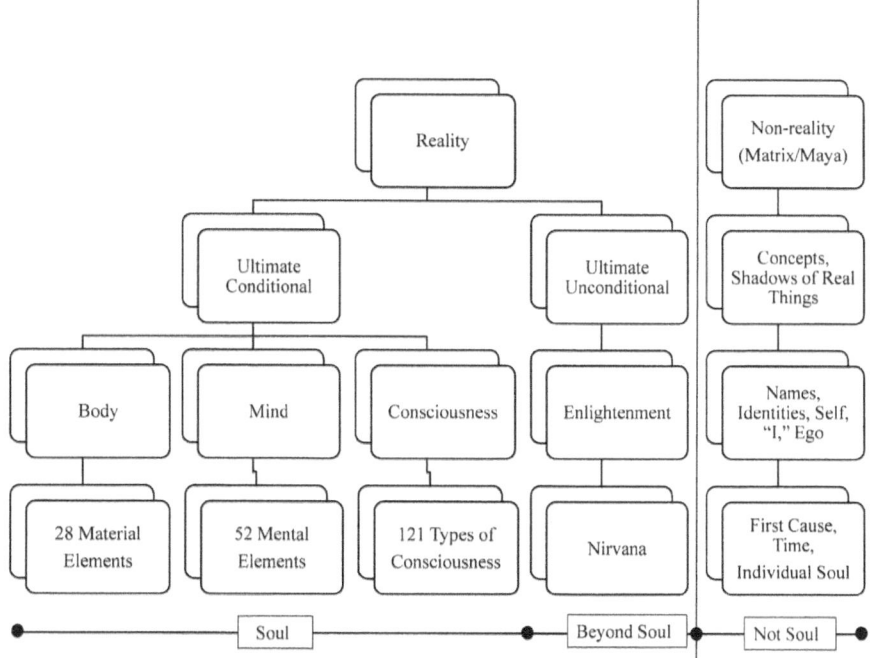

Figure 2.1. Types of reality and non-reality: In order to realize soul, understanding what is not real is as important as understanding what is real.

Non-reality

After having understood what reality is, it is quite obvious that non-reality is that which does not exist as a distinct phenomenon possessing its own intrinsic nature. It is that which is conceived, but that which cannot be experienced. It is non-universal.

Water is real. The phrase "Colorado River" is not. It is a name, a geopolitical *concept* denoting a body of flowing water. We can experience flowing water just as a fish or a bird can. But we cannot experience "Colorado River," which is a mental construction and linguistic tool so that we may communicate with one another. A fish and a bird obviously do not know what "Colorado River" is. In other words, "Colorado River" is not only *not* experiential it also is *not* universal. So it is not real.

Similarly, a "table" is not real. It does not exist. What really exists is wood (or metal, or plastic). Table is the name given to a particular form or assembly of wood. It is an abstraction.

41

Please understand that conventions and concepts are not universal because they do not exist by the virtue of their own natures. There is no experiential evidence for them. "Table" does not have universal existence because it does not mean anything to an ant or to a woodpecker. But wood is the same for all beings, whether human, ant, or woodpecker.

This may sound a bit dimwitted right now, but bear with me a while longer so I can prove to you the profound implications of what we are discussing.

A tree, man, woman, nation, and so on are additional examples of non-realities—mere words, mere names, mere concepts. A man or a woman actually does not exist. An Israeli, a German, or a Palestinian does not exist. What actually exist are bundles of consciousness, mind, and matter conventionally called a man, a woman, an Israeli, a German, and a Palestinian.

A nation does not exist. What actually exists is a piece of land. A national boundary is simply a line drawn by politicians on a piece of paper. It does not exist by its own nature because it is not universal. Otherwise a camel or an earthworm crossing the border between Israel and Palestine or India and Pakistan would experience it just as (deluded) humans do. The land is the real thing (and not a nation) because it is experienced *as land* by all beings, including camels, earthworms, and people.

The demarcation of land as various nations might be necessary for political, economic, and cultural convenience, however, when a nation itself becomes an identity or a subject of pride for some, there is fighting and killing over it, which leads to immense suffering for millions of innocent people at large.

If Hitler had not been driven by national and racial concepts, the world would not have endured the Holocaust. If these types of non-reality did not blind recent political, social, and religious leaders and their followers we would not have experienced bloodshed in Israel-Palestine, India-Pakistan, Iran-Iraq, and Sierra Leone. New York would not have been attacked on September 11, 2001. The list is long.

CHAPTER 2 WHAT IS NOT SOUL?

Two easy qualifying tests help us to identify and understand the world around us and ourselves so that non-reality is not mistaken as reality. These are "experience" and "universality." Anything that fails these tests is only a concept or a network of concepts, which in Sanskrit is known as *maya* (see figure 2.2).

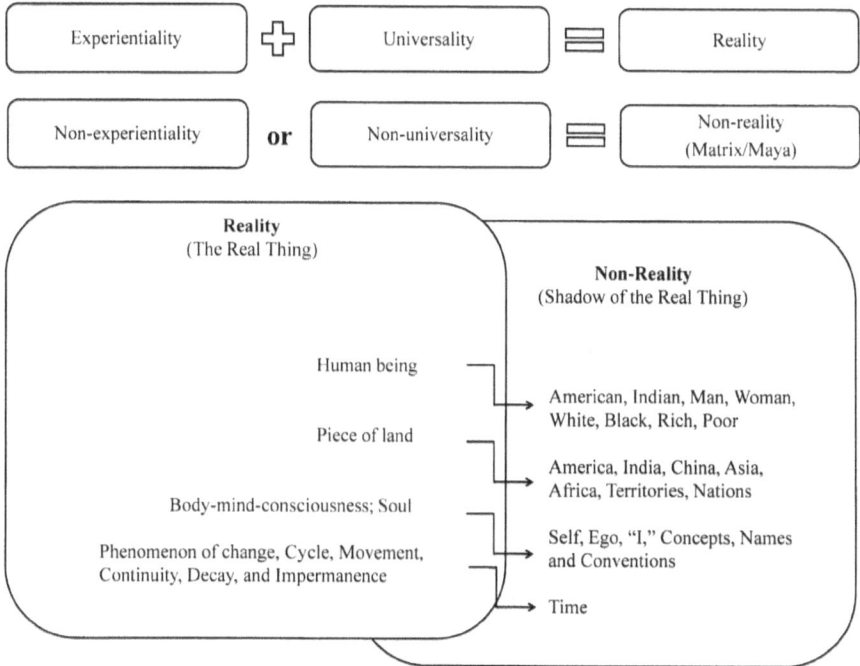

Figure 2.2. Tests for identifying reality and non-reality: experience and universality.

Maya: A Network of Non-reality

In some ancient eastern philosophical discourses, the word "maya" has been incorrectly used to describe the material world or the world of the senses. The material world exists, as it is composed of the elements earth, water, fire, and air. Inanimate matter exists. Animate matter exists. Our senses also exist. What do not exist are the various concepts that we derive from these real things: the shadows of real thing (see figure 2.2).

We live in a vast and layered network of conventions, or shared concepts, which is somewhat like the computer matrix depicted in the 1999 movie *The Matrix* about the enslavement of mankind in a virtual world. Although limited in scope, that fictional proposition was a good simulation of maya. The matrix I'm referring to is primarily responsible for the imprisonment of our intellect and the consequent human suffering on an unimaginable scale.

Due to maya, we have developed various layers of delusion, such as nationalities, religious affiliations, social affiliations, occupational identities, family relationships, personal images, and so on. None of these forms of identification is real. These layers of delusion have only led to conflicts between nations, between races, between communities, between businesses, between family members, between sexes, and so on. When a person says, "I am Hindu," or Christian, an Indian or an American, black or Caucasian, a trader or a doctor, a father or a mother, a brother or a sister, and the person genuinely means it, then that person is blinded by maya. You could also say that person is "plugged into the matrix."

Let us look at couple of examples that illustrate why maya works adversely at all levels, starting with a fictitious organization that we'll call TransWorld Inc.

TransWorld Inc., a multinational company, does not actually exist (and not just because it is fictitious). TransWorld Inc. is a name adopted by a group of people who work together in an organized manner to achieve common goals. What really exists is a group of people. That is the actual reality of TransWorld Inc.

What usually happens in today's corporate world? People are forgotten or rated second while the company name or its image is treated as the real matter of importance. The name of an organization is necessary for the convenience of doing business, however when the name or the company itself becomes an entity, the employees who make up the company suffer.

If the owners and managers of the company were to realize this, the employees would not be treated simply as a "resource" (human

CHAPTER 2 WHAT IS NOT SOUL?

resource) to be utilized for generating profits and establishing a brand. Employees would be given top priority and treated as the real company—because that's what reality is—rather than the name, image, or brand of the company.

An Indian cricket team or an Australian cricket team does not exist. These are just names. What really exist are two groups of people who play the same game. But what happens when people watch the game? People who identify themselves as Indians tend to cheer for players on the Indian team. People who identify themselves as Australians do the same for the Australian team players. Instead of watching the game, people watch to see if their team will win.

If all the sports fans of all sports were to realize this, they could learn a great deal about human skill and athletic power by simply watching a game, which is a real thing, rather than focusing on the unreal: names, nationality, league, image, affiliation, or identity of the players. Wouldn't it be lot more beneficial to sports fans if they were to watch the game because they love the game, and then learn and derive inspiration from it? Why develop a craving for one team and an aversion for another? That's beneficial only to the owners and organizers of the teams.

Non-realities are skin-deep. A New York Yankee and one of the Red Sox, a white man and a black man, an American and a Japanese all look the same when X-rayed.

If you simply "look through" them, it is obvious that sports media, marketing media, political media, religious media, and the entertainment industry thrive on the matrix for the most part. Without the popular perceptions (such as leagues, rankings, awards, lists, memberships, charts, associations, names, brands, and so forth) and herd mentality that they create and promote, they cannot make fortunes off you and me. Pop culture and the paparazzi could not function without the consumers who fall for maya or get carried away by the matrix.

Competition, trends, peer pressure, stress, and hysteria are but a few examples of the byproducts of maya or the matrix. Although we have to apply specific means of identification, qualification, and quantification to function in this world, we don't have to get hooked on it as if it is the real thing. We don't have to swear or be driven by it. We don't have to become crazy about anything or develop aversion to anything. We only have to give importance to real things (the skill, art, fineness, and excellence demonstrated by extraordinary people from all walks of life) in order to learn from it.

It is important to understand that whenever we are under the spell of unreal things we are blinded by craving and aversion. Why is this important? Craving and aversion are two great evils that support, strengthen, and protect the ego and cover up our true nature: soul. This is the reason why we suffer and cause suffering for others. Layers of identification (maya) have to be peeled off so we can expose and eradicate the ego (the subtlest of all identifications), which is at the core of all human conflicts and suffering (see figure 2.3).

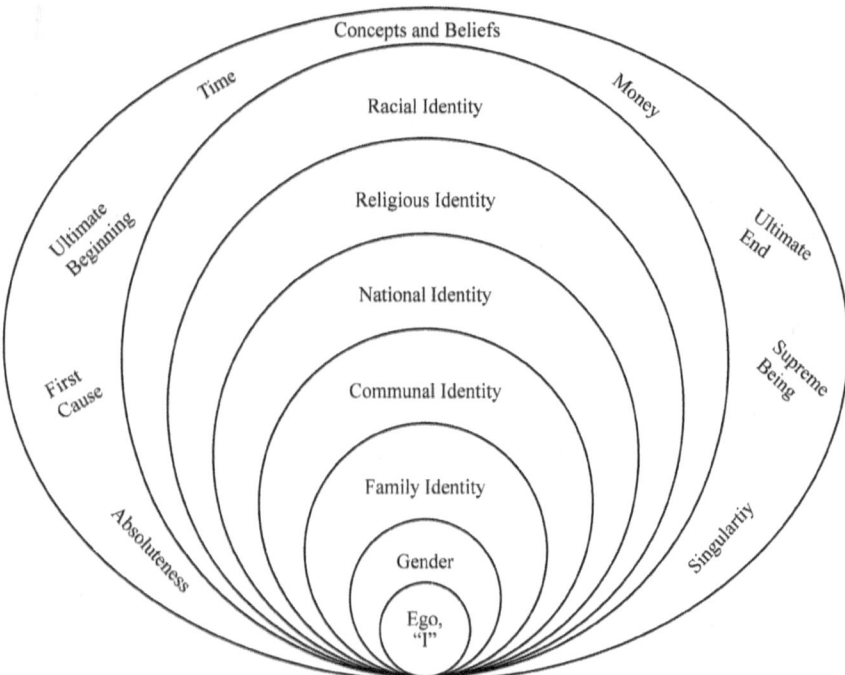

Figure 2.3. Layers of non-reality (maya): the source of human conflict and suffering.

There is huge significance to the realization of the existence of delusions created by maya. As you remove delusions, intelligence is purified and developed, which leads to removal of the ultimate delusion: the delusion of the separate self, or the ego, which is hidden behind names, conventions, and concepts. Maya is the ego's protective layered armor, which must be shattered and removed in order to awaken the ultimate human potential.

The Ego: A Non-reality

Psychologically, we could say that ego is the manifestation of various unwholesome mental elements, such as delusion, greed, and hatred. In this sense, ego is an attribute of the ultimate reality of mind. However, the ego really does not exist itself as an ultimate reality with its own intrinsic nature. As you'll learn in upcoming chapters, it is simply an attribute of a deluded mind.

Philosophically, we could say that the ego is an expression of ignorance or mental blindness. Here, ignorance means not knowing or not understanding the real nature of body-mind-consciousness. It means choosing to ignore or deny the truth about the nature of reality. Because of ignorance, the interaction between the reality of body, mind, and consciousness and their seemingly continuous co-existence is not experienced as *soul* but imagined as a separate *self*.

You might be questioning, "If ego is a non-reality then how can we eradicate it? How can we eradicate something that does not exist?"

Eradicating the ego is like eradicating the darkness in a room by turning on the lights. Darkness is essentially the "absence of light," meaning it is an attribute of light, so light overrides darkness. Ego is the "absence of wisdom (or perfect intelligence)." In order to override ego, we develop wisdom. As wisdom emerges, eradication is automatic. Nothing else is needed.

The point is: We do not try to eradicate the ego *directly*. Instead, we develop wisdom, which automatically removes layers of identification and then ultimately results in the eradication of the ego. It is just like turning on the lights to remove darkness in a room instead of trying to shovel out or erase the darkness.

Time: A Non-reality

Time is a concept. It is not real, as it is neither universal nor experiential. We cannot experience time like a sensation of heat or cold, or a feeling of joy or sorrow. Time is just a name given to the phenomenon of movement, cycle, change, continuity, decay, and impermanence. These phenomena are real because we can experience them and they are universal. They are the same for everything that exists in nature. Time is a conceptual means to measure and quantify these phenomena.

Time is an illusion in the same way that the idea of "separate self" is an illusion. Time, even as an illusion (clock time), is not the same for all—meaning, it is not universal. Time is different depending upon people's locations within different time zones.

Time also is not the experience of the past and the future. The past and future exist only in our memories, conceptions, thoughts, and imaginations. We can only remember the past. We can only think about the future. Our thoughts about past and future always occur in the present. Only the present moment is real and can be experienced. Past and future are mere conventions.

Aim to live in the real moment, which is the present. It is a more empowered approach to life to rule your memories than to allow them to rule you. Plan, arrange, prepare, and be proactive, but do not become attached to the deadlines or results that you may or may not see in the future.

Aim to be punctual, but do not go time crazy. Meet your commitments while working without being pressurized by deadlines. By this I mean work on Monday in the same manner that you work on Friday. Did you know that besides human beings no other living creatures see any difference between Monday and Friday?

The Non-reality of Ultimate Beginning and End

Human beings have a tendency to think in a linear manner. Due to the spell of time, we tend to think in terms of beginning and end. Therefore it is easy to believe that ultimate realities would have a beginning and an end. However, the word "ultimate" does not relate to the beginning of the world or a primordial reality. It simply means "the subtlest mode of experience." If you imagine that consciousness is subtler than mind, you are thinking linearly.

In this sense, there is no such thing as the ultimate beginning or end of the world. These are mental concepts that arise due to the habit of linear thinking and the illusion of time as a linear entity. Ultimate beginning and end actually do not occur in nature. There are no such things. Trying to find a beginning or an end always results in an infinite regression.

What is the beginning and end of the physical extent of your country? Where another country ends, your country begins, and where your country ends, another country begins. Because we live on a sphere, if you continued pursuing this question from country to country you would eventually arrive back at your own country. The beginning is the ending. Time-space works just the same way. The true "beginning" is where you begin. The true "end" is where you begin again. There is no absolute or first beginning, no absolute or last end.

Can we point out the beginning of the surface of Earth and the end of it? Can we locate the beginning and end of space? We cannot, because beginning and end are mental concepts. They are conventions. They do not exist. They are not intrinsically real. They do not have essential natures that can be realized.

Many intellectuals get bogged down and discouraged when they do not find answers to the questions of ultimate beginning, ultimate end, first cause, absolute reality, and similar concerns. Some then unknowingly pick up a religious or doctrinal path in search of the answers, which then hampers their spiritual growth. Some theologians and religious pundits spend their lives conceptualizing, theorizing, and dogmatizing in a vain effort to provide answers. But these questions are not valid in the first place!

God: A Reality or a Non-reality?

One of the biggest challenges many people have had—also the biggest challenge I experienced years ago in studying the four ultimate realities (matter, mind, consciousness, and enlightenment)—is an attachment to the idea of a deeper unconditional and absolute reality underlying them. Why is it not possible to have one single ultimate reality or principle, like an ultimate being, such as God, that underlies everything else?

My conclusion is that the term "God" can be used to denote all ultimate realities in union. You may also use this word to denote enlightenment, which means, "perfect intelligence" or "pure awareness." But you cannot say that there is something beyond the four ultimate realities or that some single underlying *absolute* or *separate* entity exists.

Notwithstanding, I must suggest that you do not abandon the idea of God. Instead, try to explore it. Try neither to believe nor to disbelieve in a particular concept of God. Believing or not believing is the same thing: a belief! Just keep an open mind until you know all four ultimate realities *experientially*.

Become an explorer rather than a believer or a non-believer. Investigate rather than accept or reject, and, most importantly, keep exploring and investigating without ever ending the quest. The questions related to God and such matters are best dealt with as open-ended questions in order to avoid human conflict and the suppression of truth.

Imagine what would have happened if all people simply believed in ancient religious texts about the origin of the Earth and life and did not care to explore further. Because some humans did explore, today we know so much more about the origin of the Earth and life. Not that these explorers were disbelievers or anti-religious, they simply went beyond to find the truth for themselves. Many eminent scientists (such as Einstein) have been deeply religious, but that did not stop them from exploring ultimate realities of the world.

The Importance of Understanding Non-reality

Understanding non-reality matters significantly, because the aim of genuine spiritual endeavor is to purify the intellect, which means penetrating and destroying layers of belief: religious views, perspectives, affiliations, doctrines, dogmas, conventions, and traditions. It is the first and foremost step for an authentic spiritual practitioner.

CHAPTER 2 WHAT IS NOT SOUL?

Your intellect (and my intellect) cannot comprehend anything beyond what you (and I) already believe in. If your religious view is that you can go to heaven by killing another human being in God's name, or if your religious perspective is that your sins are cleansed by accepting someone as your savior, or if you follow a tradition that says that only a guru can purify your mind and give you salvation then you can never reach the depth of reality—the soul—because your intellect is covered with layers of belief: non-reality.

Unless we dissolve these layers, it is not possible to know the soul experientially. Why is it not possible? The intellect has to be freed from the clutches of non-reality before it can recognize reality as it is.

There is no choice but to know the soul experientially. Without this, we simply cannot eradicate the ego. Unless we eradicate the ego, we cannot attain perfect intelligence. Without that, everlasting peace and happiness are not possible.

To you, my reader, I would respectfully throw down a challenge to cross-examine your *beliefs* so that you can develop *faith*. As I said earlier, beliefs are nothing but layers of concepts. Faith, on the other hand, is the understanding that is derived from exploring, investigating, studying, contemplating, *and* experiencing.

In order to develop faith in the message of this book (or in anything else for that matter) may I humbly request you to set aside preconceived notions, to neither believe nor disbelieve, and to simply stay open to all possibilities?

Unless we study, contemplate, and make an effort to experience, we cannot remove preconceived notions or wrong views or beliefs about the nature of reality. Some people believe that there is no such thing as a phenomenon of body-mind-consciousness. Some believe that there is only matter and there is no such thing as consciousness. Some believe that God has created them and there is nothing one can do about it. Some believe that they should not try to do anything about the way they are because they are the children of God. Some believe that there is no such thing as ego. Some believe that there is no imperfection and everything is already perfect. Such preconceived notions have to be removed (or at least set aside for the time being) or else we simply cannot open up the intellect to make it a guiding and clearing force in our soul journey.

The impure intellect misleads itself and becomes a roadblock. When that happens, it becomes very difficult even to embark upon the soul journey or to continue the soul journey without losing the track and getting lost in a jungle of wrong views and beliefs.

Wrong views and beliefs are like weeds that grow wild. Just as the farmer has to first remove weeds from the field prior to cultivating a profitable crop, a spiritual aspirant has to first remove wrong views and beliefs from the intellect prior to cultivating right views and faith, which are necessary conditions for the attainment of perfect intelligence.

* * *

Chapter 3

What Is Beyond Soul?

In our discussion so far, sincere efforts have been made to introduce you to the various phenomena that make up the ultimate building blocks of soul. By now, I hope you have developed a basic understanding of what is and is not soul. Let us now talk briefly about what is beyond soul: enlightenment.

If you are seeking perfect intelligence, gaining a theoretical understanding of enlightenment is an appropriate beginning goal.

Enlightenment

Enlightenment is the reality that transcends soul. What I mean is that it is a reality independent of the realities of our human experience. It cannot be conditioned by consciousness, mind, or matter. In other words, enlightenment is an *unconditional reality*.

Unconditional reality cannot be properly explained in words or in terms of experience since words and experience are phenomena of body-mind-consciousness. Nevertheless, let me try, using an analogy.

Space—meaning the room around us, the distance between objects, and the emptiness of outer space—is not conditioned by anything that exists within it. Yet it appears to exist and encompass everything within it. We cannot say we are experiencing space, yet it is the most fundamental aspect of experience because all events and things happen within space. We cannot imagine or conceive anything beyond space because it seems endless. It is always there, without a beginning and without an end. Everything arises and ceases within space without affecting it. We cannot even prove the existence of space without naming what lies within it. It has no substance because it is nothing, a void. Space is free from all that is conditioned, making it identityless and changeless. It cannot be desired because it is always there, omnipresent.

Unconditional reality shares these qualities of space. However, we should not think that the actual space we see or the vastness of outer space is an unconditional reality.

Silence is another analogy for understanding the nature of unconditionality. Nothing can change or condition silence, and yet all sounds arise out of silence and ultimately cease into silence. There is no beginning to silence, nor will it ever cease to exist.

Space and silence are like two sides of the same coin—the coin of unconditional reality. Space and silence are always present; therefore we cannot say we experience them. For experience to occur there has to be a beginning and an end.

Space and silence cannot be expressed. We cannot actually point out, "This is space," and obviously we cannot express silence. Similarly, enlightenment itself cannot be expressed or experienced. It is just not possible to make *something* out of enlightenment while trying to explain what it is. It is a different dimension altogether.

Psychologically, we can say that egolessness is the expression of enlightenment. Philosophically, we can say that pure understanding is the expression of enlightenment. Spiritually, we can say that oneness or pure consciousness is the expression of enlightenment. Even though they lay in the realm of experience, these expressions are the closest thing we can experience to enlightenment. They are like the last pointers or flag posts denoting its arrival.

Principally, what I am saying is that the transcendental quality of egolessness, pure understanding, and pure consciousness must also be transcended to realize enlightenment.

Enlightenment is not an achievement or an accomplishment because it is a state of no cognition and no experience. It is beyond action, beyond good and bad, beyond time and no time, beyond existence and non-existence, beyond any support, beyond any identification, and beyond everything else we could imagine.

Enlightenment is the cessation of everything, yet it is not death. An enlightened master does not die at the moment of enlightenment. Consciousness, mind, and matter remain since the enlightened master still lives after enlightenment. But there is no "enlightened master" left, no person or being left. There is no identification, separate self, ego, or "I" remaining after enlightenment. Thus enlightenment implies the death of the ego but not of the live body of an enlightened master.

Enlightenment leads to a state of non-being known in the Eastern world as *nirvana*. When the body of an enlightened master dies, there is ultimate unconditional liberation, known as *parinirvana*.[1]

If You Are Seeking Enlightenment

Does the idea of enlightenment sound mystical to you? If yes, this may be because you have not experienced soul or your mind is trying to make something out of the word "enlightenment." You could be thinking about enlightenment as some magical thing or as some spiritual destination. If so, you are only trying to "figure it out" intellectually.

It is not possible to thoroughly understand enlightenment exclusively through using the intellect. The intellect is necessary, but not sufficient. In addition to intellectual understanding, we have to experientially understand the egoless aspect of our existence, which means, we have to experience the soul, at least momentarily, now and then. Real understanding of enlightenment is possible only after that.

Neither thinking only, nor non-thinking only can bring about enlightenment. Not even meditative absorption or deep contemplation can, especially if we are striving for it. One key thing to know about enlightenment is that exertion does not make it happen. We cannot chase it. We can't acquire it. We cannot achieve it. We cannot arrive at it.

How does someone become enlightened?

Enlightenment is the result of tireless efforts directed towards the purification of body-mind-consciousness and the perfection of intelligence. The best strategy is to let go of the desire to attain enlightenment and simply to walk the path of purification and perfection, consistently and ardently, without leaving any trace behind, like a bird flying in the sky. Sooner or later the path ceases and the one on the path also ceases—completely. What then gradually unfolds is the dawn of enlightenment.

Enlightenment ultimately results in the state that is beyond soul: the state of perfect intelligence. This state is none other than the pure awareness of the laws of the universe, as they are. It is *pure* because it arises without clinging to a separate self or to anything in the world. Once you experience the soul in its genuine egolessness and go beyond it you will automatically know enlightenment.

For all practical purposes, becoming enlightened can be understood as a two-step process. Step one is theory: to explore and understand philosophically, psychologically, and phenomenologically the nature of soul and the nature of intelligence. Step two is practice: to use the theoretical knowledge and, through relentless, but gentle spiritual practice, develop intelligent attitude, body, senses, mind, and heart (in that order of attainment), so that eventually soul can be experienced as it is *and* transcended, to arrive at the final destination: the state of perfect intelligence.

* * *

Chapter 4

How Soul Works: A Journey Beyond Quantum Mechanics

So far, we have been primarily discussing the "what" questions about soul: what it is, what it is not, and what is beyond it. I hope these questions have been adequately answered. If they have been, then my guess is that you are now wondering about the "how": How does it all work?

The purpose of this chapter is to begin answering this new question as simply as possible without being dry. However, let me caution you that although the answer is simple (as in plain and clean) it might not be simplistic (as in crude and basic). So, please bear with me during moments of ambiguity and just keep moving forward. By the time you are done with the whole chapter (and subsequently with the whole book), I promise you will find clarity.

Soul Mechanics: A New Scientific Frontier

In theoretical physics, "how" is generally answered with the help of "mechanics" —the rules of how physical objects behave when subjected to force or displacement, as well as the subsequent effect of their behavior on the environment. Classical (Newtonian) mechanics tell us about the behavior of macroscopic physical objects, ranging from pebbles to planets. Quantum mechanics tell us about the behavior of microscopic physical objects, ranging from molecules and atoms to electrons. But neither explains the full workings of the universe. Scientists believe they would be able to solve the remaining mysteries if they could find a force that unifies all the known forces described by the two existing mechanistic theories. Popularly they are searching for a theory of everything (TOE).[1]

In order to solve the mechanistic mysteries of the universe (or to understand the workings of the soul), we need to go beyond classical and quantum mechanics, both of which describe only the mechanics of physical objects. We need to start thinking about the mechanics of non-physical objects (if I may), such as mind-consciousness. The formulation of soul mechanics is such an attempt. In fact, this might be the only way to formulate the TOE. I say so because scientists have not succeeded so far in their TOE efforts despite several decades of intense research. Even Einstein failed in his attempt, despite working consistently on TOE for more than 30 years until the end of his life.[2]

The theory of soul mechanics, which I am going to introduce here and throughout the book, might provide clues for a breakthrough in formulating TOE, as it describes the workings of mind-consciousness. It may also transform existing theoretical and experimental physics into experiential physics, and thus instigate a third revolution in physics (the first being the revolution of classical mechanics and the second being the revolution of quantum mechanics). Soul mechanics may even earn the status of being a new scientific frontier.

Volitional Action: Karma

Just as the ideas of physical action (force or motion) and space-time are pivotal to describing the mechanics of physical objects, the idea of volitional action is pivotal to describing the mechanics of non-physical objects.

Volitional action means mental action, but not just any action, such as thinking or feeling. It is a mental action that has an ethical quality of wholesomeness (good) or unwholesomeness (bad).

As we discussed in chapter 1, all mental phenomena involve volition, the universal mental element that is ethically neutral. When volition combines with wholesome or unwholesome mental elements, it gives rise to either unwholesome mental action or wholesome mental action: the two types of volitional action. Thus, a volitional action is always ethical. Here, ethical does not mean moral, but having the mental quality of being good or bad.

Water is colorless. When you add blue or red color to it, it becomes blue or red water. Volition is like water and volitional action is like blue or red water.

As volitional actions occur they accumulate and form volitional patterns due to grasping or clinging by a person's mind. These are known as volitional formations. For example, non-greedy actions done over a period of time give rise to a formation of generosity. Non-hateful actions done over a period of time give rise to a formation of love and kindness.

Karma is a popular Eastern term primarily used in regard to volitional action, but also in regard to volitional formations. Many people wrongly assume that there is an individual soul that generates karma. Many also misunderstand karma as a storehouse of things or deeds possessed or owned by an individual soul. Contrary to these beliefs, you don't carry around good or bad karmas (volitional formations) in your spiritual suitcase. Karma is simply a volitional (mental) phenomenon that underlies the mechanics of soul.

Volitional Force

Together, three non-physical phenomena—the element of volition (which can be considered as the seed of volitional action), volitional action itself, and volitional formations—give rise to a non-physical force known as the "volitional force." The difference between the three non-physical phenomena lies in the difference in their potency to generate the volitional force.

The volitional force is the result of karma. It lies at the heart of soul mechanics (see figure 4.1).

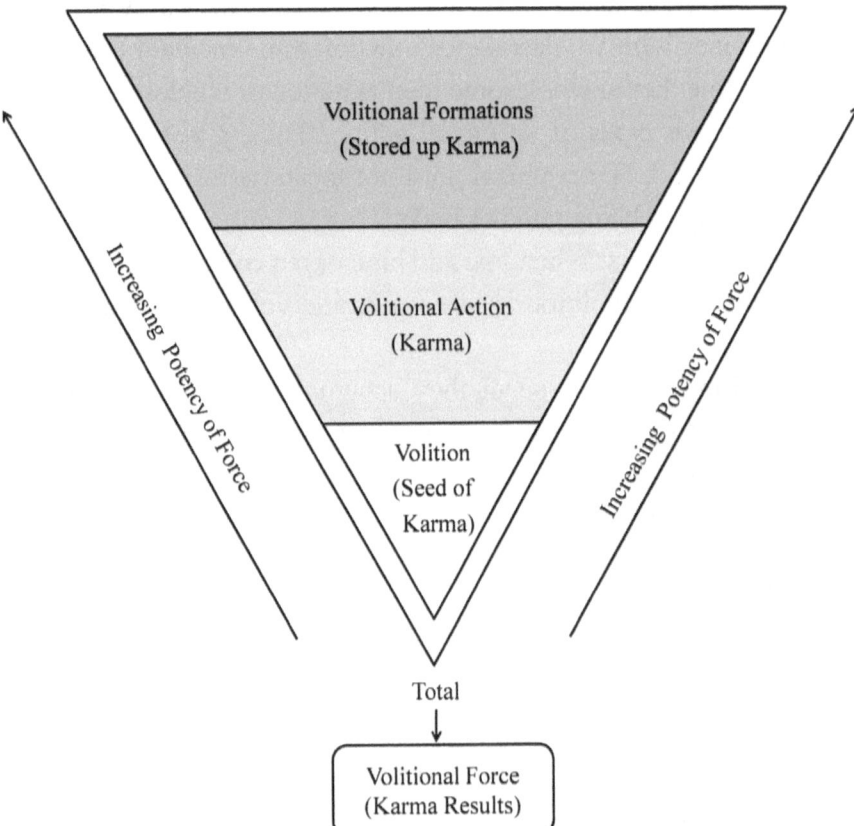

Figure 4.1. Volitional force and the karmic phenomena: the heart of soul mechanics.

Volitional force may also be known as ethical force or mental force. There is a difference between a physical force, such as gravity or

CHAPTER 4 SOUL MECHANICS

electromagnetic force, and a mental force. Physical force arises out of physical energy which simply *conserves*.[3] Volitional force arises out of volitional energy which *evolves*. Volitional energy (or force, as will be discussed later) evolves because it *learns* from its effects on the environment and vice versa. Moreover, it does not directly cause motion of any kind, but gives rise to physical energy (or force), which in turn causes motion (effects) in space-time.

Our evolution is the proof that volitional forces exist. Without volitional forces, a monkey could not have become a man. Without volitional forces, a man could not have stepped out of the cave and reached the Moon. The presence of volitional forces is what makes the human brain different from a computer. A computer works only on physical forces. Our brain works not only on physical forces but also on volitional forces, making it an evolving and learning machine.

You cannot wiggle your toes unless there is volition to do so. If you contemplate and go deeper, you will realize that, similar to a voluntary action, an involuntary action, such as a heartbeat or breathing, could not occur unless there was volition to live. If you go even deeper, you will realize that volition to live itself cannot arise unless there are additional underlying volitional forces.

On an individual basis, volitional force causes motion expressed as individual life. On a universal basis, it causes motion expressed as universal life. Just as you are alive, the universe is also alive! Just as various parts of your body (from the whole body all the way to cells and subatomic particles) are moving, various objects in the universe (from the whole universe all the way to galaxies, planets, atoms, and subatomic particles) are moving, *ultimately* due to volitional forces.

At least, on an individual basis, we experientially know that without volitional action there is no physical action. We cannot personally move or exert force on an object without the underlying force of volition. As we become more and more intelligent, one day we may realize that on the universal basis the same is true: Celestial bodies cannot exert force on each other and move without the underlying (and unifying) force of volition. That day of realization will bring forth a new, third revolution in physics.

The above paragraphs may sound like bunch of audacious reductionist statements right now. But if you contemplate what I'm communicating with an understanding of the interdependence and interconnectedness of matter and mind-consciousness, you will begin to see its depth (individual application) and breadth (universal application).

I strongly feel that volitional force is an attribute of the grand unifying force that has eluded scientists for so many decades. Exploring and understanding the nature of this force has tremendous scientific value because, one day, it may help us confirm that ours is a volitional universe, an ethical universe, a thinking universe, a living universe and not just a void filled with material/physical objects.

Volitional Energy

As stated earlier, the element of volition is not entirely volitional action. It is the most important factor responsible for generating volitional action because it is the mental element that facilitates the grouping of various unwholesome (bad) or wholesome (good) mental elements. Thus it causes good volitional action or bad volitional action. So, always think of the element of volition itself (and not "you") as being the seed of volitional action (or karma).

You might be wondering, "If it is not me, then where does the seed come from?" The answer: It comes from volitional energy. Note that volitional energy is nothing except for a term used to express the potentiality for generating the volitional force.

Think of a dam with a reservoir of water behind it. The potentiality of this dam (known as potential energy) to generate a downstream flow of water depends upon how big a reservoir it has created. Analogically speaking, a reservoir is like a storehouse of volitional formations and the potential energy of the dam is like volitional energy. The reservoir's essential content or seed— water—is like the element of volition and the force of the downstream flow coming from the spillway is like volitional force (see figure 4.2).

CHAPTER 4   SOUL MECHANICS

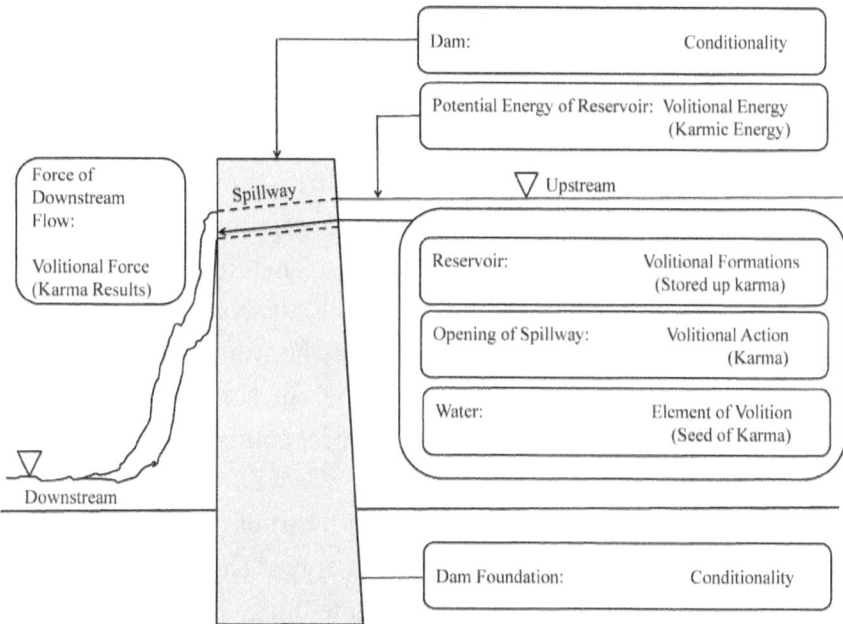

Figure 4.2. Soul mechanics: an analogy.

Just as the force of the downstream flow of water coming from a spillway depends upon the potential energy of the reservoir (the dam), the efficacy of a volitional force depends upon volitional energy. Just as the force of a downstream flow of water can generate electrical force due to specific conditions of turbines and other hydroelectric power apparatus, the volitional force can generate physical force due to specific conditions of matter, mind, and consciousness. Generated physical force manifests as physical actions and, we could also say, as physical objects and their motion.

All volitional actions do not necessarily lead to physical actions. However, they always lead to the creation of volitional formations, which in turn generate volitional energy. For example, if you are a heterosexual man and see a barely dressed woman on the beach, a lustful volition may arise in your mind. You may fantasize about things but not follow up with a physical action of chasing her and fulfilling your lust. In this case, because you did not follow up with a physical action does not mean you have not caused any harm to yourself or not done anything wrong. Mere lustful fantasizing (a mental act) has enough potency to generate bad volitional energy.

Similarly, just because you are not verbal about your hatred towards a competitor, this does not mean you are not generating bad volitional energy. The mere thought of hatred is enough to generate it. All mental actions generate volitional energy with or without the occurrence of subsequent physical actions. Therefore, being vigilant about the quality of mental actions (which always precede physical actions) is of utmost importance for those who want to avoid generating volitional energy, especially a bad one. Such a vigil is necessary because volitional energy determines the probability of the occurrence of good or bad actions in future.

Note that probability (a mathematical term) or potentiality (a mechanical term) is always a function of energy. "The unmanifest" is a philosophical term for describing the same thing. Therefore, we may consider volitional energy as the unmanifest non-physical phenomenon that expresses itself through volitional action as well as through volitional force. Such understanding will soon come handy as you dive deeper into the ocean of soul mechanics.

An artist cannot paint a picture unless he is alive (meaning, he has the volition to see, hear, and so on) and unless he has an artistic mind (volitional formation). Due to these two conditions, a third condition, the volition to paint, arises in his mind (volitional action). Due to these three conditions, he is able to visualize (volitional force) a painting he plans to create. The energy (volitional energy) required to visualize the painting depends directly upon the three conditions. Then the artist starts painting using physical energy. A completed painting is thus an outward expression or manifestation of the volitional and physical energies. Similarly, our world and the human experience of it are the expressions of various volitional and physical energies.

Understanding that our world is the expression not only of physical energies *but also* of volitional energies can have a significant impact on how we abide in it as a species. For example, realizing that it's not just carbon dioxide (CO_2) but also our greed that is responsible for global warming, may help us develop regulations that will not only minimize CO_2 emissions but also our greed. Such understanding can also serve as a foundation for personal development, especially if we take the following four laws of soul mechanics into consideration.

The First Law of Soul Mechanics: Accountability of Mental Action

Wholesome volition produces wholesome volitional force. What are the effects of this force? Fundamentally, it results in states of wholesome consciousness such as contentment, generosity, loving-kindness, faith, tranquility, happiness, and peace.

Similarly, unwholesome volition produces unwholesome volitional force. What are the effects of this force? Fundamentally, it results in states of unwholesome consciousness such as craving, aversion, stupidity, vanity, pride, pain, suffering, misery, and ego.

Wholesome or unwholesome volitional force is like a particular mould of the mind. They are a bending of mind. They bend a pure mental phenomenon by imparting their qualities to it, thereby giving rise to wholesome or unwholesome states of consciousness.

This is the first law of soul mechanics, which accounts for the ethical quality of action.

A seed of mango can only generate a mango tree that bears sweet fruit. A seed of lemon can only generate a lemon tree that bears sour fruit. A seed of lemon cannot generate a mango tree. A seed of mango cannot generate a lemon tree.

We cannot perform unwholesome deeds, such as murder, theft, lying, and slander, and get away with them. Such actions will always lead us to misery and suffering, even if these outcomes might not be obvious or show up right away. Similarly, we must not stop performing wholesome deeds, such as meditation, service, giving, reverence, and virtuosity, even if they do not produce immediate benefits. Good deeds will eventually lead us to happiness and peace although we might not feel those states right away. So do not stop being nice to someone although your kindness might not be reciprocated or you might be taken disadvantage of. Sooner or later, the benefits will come.

Just as a mango seed cannot generate a mango tree unless there are favorable conditions (soil, water, minerals, warmth, and so on), a volitional force cannot produce results or states of consciousness unless favorable conditions of matter (body) and mind exist. A seed of mango, a mango, or a mango tree does not take its form instantly. It acquires a particular form due to the accumulation of matter. Similarly, the effects of unwholesome volitional force are formed due to the accumulation of greedy or hateful reactions over a vast period of time, and the effects (the benefits) of wholesome volitional force are formed due to the accumulation of generous or faithful actions over a vast period of time.

The law of accountability of mental action is a perfect accounting system. If you develop faith in it, it will automatically give rise to fear for wrongdoing and strong will for right doing.

The Second Law of Soul Mechanics: Mental Action-reaction

A volitional force generates further volition bearing the same qualities as it, just with higher intensity. That volitional force augments as it cycles is the second law of soul mechanics.

A seed of mango generates a mango tree. This newly generated tree can only produce mango fruits that contain mango seeds only. Moreover, one seed generates many. Similarly, the volitions of greed or hatred can only generate greedy or hateful actions. These actions result in states of unwholesome consciousness that will cause the volition of greed or hatred to arise again with greater intensity. Thus the unwholesome always begets and augments the unwholesome, and the wholesome always begets and augments the wholesome.

You can't say, "Let me be greedy just for few years, make some money for my kid's education, and then I will stop and become generous" or, "Let me lie and cheat a bit for now and once this situation is over, I will become honest; after all I am doing it to help someone,"

CHAPTER 4 SOUL MECHANICS

without repercussions. If you are greedy at this moment, you are bound to become greedier the following moment. What I am trying to say is, "Change begins now, no matter what. If you cannot do it now, then most likely you will never do it because it is going to get increasingly difficult."

Every time we perform a greedy or hateful action, we produce a brick, which self-replicates and forms more bricks. Soon these bricks of action-reaction-action-reaction turn into brick walls that imprison us. However, due to delusion, we do not see these walls as prison walls but as the walls of a castle. We even color them gold and proclaim that we are living in a golden castle. This phenomenon of "gilding the walls" is most obvious in self-righteous people who justify their greedy and hateful actions in the name of personal responsibility, family obligation, a social cause, fighting for justice, public service, a commitment, duty, honor, and so forth.

The second law of soul mechanics is a form of imprisonment that all human beings live in. But it is a self-imprisonment. We can break the walls and gain freedom from imprisonment if we take the following three steps.

1. Realize that not only bad actions do not go unnoticed (the first law) no matter what kind of curtain or cover we put on them, but also they replicate, accumulate, become stronger, and make the prison walls thicker (the second law).
2. Based on the above realization, immediately start minimizing bad actions and start performing good ones.
3. If bad actions do not subside or if good actions do not produce results right away, do not be discouraged. Keep maximizing good actions until the force of wholesome volition starts crumbling the prison walls.

If there is greed, continue performing generous actions. If there is hatred, continue practicing loving-kindness. Continue until you nullify the unwholesome forces. You cannot extinguish fire unless you first realize that it is fire, second you stop adding fuel to it and start hosing it with water, and third you do not give up.

The Third Law of Soul Mechanics: Perfect Action

When the first and second laws of soul mechanics are properly implemented and continuously practiced, a time consequently comes when unwholesome volition no longer arises due to purification of mind. Mechanistically, you could say, the force *evolves* from unwholesomeness to wholesomeness.

As the force continues to evolve due to established wholesome actions, a stage eventually comes when volitional actions no longer give rise to volitional formations. There is no longer mental clinging to anything or mental grasping of any kind, due to the arising of non-delusion. If you recall, volitional formations arise only when clinging occurs due to person's mind (the presence of delusion, sense of separate self). Non-clinging or non-forming is somewhat like escaping a prison and becoming a bird that flies in the sky without leaving a trace behind. This is the state of selflessness, the highest state of mental evolution. From this moment onwards, there is only action. There is no reaction. Because there is no reaction, selfless actions are perfect actions and selflessness is the perfect state of being.

Not generating volitional formations means that a person's actions are not rooted in the specific cravings and aversions that arise due to having a sense of separate self. Any action that arises without craving or aversion liberates us from self-imprisonment and leads us in the direction of mental evolution. For attaining the highest state of evolution, the necessary condition is performing selfless actions from moment to moment.

Selfless action sometimes is misunderstood as self-sacrifice or ignoring oneself. In fact, self-sacrifice is not much different from selfishness. Both are contaminated with the sense of separate self. People who are attracted to sacrifice and self-annihilation must do the following if they are truly interested in attaining selflessness. They must:

1. Consider the welfare not only of others, but also of themselves (in other words, they must aim to create win-win rather than lose-win scenarios).

2. Remove the barriers between themselves and others by getting rid of the egoistic sense of duty or responsibility and by eradicating the delusion of being a leader or a servant.
3. Transcend the self, as if shifting their attention from inside their body to being part of the surrounding space and then looking at all beings (including themselves) from a bird's eye view, and acting from that perspective. This enables them to look at all beings (including themselves) as worthy of loving-kindness and compassion.

Transcending the self always gives rise to effortlessness and non-striving in action because there is no burden, no guilt, no competition, no power struggle, no goals, and no finish lines to reach. You are in it for one and all, *including yourself.*

Enlightened masters perform selfless actions, which is what makes them effortless functionaries. There is no striving in their actions. They do for the sake of doing that which benefits one and all. Effortlessness or non-striving is the hallmark of selflessness. Selfless action is the hallmark of perfection in action.

Ultimately, selfless action means performing an action without ego. If you help someone thinking that "you" are helping, then your action is rooted in ego. If you help someone thinking that a wholesome volition to help has arisen and is manifesting itself, then your subsequent action will be egoless. Try this out and pay attention to how you feel. In the first case, you will notice a sense of striving and in some situations a subtle expectation of reward or appreciation. In the second case, you will always feel at ease. In the first case, there is subtle self-interest (which is extremely hard to detect). In the second case, there is selflessness. Whenever there is no sense of doer, performer, achiever, executor, and so on in your actions, you'll observe that the actions become easy, flowing, smooth, impeccable, flawless, immaculate, and perfect.

The law of perfect action is subtle and profound. It becomes crystal clear only if it is applied in daily life, wakefully. As an experiment, try performing all your actions selflessly perhaps an hour a day for one week. You will soon notice how your actions become more and more playful and delightful and how you get better and better results from your actions ultimately leading to perfection.

The Fourth Law of Soul Mechanics: Emptiness and Timelessness

As we have discussed, volitional force (the force) arises out of volition, volitional action, and volitional formations (the three). However, the force and the three are entirely distinct phenomena. Although the force depends wholly upon the three for its creation, the three neither remain inside the force, nor is there any force inside the three at the beginning. In other words, the force is simply the outcome of the three having undergone a transformation. There is no outer or inner fixed entity, a force creator, which creates the force using the three as ingredients. Let us try to understand this with the following analogy.

In order to make ghee (a highly distilled form of butter from India), one has to first make milk into curd and then curd into butter. One has to then heat the butter for a long time until it turns into the liquid called ghee. Analyzing this process, we could say that milk is a basic ingredient and curd and butter are other ingredients in the manufacturing of ghee. However, no matter what you do to the ghee, you cannot retrieve milk (or curd or butter) from it. Similarly, no matter what you do to the curd or butter, you cannot find milk in it. It is so because neither milk, nor anything else is a permanent entity underlying the milk-curd-butter-ghee phenomenon. There is no unchanging substance that is transmigrating from milk to curd to butter to ghee.

Now, in the soul mechanics context, volition is the basic ingredient in the creation of action, formation, or force. However it cannot be retrieved or separated from them. There is no unchanging entity that can be found in the three and in the force. If there was an underlying fixed creator, we would be able to identify it in all of them.

CHAPTER 4 SOUL MECHANICS

If you apply this in a human context, you will realize that childhood-youth-adulthood-old age-death is merely a phenomenon of transformation. You cannot find a permanent, unchanging being (an individual soul) that is growing from childhood to adulthood and then dying. There is no entity transmigrating through different stages of life. There is no "you" being born, maturing, degenerating, and dying. At the same time, there is no maturation, aging, and death without birth. These conditions are just mutually interdependent phenomena driven by volitional and physical forces and the conditionality of matter, mind, and consciousness.

Even though we live with a sense of linear time, nothing fixed or permanent (such as a time entity or a self entity) is moving from past to present to future. The "past" is a term used to describe *conditions* that existed before the present. The "present" is a term used to describe *conditions* that currently exist. The "future" is a term used to describe *conditions* that are probable based on the present. There is no present without the past and there will be no future without the present, like the milk-curd-butter relationship.

As a thread between the conditions of past, present, and future, the volitional force creates the illusion of continuity (known as time) between past-present-future. In actuality, only the phenomena of soul fueled by the volitional force flow on—not time. Soul phenomena underlie everything in existence and yet they are empty (of self) and timeless. You and I neither have eternal life nor time-bound existence. Body, mind, consciousness are simply transforming in accordance with the laws of soul mechanics.

The four laws of soul mechanics are fixed, meaning they cannot be changed. No outside or inside power ensures their efficacy. The laws themselves are supreme (see figure 4.3).

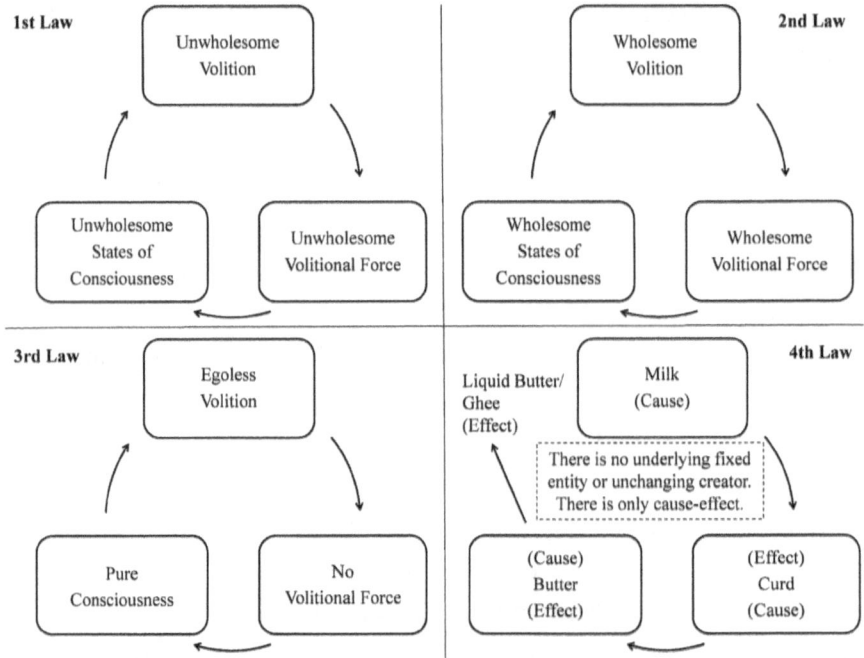

Figure 4.3. The four laws of soul mechanics.

What about Choice or Free Will?

You might be wondering, "If the laws of soul mechanics are supreme, then what is the nature of choice? Don't we make choices in our lives? Are we only living machines run by these laws?"

Choice is nothing except for a volitional phenomenon. All choices arise at the climax of the cognitive process of consciousness. I cannot discuss this in detail just yet, but if you were to simply understand choice-making as a climactic volitional activity, you would appreciate the crux of it. However, there isn't a choice maker behind choice.

A choice is an action or a reaction. It is primarily a reaction when unwholesome volition arises and it is primarily an action when wholesome volition arises during the cognitive process. Because of delusion (ego), we feel that we have made a choice. In both cases, whether action or reaction, what is actually happening is a volitional activity.

Let us say you were extremely hungry and you were asked to choose between a healthy salad and a less healthy double-cheese pizza. Even

CHAPTER 4 SOUL MECHANICS

though you prefer eating pizza, in this case you ignored it and *chose* the salad. What happened was as follows: The moment you saw food, there was a desire to eat. This desire was nothing but the arising of sense-consciousness rooted in greed, a manifestation of impulses caused by the volitional force that arose at the climax of the cognitive process. Assuming you were mindful and non-reactive, a strong wholesome volition for nourishment and health arose and counteracted the impulses. It reduced the strength of the volitional force and overcame it. That's why you ended up ignoring the unhealthy pizza and chose the healthy salad. Instead of reacting, you acted. If wholesome volition had not arisen, then you simply would have succumbed to the impulses.

The volitional action that overpowered the volitional force is called "choice" in common language. While an impulse is also commonly referred to as choice, really it is just a reaction. So, the correct thing to say would be, "Wholesome volitional action is a right choice and unwholesome volitional action (or impulse) is a wrong choice."

In the preceding case, notice that wholesome volition arose and overpowered the impulse for eating tasty, but unhealthy food because there was mindfulness and non-reaction. In life, we encounter many other impulses (such as lust and anger) that have formidable power. To counteract them, we not only require mindfulness and non-reaction, but also concentration and wise attention. From here on, I shall collectively refer to these four mental faculties as "meditativity." Meditativity can be understood as a powerful wholesome volition or right choice.

We are going to discuss a lot about how to develop meditativity so that more right choices are made and wrong choices are entirely eliminated. If you ardently and consistently develop meditativity, I am confident that a stage will come in your life when you will make no more wrong choices. There will be no more reactions.

It is harmful to live in a reactive mode of life, because all kinds of suffering arise when greed, hatred, and delusion are running the show. It is much preferable to live in the mode of taking actions that are rooted in non-greed, non-hatred, and non-delusion. A spiritual practitioner sooner or later realizes beyond a shadow of doubt that such actions cannot arise without the volition of meditativity.

I strongly urge you to develop meditativity. It is, overall, the best choice you can make in life. The soul meditation practices that I will discuss later in the book are designed for this purpose. These meditations are not typical "sitting down with closed eyes" kinds of meditation. They are a lot more than that. They can be practiced with open eyes and while doing chores or anything else. They are designed so that they become a way of life.

Do everything you do in life as a meditation so that meditativity can arise during action. Meditativity can only bring perfection to actions, including actions that may be as trivial as plucking a flower or as significant as saving someone's life. Meditate! Practice, practice, practice! And then leave the rest to the four laws. The laws are foolproof. They work flawlessly. In the presence of meditativity, they will surely bring you to a state of perfection.

What about Desire?

It is hard for many of us to accept that choice is a volitional phenomenon and there is no choice maker. We make (or think we do) various choices in our lives in order to fulfill our desires. So many of us wonder how we can have desires and why we should have desires if we are not making choices.

The real issue behind such questioning is that most of us are so self-centered and deluded that we cannot perform actions without self-interest. We cannot even conceive of such a possibility. That is why we suffer and create suffering for others.

In order to attain a high degree of perfection in action, we need to perform desireless and choiceless actions—just as an infant performs its actions, just as flowers bloom, and just as birds fly in the sky—but with awareness and wisdom of the four laws. We need to perform only wholesome actions rooted in the wisdom made evident to us by the four laws.

CHAPTER 4 SOUL MECHANICS

Actions can be performed without being an actor or a choice maker. Actions can be performed without pursuing a particular desire. When we do something as a hobby, we don't necessarily have any desire to achieve anything, even if we spend hours pursuing the activity. We just play guitar, paint, or make clay pots. There is no wanting in performing the activity, no sense of desiring in terms of achieving or go-getting something. Desireless, choiceless actions are kind of like that. They arise without having to have selfish desires or goals.

When there are no selfish desires or goals, the *purpose of life* is illuminated in our consciousness. From this perspective, you may realize that the real purpose of your life is invariably rooted in desireless, choiceless actions. If you can discover this real purpose, you can change your life from misery to mastery.

A simple, pragmatic way to find your life's purpose is to start minimizing unwholesome actions and start maximizing wholesome ones. Whenever there is a sense of greed or hatred, you ought to abandon the action. Whenever there is self-interest or delusion, you ought to abandon the action. See examples in the two lists below.

Table 4.1
Unwholesome Actions (To Be Minimized)

Greedy Actions	
Acquiring	Hoaxing
Accumulating	Intoxicating
Attaching	Lying
Clinging	Longing
Conning	Lusting
Corrupting	Stealing
Craving	Scamming
Dominating	Sexually overindulging
Exhibiting	Passion
Excessive cheering	Patronizing
Excessive consuming	Pestering
Excessive entertaining	Possessing
Excessive partying	Showing off
Flattering	Stalking
Gambling	Womanizing

THE ELEMENTS OF SOUL

Table 4.1
Unwholesome Actions (To Be Minimized) (Continued)

Hateful Actions	
Accusing	Fighting
Aggravating	Forcing
Arguing	Getting bored
Antagonizing	Hating
Being Mean	Killing
Competing	Punishing
Complaining	Polluting
Condemning	Regretting
Crying	Resenting
Envying	Slandering
Deluded Actions	
Advertising	Manipulating
Becoming suspicious	Judging
Believing	Justifying
Bewildering	Mystifying
Celebrating	Opining
Dogmatizing	Overreaching
Endorsing	Performing rituals blindly
Fearing	Politicizing
Feeling restless	Standardizing
Forgetting	Self-mortifying
Grieving	Self-aggrandizing
Holding back	Self-satisfying
Indoctrinating	Worshipping without understanding
Lazing out	Worrying

Table 4.2
Wholesome Actions (To Be Maximized)

Admiring	Neutralizing
Agreeing	Meditating
Appreciating	Moderately consuming
Attending wisely	Neither believing, nor disbelieving
Balancing	Non-adhering
Befriending	Non-discriminating
Caring	Non-disturbing
Concentrating	Non-forgetting

Table 4.2
Wholesome Actions (To Be Maximized) (Continued)

Contemplating	Non-hindering
Cooling	Non-opposing
Cooperating	Non-resisting
Detaching	Non-wobbling
Developing pure understanding	Observing silence
Devoting	Penetrating
Discovering	Promoting virtue
Empathizing	Promoting welfare
Enabling	Purifying
Enjoying	Rejoicing
Equalizing	Remembering
Establishing faith with understanding	Removing others' suffering
Fearing wrongdoing	Renouncing
Forgiving	Resolving
Gifting	Respecting
Giving	Resting
Gladdening	Serving
Guarding mindfulness	Simplifying
Healing	Smiling
Helping	Studying
Honoring	Sympathizing
Investigating	Thanking
Just being	Trusting
Lightening up	Wielding
Listening	Wondering
Neutral observing	Worshipping with understanding

We need to perform only wholesome actions. Most importantly, we need to perform all actions with meditativity. If we do so, a stage automatically comes when our actions eventually are driven by the real purpose of our lives. This stage comes in the lives of those few people who consistently strive for self-improvement and self-realization. Most often, this stage comes during the mid-life period (between the ages of 35 and 45 years). It is commonly and mistakenly known as a mid-life crisis, because it is often accompanied by emotional pain. But it actually is not a crisis. It's a blessing. We can see the blessing in this period if we develop meditativity. The majority of people miss this golden opportunity and end up living in a rut forever chasing endless desires that can never be fulfilled.

Once we discover our real purpose in life and act on it meditatively, then our creativity unfolds. The newfound work becomes tireless and delightful. There is joy in what we do. There is bliss in action. And this represents real success. Eventually, through such creative, joyful, and blissful actions, wise people establish themselves in the purity of non-self. This is the way of purification by action.

People often want to own the fruits of all their actions or they want to take no action. They simply cannot let go of the self-identity. They cannot understand the middle way—the perfect way—*the way of performing actions without being attached to the results of action.*

What about Chance, Fate, Destiny, and Luck?

Many deterministic thinkers do not like the idea of finding the real purpose of life because they believe everything is destined. They believe in fate and providence, and so live passive lives. Some who happen to be unsuccessful in life consider themselves unlucky and some who happen to be successful in life consider themselves lucky.

Even great physicists like Isaac Newton and Albert Einstein firmly believed that whatever happened in the universe had to be predestined. According to them, the universe ran like a clock. In classical mechanics, there was no such thing as chance. Everything was bound by fate or destiny as determined by the known laws of physics. This was most exemplified by Einstein's famous statement, "God does not throw dice."[4]

Although later developments in quantum mechanics decisively proved that everything in the microscopic world is probabilistic and happens by chance (based on conditionality), Einstein was not willing to accept this fact. He even modified his theories of relativity to remove aspects of chance (probability) from quantum mechanics. Another physicist, Niels Bohr, once chided him, "Don't tell God what to do!" Eventually Einstein gracefully accepted his mistake with a statement, "I have earned the right to be wrong."[5]

CHAPTER 4 SOUL MECHANICS

Classical mechanics does not allow chance, and quantum mechanics relies solely on it.[6] In soul mechanics, on the other hand, chance, fate, and destiny are fundamentally similar except for their potency in generating a particular manifestation of the volitional force. Fate is stronger than chance. Destiny is stronger than fate. On a scale of probability of generating a particular manifestation, you could say that chance is at the lowest level. Fate is in the middle, thus having a greater chance. Destiny is at the top, thus having the greatest chance. Most of the significant events in our lives occur due to fate or destiny, rather than by chance or luck (see figure 4.4). Luck is just another word for *chance taken personally*.

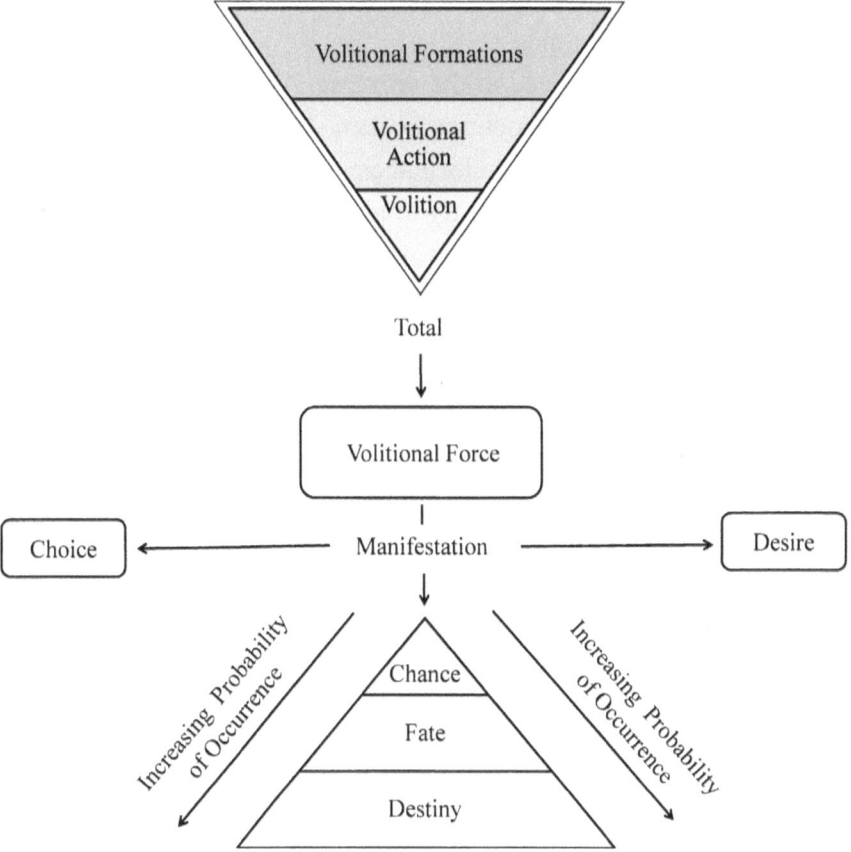

Figure 4.4. Chance, fate, destiny, and luck: The manifestation of the volitional forces (karma).

79

There is a greater chance of leading happy, peaceful lives if we generate wholesome volitional forces. There is a greater chance of leading painful, unhappy lives if we generate unwholesome volitional forces. Those of us who perform wholesome deeds have a greater chance of having good fortune than those who perform unwholesome deeds. If we choose to perform only wholesome actions and abandon unwholesome actions, consistently and ardently, we can change the direction of our fate and destiny. However, we must not wait. We must make right choices right now. The longer we wait, the harder it is to change our fate or destiny for good.

In short, we always have a chance in life to make it better. We are not bound by some fixed fate or destiny. So we need not blame fate or destiny for our misfortunes.

Nothing goes unnoticed in the universe. As was said earlier, soul mechanics is a perfect accounting system. It produces immediate results, as well as long-term results that can eventually change our luck. However, do not overreach and try to identify with it or to own it. Just as there is choice without a choice maker, there is luck, but no owner of it. There is fate, but no owner of fate. There is destiny, but no owner of destiny.

Chance, fate, and destiny are simply volitional phenomena that produce a karmic drama. In this drama, you are stuck playing the lead role as long as you identify with it or "own it" due to ego. When ego is finished, the drama ends, and real life begins. What begins is the unfolding of your real life purpose, leading to happy abiding and bliss.

* * *

Chapter 5

Soul Intelligence: A Journey beyond Emotional and Spiritual Intelligence

The topic of soul mechanics is exciting and vast. It has the potential to address many intriguing existential issues, such as the origin and development of life (creation and evolution), the boundary conditions of an individual life (birth and death), the continuation of an individual life (reincarnation or not), the hierarchy of life (other worlds of existence or not), and so on. These issues form the hot topics (if not the holy grail yet) of a current scientific community, which is composed of evolutionary biologists, life scientists, bio-engineers, genomists, biochemists, astrobiologists, astrophysicists, cosmologists, futurists, and the like.[1] Soul mechanics can provide a thorough philosophical framework to address these issues, but due to its vastness and complexity it cannot be discussed further beyond the introduction given in the previous chapter. Nonetheless, what I intend to do here is to prepare an intellectual foundation for such a framework. Soul intelligence is that foundation.

The premise behind soul intelligence is that the deepest mysteries are invariably rooted in the mystery of "you." And this is precisely the problem we have in investigating them. With our two eyes we can look through the telescope and microscope and explore the world *out there,* but our two eyes cannot explore the world *in here.* We need a "third eye" that can provide us with a unique "vision" so we can look "within" and then "without" to unravel the universe's deepest mysteries.

I am proposing soul intelligence is the third eye.

What Is Intelligence? A Mainstream Perspective

The nature of intelligence is a question that for decades has eluded psychologists, as well as other mainstream scientists and educators. There are as many definitions as there are definers. Intelligence has been defined variously as goal-directed adaptive behavior, judgment, a mental faculty for adapting to circumstances, rational thinking, purposeful thinking, initiative, practical sense, a set of problem-solving skills, the ability to deal with cognitive complexity, innate cognitive ability, creative adaptability, memory, the capacity to figure things out, making sense of things, and so forth.[2] Considering the variety of definitions, it seems as if the word "intelligence" is more of an umbrella concept than a specific term.

Although there are many definitions of intelligence, currently there aren't many ways of understanding or testing it. The most widely known method is based on psychometrics. This method utilizes the IQ test and other aptitude tests, which measure the general intelligence factor "g" that correlates rather well with genetic, biological, and social parameters. However, this method is not universally accepted. Howard Gardner, a well-known intelligence theorist from Harvard

CHAPTER 5 SOUL INTELLIGENCE

University, believes that there is no such thing as "general" intelligence (g) or IQ that can fully describe cognitive ability.[3]

It seems there are computationalists from the field of computer science and logic who also think the whole idea of psychometric or general intelligence is weak. They argue that computers or robots (known as computational agents) can perform and will perform all of the IQ tasks defined under the umbrella of intelligence even better than people. They cite the example of a computing machine called Deep Blue, which defeated the reigning chess champion Gary Kasparov in 1997.[4] Does this mean that Deep Blue, a machine, is intelligent? According to futurologists (a new science of probability), a desktop computer will be close to becoming a brain and will be able to perform all the above defined tasks of intelligence by 2029, a probability derived from Moore's Law, which says that computing ability doubles every 18 months.[5] Does this mean that in the future we will have intelligent computers and robots doing our bidding? Does a calculator become intelligent because it can compute? It has a far better ability to compute than the highest IQ test scorer.

It is obvious that the IQ model of intelligence is inadequate. In order to complete the model of intelligence, a new area of psychological research began to account for factors (such as emotions, motivations, intentions, desires, fears, and so on) that go beyond IQ. Concepts of emotional intelligence (which is popularly known as EQ) were introduced, developed, and popularized by psychiatrists, psychologists, and journalists, such as Wayne Payne, Stanley Greenspan, and Daniel Goleman. In fact, seeds of EQ were planted years ago by Charles Darwin, creator of the theory of evolution, who postulated that emotional expression is significant for survival, as well as by behaviorists and educational psychologists like the late Edward Thorndike, who conceived of the idea of social intelligence. Howard Gardner introduced the model of multiple intelligences (interpersonal and intrapersonal intelligences), which referred to EQ. However, it wasn't until *New York Times* reporter Daniel Goleman published his book *Emotional Intelligence* (Bantam 1995) that EQ became a popular term.[6]

The arguments and the amount of confusion in the EQ field are so intense that there is no consensus to date. Current definitions are being constantly modified due to rapid, ongoing research. Although there are various definitions and a few measurement models (such as ability-based, trait-based, and competency-based), these models are generally viewed as being too broad and not stable. Some of the models, such as the competency-based model proposed by Goleman, are criticized as being pop psychology.[7] Some modern researchers such as Hans Eysenck and Edwin Locke suggest that EQ is not even a form of intelligence![8]

The third category of intelligence is known as spiritual intelligence (SQ). This has been proposed by philosophers, thought leaders, and spiritual advocates to account for intuition, integrity, compassion, the sense of belonging, believing, having faith, having purpose, and so on. The term itself reportedly was coined by Danah Zohar, a multidisciplinary graduate of MIT and Harvard University, who categorized SQ as the intelligence of the deep self, self-awareness, integrity, leadership, and the ability to ask the deepest questions about ourselves. Other thinkers, among them Tony Buzan, Kathleen Noble, and David King, have defined SQ as the mental ability for transcendence, choosing between ego and spirit, heightened states of consciousness, mental ability for non-materialism, unity consciousness, oneness, awareness of spirit, inspiration, and so forth. Howard Gardner excluded SQ from his theory of multiple intelligences and called it an existential intelligence. Definitions are thus varied and without a universal model of measurement.[9]

Why Soul Intelligence?

Having briefly reviewed the existing concepts of intelligence (IQ, EQ, and SQ), I would venture to say that although we may develop a broad understanding of intelligence from these concepts, a complete understanding is not possible. I prefer to call these concepts incomplete rather than flawed because they have a pragmatic value that has been demonstrated over the years. This is somewhat similar to the incomplete nature of Newtonian mechanics, which we discussed earlier.

CHAPTER 5 SOUL INTELLIGENCE

Although Newton's laws of motion and gravity are based on absolute space-time, a concept that has been proven flawed beyond doubt, the laws still work beautifully in day-to-day matters and thus carry immense practical value. Without these laws, we would not be able to design and use various small and large mechanical devices, including spaceships! However, these laws break down beyond a certain threshold (atomic scale and near the speed of light).[10] We cannot use them to design TVs, cell phones, GPS systems, computers, or laser equipment. Similarly, all the existing theories of intelligence break down when we reach the threshold of the self.

Here is why. A careful scrutiny reveals that current theories of intelligence appear to be based on two assumptions: 1. A permanent self exists. 2. Intelligence is an entity (a separate reality), which can be acquired or possessed by the self. Excluding just one or two definitions, all others seem to be underlain by an assumption of the self as separate from intelligence. This assumption makes current theories break down at the threshold of the self, rendering them incomplete.

In an earlier chapter, I introduced the idea of soul mechanics to integrate and go beyond Newtonian and quantum mechanics. Here I am introducing the idea of soul intelligence to integrate and go beyond IQ, EQ, and SQ, so that we might one day develop a complete, flawless theory of intelligence.

Redefining Intelligence

From the perspective of soul intelligence, we can define intelligence simply as the "mental ability of consciousness." Intelligence is not quite the adaptability or computability or cognitive ability of a person or a being. Rather, it is a mental phenomenon, or conditionality, which facilitates understanding reality *as it is* without the need of a being. In other words, soul intelligence is *pure* understanding, which is commonly known as "wisdom." The word "pure" is emphasized to indicate that intelligence is a phenomenon devoid of any being. However, it cannot exist independent of consciousness.

You might know that the word intelligence itself comes from the Latin verb "intelligere," which means, "to understand." It understands, so it is intelligence.

Ultimately, intelligence is a state of knowing (the reality, the truth) without a sense of being a knower. Soon I will shed more light on this phenomenon and illuminate its profound practical implications.

The philosophical model of intelligence that I am going to propose here is based on the ideas of mental elements and consciousness that were introduced in chapter 1. Let us call it the soul model. According to this model, intelligence is a phenomenon that takes place when groups of mental elements arise together in consciousness. Conventionally speaking, "intellect" and "intelligence" are both just terms used to convey that this is occurring.

Because I have grouped various mental elements as various mind types (universal mind, unwholesome mind, wholesome mind, special mind, and so on) we could say that intelligence is essentially the outcome of interactions between various mind types that arise in consciousness.

Mechanistically, we could say that volitional force is a subtle nonphysical disturbance caused by intelligence. It is somewhat like a relationship between a force and a field.[11] Intelligence is like a field (related to volitional energy) that generates volitional forces and vice versa.

Depending upon the nature of arising mental elements (neutral or ethically variable), any currently forming intelligence may be classified into three known categories (IQ, EQ, SQ), various subcategories, and the fourth category of soul intelligence. These four categories are not separate from each other. Rather they indicate an ethical hierarchy somewhat like an evolutionary ladder. IQ is basic intelligence, EQ is higher than IQ, and SQ is higher than EQ. I am proposing soul intelligence as the top rung on the ladder. There is no EQ without IQ, and no SQ without IQ and EQ. Similarly there is no soul intelligence without IQ, EQ, and SQ.

CHAPTER 5 SOUL INTELLIGENCE

What about Artificial Intelligence?

If there is no consciousness, there is no intelligence. That is why initially we defined intelligence as the mental ability of consciousness. What this means is that there can be no such thing as artificial intelligence (AI).

Machines are not conscious beings, so the computing or logic abilities of computers, no matter how incredible, cannot be attributed to intelligence *per se*. There have been endless philosophical discussions in the AI field over decades regarding whether or not machines can think and whether or not a human brain can be duplicated in a machine.[12] For me or anyone else who understands the *conscious* nature of intelligence, the answer is a very simple "no."

As we will soon discuss, the element of "feeling" is a primary mental element in all types of intelligence (except in soul intelligence, where it exists in a residual form because it is transcended). You cannot become conscious or think or perceive or know *unless* you feel.

The status of the element of feeling from the chart of mental elements (as introduced in chapter 1) is analogous to the status of the element of hydrogen from the periodic table. Unless the element of hydrogen was created at the big bang, we would not have had other elements and the matter that we see around us.[13] Likewise, without the element of feeling there would not have been any intelligence created. What I am suggesting is that if we consider hydrogen the most primitive element of matter, we could in the same way consider feeling the most primitive element of intelligence. In my opinion, the element of feeling is directly related to the formation of intelligence through the process of evolution (or learning).

Unless we make machines that can feel, we cannot have AI. This does not mean that AI is not possible. It's just not going to happen soon. Once a feeling machine (and not just a sensing machine) is built it might take hundreds or thousands of years for the generation of intelligence through feeling and learning unless radically different computational and logical models (which account for feeling) are also formulated. Note that nature took several million years to build the human brain from amoeba, the most primitive intelligent organism.[14]

To the great thinkers and leaders of the AI industry, I would humbly make the request that they ponder soul mechanics and other such matters. The possible reason that many scientists do not have a good understanding of AI and the reason why AI is still a largely mysterious field is that scientists do not account for consciousness, feeling, or the volitional forces that form the root of all forms of intelligence. Although the known laws of physics do not prevent us from creating AI, we are still nowhere close to building a thinking machine. I suggest this might be happening because we are overlooking the fact that the known laws of physics are incomplete without considering the volitional forces of soul mechanics.

My view about the near impossibility of creating AI is shared by renowned mathematical physicist Roger Penrose of the University of Oxford, philosopher John Searle of the University of California at Berkley, and Colin McGinn of Rutgers University.[15]

We can create robots and computers like Deep Blue that have far greater computing capabilities than humans, but we cannot currently create emotional robots that can feel, think, and find meaning in what they sense. A robot can see and hear far better than any human can but it cannot derive meaning from what it sees or hears. For a robot, a rock or a metal or a child is just a bunch of video pixels. It will crush or destroy what it sees if it is asked to do so. It does not have volition of its own and hence it has no volitional or ethical force for generating intelligence. It has no understanding. A robot can be a master of syntax, but it cannot master semantics. It can never know what love or hate *means*, although it can effortlessly translate the words into any language. Why? It has never *felt* those emotions, which arise due to volitional forces developed through evolution.

Levels of Intelligence

Intelligence is an evolutionary phenomenon. I suggest it develops as volitional forces evolve from unwholesome to wholesome.

CHAPTER 5 SOUL INTELLIGENCE

Depending upon the degree of such development, we perform the act of knowing at four different levels.

Let us say four people are asked to describe a red apple placed on a plate in front of them. The first person looks at the object and describes it as a red, smooth, round object. The second person describes it as an apple, a sweet fruit. He sees and perceives it as such due to past knowledge, inference, judgment, and memory. He may also describe it as the "king of fruit" or as his "favorite fruit." The third person touches the object, smells it, tastes it, and then describes it as a red, smooth, round-shaped fruit that tastes sweet. He penetrates deeper into the nature of the object by becoming conscious of it through direct experience. The fourth person not only eats the apple, he also meditates and contemplates the apple's nature. Consequently he describes it as a red, smooth, round, and sweet piece of *matter* made of various elements, including wholesome fibrous nutriment. His understanding penetrates the characteristics of the apple and reaches the level of its essence: the elemental nature of having nutritious value.

Four people know the same object differently due to their different levels of intelligence. The first person is at the level of IQ, the second person is at the level of EQ, the third person is at the level of SQ, and the fourth one is functioning at the level of soul intelligence.

The preceding example was a crude way of illustrating the subtle differences between the four levels of intelligence. It should not be followed literally. What I mean is that even though one may understand apple as nutritious matter, one need not stop using the word "apple" while communicating with others.

If our four subjects were now asked to describe themselves, the first person would describe himself as a mammal, a human body. The second person would describe himself as somebody who resides in a body. He knows his body as his self. He perceives it as such due to his attachment to it. The third person would describe himself as a bundle of body-mind-consciousness. He has become conscious of three distinct phenomena through experience. However he would describe it as the carrier of his (individual) soul, because he still considers himself the owner of the bundle, and he feels and experiences it as his own.

The fourth person would not describe himself as someone carrying the body or the bundle of body-mind-consciousness. He understands body-mind-consciousness as a group of phenomena that exists on its own accord. He understands that there is no owner of these phenomena and no self in them. He understands that there is only soul and no individual soul. He also understands the impermanence in the phenomena. He understands that physical, mental, and conscious phenomena arise and pass away. Nothing lasts forever. He sees that he does not have control over it. He cannot make it the way he wants it. Having thus penetrated the deepest level of understanding, he then describes himself as "pure awareness" because he has been asked to describe himself in words (otherwise he wouldn't say anything). He goes beyond the threshold of the self because he is rooted in soul intelligence.

In the human context, the four levels of intelligence can be understood psychologically as follows. (As stated earlier, the element of feeling is present in all three levels and in a residual form in the fourth level).

- *Level 1 (sensing and feeling):* Sensory and mental acts of mere knowing that are rooted in the universal and special mind, specifically in the mental elements of sensation, feeling, and thinking. Such acts of knowing are ethically neutral and mostly related to IQ.
- *Level 2 (feeling and perceiving):* Mental acts of interpreting, distinguishing, recognizing, identifying, judging, and evaluating that are rooted in the universal mind and the special mind, as well as the wholesome mind and the unwholesome mind, specifically in the mental elements of feeling, perception, greed, non-greed, hatred, and non-hatred. Such acts of knowing are ethically variable (good or bad) and they are mostly related to EQ.
- *Level 3 (feeling and cognizing/becoming conscious):* Experiential acts of knowing that are rooted in the universal mind and the special mind, as well as in the wholesome mind, specifically in the mental elements of feeling, perception, non-greed, and non-hatred, and most prominently in the element of equanimity. Such acts of

CHAPTER 5 SOUL INTELLIGENCE

knowing are mostly related to SQ and always have a wholesome ethical quality. *Becoming conscious* is the real act of cognition. It is subtler and more penetrative than simply feeling and perceiving. Note that the unwholesome mind does not partake in SQ.

- *Level 4 (understanding):* The fourth and the subtlest act of knowing, which is beyond cognizing. It is cognizing without being a cognizer. It simply understands by itself. It is something that is beyond mind-consciousness yet not separate from it. It is the act of knowing at a selfless level of consciousness. It is ultimate knowing rooted in non-delusion at the level of essence. There is no further penetration of knowledge beyond understanding. Such understanding, which is pure consciousness, is conventionally called *wisdom*. This fourth level of knowing is the third eye (aka spiritual vision). It facilitates understanding of extremely subtle existential phenomena. It unravels mysteries and brings forth perfection (see figure 5.1).

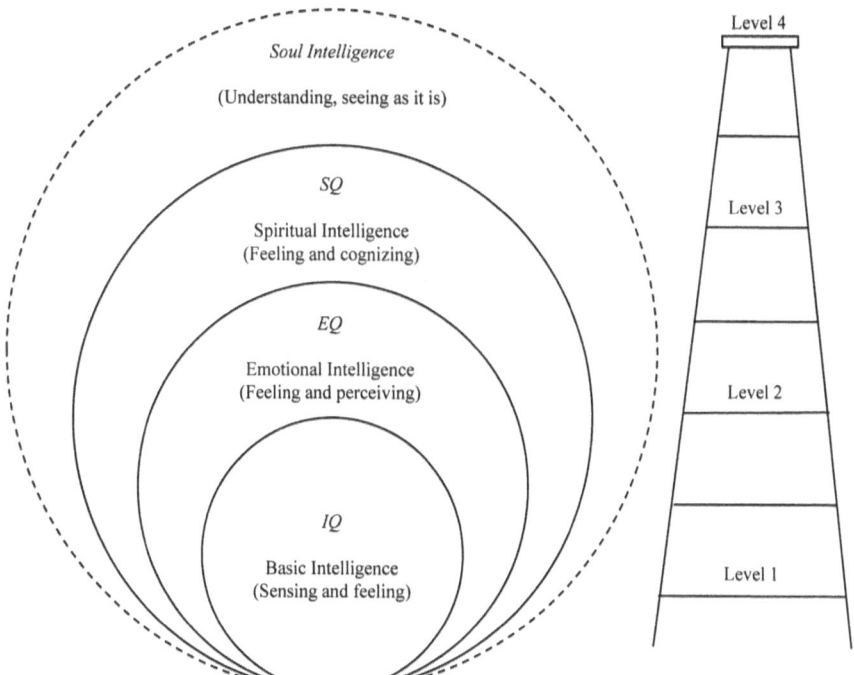

Figure 5.1. The levels of intelligence. Notice the psychological makeup of the four levels of intelligence. The element of feeling is present in all of them except in level 4, where it is present only in residual form.

Many times I have been asked questions like, "What difference does soul intelligence make in everyday life?" The following answer illustrates the benefits.

What you do when someone gets angry with you? Most likely, you perceive the other's anger as a personal attack. You get offended. Your heart burns with hatred towards that person. You perceive anger as something belonging to someone. You perceive it as a weapon directed towards you. This happens because you know anger only through IQ and EQ.

If you do not get offended and observe anger with equanimity, most likely you will begin to realize that the angry person does not look happy. You will also realize that you don't feel good either. You will thus recognize that anger is an unpleasant feeling, an unwholesome mental phenomenon through in and throughout. When you know anger in this way, through SQ, through *becoming conscious* (real cognition) of its nature, you will no longer pursue it as belonging to someone or as something directed towards you.

If your intelligence evolves even further, most likely you will realize that anger does not last forever. It arises temporarily due to unwholesome mental elements (or conditions rather than due to you or anyone else) and eventually ceases. You will realize that anger is an impermanent and impersonal unwholesome mental phenomenon. When you know the essence of anger in this way, through soul intelligence—the mode of understanding—what happens to you? You see the angry person as diseased and suffering just like you would see a person with cancer. Due to spiritual vision, compassion and loving-kindness will arise in you and you will no longer feel hatred towards the angry person. Hatred will be replaced by the divine feelings of compassion and loving-kindness. Suffering will be replaced by wisdom! This is how soul intelligence can make a tremendous difference in everyday life.

Much effort in the psychological and educational communities is spent on improving IQ. From childhood to adulthood, we are mostly learning how to think, investigate, determine, calculate, and so on. Unless we have guidance, we rarely discover how to remove greed,

CHAPTER 5 SOUL INTELLIGENCE

hatred, or delusion from our intellect. That is why, no matter how intelligent we become in a worldly sense, we still suffer and live only moderately happy, and often downright unsatisfactory lives.

A Nobel Prize-winning physicist may have great intelligence, but her intellect is still basic if she hasn't developed soul intelligence! That is why, even though some such winners might have reached the pinnacle of IQ, they did not necessarily live happy and peaceful lives. Ludwig Boltzmann, who could be called the father of atomic theory, killed himself, apparently because he could not handle being ridiculed by those who thought atoms did not exist. Hans Berger, the German neurologist who devised the first EEG machine for use on human objects, committed suicide because he was disturbed by war. Edwin Armstrong, the inventor of FM radio, jumped from the 13th floor of a building and ended his life due to extreme pessimism. George Eastman, the inventor of Kodak, a brilliant but deluded man, ended his life saying, "The work is done, why wait!"[16]

The most heartbreaking story of all is that of British scientist Alan Turing, the father of computer science and mathematical logic. Without his work, none of today's computers and other such products could work. He took his own life because he could not tolerate the humiliation he felt after the exposure of his homosexuality.[17] And Albert Einstein, who could easily earn a genius score on an IQ test, lived a sad life, especially during World War I. In fact he contemplated ending his life due to many failures in the early part of his career.[18] The list is surprisingly long and filled with great achievers not only in science but also in music, art, industry, religion, and politics. Some great IQ achievers not only have lived sad lives, they also have directly or indirectly generated great harm by facilitating the production of nuclear weapons and other harmful byproducts.

Enlightened masters and spiritual aspirants may not know how to solve mathematical equations, but most of the time they are happy and peaceful. Using IQ and EQ, they sharpen and purify their minds and make them wholesome. Then, using SQ, they develop equanimity. Eventually, using soul intelligence, they perfect the mind by cultivating non-delusion. Instead of simply developing a mathematical model or an experimental model for understanding the material world (like most IQ masters would do), enlightened masters and spiritual aspirants think, contemplate, and *figure out* how to remove anger, lust, greed, and delusion from their consciousness, and how to develop love, compassion, happiness, and peace.

Can you imagine what would happen if our educational systems were to focus more on purifying and sharpening the mind to wholesomeness (EQ and SQ) than on developing IQ? Can you imagine what will happen if many of our spiritual and religious traditions were to focus on perfecting the mind (soul intelligence) than on developing theologies, institutions, and memberships? Human civilization will be radically transformed in every area from science to art to governance to economy to religious harmony.

Having said these things, I must point out that a person possessing tremendous IQ, such as a scientist, has a much better chance of developing EQ, SQ, and soul intelligence than the average person. The problem is that most don't know how to do so.

In this book, I am primarily focusing on how to develop soul intelligence, which is not attained exclusively by worldly knowledge (IQ), wholesome emotionality (EQ), mental conditioning (EQ), or equanimity (SQ), but rather by a combination of these. Because soul intelligence is at the top of the ladder of intelligence, as you develop it, your IQ, EQ, and SQ automatically build up and, as the top of the ladder is approached, eventually lead to generating everlasting happiness and peace by revealing the true nature of things. At the top of the ladder, due to soul intelligence, the illusion of separate self (the ego) is removed and intelligence is perfected.

Because soul intelligence goes beyond sensing, perceiving, cognizing, and becoming conscious (the lower acts of knowing that are tainted with ego) it is capable of completely eradicating the ego through the understanding of impermanence and non-self. Perfection is impossible unless these two ultimate truths of our life experience are known. Therefore any spiritual practice or mental training geared towards attaining perfect intelligence should be dedicated to the development of soul intelligence.

How does one develop soul intelligence?

One practices soul meditation, a unique form of mental training described in the next chapter.

* * *

Chapter 6

Soul Meditation

In common language, the word "meditation" loosely refers to the activity of sitting down and concentrating on a physical or mental object, such as a flame, a dot, a mantra, a sound, an image, or a thought. The word also refers to a variety of reflective and introspective practices taught by different spiritual traditions.

The practice of meditation rings a mystical or supernatural tone for religious people. For martial artists, some monks, and some yogis, it is a way of developing their physical and mental muscles. For secularists, it represents a form of relaxation, sensual awareness, and biofeedback. For a scientific community composed of medical doctors, physiologists, psychologists, and psychiatrists meditation is a form of therapy and the subject of mind-body research. Last but not least, for some New Age enthusiasts and some of the Hollywood moviemakers, meditation is considered cool and trendy.

What Meditation Really Is

In reality, none of the preceding descriptions indicates the essence of meditation. Meditation does not only mean sitting down and concentrating. That is a limited practice. So whenever the word meditation comes to mind and you visualize a person sitting cross-legged with closed eyes, immediately rid your mind of that image. Otherwise, you will never fully understand the essence of meditation.

Meditation also does not mean reflection, introspection, relaxation, biofeedback, therapeutic treatment, or a way of developing physical and mental prowess. That is just a partial scope of it. Meditation is neither mystical, nor supernatural, and it definitely does not belong to pop culture.

Meditation is essentially the phenomena of mental development. It is basically the procedure by which we develop intelligence and thereby experience mental development. It is a procedure, as well as an experience.

We could also say that any experiential procedure that develops any level of intelligence (IQ, EQ, or SQ, all the way to soul intelligence) is a meditation. The necessary condition is the development of intelligence.

Chanting or relaxing can become a true form of meditation provided it incorporates the development of intelligence. For example, while you are trying to relax by listening to soft soothing music, if you simply become aware of how you are feeling, you may develop an understanding of the relationship between the softness of sound and the softness of feeling. You may then use this knowledge to change your feelings by simply changing the characteristics of sound in you and around you. By simply making your voice softer, by removing noise and harshness from your immediate environment, or by removing yourself from a noisy environment, you may be able to improve your feeling state to better.

Similarly, while chanting a mantra or a word such as "om" or "love," if instead of simply uttering it you focus on the *meaning* of it, you may be able to cultivate it in your mind and make it your nature. Likewise, simply praising or uttering your deity's name may be relaxing and may even assist you in minimizing discursive thinking, but it won't become a meditation until you focus on the *qualities* of your personal god. When you do that, you are automatically inspired by those qualities and you start developing them. For example, if you recollect and concentrate on the qualities of Jesus (such as loving-kindness, compassion, mercy, and forgiveness) while listening to or singing his name in prayer, you are more likely to become like him.

An ascetic concentration practice of a martial artist, a monk, or a yogi can become a meditation if it is used for sharpening the mind (developing penetrating focus), so that subtle realities about the ego can be pierced, exposed, and purified. A mere ritualistic training of concentration for becoming powerful does not qualify as true meditation unless it leads to purification of mind.

Note that "purification" is a spiritual word for phrases like "evolution" and the "development of intelligence."

Soul Meditation: A Vehicle for Developing Higher Intelligence

True to its essential nature, as clarified above, I have developed a meditation practice called *soul meditation*. It is a unique form of meditation, which is specifically designed to develop all four levels of intelligence by way of purifying, sharpening, and perfecting the mind.

Soul meditation is the result of my awakening experience (described in the Preface). Although I say I developed it, what really happened was a spontaneous creation. Here, I am conveying it to you in a structured manner that is the result of further reflection.

Soul meditation is like a spiritual vehicle with a four-wheel drive. The four wheels are analogous to the four intertwined practices of mindfulness, non-reaction, wise attention, and concentration that make up soul meditation. The practice of *mindfulness* develops present-moment-awareness and serves as a foundation for mental development (somewhat equivalent to IQ). The practice of *non-reaction* eliminates mental impurities, such as greed and hatred (equivalent to EQ plus the emergence of SQ). The practice of *wise attention* removes delusion, generates equanimity, and fuels understanding (equivalent to SQ plus the emergence of soul intelligence). When mindfulness, equanimity, and some degree of understanding are combined with higher levels of *concentration*, the mind is purified, sharpened, and perfected, ultimately leading to the awakening of soul intelligence. The stronger, the better tuned, and the better balanced the four wheels are the faster will be the development of higher intelligence.

If you were to thoroughly investigate the depth and breadth of human suffering, you would come to realize that they are the direct manifestation of the lack of mindfulness, non-reaction, and wise attention. Because these elements are always present in soul meditation, it is a sure way to attain freedom from suffering (see figure 6.1).

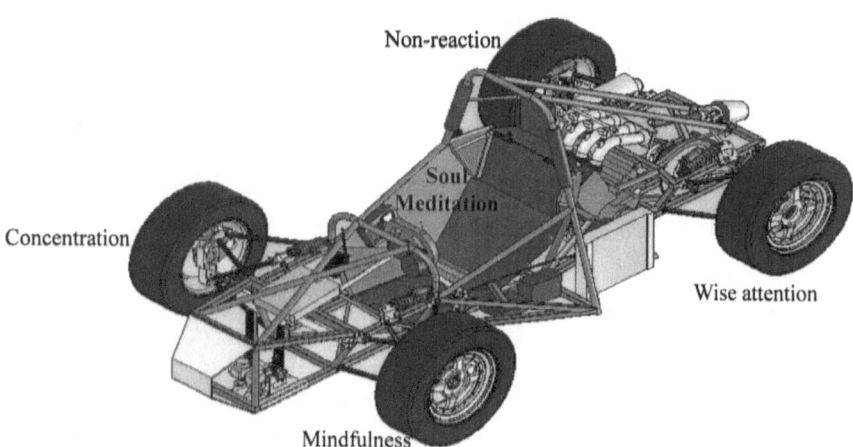

Figure 6.1. Like a four-wheel drive car, soul meditation requires four intertwined practices to be effective: mindfulness, non-reaction, wise attention, and concentration.

As you'll soon experience for yourself, soul meditation is active as well as passive. Just as any action that involves the four practices, such as walking or chanting, is considered a soul meditation, any non-action that involves the four practices, including sitting with closed eyes and observing the breath, would also be considered a soul meditation. Anything you actively or passively do that leads to wholesome

CHAPTER 6 SOUL MEDITATION

mental development is soul meditation. There is no actual set meditative activity (or ritual) *per se*.

Yes, this gives you a lot of freedom to choose when and how to practice soul meditation once you develop a basic understanding of it. That is part of its beauty. It teaches self-mastery and eliminates the need for gurus and teachers who are sometimes dogmatic, strict, and even intimidating.

Any wholesome practice could be a soul meditation, including a breathing practice, chanting, prayer, and physical exercise. For instance, while you are doing a workout at the gym, you could become *mindful* of the bodily sensations of stretching, lifting, pulling, and pushing. You could learn *not to react* to pain and pleasure arising out of those sensations. You could give *wise attention* to their arising and cessation. And you could develop *concentration* by focusing on the movement of your breath. You could learn a great deal about yourself through your body and breath simply by applying these four practices to your physical activity.

It is not possible to understand soul meditation simply by hearing, thinking, or reading about it. As jumping in the water and swimming is necessary to understand swimming fully, you also have to directly experience the phenomena of mindfulness, non-reaction, wise attention, and concentration in order to know what soul meditation really is. Real understanding of soul meditation will come only through actual practice. Nevertheless, let us first try to comprehend its basic tenets through the following illustration.

Let us say that one cool autumn day you are walking along the beach and for some reason you decide to become deliberately aware of each step you are taking. You become aware of the coolness of sand as it touches your feet, and of the overall pleasant feelings that come to pass. You also deliberately remain conscious of any desires that arise, such as the desire for continuity of a pleasant experience arising from coolness of sand. In addition, you deliberately try to understand the cause-effect relationships behind the arising desires you perceive as you are walking.

If you try to do one or all of the above to some degree then you are doing a soul meditation. Note again that you are not sitting with closed eyes, but rather walking.

Now, on another occasion you are walking along the same beach. This time it is a hot summer day. Again you decide to become deliberately aware of each step you take. You become aware of the hotness of the sand as it touches your feet and the overall unpleasant feelings that come to pass. You also deliberately remain conscious of any desires that arise out of those feelings, such as the desire for cessation of unpleasantness arising from the hotness of the sand and a desire or longing for coolness. In addition, you deliberately try to understand the cause-effect relationships behind the arising desires you perceive as you are walking.

In both of the preceding scenarios, being mindful means being aware of your steps, the touch of the sand (coolness or hotness), the mood of liking or disliking the sensations, and the cause-effect relations—in this order of increasing mindfulness. When you become mindful, your mind is neither in the past nor in the future. You are not reminiscing about the past, nor are you planning ahead. You are abiding in the present moment.

This abiding is not a mundane presence of mind. Rather, it is an *awareness* of what is happening on the body level (the steps), the mind level (the feeling of coolness or hotness), the conscious level (the mood of liking or disliking), and the level of causal laws (the cause-effect relationships or the conditionality of experience).

At first, practicing mindfulness may be the full extent of your soul meditation. But once mindfulness becomes a habit you can begin to realize that the mood of liking or disliking is your *reaction* to feelings of coolness and hotness that resulted from external environmental conditions, such as weather and sand, and the condition of your body-mind. Once you realize this, you practice remaining aware and not reacting to the feelings that arise, which means you aim to remain neutral and not to develop liking (for coolness) or disliking (for hotness).

CHAPTER 6   SOUL MEDITATION

When you remain mindful and non-reactive in this way, you purify consciousness. You remove greed (liking) and hatred (disliking) by not reacting. This results in equanimity.

Once mindfulness and non-reaction become a habit due to regular practice, you can then begin to give wise attention to your experience and realize experientially that all feelings are simply coming and going dependent upon the external and internal conditions mentioned above. Due to such wise attention, you eventually stop identifying with the feelings, which means that you look at feelings as *mere feelings* that arise due to conditionality. When that happens, your desires (longing for coolness when it is hot or longing for heat when it is cold) begin to lose their strength, subside quickly, and help you remain in equanimity.

Sooner or later, due to an increasing degree of wise attention you begin to realize that feelings or desires are impermanent in nature. You also begin to realize that there was really no "you" in the experience of coolness or hotness (feelings) or in the desires that resulted from it. You realize that "you" got created every time there was a reaction or identification with those feelings or with the desires resulting from those feelings. You also realize that "you" got created due to a perception of being separate from the conditionality (the environment) that gives rise to feelings and desires.

Wise attention eventually brings about an understanding of impermanence and non-self and removes delusion about the separate self (the ego). With further practice, it is possible to perceive coolness and hotness, pleasantness and unpleasantness, and liking and disliking merely as phenomena of body-mind-consciousness driven by conditionality and not as things that are happening to you.

With ardent and consistent practice, due to increasing mindfulness, non-reaction, and wise attention, your mind and consciousness begin to concentrate (or focus) at higher levels. They begin to work evenly, harmoniously, unscatteredly, undistractedly, and unwaveringly around a single object. As this focus becomes increasingly one-pointed, you begin to further sharpen and purify the mind until you are thoroughly established in *equanimity* and in *non-delusion*. If you recall, these are the two most prominent mental elements of SQ and soul intelligence. Exactly how this all happens is the matter of the chapters that are forthcoming in Part III.

In the preceding example, because you applied mindfulness, non-reaction, wise attention, and concentration (the four fundamental constituents) to a walking activity along the beach and developed intelligence, the walking activity became a soul meditation. In short, any activity, practice, or experience that involves the four fundamental constituents is a soul meditation. Although the four constituents are not always present with the same intensity, there is always a trace of all of them when you are practicing soul meditation.

How to Develop a Lifestyle of Meditation

Performing or transforming any activity into meditation is not an easy task. You first have to prepare yourself for meditation. Second, you have to develop an experiential understanding of the four fundamental constituents by performing a daily, seated practice, which I will soon discuss. A daily, seated practice is not absolutely necessary, especially for those who are currently performing other meditations. It is, however, necessary for those who have not meditated before. In any case, once you have actually experienced the four constituents you can apply soul meditation effectively to other spiritual practices and to non-seated practices, such as walking, exercising, chanting, and so on, and ultimately to all life situations.

You might be thinking that I am contradicting myself here. Earlier I said there was no set practice to do, and now I am recommending one. The reason is that unless you regularly tune up your vehicle of intelligence (the soul meditation), the vehicle does not run efficiently. Daily, seated practice of 15 to 30 minutes in the morning will get you going for the rest of the day and bring fantastic results in terms of being able to effectively remain mindful, non-reactive, and wisely attentive in situations that are otherwise unusual or emotionally challenging. Also, it will help you develop the *habit* of meditativity that we talked so highly of in the soul mechanics chapter.

CHAPTER 6 SOUL MEDITATION

Personally speaking, because I have prepared myself for soul meditation over the years through daily seated practice, I have been able to invoke the four constituents whenever necessary. At times, I have been able to wisely handle extremely difficult life situations by simply closing my eyes for a few moments, quickly running through the seated practice in my mind, and then miraculously finding a peaceful solution.

Although a daily practice is not absolutely necessary, I highly recommend it. Ultimately, it is your choice. As long as you experientially understand the four constituents, you are with me.

Now, let us talk about how one prepares for soul meditation.

Simple: By removing clumsiness and becoming skillful in the way of daily living, in the way of socializing, in the way of applying effort, in the way of arousing volition, in the way of recollection, and in the way of developing equanimity.

Soul meditation does not require goal setting, hard work, effort, or even passion, only pure skill. In order to develop such skill, I recommend adopting the following principles.

- Choose a living place free of dust, heat, smell, insects, strong wind, noise, and nuisances
- Choose healthy foods that are suitable for your climate and eat them in moderation
- Maintain silence most of the time. Speak in moderation and only if necessary
- Live in the company of virtuous and wise people. Avoid worldly-minded people
- Study the qualities of enlightened people
- Stimulate your mind by contemplating the benefits of meditation, such as attaining higher levels of intelligence, as well as peace of mind, serenity, and bliss
- Practice meditation only when it is appropriate to practice. Do not force yourself to meditate. Exert the mind only to such an extent that it does not feel forced. If you feel agitated, then you are forcing the mind. When the mind is not at all willing to meditate,

become aware of the fact that you are not able to meditate and simply let go for a while. Before trying again, read inspirational books, listen to spiritual discourses, do physical and breathing exercises, or simply take a walk in the woods
- Give importance to developing an inclination for meditation. Develop a sense of urgency for practicing it. However, do not crave it. Do not *try* to do it. Just meditate and let go of any desire for the end results. Just let it happen

Most importantly, develop an experiential understanding of the four constituents of soul meditation. For this purpose, as I recommended earlier, meditate daily, at least in the beginning. Become firm and unwavering in your daily practice.

For a daily, seated meditation, you need a perfect object to meditate on. Use your natural breath, because the natural breath is:
- Unadulterated, unmodified, and unmixed, and thus it provides us with purity, which is an important aspect in maintaining wholesomeness of meditation,
- Non-religious and non denominational, universal and common to all people,
- Unlimited in supply and it always accompanies the meditator,
- Beneficial—even prior to meditation it provides nutrition and supports physical life,
- An easy and quiet object. It does not create sound or thought. It is neither repulsive, nor attractive. It is neutral, peaceful, and sublime in its own individual essence,
- The closest link between the body and mind, so it serves as a portal for mind-body conditioning,
- An internal as well as an external object, thus providing totality during observation,
- Accessible to people at all levels of meditative absorption, from preliminary to advanced, and
- An aspect in the development of equanimity, tranquility, sublimity, and peace.[1]

CHAPTER 6 SOUL MEDITATION

Last, but not least, when you use natural breath as an object of meditation, you develop *breath awareness:* a sublime quality of consciousness. As we will discuss in the following paragraphs, breath awareness arises when you become mindful of inhalation and exhalation due to the sensations in the nostrils that arise from the touch of the natural breath passing through the nostrils. When you anchor your attention on these sensations occurring in the small triangular area of the nose (the nostrils), your mind takes refuge in that area due to anchored attention.[2] The triangular area of the nose becomes an island, a safe haven for the mind, due to breath awareness.

If you are looking for a place on Earth where you can be 100 percent secure, safe, and sound, you won't ever find it. No matter how much you protect yourself from external forces, you cannot get out of harm's way until you develop a quality of consciousness such as breath awareness. You may be driving the safest car or living in an invincible fort, but you can still be harmed if you are not aware of yourself and your surroundings. Breath awareness facilitates that awareness by helping you remain highly sensitized and by keeping you rooted in the present moment. It keeps the mind focused and does not allow it to wander. After dedicated practice, it also provides much needed equanimity through the application of non-reaction to cravings and aversions, thus protecting you from unwholesome reactions.

Whenever you experience fear or anxiety, simply arouse breath awareness and notice how anxiety fades and how quickly you can take care of any situation. Whenever you realize the advent of anger or lust, simply initiate breath awareness and notice how effectively you can deal with these unwholesome driving forces. Whenever you feel you are being swept away by the flood of greed or desire, quickly take refuge in breath awareness and observe how easily you can survive those dangerous floods.

No amount of material things can create a safe haven like breath awareness can. No amount of prosperity can generate emotional stability as much as breath awareness can.

Developing Breath Awareness: A Daily Practice of Soul Meditation

Although we are still in the theoretical part of this book, I am introducing you to a seated meditation practice. The purpose is to get you started in developing meditativity, which will be extremely helpful to you as you are diving deeper into the elements of soul.

Practice the following seated meditation for 15–30 minutes in the morning. It has ten steps so you may not be able to cover them all in one sitting on one day. Start by learning the first couple of steps. Become proficient in those. Then add another step, and another, and so on. If necessary, increase the duration of your practice as you add more steps.

Do not consider the following list of steps as a "how-to" manual. You do not have to keep the list in your lap while meditating. Simply use the list as a set of guidelines. Read the guidelines, study them, try them, and modify them if necessary as long as the final goal of developing breath awareness and understanding the four constituents of soul meditation is well understood.

Step 1: Sit in a comfortable posture in a closed room with cool air, gently close your eyes, and mentally review the benefits of breath awareness, which we just discussed.

Now, take your attention to the triangular area of the nostrils (the entire nose area) and anchor it there. Take a couple of long, deep inhalations and release a couple of long, deep exhalations with the intention of feeling sensations in the nostrils as the breath passes through the nostrils. Continue breathing in and out deeply, until you become aware of the sensations in your nostrils. Because you are taking long, deep breaths, it is easier to feel their touch in the nostrils. In fact, if your attention is well anchored you will feel a cool sensation in the nostrils while inhaling and a warm sensation while exhaling. This will happen because the air in your meditation room is cooler than the air inside the body.

Step 2: Once you are established in the awareness of sensations in the nostrils due to *intentional* long breaths, you no longer have to use them. So, abandon taking long breaths and simply let the natural breath come and go. In other words, now breathe normally without intentionally taking long breaths. Observe the normal, natural breath as it comes and goes by feeling its touch in the nostrils, and stay with the sensations arising in the nostrils due to that touch. At this stage in the meditation, breathing normally and naturally without any conditioning (such as the lengthening of the breath) is important.

If your attention is hijacked by any thoughts arising in the mind you may forget to observe your natural breath and simply flow with those thoughts. Sooner or later, when you realize that your attention has run away, gently bring it back to your breathing without aversion. Do not strive or crave attention. Do not develop an aversion for non-attention if you are unable to bring your attention back to your breathing quickly. Simply keep bringing your attention back to the object of your focus whenever it roams.

Step 3: After a few minutes of continuous practice, you will develop breath awareness due to sustained observation of sensations in the nostrils. Breath awareness will give rise to an experience of pleasantness, a natural outcome of the higher level of concentration.

Do not get immersed in the pleasantness of sensations and lose awareness. Simply keep observing the breath, without developing a liking for pleasantness, without craving pleasantness.

Step 4: At the end of step 3, you will have been seated for at least 15–20 minutes. So, you will begin to experience pain or stiffness in some parts of your body, such as your knees, ankles, lower back, and shoulder joints. Knowingly, move your attention from your breath to any painful or stiff areas and try to observe the pain or stiffness as a bundle of bodily sensations just as you were observing the breath by virtue of sensations it created in the nostrils. Try not to react to unpleasantness of pain or stiffness in the same manner that you did not react to the pleasantness in step 3. In other words, do not develop an aversion to the unpleasantness. This is possible only if you observe pain or stiffness as bodily sensations while you take your attention to the painful or stiff areas and anchor it there.

Observe unpleasantness only until it is bearable, which means, until there is no aversion. Do not fight it or control it. If necessary, change your posture or physically rub the painful area and again get back into meditation. Do all transitional movements knowingly so that your movements are not driven by reaction to pain but by awareness of pain.

At times you may feel like itching or like getting up and doing something. You may become overwhelmed by boredom and want to open your eyes and look around. As much as possible, simply observe all these bodily and mental feelings without reacting to them. Don't succumb to them out of aversion.

No itch lasts forever. So you may want to temporarily make an "itch" the object of your meditation and continue observing it until it passes away. Similarly, you may want to continue observing a feeling of boredom until it subsides. In this way, observe all unpleasant bodily and mental feelings with the understanding that sooner or later they will cease. However, this is possible only if you observe them without aversion. Notice that there is neither suppression, nor control, but merely non-reactive observation.

Step 5: As you attain higher and higher levels of stillness and non-reaction, at times there will be intruding thoughts of happiness or sadness arising from memories. Deep-rooted desires will come to the surface of the mind. Various moods will manifest themselves as various frames of minds. Observe all these thoughts, desires, moods, and so on without getting carried away by them. Observe them without reacting with craving or aversion. Let them simply come and go, as it is their nature to do so. Knowing that nothing lasts forever, simply maintain non-reactive awareness of all that is happening at the level of body, mind, and consciousness so that equanimity can arise.

Step 6: Equipped with equanimity, take your attention back to the breath knowingly and gently. Give wise-attention to the natural breath as it moves in and out of the body by feeling its touch. Become aware of the fact that the breath is changing from an in-breath to an out-breath, and then again to an in-breath, thus moving in and out of the

CHAPTER 6 SOUL MEDITATION

body naturally. Then reflect and contemplate on the changing nature of the breath and understand the impermanence of the in-breath as well as the out-breath. In other words, understand that no in-breath or out-breath lasts forever. All change constantly from one to the other. Develop that wakefulness.

Step 7: Now, try to realize that the breath is arising and passing away *on its own accord*, constantly changing naturally from an in-breath to an out-breath without a need for you to intentionally change it, or without a need for you to tell the body to change it. Become aware of this whole involuntary phenomenon of movement of air as "breathing." In other words, try to become aware of the fact that "it is the body that is breathing on its own accord" and not "you."

Step 8: Continue to reflect upon this fact and try to look at the breathing body as a third person. It is like putting your attention in front of the body and looking at the body with a bird's eye view. With such vision, try to look at the breathing body and understand that the breath is bound with the body and that it is a bodily phenomenon.

Step 9: By now, you will have developed some wakefulness, vision, the understanding of the impermanence of breath, and the understanding of the origin of breath as a bodily phenomenon. Now, try to find the one who is breathing amidst the understanding that it is really the body that is breathing and not you.

You will not be able to locate the breath-taker.

Then, ask a simple question, "Why am I still feeling that I am the one who is breathing?"

Continue giving wise attention to the breath in search of an answer. Soon, you will realize that it was the "awareness of breathing" that was mistaken as a breath-taker! The "awareness" was misunderstood as the "I."

Such realization will automatically generate a smile on your face and bring you spiritual joy.

Simply abide in that joyous realization and develop clear comprehension of what you have realized. In other words, clearly comprehend breathing as strictly a bodily phenomenon having an impersonal nature. Clearly comprehend the fact that there is only "awareness of breathing" and there is no "breath-taker."

Step 10: Become established in such mindfulness without a sense of being mindful, being aware, or being a knower, and without clinging to anything in the world. This stage of mindfulness is pure awareness—the perfect stage of mindfulness that leads to perfect equanimity and non-delusion: the two most prominent elements of SQ and soul intelligence.

* * *

In the initial stages of practice, you might find step 7 through step 10 quite difficult to comprehend and to practice. Do not strain yourself. Simply keep trying with an open and relaxed mind. Do not stop at a particular step and wait until you have realized its essence. Simply follow all the steps mechanically in anticipation of realizing the essence of each step. This process is like taking a virtual tour and preparing the mind for the real thing, which is bound to happen sooner or later.

In this way, develop mindfulness starting with breath awareness (steps 1–5) and then moving onto wakefulness (steps 6–7), to vision (step 8), to clear comprehension (step 9), and ultimately to pure awareness (step 10). Let mindfulness evolve in this way through seated meditative practice. As soon as you have attained some degree of wakefulness, start applying it to non-seated practices and to daily life situations. You do not have to wait until you have attained the level of pure awareness.

During steps 1–10, you will have experienced the entire spectrum of mindfulness, during steps 2–5, the element of non-reaction, and during steps 6–10, the element of wise attention. The element of concentration will have been experienced as an undercurrent throughout the entire meditation. In this way, through experience, you will have understood the four constituents of soul meditation.

The ten-step seated meditation is just one of many possible seated soul meditations. Once you have practiced it for several months, depending upon your progress, you can then start devising your own seated meditation to address a personal issue that you are facing, so that your meditation time is actually used to solve your problems on a daily basis. For example, let us say on one particular day you are worried and experiencing irritation. On that day, during the seated meditation, give wise attention to the movement of your breath. Notice how your breath changes with changes in levels of concentration. Notice how it becomes harsh and fast if thoughts of worries or anger arise while concentrating. Notice how it becomes soft and slow if worries and anger are replaced with letting go and compassion. Notice how the same effect can be achieved by intentionally making the breath soft and slow. In this way, apply wise attention to understand the link between the mind and the breath and implement this knowledge to change your state of mind.

Alternatively, give wise attention to the external conditions that gave rise to the worries and irritation you are feeling. Find out how you can eliminate those conditions and thereby eliminate the worries and irritation. If you cannot change those conditions, find out whether your worries and irritation are the result of internal conditions, such as your reaction (aversion) to certain unpleasant memories or frames of mind that are arising to the surface. Try to observe those memories or frames of mind without aversion and with the understanding that they will not last forever. By simply applying non-reactive observation you will be able to eradicate worries and irritation.

Similarly, if you are experiencing bodily pain, say pain in your lower back due to putting in too much overtime at work, give wise attention to that. Notice how it becomes aggravated if you dislike it and lessens if you simply let go of it by observing it simply as bodily sensations without aversion.

The rewards of a seated practice will increase many times over once you start applying the combined effects of the four constituents derived from the daily practice to all other practices and to all life situations. In fact, if you are really serious about climbing the ladder of

THE ELEMENTS OF SOUL

intelligence, I encourage you to perform all physical, verbal, sensual, and mental activities as soul meditations. In other words, do everything with mindfulness, non-reaction, wise attention, and concentration. If you do so, you will develop tremendous power.

After all, what is power?
Essentially, intelligence!

* * *

Part II
Soul Exploration

I hope you have enjoyed studying soul theory and practicing soul meditation as described in Part I. Assuming you have developed a degree of meditativity, I invite you to dive deeper into the three key elements of soul. Here I encourage you to explore the ultimate building blocks of matter (chapter 7), consciousness (chapter 8), and mind (chapters 9–16).

In chapter 7, you will discover the smallest recognizable units of animate and inanimate matter, such as soul atoms, I-atoms, and the material elements, which form the ultimate basis of all material existence. Most likely, you will be exposed for the first time, at least theoretically, to the nature of what ultimately lies beyond the quantum mechanical reality of the world. You will also learn about the ultimate origins of matter.

In chapter 8, you will learn to discern various types of consciousness and discover how they partake in the phenomenon of cognition. You will be introduced to the dynamic nature of consciousness and be shown how such knowledge can liberate you from imperfections and bring you real happiness and peace.

In chapters 9–16, you will survey the ultimate building blocks of mind, the mental elements, which will forever change the way you think about the nature of mind. Your exploration of each mental element will bring about a unique perspective on various mysteries of mind. You might also begin to feel that you know your mind so intimately that you can wield and master its incredible powers.

* * *

Chapter 7

Exploring the Ultimate Building Blocks of Matter

Matter is not yet fully defined by the scientific community. Although *matter* is loosely understood as "something that occupies space and has mass," at present there is no agreement as to what matter really is. Many physicists simply adhere to concepts of mass, energy, and particles to describe matter and do not even use the word "matter."[1]

Matter is conventionally known as that which is subject to deformation, degeneration, decay, or increase in entropy. We generally recognize matter *as* matter because it deforms under conditions of pressure and temperature, such as cold and heat. For example, water evaporates when subjected to heat. Rock erodes and turns into soil, wood rots, and uranium decays radioactively. The human body grows old and degenerates due to various physical and environmental conditions. Everything in the material universe is subjected to increase in entropy.[2] Such is not the case with mind and consciousness, which do not undergo deformation, degeneration, decay, or increase in entropy.

We are going to go a step beyond convention and define matter as *that which is devoid of experience by itself.* A piece of rock, for instance, is material because it is devoid of experience. Similarly, a human corpse (a body lacking mind and consciousness) is exclusively material because it is devoid of experience. Your living body is also material, however it is matter that is not exclusively material but clung to by mind-consciousness. Soon, we will discuss this in more detail.

In chapter 1, we mentioned that matter is a *material phenomenon*: a flow, a flux, or a constantly changing reality—just as mind is. However, matter is not mind. Nor is mind matter. Mind is that which experiences matter, although mind cannot experience without matter. Mind and matter are interdependent and inseparable within each of our experience. But they are distinct. It is important to understand this so that confusion does not arise if you are a student of a philosophy such as materialism or anti-materialism in which mind is considered "spiritual matter" or matter is considered "physical mind." Throughout this book, we shall treat mind and matter as separate, yet interdependent elements of soul, both being experiential (by virtue of each other) rather than intangible or tangible.

Matter is an ultimate reality, just as mind is. This means matter exists by reason of its own intrinsic nature, because of which it is possible to investigate matter and make it known.

Material Elements

Just as various mental elements produce mental phenomena, which we collectively call "mind," various material elements produce material phenomena, which we collectively call "matter." In chapter 1, you were introduced to 28 such elements in the chart of material elements.

The elements of which I am speaking here are not atomic or subatomic particles (such as fermions, baryons, quarks, electrons, protons, and neutrons) or the chemical elements of the periodic table, or objects that have size, shape, weight, mass, or charge. Material elements are neither mysterious primordial substances, nor packets of energy. Rather they are fundamental physical phenomena that are experienced as matter. The word "phenomenon" has great significance in this instance,

CHAPTER 7 EXPLORING MATTER

since it helps us to go beyond our notion of matter as being a fixed, solid substance. In deeper scrutiny, the word "phenomenon" also helps us to transcend the notion of matter being a quantum of physical energy.

Modern science considers the atom to be the smallest recognizable unit of matter. Atoms are so small that we could fit several million of them on the tip of a needle. Each atom is known to consist of subatomic particles, which in turn are made up of sub-subatomic particles. In future, there will be discoveries of sub-sub-sub . . . subatomic particles. I feel, these discoveries will continue until a day comes when modern science will merge with soul science to realize the presence of ultimate realities of matter: the material elements that we are going to discuss here.

Material elements are ultimate realities of matter because, first, they are a phenomenon and, second, they can be known only through experience and not just through experiment. Since nothing else remains to be penetrated or investigated beyond experience, the material elements are rightly termed the ultimate building blocks of matter.

Think of an apple for a moment.

At the gross and objective level, the matter of an apple contains seeds, pulp, and so on. At a deeper level of scrutiny it is made of apple cells. Apple cells are made of molecules, which are made of atoms that, in turn, are divisible into electrons, protons, and so on. Such physical knowledge of the matter of apple does not lead, however, to the ultimate understanding of apple. Understanding arises only when you experience it—meaning, only when you see, touch, smell, and taste the apple. You will not know what an apple really is without experiencing it no matter how powerful or advanced a microscope you use to study its material nature.

When you *experience* an apple, you realize that it is *essentially* a "soft/hard, watery/fluid, warm/cool, and stiff rounded bundle of matter." These experiential aspects of the apple are none other than the material elements we are talking about. In chapter 1, we introduced the four ultimate and essential material elements: earth, water, fire, and air (numbers 1–4 on the chart of material elements). In the case of an apple, the earth element is the *experience of softness/hardness* of apple matter, the water element is the *experience of wateriness or fluidity* of apple matter, the fire element is the *experience of warmth or coolness* of apple matter, and the air element is the *experience of distension or stiffness* of apple matter. These four experiences are fundamental in that they are essential for knowing apple as matter at the ultimate level.

Just as the four essential elements together produce the essential or the most fundamental experience of apple as matter, they also produce the experience of the entire material world as matter. They are essential for experiencing or knowing matter *as* matter. So, they are considered *essential*. In this sense, they are the fundamental building blocks of the material universe that we experience (see figure 7.1, below, and figure 7.2, on page 126).

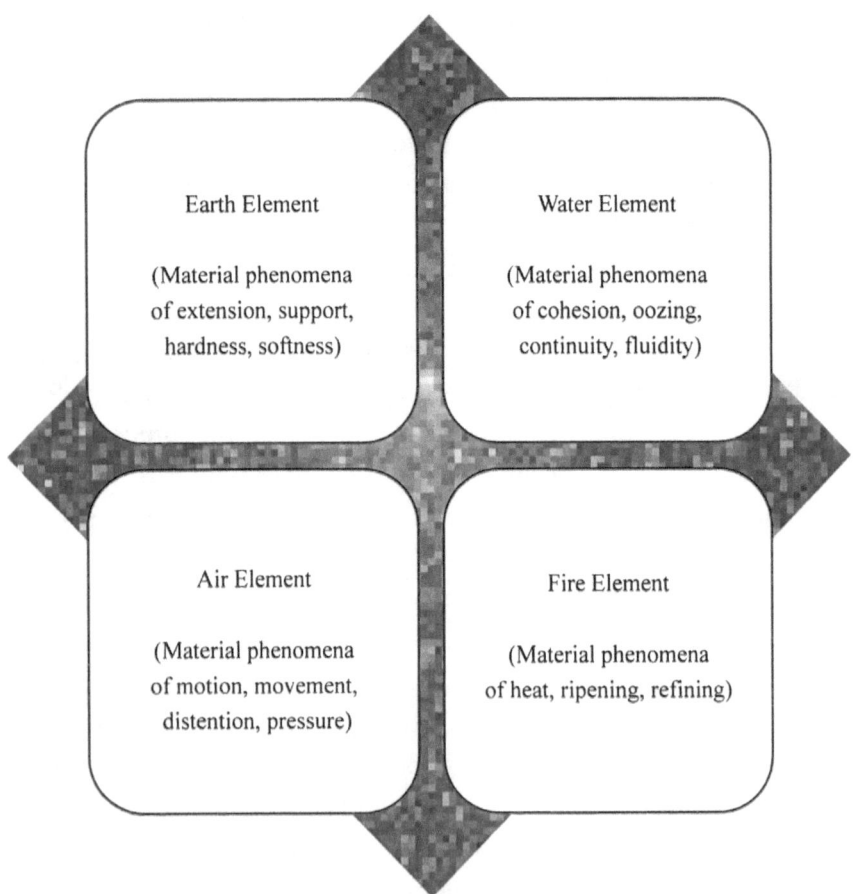

Figure 7.1. Four essential material elements (earth, water, fire, and air) make up the ultimate reality of matter, which is experiential rather than experimental. Nothing is subtler in matter than these four material phenomena.

Do not mistake the four essential elements for solid earth, flowing water, burning fire, or blowing air. Earth, the element, is basically a *phenomenon* of extension, support, hardness, softness, and so on. We predominantly experience the soil we see in the manifested world as the earth element because it predominantly possesses qualities of earth.

Water, the element, is a *phenomenon* of fluidity, cohesion, oozing, continuity, and so on. Oceans, lakes, and rivers are considered water because the qualities of the material element of water are most predominant in them.

Similarly, the fire element encompasses all *phenomena* related to heat and cold.

The material element of air relates to *phenomena* of motion, movement, distention, and pressure, which is not the wind we feel or the atmosphere we breathe, but a subtler level of reality (experiential reality) that is predominant in the wind or the atmosphere.

Such understanding as well as the knowledge of other salient features of the four essential material elements can arise only by studying and contemplating their nature.[3]

Each material element is a unique material phenomenon and not an object or a "thing" having a certain size, shape, weight, mass, or charge. Having certain characteristics, functions, and manifestations, these elements are experiential in nature. They have to be experienced by the knower to be known to the knower. They cannot be known or identified objectively using microscopes or particle accelerators.

Material Elements: A Historic Background

The idea of earth, water, fire, and air as being the essential building blocks of matter is old. Although not the same as what has been presented in this book, the idea has been proposed in different shapes and forms in various cultures since ancient times. The Ancient Greeks called them classical elements and used them to describe phases, patterns, or states of matter. Pre-Socratic Greek philosopher Empedocles, who was alive around 500 B.C.E., first used them in the West to explain the ultimate structures of nature.[4] He called them "roots" of matter.

It was Plato, a mathematician and philosopher, student of Socrates, teacher of Aristotle, and the founder of the first institution of higher learning in the western world, who popularized them as the "elements."[5] Hippocrates, the father of medicine, used them as four *humors* of the body.[6] According to his theory, the body is primarily made up of four humors that are directly related to the four elements and disease is the result of an imbalance in the proportions of the elements.

Before the Ancient Greeks, in the East around 500–600 B.C.E., Buddha attributed the four elements to the part of *kalapa*, which he referred to as the smallest particle (or event) of matter.[7] Japanese called the elements *go dai*. Chinese neo-Confucians called them *go gyo*.[8] Apparently before Buddha and everyone else, around 1500–3000 B.C.E., the Hindu philosophers of Indus valley in the Himalayas had used the elements (called *mahabhutas*) to describe the substructure of the manifested world. Ayurveda, the 5,000-year old Hindu system of medicine still in use today, which originated in the era of 1500–3000 B.C.E., called them *doshas* (humors of the body) and used them to diagnose and to treat diseases.[9]

In modern times, which are dominated more by science than philosophy, the four elements are not used as a scientific basis for describing matter or treating diseases, however, they have been extensively used thematically in art and cinema.[10]

The Soul-atom: The Smallest Recognizable Unit of Matter

Now, let us go back to thinking about an apple.

Besides the four essential experiences of an apple as matter that we discussed earlier, there are four other derived experiences that constitute the totality of the experience of an apple as matter: the sweetness of the apple, its color or shape, its fruity aroma, and its nutritious nature (its energy in terms of fructose/vitamin C/pectin/and so on). These four derived experiences can be known as the four derived

CHAPTER 7 EXPLORING MATTER

material elements of taste, color/form, smell, and nutriment, respectively (numbers 5–8 on the chart of material elements). Thus, in order to know an apple thoroughly, to *recognize* (or experience) the apple as matter, we need a bundle of eight material experiences: the four essential ones and the four derived ones. Together these create a bundle of earth-water-fire-air-taste-color/form-smell-nutriment. We cannot separate the experience of an apple's softness from its shape or color, or from its taste or smell. We can know an apple only as a *bundle* of eight experiences (the eight material elements). I call this bundle the *soul-atom*.

Just as the atom (a bundle of electrons, protons, and neutrons) is the smallest recognizable unit of matter in quantum mechanics, the soul-atom is the smallest recognizable unit of matter in soul mechanics. Notice that atom or soul-atom is the smallest *recognizable* unit of matter and not the smallest unit of matter. What that means is that we cannot identify matter *as* matter beyond the level of an atom (in quantum mechanics) or a soul-atom (in soul mechanics).

The critical question is: Which atom is subtler?

To me, the obvious answer is the soul-atom because it is experiential in nature, it incorporates the observer, and it is phenomenal, rather than physical.

Such understanding has deep scientific implications. For example, one of the most daunting questions that contemporary scientists face is if matter exists without mind-consciousness. In other words, does an apple exist without an observer? I feel the answer is a simple no. Matter cannot exist independently of its experience (or mind-consciousness). In other words, the ultimate existence of matter lies in soul-atoms (see figure 7.2). It neither lies in the atoms of quantum mechanics, nor in the subatomic particles of the famous standard model of fundamental matter developed by 20th-century physicists.[11]

THE ELEMENTS OF SOUL

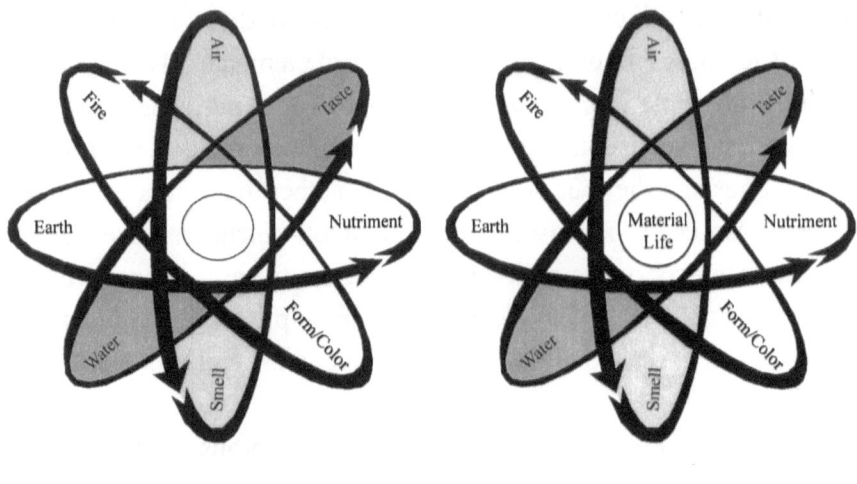

Soul-atom   I-atom

Figure 7.2. The soul-atom consists of an inseparable bundle of eight material elements.

The Soul-atom and String Theory

Now, let us think about water. Water is made of molecules of H_2O. Each H_2O molecule is made of two hydrogen atoms and an oxygen atom, which are, in turn, composed of electrons, neutrons, and protons. These atomic particles are made of quarks and other sub-subatomic particles now being considered by many modern physicists as different modes of a single vibrating string. According to string theory, a vibrating string is a physical entity that could be one billion billion times (10^{-20}) smaller than the diameter of a proton, thus making it possibly the smallest known form of matter. In fact, a vibrating string is so small that it is more mathematical than real. It becomes real in terms of its vibrating modes that manifest as zero-dimensional point particles of atom. Just like a guitar string produces different musical notes, a vibrating string produces various subatomic particles that make up atoms.[12]

Mathematically speaking, we will always be able to go even deeper than a vibrating string and quantify smaller and smaller entities of matter in terms of size or shape or charge. However, as long as we do

CHAPTER 7 EXPLORING MATTER

that we will never reach the ultimate or subtlest reality of matter. Such reality is not mathematical or physical, but experiential. Such reality is not quantitative, but qualitative. I propose going beyond mathematics (or developing entirely new mathematical tools) so that we can look at matter in relation to how it is experienced, in relation to mind-consciousness, not as an independent entity. If we do, we might find that the vibrating string of string theory is not the fundamental constituent of matter but a manifestation of the soul-atom (see figure 7.3).

The substantiality of what I am trying to propose here can be easily grasped by at least two groups of people: the meditators who experi*ent*ially know that matter cannot exist without mind-consciousness and the modern physicists who experi*men*tally know that the observer can no longer be separated from the observed system.[13]

String theory is currently the most promising candidate for formulating a theory of everything (TOE).[14] I strongly feel that if we try to apply the ideas of the soul-atom, as described here, and the volitional force, as described in earlier chapters, we might develop key insights into the formulation of TOE. These ideas might also provide insight into the workings of gravity at the quantum level and facilitate the completion of the famous standard model, which is widely accepted as the theory of *almost* everything.[15]

Philosophically, how that might be possible is the subject of my study, which I intend on publishing later in a separate book to be entitled *Soul Mechanics*.

THE ELEMENTS OF SOUL

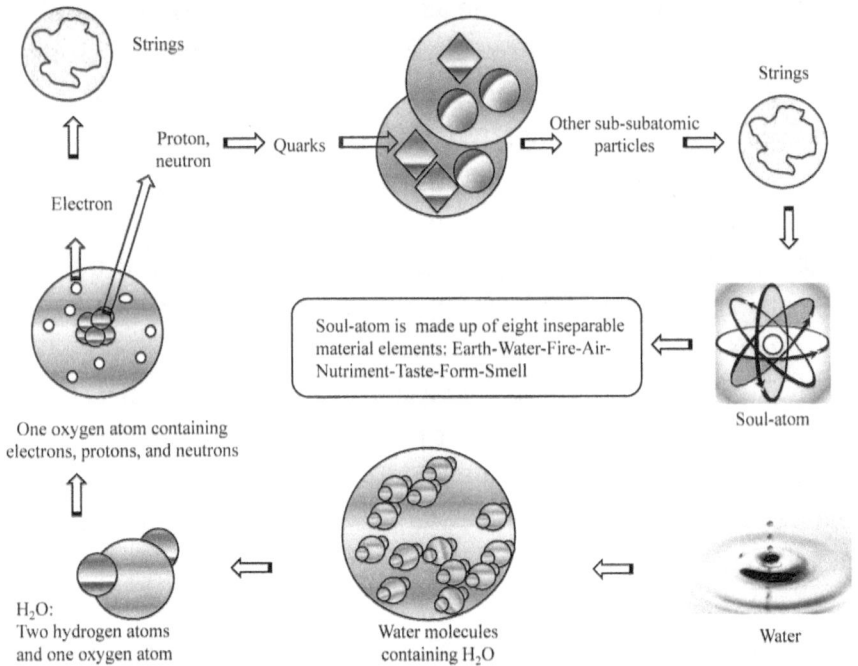

Figure 7.3. The smallest "realizable" or "recognizable" unit of water (or any matter) is the soul-atom.

For now, in accordance with soul mechanics, I would like to put forth the following hypotheses:

- *Hypothesis 1:* A soul-atom gives rise to a vibration when it combines with mind-consciousness (internally) and temperature (externally).
- *Hypothesis 2:* An induced vibration is nothing but a conscious soul-atom.
- *Hypothesis 3:* A conscious soul-atom is subjected to motion due to volitional forces.
- *Hypothesis 4:* A soul-*atom*, volitional *force*, and the *field* of intelligence are the three phenomena that can take us beyond quantum mechanics.

A string theorist with a philosophical background might relate the vibration (hypothesis 1) to the lowest mode of vibration of a string (even lower than a mode of vibration that is attributed to gravity). A spiritualist, an eastern mystic, or a yogi might recognize the vibration

CHAPTER 7 EXPLORING MATTER

as the primordial sound, *om*. A religious person might relate it to the "word of God." In other words, a vibrating string of the string theory, a primordial sound, or the "word of God" might just be different expressions for the phenomenon of *soul-atom becoming conscious of itself.*

Today, these ideas about the soul-atom may seem preposterous, just as the idea of the atom was a century ago and the idea of string theory was a couple of decades ago.[16] In fact, until recently, the opponents of string theory have been calling it the theory of nothing because it was impossible to experimentally prove its existence.[17] According to theoretical physics, we would have to create an entire galaxy in the laboratory to experimentally prove the existence of strings as proposed by the string theory. Because of such difficulties, string theory almost became the domain of unemployed physicists. But now, the tide is changing. String theory and related work are now in vogue at the top research universities. Today, we are spending millions of dollars on projects such as Laser Interferometer Gravitational Wave Observatory (LIGO) and Big Band Observer (BBO) to indirectly prove the existence of vibrating strings by detecting gravity waves: the lowest anticipated vibration of a string.[18] The direct proof is not possible in the foreseeable future, but the indirect proof seems to be almost within our reach.

Similar is the case with soul-atoms. In my opinion, the only way to objectively prove their existence is to create an entire universe in the laboratory (and not just a galaxy as in the case of string theory). This obviously is not possible by today's technological standards or in the foreseeable future. But there is hope for the idea of the soul-atom, especially if you develop an inclination towards understanding its *experiential* nature.

The Soul-atom and the Sound Element

One way to know the existence of the soul-atom objectively is by virtue of the sound element. Do you hear a subtle sound in your head when you are reading these pages? Is there a voice? How about the constant humming sound that you hear when there is silence? How about the sound of your thoughts? How about the sound of the silent chanting of a mantra or a prayer? Aren't all of these sounds subtler and different than the sounds you hear with your ears?

There is a unique material phenomenon happening inside as well as outside you, because of which there is the experience of this subtle sound. This experience is called the *sound element* (element 18 on the chart of material elements). I propose the sound element as the subtlest and purest manifestation of the soul-atom, an indirect proof of the existence of soul-atoms.

I-Atom: The Smallest Recognizable Unit of Living Matter

By now, you might be wondering, "What about living matter, such as the matter of the human body?" What is that ultimately made of? Vibrating strings? Soul-atoms? The sound element?

At the gross level, the human body contains blood, muscles, bones, skin, and so on. This matter is made of cells. Biologists consider cells the smallest units of living matter. A cell is two-thirds water and one-third a combination of various other types of molecules, such as carbohydrates, lipids, and proteins. Proteins are made up of small biochemical building blocks called amino acids and genetic material called nucleic acids (DNA, RNA).[19] These building blocks consist primarily of carbon, hydrogen, oxygen, and nitrogen atoms. As we know, atoms are, in turn, composed of electron, proton, neutrons and sub-sub-atomic particles. These, in turn, are made of strings. And, as I proposed earlier, strings are manifestations of soul-atoms. So, like the molecules of an apple or water, the molecules of the human body are ultimately made of soul-atoms. However, there is a difference.

In the human body, soul-atoms are not *pure* but clung to (or entangled with) a volitional force that arises from an inherent desire to live or to have sensual experience. It is as if a soul-atom wants to know itself by experiencing itself sensually. This volitional force gives rise to a unique kind of material phenomenon called *material life*. The material life phenomenon is distinct from the eight elements of the soul-

CHAPTER 7 EXPLORING MATTER

atom and the sound element. Therefore it is listed as a distinct material element (element 16 on the chart of material elements). This clung to or entangled form of soul-atom is what I call the *I-atom*. This I-atom, the smallest recognizable unit of *living* matter, manifests as the matter of all living beings as described below (see figure 7.4).

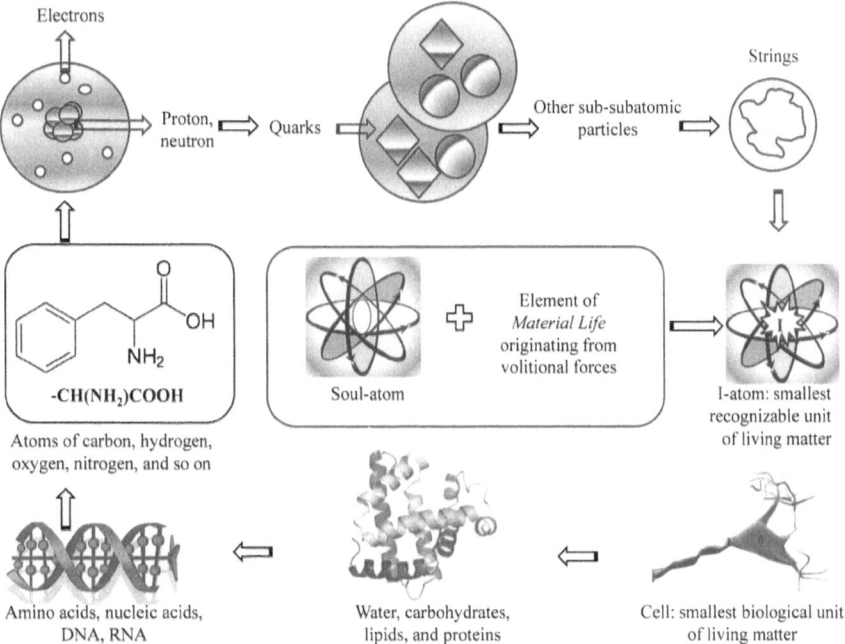

Figure 7.4. The smallest "realizable" or "recognizable" unit of living matter is the I-atom.

Let us now consider hydrogen, the simplest form of atom and the first element on the periodic table. An atom of hydrogen gives rise to the heavier and more complex atoms of helium, carbon, oxygen, and so on, due to nuclear processes called nucleogenesis, nucleosynthesis, and nuclear fusion. These heavier atoms are identified as distinct elements of the periodic table. In a way, hydrogen is the mother of other elements of the periodic table. When hydrogen, the mother element, combines with other elements such as the oxygen, we get a molecule of water. When it combines with carbon, we get a molecule of hydrocarbon, and so forth. Thus, the element of hydrogen gives rise to various molecules of matter. In this simplest way, we can understand how elements (or atoms or molecules) form the basis of inanimate physical matter that we see in the universe.[20]

Analogous to the hydrogen atom, the I-atom gives rise to higher (more evolved) forms of I-atoms that make up the sensual matter of five senses, sexual matter, and the subtle-heart matter of the heart and the blood. Evolved forms of I-atoms arise primarily due to volitional forces. Exactly how that happens is the theme of *soul genesis,* a subtopic of soul mechanics, which I am leaving out of this discussion due to its vastness and complexity. It will be addressed in the sequel to this book.

For now, I invite you to consider the following:

- An I-atom gives rise to five types of living matter due to a volitional force (aka a desire) to hear, see, smell, taste, and touch. These higher forms are the material phenomena of ear sensitivity, eye sensitivity, nose sensitivity, tongue sensitivity, and body sensitivity (elements 9–13 on the chart of material elements). The higher forms eventually generate sense matter of the five sense organs when the conditions of consciousness, temperature, and nutriment are present. The five sense organs grow inside the mother's womb because these conditions are present there. Throughout life they continue growing, as long as the person is alive (the condition of consciousness), as long as there is temperature (necessary for digestion and metabolism), and as long as the person is fed (the condition of nutriment).

- An I-atom gives rise to two additional types of living matter due to a desire for the propagation of the species. These two higher forms are the phenomena of male-sexuality and female-sexuality (elements 14 and 15 on the chart of material elements). They eventually generate the sexual matter of the sexual organs as well as the sexuality of the whole body when the conditions of consciousness, temperature, and nutriment are present.

- An I-atom gives rise to another type of living matter due to a desire to feel, perceive, and think (and not only sense and propagate), a desire that is higher than a sensual one or a sexual one, a desire that is responsible for the generation of mind-body and not just body. This highest form is the phenomena of *mind sensitivity* (element 17 on the chart of material elements), which underlies the sensitivity of the five senses. It is also known as the subtle matter of the sixth sense. It eventually generates the subtle matter of the heart and the blood when the conditions of consciousness, temperature, and nutriment are present.

In this way, due to various volitional forces (desires), an I-atom gives rise to more and more evolved forms of I-atoms. These in turn generate the living matter of the human body.

You might be wondering how brain matter is formed. I propose that brain matter (including the nervous system) is actually *derived* matter (through further evolution) and does not form directly from the various I-atoms that we have discussed so far. Maybe that is why the body can continue living even if we are brain dead.

Those who find the preceding statements about various I-atoms puzzling might want to consider them in light of genetics. As we now know, our bodies take form starting with a single cell (zygote).[21] This is possible because a zygote contains DNA molecules, which are loaded with all the information necessary for the creation of a body. Where does this information come from? I propose it comes from the I-atoms we have been discussing.

Origin of Matter

If the propositions that I have made are accurate, it is obvious that volitional forces are what set in motion the creation of living matter. From previous discussions, we know that volitional forces originate from volitional energy. So ultimately it is the volitional energy that is the creator of living beings. However, volitional energy is not strong enough to create tangible living matter. It needs the presence of consciousness, temperature, and nutriment, as discussed above.

Thus, we can say that there are four causes (origins) of living matter. I propose that there is no single cause.

Modern physics tells us that first atoms were formed due to nuclear reactions soon after the Big Bang. Hydrogen is supposed to be the first atom derived from subatomic particles that were generated at the time of Big Bang. However, no one yet knows where the first subatomic particles came from. One speculation in the scientific community is that they came from nothing, a vacuum that is also broadly known as *dark energy*.[22]

An interesting aspect of this energy is that it cannot be calculated mathematically. Although its presence is confirmed through observations and inference, an attempt to calculate it results in the biggest mathematical blunder ever (off by 10^{120})! This energy is most obvious in the universe because it is abundant and occupies two-thirds of universal space.[23] And yet, ironically enough, it is not possible to put it in a mathematical or theoretical or physical equation. It seems this energy, the source of matter, is not quantifiable.

Is it possible that the source of matter is not quantifiable because it is fundamentally rooted in soul-atoms and I-atoms, which are *qualitative* material phenomena? Is it possible that the energy of nothing is none other than the volitional energy that gives rise to soul-atoms and I-atoms?

Atoms of elements on the periodic table can be created in the laboratory using particle accelerators or nuclear reactors. However, soul-atoms and I-atoms, which are subtler than atoms of the elements on the periodic table, cannot be created by physical efforts. Of their own accord, they arise out of the four causes. In other words, all the matter in the universe *fundamentally* originates from volitional energy, consciousness, temperature, and nutriment.[24] How this happens in the simplest manner possible is illustrated in figure 7.5.

CHAPTER 7 EXPLORING MATTER

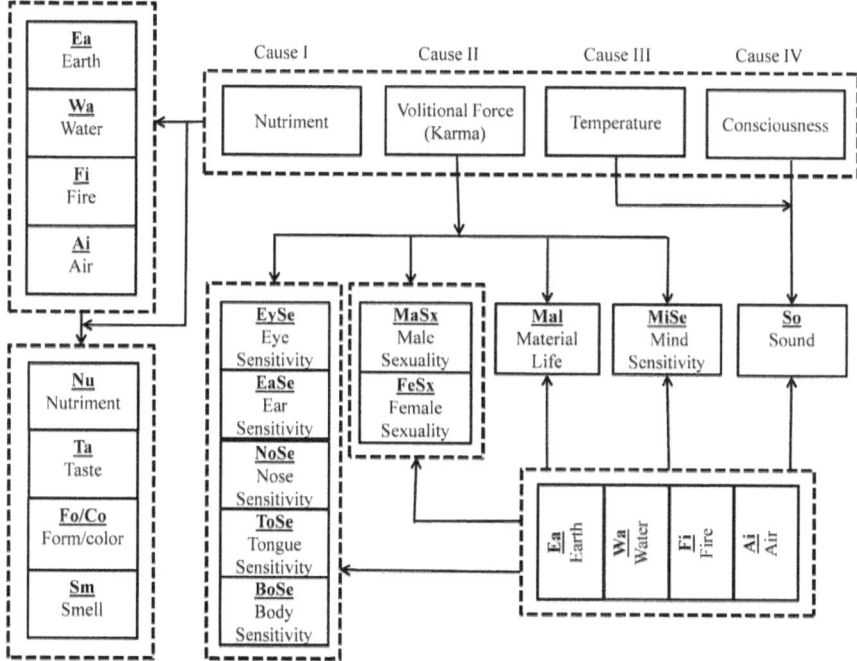

Figure 7.5. The origin of matter. This flow chart illustrates the creation of the ultimate building blocks of matter from four ultimate causes: consciousness, volitional force, temperature, and nutrient. Note that there is no single ultimate cause.

Many people wonder about what might have existed before the four causes. Many are interested in finding out the absolute first cause. There are those who simply attribute it to an almighty figure, such as a creator God, that is presumably beyond cause and effect. To such people, may I humbly suggest that there is no absolute first cause because:
- A cause cannot exist without conditions,
- Everything is relative and interconnected,
- There is no absoluteness in the universe, and
- Nothing can exist outside of or separate from the universe, since this would defy the law of cause and effect (in terms of conditionality).

Asking whether or not anything existed before the four causes or what was the *absolute* first matter is not particularly helpful. It is like asking, "What is the diameter of a cube?" "What is the distance to the horizon from where you are?" or, "What is the beginning point of the surface of the Earth?" We cannot answer such questions because the questions themselves are wrong! Diameters are mathematical means of measuring circles and spheres, not cubes. The horizon is an optical illusion. You can never reach it. The surface of the Earth is spherical. It cannot begin or end at one surface point. In short, what I am suggesting is that it is not possible to know what the absolute first matter or first cause is because it does not exist.

Another often-debated question is whether non-material stuff (volitional energy and consciousness) or material-stuff (temperature and nutriment) creates matter first?

An even more contentious question is whether mind creates matter or matter creates mind?

I feel a better question to ask is: What is the fundamental (ultimate) cause of matter?

Remember that the word "ultimate" means *the subtlest mode of experience—that which cannot be penetrated or further reduced*. It also means *the level of phenomena*. So the answer is that matter ultimately arises out of non-material stuff as well as out of material stuff, and it is up to us to choose one as the origin and go forward from there. After all, at the level of phenomena, there remains no *absolute* or *objective* boundary between material and non-material stuff.

Space and Abstract Elements of Matter

Some people believe that space existed before matter and therefore it could represent the origin of matter or the subtlest material element. From ancient times to the medieval era, philosophers attributed the origin of matter to an entity called *akash* or *ether*, which means space.[25] Even Newton believed in a preexisting absolute space in which matter came to be.[26]

It seems like common sense, but it is not true. A scientific fact widely accepted by modern cosmologists is that the universe was in an "infinitely dense" state at the time of the Big Bang. Materially speaking, infinite density should mean zero space. In other words, there was no space at the origin of the universe. Space (or space-time, as it is currently known) was created as the universe expanded or, more precisely, inflated.[27] It is somewhat like inflating the balloon. As you blow air in it, it inflates and creates space. Here, space is analogous to the inflated surface of a balloon and not the inside of a balloon. Another way of understanding is to consider the Big Bang the explosion *of* space rather than something that happened *in* space.

Those who think space preceded matter might be mistaking space for the elements of mind or consciousness.

I suggest that space is not the origin of matter. Moreover, it is neither an entirely material phenomenon, nor a non-material phenomenon. Rather it is an *attribute* of material phenomena. It is there (as an attribute) because matter is there and vice versa. In other words, space exists because real matter exists and not necessarily the other way round!

Empty space, the distance between objects, does not arise *directly* out of the four causes of matter the way soul-atoms and I-atoms do. Therefore space is not matter in the way concrete matter is. It is the absence of matter. In this sense, space can be known as the non-concrete matter.[28]

Conventionally speaking, matter is recognizable *as* matter because it deforms. Space bends and curls in relation to matter. In fact, the reason we experience gravity is because of the bending of space due to the mass of planet Earth. Gravity is the proof that space exists—however, only in relation to matter. I intuitively feel that it is bent space that pushes us down towards Earth (technically, this phenomenon is gravity), rather than the Earth pulling us down towards itself! Or maybe it is both. You may feel the same way if you study and contemplate Einstein's theory of general relativity.[29]

Experientially, we can recognize the abstract material phenomenon of space as the quality of *material voidness*, which is called the *space element* (element 28 on the chart of material elements). We experience this space element as gaps, voids, cavities, apertures, and so on. The space element separates material objects and makes it possible to perceive objects as distinct. Its characteristic is to define the boundaries of matter and its function is to display these boundaries. We can experience or perceive space element only in relation to other material elements.

In addition to the space element, there are nine other abstract material phenomena: the elements of lightness, flexibility, pliability, production, continuity, decay, bodily-intimation, vocal intimation, and impermanence (elements 19–27 on the chart of material elements).[30] Like the space element, these elements are not matter but simply *attributes of matter*. They will be described in detail in the sequel to this book. They represent abstract qualities found in the real material world (see Appendix A, "The Material Elements in Terms of Their Characteristics, Functions, Manifestations, and Proximate Causes," on page 367).

In summary, our material world (including the human body) is the result of 18 concrete material phenomena and 10 abstract material phenomena. More precisely, these 28 material elements—the distinct material phenomena or experiences—are what we collectively refer to as the material world.

So What?

Knowing the body as a bundle of 28 material elements that are constantly arising and passing away on their own accord, we can develop a sense of impermanence and impersonality, and reduce our bodily attachment and the suffering that arises from it. For example, look at any pain you feel as a bundle of intensified fire elements that are arising and passing away in a flux and find out if that makes any difference to you. Personally, I have noticed an increase in my ability to handle pain when I look at pain as "intensified fire elements" rather than "pain in *my* body." From this perspective, I am able to focus on the impermanence and notice how long the pain lasts, as opposed to instantly reacting and worsening the pain. This gives me time to deal with the pain before it becomes unbearable. It also helps me in not grabbing an aspirin in reaction to the smallest degree of pain. I am

CHAPTER 7 EXPLORING MATTER

able to better manage pain and take medication only when necessary, therefore doing less harm to my body.

In the advanced stages of understanding that come after practicing the various meditations described in upcoming chapters, we can reduce body-centeredness by observing the body simply as a continuum of material elements that arise and pass away due to the four causes. We can experientially understand how these elements come and go of their own accord without us having any control over them. We can experientially realize that the body we live in is "a body, a bundle of 28 material elements," and not *our* body. After such realization, we automatically begin to dis-identify ourselves with the body due to *experiencing* its non-solidity, impermanence, and non-self nature.

Eventually, we become detached from the body. This is not to say that we abandon or neglect the body, but that we simply stop craving it and start looking beyond it. Due to bodily detachment, we become less afraid of pain, disease, aging, and death.

Remember that the *experience* of non-solidity, impermanence, and non-self cannot arise from the knowledge of conventional material entities, such as electrons, protons, quarks, or strings, because these material entities cannot be felt the way that material elements can be. This experiential nature and the wisdom of impermanence, and impersonality that arises from it really are the two main reasons behind knowing the body in terms of the material elements. Ultimately, experiential wisdom can only remove the confusion in the philosophies of materialism and anti-materialism, and pave the way for the development of perfect intelligence.

* * *

Chapter 8

Exploring Consciousness

There is no universal consensus on what consciousness is. As far as I know, no one has come up with a suitable definition so far that everyone can agree upon.[1] But I strongly feel, and you may agree, that we came close in chapter 1.

The subject of consciousness has been discussed *ad nauseum* by modern thinkers and philosophers, and overlooked by scientists and psychologists. Consciousness really is not so hard to understand if we define it as *a phenomenon of experience (cognition)*. Instead of debating whether or not this is true, why not to try to categorize all experiences into various types of consciousness and build a meaningful model so we can understand the totality of human experience? At the same time, let's use that understanding to purify our minds.

Types of Consciousness

Categorizing all experiences into various types of consciousness facilitates mental purification through the development of non-delusion, because it allows us to account for all experiences (seeing, hearing, smelling, tasting, touching, and knowing) without introducing into the mix a fictitious entity: the experiencer. When we know that various types of consciousness perform all the cognitive functions that are necessary for an experience to occur, we are not left with any unknowns. In most cases, various fictitious entities (such as the separate self, the super self, the higher self, the individual soul, the super soul, atman, almighty, and so on) are introduced when we are trying to account for the unknowns.

In chapter 1, we introduced the idea of four primary types of consciousness and 15 subtypes of consciousness. We discussed how consciousness acquires the ability of cognition due to the mental elements that arise with it and impart their qualities to it. Using this knowledge, let us try to explore the types of consciousness further.

1. *Unwholesome consciousness*: Consciousness rooted in one or more unwholesome mental elements: greed, hatred, and delusion. We consider it unwholesome firstly because it adversely impacts experience, thereby inflicting pain and suffering. Secondly, it is unwholesome because it generates unwholesome volition.

Unwholesome consciousness can be sub-classified as:

- *Greedy:* Consciousness that is predominantly rooted in greed is primarily responsible for experiences of selfishness, passion, lust, attachments, indifference, sensual pleasure, convictions, beliefs, and so on.
- *Hateful:* Consciousness that is predominantly rooted in hatred is primarily responsible for experiences of displeasure, and for the entire range of aversions ranging from minor irritation, resistance, and negativity to violent anger.
- Deluded: Consciousness that is predominantly rooted in delusion is primarily responsible for experiences of impatience, agitation, skepticism, indecisiveness, indifference, brazenness, laziness, and so on.

2. *Wholesome consciousness*: Consciousness rooted in one or more wholesome mental elements: non-greed, non-hatred, and non-delusion. We can consider it wholesome firstly because it positively

CHAPTER 8 EXPLORING CONSCIOUSNESS

impacts experience, thereby generating happiness and peace. Secondly, it is wholesome because it generates wholesome volition. Wholesome consciousness can be sub-classified as:
- *Non-greedy*: Consciousness that is predominantly rooted in non-greed is primarily responsible for experiences of joy, generosity, sympathy, empathy, letting go, non-craving, non-clinging, detachment, unselfishness, renunciation, dispassion, contentment, effacement, wealth, happiness, peace, and so on.
- *Non-hateful:* Consciousness that is predominantly rooted in non-hatred is primarily responsible for experiences of loving-kindness, patience, forbearance, equanimity, sociability, agreeableness, amity, gentleness, friendliness, calmness, softness, coolness, pleasantness, delight, happiness, bliss, concentration, energy, and so on.
- *Non-deluded:* Consciousness that is predominantly rooted in non-delusion is primarily responsible for experiences of freedom, purified views, clear comprehension, pure understanding, pure knowledge, wisdom, mental perfection, sainthood, holiness, spaciousness, oneness, infiniteness, egolessness, and so on.

3. Resultant consciousness: Consciousness that is the fruition of accumulated volitional forces (karma). Although it is comprised of the *results* of the first two types of consciousness, it is neither unwholesome nor wholesome in itself.
Resultant consciousness can be sub-classified as:
- *Five sense types*: Eye consciousness (responsible for seeing an object), ear consciousness (responsible for hearing an object), nose consciousness (responsible for smelling an object), tongue consciousness (responsible for tasting an object), and body consciousness (responsible for touching an object).
- *Receiving:* Immediately following sense consciousness, an object is apprehended due to this type of consciousness. For example, once eye consciousness senses an external visual object, the object cannot actually be seen unless it is mentally received by receiving consciousness.

- *Investigating*: Immediately following receiving consciousness, an apprehended object is investigated or examined by this type of consciousness.
- *Registering*: Immediately after all the types of consciousness we have mentioned so far have arisen and ceased, this type of consciousness arises and registers the object. It is responsible for creating memories, impressions, volitional formations (accumulated volitions that form mental patterns), and so on.
- *Birth and death*: These types of consciousness arise at the moments of conception and death, respectively. They are the manifestation of the subconscious, which we will soon discuss. Understanding these two types is necessary for exploring the boundary conditions of human lifespan.

4. *Functional consciousness*: Consciousness that is none of the above (unwholesome, wholesome, or resultant) is functional. It performs the activity of enabling, referring, or determining an object. However, it is not potent enough by itself to generate an experience.

Functional consciousness can be sub-classified as:

- *Sense-enabling:* This consciousness precedes the five types of sense consciousness. It is the first one to arise in any experience or cognitive process related to seeing, hearing, smelling, tasting, and touching. By its arousal, it enables the functioning of the five sense consciousnesses so that an experience can occur. An eye can sense a visual object because this type of consciousness refers eye consciousness to a visual object. Without its arousal, none of the five sense consciousnesses would know what to look for. Using the five material bases (as we have previously discussed) as a meeting place, this consciousness initiates and facilitates interaction between the external world of sense objects and the internal world of senses.
- *Mind-enabling*: This consciousness precedes all types of consciousness (collectively known as mind consciousnesses) except the five of sense consciousnesses. It is the first one to arise in any

CHAPTER 8 EXPLORING CONSCIOUSNESS

experience or cognitive process related to thinking and knowing. By its arousal, it enables the functioning of mind consciousnesses so that a mental experience such as thinking or knowing can occur. We can think because this type of consciousness refers mind consciousness to mental (non-material) objects, such as thoughts, memories, and impressions. Without its arousal, mind consciousnesses would not know what to look for. Using the sixth material base (previously discussed, see page 31) as a meeting place, this consciousness initiates and facilitates interaction between the internal world and the sub-internal world, which we shall discuss momentarily (see figure 8.1).

- *Determining type*: Immediately after the investigating consciousness, this type of consciousness arises and determines and categorizes the object. It is responsible for concluding the discrimination phase of the cognitive process, as we will soon discuss in detail.

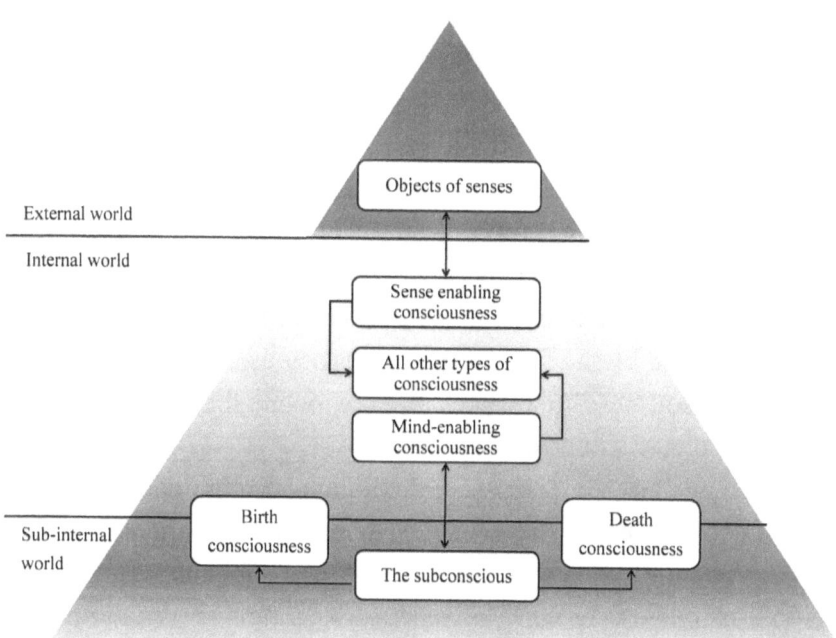

Figure 8.1. Interrelations between functional consciousness and all other types.

145

Depending upon their constitution in terms of mental elements, the four primary types and 15 subtypes just described can be further classified into sub-subtypes, giving a total of 121 types of consciousness (see Appendix B, "The 121 Types of Consciousness," on page 371).[2]

Let me remind you that there can be no rigid classification of consciousness. Wholesome consciousness can be wholesome resultant or wholesome functional, and so on. Mind-enabling consciousness can also be determining, depending upon which of the six material bases it uses as its support. Nonetheless, the four primary types and 15 subtypes are distinct from one another in that their constitution of mental elements is unique.

The Subconscious

The subconscious is a dormant, underlying state ("sub" means "under") of consciousness. It is the *potentiality* for consciousness. Like a seed of consciousness, it is a *state* that won't become consciousness until it gains enough strength. Just as a seed does not become a seedling unless it is planted in soil and receives adequate sunlight, the subconscious does not become consciousness unless appropriate conditions of matter and mind are present.

The subconscious is the foundational and conditional principal of our existence because it serves as an undercurrent and reason for any experience or act of cognition. It is always present in a dormant or underlying state, and arises as consciousness if no cognitive process is taking place. For example, in dreamless sleep or in a coma our existence is upheld by the flow of the subconscious. As soon as another type of consciousness arises, such as a dream or a thought, the flow of the subconscious is interrupted.

As we have already discussed, the body and mind cannot survive without consciousness. So whenever there is no volitional or cognitive activity (meaning, no consciousness) the subconscious sustains the flow of our existence. The subconscious thus serves as the life continuum or undercurrent of our existence. Like a stream of fuel, it flows continuously, burning up in a *passive* manner, and thereby

CHAPTER 8 EXPLORING CONSCIOUSNESS

running the vehicle of existence. For example, in a state of deep meditation or mental absorption an enlightened master is sustained by the flow of the subconscious, because there is no volitional activity in such a mental state.

The subconscious is always operational. It is not a static, permanent, or eternal entity (as a Hindu *jiva* or *atma* would be). It is a resultant and dynamic state that arises whenever consciousness is absent, and it ceases whenever consciousness intervenes.

In the beginning, we can simply understand the subconscious as a gap between thoughts, or as memory, intuitional faculty, and a storehouse of cognitive power. We can also understand the subconscious as the phenomenon that makes the heart beat, makes cells grow and multiply, and makes all unintentional mental and physical phenomena to occur.

We can also look at the subconscious as a field of dormant consciousness that is permeated by the volitional force just as the gravitational field is permeated by the force of gravity. The volitional force transforms the subconscious into consciousness, just as the force of a tossed pebble makes a ripple in a still pond. Consciousness is the ripple; the subconscious is the pond.

Birth consciousness is the most obvious manifestation of the subconscious. Due to volitional force (in this case, a strong desire to live) transforming the subconscious, birth consciousness arises in the mother's womb at the moment of conception, where along with other conditions of matter it causes life to begin. The subconscious also manifests as death consciousness, which is the last consciousness in a lifespan. This type of consciousness arises because volitional force no longer has enough strength for manifestation. It results from deterioration and the cutting off of body-mind conditions.[3]

A lifespan begins with birth consciousness and ends with death consciousness. Birth and death, like everything else in the realm of human experience, are phenomena of consciousness. In light of this knowledge, would you not wonder whether there is really such a thing as *a person* taking birth and then dying?

Dynamics of Consciousness: The Cognitive Process of Soul

Let us now look at how various types of consciousness and the subconscious function together to facilitate cognition.

A cognitive process is that by which we experience and know the world. As you already know, there are six fundamental cognitive processes: seeing, hearing, smelling, tasting, touching, and knowing. The first five are connected with our physical senses and the sixth is connected with mind. Cognition occurs only when essential conditions of matter-mind-consciousness are present.[4]

In other words, we can hear only if there is:

- *Matter:* A physical ear and the brain, ear sensitivity, sound, and space (a medium for sound to travel in)
- *Mind:* Attention (always accompanied by volition—in this case, the volition to hear)
- *Consciousness:* Ear consciousness, in this instance

We can see only if there is:

- *Matter:* A physical eye and the brain, eye sensitivity, a visible object, and fire (light)
- *Mind:* Attention (accompanied by the volition to see)
- *Consciousness:* Eye consciousness, in this case

We can smell only if there is:

- *Matter:* A physical nose and the brain, nose sensitivity, odor (chemical molecules), and air (a medium for smell to travel in)
- *Mind:* Attention (accompanied by the volition to smell)
- *Consciousness:* Nose consciousness, in this instance

We can taste only if there is:

- *Matter:* A physical tongue and the brain, tongue sensitivity, flavor (chemical molecules), and water (saliva)
- *Mind:* Attention (accompanied by the volition to taste)
- *Consciousness:* Tongue consciousness, in this case

CHAPTER 8 EXPLORING CONSCIOUSNESS

We can feel touch only if there is:
- *Matter:* A physical body/skin and the brain, body sensitivity, earth (tangible data)
- *Mind:* Attention (accompanied by the volition to touch)
- *Consciousness:* Body consciousness, in this instance

We can know or think only if there is:
- *Matter:* Heart, brain, and mind sensitivity
- *Mind:* The volitional force
- *Consciousness:* Mind consciousness (which includes all types of consciousness except the five sense types)

The act of knowing is different from the five sensual cognitive processes. Although it is independent of the five, it takes on the same object as is taken by the five. Any one of the five sensual cognitive processes is not complete unless knowing immediately succeeds it. In every complete cognitive process, sense consciousness is succeeded by mind consciousness.

Let us say, you are taking a walk in Central Park in Manhattan and suddenly you see an old acquaintance (of whom you have bad memories). The moment you look, the element of attention (which is always combined with volition) vibrates the subconscious, thereby arresting it and facilitating the beginning of a conscious process. As soon as there is a contact between your eyes and your visual object, which in this case is your acquaintance, sense-enabling consciousness arises and refers your old acquaintance to eye consciousness. Eye consciousness immediately *sees the object*.

Next, receiving consciousness receives the *seen object*. Then, investigating consciousness investigates the *received object*. Finally determining consciousness discriminates and perceives the *investigated object* as an old acquaintance. All these various types of consciousness arise and cease so rapidly that you interpret them as happening in one continuous stream.

As soon as the process of discrimination ends, there is an impulse for mental action (or reaction), which could lead in myriad directions. One of these might be to avoid the acquaintance due to past unpleasant experiences: a reaction rooted in hatred. Another would be to say hello without judging or thinking that the acquaintance might have changed for better: an action rooted in non-hatred. Mental actions and reactions are nothing but the arising respectively of either wholesome consciousness or unwholesome consciousness.

The arising of wholesome consciousness or unwholesome consciousness subsequent to determining consciousness is the most significant stage of the cognitive process. At this stage, choices are made. A choice is a volitional action that eventually becomes the volitional force. Choice making is the climax of the process of cognition because it leads your mind to what it becomes: good, bad, happy, sad, and so on. Note that choice making is simply the arising and passing away of wholesome consciousness or unwholesome consciousness. There is no choice maker.

Registering consciousness immediately follows the making of a choice. It registers the action or reaction into the subconscious, facilitating the creation of memories, impressions, mental patterns, and so on. Then the arising of the subconscious follows the subsiding of registering consciousness if no other consciousness arises at that moment.

The cognitive process thus begins and ends with the subconscious.

Cognitive processes follow a fixed order of consciousness from which they never deviate (see figure 8.2).[5]

CHAPTER 8 EXPLORING CONSCIOUSNESS

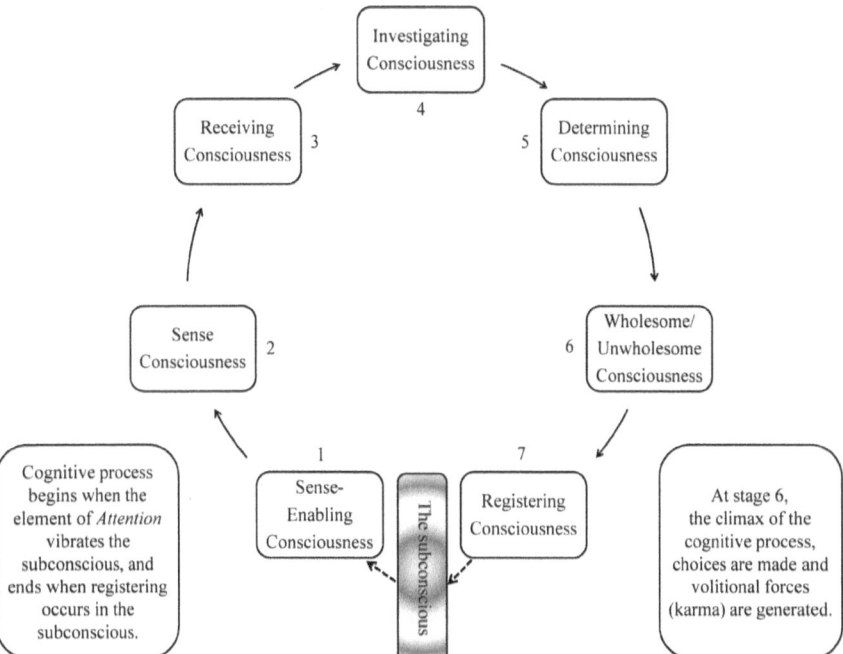

Figure 8.2. The dynamics of consciousness: Various types of consciousness—following a fixed order—facilitate the cognitive processes of soul.

You may be wondering, "What's the point in knowing all this?" The point is that understanding the cognitive process is necessary if you want to familiarize yourself with what is going on inside you.

As you study this chapter, along with later chapters, and learn ways to observe your mental activity and states of consciousness, you will begin to realize that:

- Many different types of consciousness partake in the act of cognition. No single consciousness performs all functions. No single consciousness is eternal. All arise and pass away, in the process paving the way to the next one. (Such realization will make you wonder whether there is really such a thing as an ever-lasting spirit or universal consciousness.)
- Each successive type of consciousness is conditioned by the type of consciousness that precedes it. Individual experiences are merely the outcomes of this *process of conditional interdependence of various types of consciousness*. Nothing exists inside or outside of

this process; the process goes on by itself following a fixed order. (Such realization will raise the question in your mind: "Is it possible that there is no fixed or absolute controller, overlord, or Almighty Father or Mother who rules or guides our experiences?")
- Cognition—an outcome of the dynamics of consciousness—is the only means by which we experience and know the world. (Such realization will surprise you as you begin to consider the possibility that there is no being, no person behind the act of cognition; that there is no knower in the act of knowing; that there is no thinker behind thoughts, and so on).

Work with these insights when they arise spontaneously for you. It is not sufficient for me to tell you about them. Direct experience is necessary rather than intellectual memorization. Don't believe me just because I say it. Test this information for yourself. These insights have the potential to bring about profound personal transformation, as they loosen the grip of various commonly held delusions, opening up the wisdom faculty.

The more you root your life in these insights, the less reactive and wiser you will become.

Before long, you will begin to recognize how your life is but a ballet of consciousness. You will then be able to observe the ballet without identifying with it. When that happens, you will know *experientially* what real freedom is.

* * *

Chapter 9

Exploring the Ultimate Building Blocks of Mind

There are many hypotheses about the nature of mind. Some are theological, some are metaphysical, some are philosophical, some are psychological, some are neuro-scientific (brain based), and some are a combination thereof.[1] The hypothesis of mind we introduced in chapter 1, however, is a new and different one that may serve one day as a unifying link for all the other mind hypotheses that are currently known. I say so because it is a *phenomenal* hypothesis based on the *ultimate building blocks of mind*, the 52 mental elements that are unique phenomena representing the roots of all mental activities.

Just as the study of the elemental nature of inorganic matter—atoms, subatomic particles, strings, and the elements of the periodic table—has revolutionized the sciences of physics and chemistry, and, just as the study of the elemental nature of organic matter—cells, genes, and

DNA/RNA—has revolutionized the sciences of chemistry and biology, the study of mental elements may do the same for the sciences of mind. Most importantly, the study of mental elements has the potential to provide a scientific framework for total mental development, because it addresses not only the neutral functions of mind (such as sensation, feeling, perception, volition, thinking, and so on), but also the ethical ones (such as greed, non-greed, hatred, non-hatred, conscience, and so on).

Because mental elements are ultimate realities, knowledge of them can help the scientific and medical communities in identifying the *root causes* and conditions behind various emotional and psychological disorders. So I humbly urge professionals in these fields to consider the mental elements proposed here a subject worthy of research and to use knowledge of the mental elements to integrate the fields of psychology, psychiatry, and neuroscience to create a unified framework of mind science. Such a framework could provide clues to solving various psychiatric and neurological mysteries that currently daunt us.[2] It could also provide insight for developing next-generation psychological and psychoanalytical diagnostic and therapeutic tools.

On an individual basis, if you study, contemplate, meditate, experience, and understand the 52 mental elements, you will *intimately* know your mind. So I encourage you to closely study the description of each element given in numerical order in chapters 10–16. If you already know a lot about mind, I hope you will find numerous golden nuggets of insight that will enrich your current understanding.

By the time you are done reading about the mental elements, I hope I will succeed in providing answers to many intriguing mind-related questions, such as:
- What is a feeling?
- What is perception?
- What is an emotion?
- Where does pain come from, and how can I get over it?
- What are attention, volition, and will?
- What is choice?
- What is wholesome desire and what is not?

CHAPTER 9 EXPLORING THE ULTIMATE BUILDING BLOCKS OF MIND

- What are mental powers, and how do I develop them?
- What are mental weaknesses, and how do I eradicate them?
- What is transcendence?
- What is mental refinement?
- What is intrinsically wholesome (good) and unwholesome (bad)?
- Are good and bad relative or not?
- What are ethics and morality?
- What is faith, what is belief, and how do they differ?
- What are real happiness and real wealth?
- Is greed a necessary condition for becoming rich?
- What is real success?
- What is conscience?
- What is fear, and is it good or bad?
- What is holiness?
- What is divinity?
- What is love?
- What is nobility?
- What factors lead to mental perfection?
- What does it take to achieve truly great things?

Chapters 10–16 together form a catalogue of sort of the 52 mental elements previously listed in figure 1.4 on page 26 and 27.[3] Make this catalogue your daily reference manual so that you can find solutions to the problems you face as they arise. For example, if you feel lethargic and want to get over it, study the descriptions of sloth and torpor (elements 25 and 26 on Appendix C, "The Mental Elements in Terms of Their Characteristics, Functions, Manifestations, and Proximate Causes," on page 383) to find out what is happening at the *root* of your lethargy, and then refer to the description of vigor (element 12) to come up with your own solution. If you are agitated and feeling miserable, read about restlessness (element 17), mindfulness (element 30), and tranquility (elements 34 and 35). If you are feeling remorseful, reference remorse (element 22). If you are feeling angry, immerse yourself in studying hatred (element 15) and non-hatred (element 29).

Soon you will know which of the mental elements to refer to when analyzing an emotional difficulty and seeking to formulate an effective solution. When you are in a remorseful state of mind, for instance, you will also notice that just by reading about the element of remorse you will start feeling better. Just by dwelling in the study of the elements of hatred and non-hatred, your anger will subside. You will realize that "knowingness" changes everything for the better!

Once you experience the benefits of knowing the mental elements, you may find it valuable to memorize their characteristics, functions, manifestations, proximate causes, and solutions. Appendix C was designed for this purpose.[4] Based on my own experience of several years, I confidently can say that this brief summation of the elements will soon become your anchor in understanding your mental actions and reactions, and in coming up with quick solutions to overcome your mental challenges and emotional difficulties.

These are no ordinary tools because they are rooted in the ultimate reality of mind: the 52 mental elements.

* * *

Chapter 10

The Universal Mind

We now begin with a discussion of mental elements 1–6 that perform essential and neutral functions of the Mind. These elements are present as a group in all mental activities. Mind cannot function without their presence (see figure 10.1).

Sensation *(mental element 1, Se)*

Sensation is the first mental element to function in all cognitive processes because it actually facilitates contact between consciousness (the inside world) and objects of experience (the outside world). This contact is similar to a physical *touch*, but it is more of a mental impression. It is nothing but a coming together of the senses and the objects of the senses.

When we see a flower, the eyes do not actually go out and touch the flower. When we hear a radio, the ears do not actually go out and touch the radio. Still there is a touch between eyes and flower, ears and radio. There would not be any seeing or hearing otherwise. When we see our favorite dishes, our mouths start watering. This happens without physically touching the dishes with our mouths.

We have mentally touched the dishes. Similarly, when our children are physically hurt and experiencing pain, we feel their pain because we are touched due to the element of sensation.

Here an external object, mind, and consciousness are meeting. They are coming together dependent on each other. Therefore, the best way to understand the element of sensation is to look at it as a meeting place between mind and matter, between the external world and the internal world, or between the senses and objects of the senses.

Sensation fits into a gray area between mind and matter. It has a foot anchored in both the physical and the mental fields however it is predominantly mental.

Sensation initiates mental activity, which leads to the arising of feeling. Sensation is a foundation and a necessary condition for the occurrence of feeling.

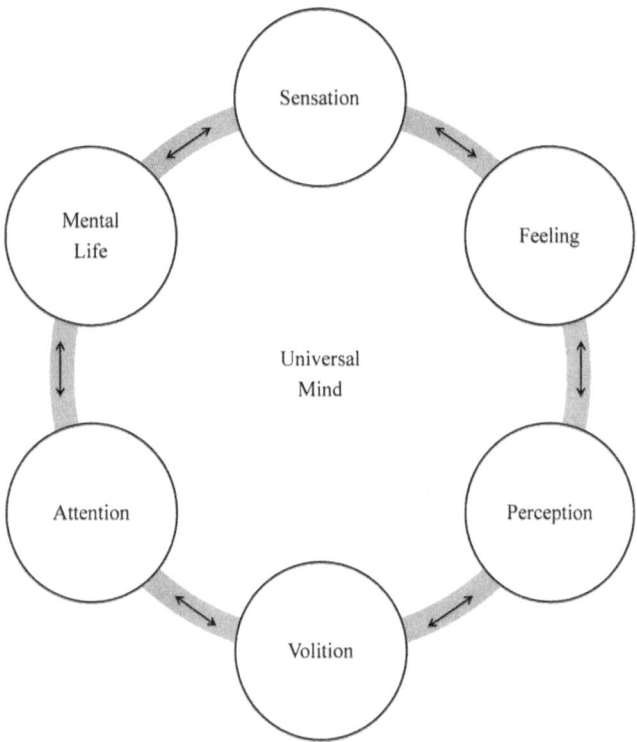

Figure 10.1. The universal mind consists of six mental elements that perform all the essential mental functions. These elements always arise together as a group. Feeling, the most primitive, is the mother of all other mental elements.

Feeling *(mental element 2, Fe)*

Feeling is the second consecutive element to function in all the cognitive processes. As such, it is preceded and conditioned by sensation.

Bare, unconditioned feeling is a mental phenomenon that "feels" objects of the senses. All experience results in some kind of feeling. Therefore, everything in the realm of experience can be understood in terms of feeling.

Feeling assists consciousness in experiencing an object directly and thoroughly. That is how we can differentiate it from sensation. It is difficult to understand our feelings without experiencing them. Right now, try to feel your breath or touch your arm with your fingertips. What you are feeling is direct and thorough. This happens due to the arising of the element of feeling.

There are basically three types of feelings: pleasant feelings, unpleasant feelings, and neutral feelings. Sensual pleasures are examples of pleasant feelings. Physical pain (from now on referred to simply as "pain") and sorrow are examples of unpleasant feelings. Equanimity is neutral: neither pleasant, nor unpleasant.

Even though sensation is the first mental phenomena to occur in any experience, the arising of one of these feelings initiates the direct experience of anything in the world. Because of the initiating and affective quality of feeling, it has tremendous potential to awaken the mind. Also, the element of feeling is somewhat unique because it initiates experience. In this sense, it is the chief mental component of every experience.

The unpleasantness or pleasantness of a feeling is not a perception. It is not a reaction to an object that makes a feeling unpleasant or pleasant. Unpleasantness or pleasantness are inherent qualities of the element of feeling, just as heat and cold are inherent qualities of the element of fire, and just as hardness and softness are inherent qualities of the element of earth.

Unpleasant and pleasant feelings are neither unwholesome (bad) nor wholesome (good). What makes a feeling good or bad is the presence of other mental elements that arise with it. Pain, for instance, is an unpleasant feeling. This doesn't mean pain is unwholesome. Pain is simply unpleasant, just as the earth element is hard and the fire element is hot. Pain becomes unwholesome when greed or hatred arises with it. In other words, if you dislike or like the unpleasantness of pain, then pain becomes unwholesome. Similarly, feelings of happiness or joy are pleasant in nature. This is so because it is their inherent quality. Feelings of happiness become unwholesome when you develop a craving for happiness or when greed arises with it.

Unpleasant feelings exist in nature. If we feel unpleasant in hot weather, it does not mean that we are reacting to the weather. If we feel uncomfortable or suffocated in polluted air, it does not mean that we are reacting to the air or that we are physically or mentally weak. We feel uncomfortable because of our physiological and psychological constitution, which is common to all human beings.

A feeling (unpleasant or pleasant) can be either physiological or psychological. Feelings primarily caused by the body (or that have matter as a proximate cause) are physiological. Feelings that are primarily mental (or that have mind as a proximate cause) are psychological. Pain can be understood as an unpleasant physiological feeling and sorrow can be understood as an unpleasant psychological feeling. Sensual pleasure can be understood as a pleasant physiological feeling, and happiness can be understood as a pleasant psychological feeling (see figure 10.2).[1]

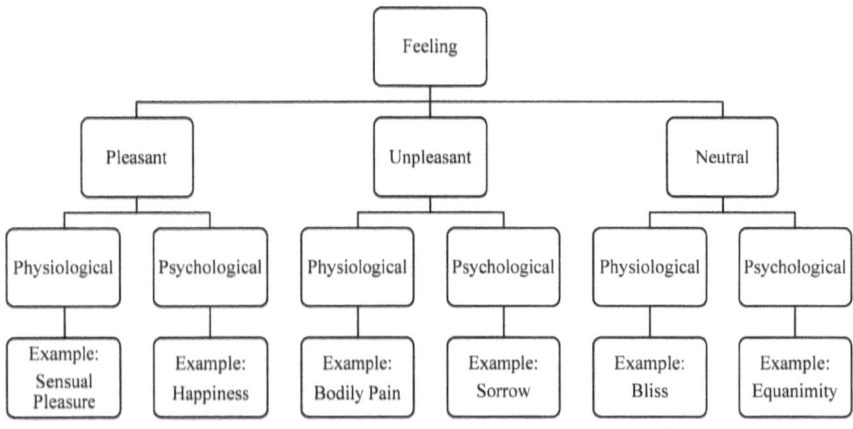

Figure 10.2. Types of feeling. Any human experience can be classified as one of six types.

CHAPTER 10 THE UNIVERSAL MIND

Feelings are mental phenomena that have physiological and psychological underpinnings. Such understanding is helpful in removing the delusions of ill-informed spiritual enthusiasts, including some ascetics and yogis. Many do not understand the nature of feelings. They criticize or look down upon others who would avoid painful feelings, wrongly considering their own ability to tolerate pain or unwholesome environmental conditions (such as polluted air, noise, and so on) as a measure of their spiritual attainment. Ignorant ascetics and yogis develop an attachment to pain and an aversion to pleasure. They shy away from pleasant feelings. But this becomes a huge hindrance to mental development. Proper understanding is also helpful in removing the delusions of worldly people who struggle to push away or suppress unpleasant feelings.

When we realize that it is the nature of a feeling itself to be pleasant or unpleasant, we begin to detach ourselves from the feeling. We stop thinking that our perception is coloring the feeling. We neither develop guilt for experiencing sensual or mental pleasantness, nor do we try to escape from sensual or mental unpleasantness. We simply dis-identify from feelings, which ultimately leads to objective observation. As we observe our feelings arising and passing away without reacting to them, this in turn leads us to become aware of our neutral feelings. Once this happens it is an indication that equanimity, a sublime quality of mind, has arisen.

Neutral feelings are elusive. Students frequently ask me if neutrality is the same thing as numbness or not feeling. They understand pleasant and unpleasant feelings but struggle to comprehend neutrality. They also commonly ask: "How can it be a feeling if it is neither pleasant nor unpleasant?"

The answer is that only one type of feeling can be felt in a particular moment. Until it has passed away, another type of feeling cannot arise. Therefore, if one remains consistently mindful of one's feelings from moment to moment, one can understand that pleasant and unpleasant feelings do not occur simultaneously. When such mindfulness (a precursor to equanimity) is established, sooner or later one begins to realize that feelings come and go of their own accord without any being having control over them. One begins to realize that feeling feels. It is just a mental phenomenon. One understands that the awareness or consciousness of feeling is being mistaken as a "feeler" and that there is only consciousness. When such wisdom arises, a feeling is experienced that is neither pleasant nor unpleasant. This is the third type of feeling: neutrality, which awakens equanimity and non-attachment.

Equanimity and non-attachment result in the occurrence of additional neutral feelings, which are of transcendental nature, meaning they transcend pleasantness and unpleasantness. They are not numbness, indifference, blandness, tastelessness, and insensitivity, as is often misunderstood. Rather they are the indirect manifestation of supra-sensitivity and wisdom. The term "neither pain nor pleasure" does not merely signify the absence of pain or pleasure, but the transcendence of those feeling states.

Transcendent neutral feelings are an indirect experience of egolessness, the manifestation of perfect intelligence. However, such feelings do not occur until there is thorough and experiential understanding of pleasant and unpleasant feelings through the practices of soul meditation and contemplation, which we will discuss in later chapters.

Going Beyond Sensual/Physical Pleasures

When we experientially understand all three types of feelings, our knowledge always gives rise to spiritual joy. For those who are inclined towards perfecting intelligence, experiencing spiritual joy is absolutely necessary because it assists us in going beyond our cravings for sensual pleasant feelings. It serves as a substitute for sensual pleasant feelings, thereby saving us tremendous energy that we would otherwise spend in pursuing sensual pleasures.

As we begin to abide in the pleasantness of spiritual joy, we start naturally abandoning sensual pleasures. We begin to spend more time reading, studying, contemplating, meditating, and so on, activities that are sure to result in the experience of deeper kinds of pleasantness, ranging from rapture, to delight, to bliss, and so on. Without experiencing such pleasantness, it would be extremely difficult to abandon sensual cravings and deal with the monumental task of eradicating all cravings. Spiritual joy is necessary for going beyond sensual pleasures.

However, you should celebrate when you experience spiritual joy, but do not get overexcited. Even if it arises out of wholesome spiritual practices, you must not develop a craving for its pleasantness. Simply allow it to arise and pass away, gladden your mind, and deepen your practice, so that equanimity ultimately can arise of its own accord.

Going Beyond Pain

Pain is a physiological feeling. Unpleasantness is its intrinsic quality. Even someone in an egoless state, such as the enlightened master, cannot change that, as it is a law of nature. Everybody feels pain as unpleasant, but once equanimity arises, there is no reaction to the unpleasantness. And when there is no reaction to unpleasantness, due to equanimity, it becomes so *refined* that it is eventually transcended. The subject and the object of pain are transcended.

A crude way to understand the refinement of pain is to perform a physical exercise in which you hold a posture (say the squat or table-top pose in martial arts) for a long time. As you hold the posture, you will begin to feel unpleasantness in your thighs. This unpleasantness will increase with time and turn into pain the moment that you react to it with aversion. If, on the other hand, you work to develop mindfulness of the unpleasant feeling and non-reaction to it, you will be able to hold the posture longer. You may feel unpleasantness, but not pain. Soon, in an advanced stage of practice, you will no longer even feel unpleasantness if the same posture is held with increasing mindfulness and non-reaction united with concentration and wise attention. The unpleasant feeling then is refined to such an extent that unpleasantness itself would be transcended.

Through increasing mindfulness and non-reaction (in union with concentration and wise attention), it is possible to become so subtle that you can actually move through oceans of feelings without getting wet. It is as if you are simply abiding in consciousness without clinging to anything in the world of matter and mind.

It is not essential to go through pain or torture to master pain. It is neither a necessary condition, nor a proper means to develop equanimity towards pain. However, many spiritualists and theologians use this unwise process, as they assume that pain can be mastered (or sins can be erased) by burning up past mental impressions related to unpleasant feelings. In some traditions, this unwise process is known as "karmic retribution."[2]

If a person inflicts pain for the purpose of mastering pain, it is not easy for that person to develop mindfulness, non-reaction, and concentration—states without which real equanimity and perfect intelligence cannot arise.

Mental pain (unhappiness, sorrow, lamentation, grief, anger, and so on) is more intimate and subtle than physical pain because it requires a higher degree of mindfulness to remain non-reactive to it than to physical pain. Therefore, when it comes to mastering pain, dealing directly with mental pain is of utmost importance. Ultimately, mental pain has to be dealt with in order to transcend any type of pain completely.

My earlier example of an exercise in the martial arts pose was given as a crude means for an experiment. If you decide to try this experiment, you should not let your unpleasant physical feelings rise to such a level that you react to them with aversion. You have to gradually and skillfully expand your tolerance zone so that you do not develop a craving or an aversion to unpleasantness. In other words, never allow unpleasantness to aggravate to such levels that it turns into pain. The moment you realize that aversion is arising, you should knowingly get out of the posture. Later try again, and each time you do increase the holding time to manageable levels of unpleasantness.

The important thing is to try to remain non-reactive in every painful situation. It is not necessary to inflict physical pain on oneself intentionally as some of ascetics, monks, and yogis do. If physical pain arises due to a natural process, like aging or disease, only then should it be used to develop the faculty of non-reaction.

As long as we live, we cannot avoid physical unpleasantness. It naturally arises through disease and the aging process, and while dying. No amount of prosperity or luxury could help us to get rid of it. Therefore we train ourselves not to develop aversion towards it.

In advanced stages of meditation practice, you should start paying wise attention to pain. You should aim to understand it as an imperfect aspect of your existence. Look at pain merely as a wakeup call for beginning the process of physical and mental purification. Use painful feelings as a constant reminder of your imperfections. Try to discover and understand the causes of pain and realize that essentially it arises due to lack of equanimity towards unpleasant aspects of life.

The meaning of non-reaction, equanimity, mental refinement, and transcendence is best experienced through soul meditation and contemplation. If you try to understand these states intellectually, it may raise more questions than provide answers.

Feeling vs. Emotion

The element of feeling is not emotion, as some people think. Emotion is a complex phenomenon that results from the combination of various material and mental phenomena, including the element of feeling and other mental elements. Emotions are felt in the same way that everything we experience is felt. This does not mean that emotions are only feelings. They are phenomena of body-mind-consciousness. Whenever we experience an emotion, there are always physical components, mental components, and consciousness in it.

Lust and anger, for example, are common emotions. Lust arises because of the arising of sexuality and body sensitivity, along with greed, delusion, and sense consciousness. Anger arises because of the arising of various bodily phenomena, hatred, delusion, and mind-consciousness. No matter what emotion or experience arises, however, the element of feeling initiates it. In this sense, feeling is the chief mental component of any emotion (see figure 10.3).

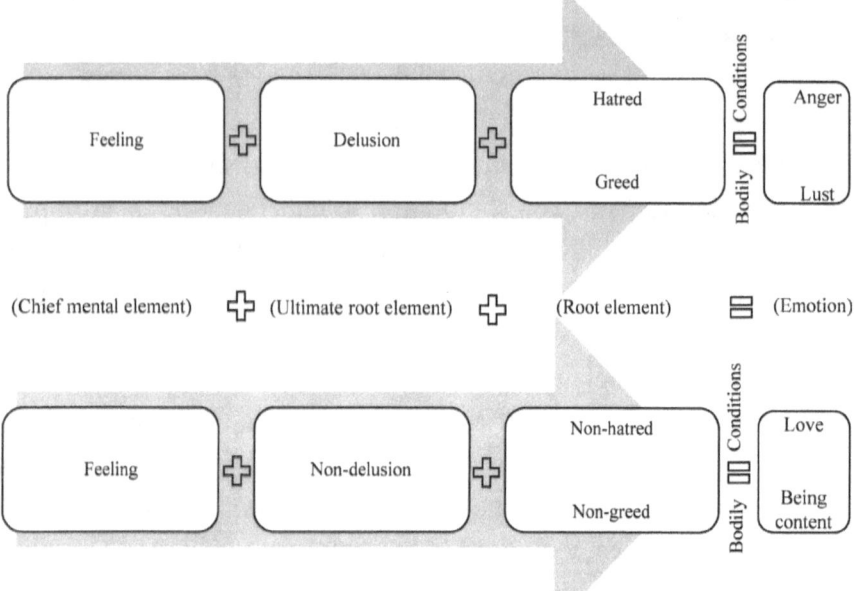

Figure 10.3. How emotions occur: Dependent upon bodily conditions, various mental elements combine and give rise to an emotion. The element of feeling is a chief mental component of every emotion.

Most of us blame external factors such as another person or situation for our emotions, not knowing that the element of feeling is the main culprit. External factors are mere triggers. When someone insults you and you become angry, what is actually happening in the background is your *reaction* to the unpleasant feeling generated by the insult and not the insult itself. This reaction is none other than aversion (hatred) towards the unpleasantness of feeling.

If we want to get rid of any unwholesome emotion, first we have to realize the makeup of various mental elements that give rise to that emotion. Second, we have to develop mindfulness of the pleasantness or unpleasantness of the feeling associated with that emotion. Third, we have to learn not to generate craving (greed) towards the pleasantness or aversion (hatred) towards the unpleasantness of feeling, knowing that all feelings are transient and will cease on their own accord. This is the most skillful way of dealing with emotions—the way of mastering them inside ourselves. Trying to control or fix the outside only leads to more suffering.

Perception *(mental element 3, Pe)*

Perception is the third consecutive element to function in cognitive processes. It is conditioned by sensations and feelings. Basically, the phenomenon of interpretation of sensations and feelings is perception. It distinguishes, recognizes, and identifies. However, perception is not same as the act of understanding or the act of cognizing.

When we see a flower, how do we know it is flower? We interpret the sensations and feelings that arise from the contact of our eyes with the flower, as "flower." We make it a flower by marking it as a "flower" the first time we see one. When a similar object is seen, we know it is a flower because of the previous mark that we made. Because of this mark, we perceive flowers as flowers again and again. If a flower is identified as a bundle of material elements that are impermanent and impersonal, then, such identification and interpretation are acts of understanding rather than perceiving.

Perception does not make a person optimistic, pessimistic, or deluded. There is no such thing as an intrinsically good perception, bad perception, positive perception, negative perception, and so on. The phenomenon of perception is neither good nor bad. What makes it good (wholesome) or bad (unwholesome) are the other mental elements that arise with it.

A person sees a piece of rope in the dark and interprets it as snake. This is a perception with delusion. A blind person touches an elephant's tail and interprets it like this: "An elephant is like a broom." This is also a perception with delusion. An ignorant person sees a body, hears sound, smells odor, tastes flavor, feels tactile sensation, has feelings, and interprets them like this: "This body is mine; I am the one who sees, hears, smells, tastes, and feels." This is also a perception with delusion. Any sense of separate self should be understood as a deluded perception.

When an ignorant person deals with an angry person, the angry person is perceived as unpleasant and irritating. Such perceptions occur because the element of hatred has arisen along with perception, making it unwholesome. A wise person does not perceive an angry person as a threat or an enemy. The person is perceived as someone diseased and sick who needs help. Such perceptions occur because the element of compassion arises with the element of perception.

Perceptions that are not wholesome, unwholesome, or deluded are indeterminate perceptions, such as the perception involved in mere seeing, mere hearing, mere tasting, mere touching, mere smelling, and so on.

Some people wonder whether our memory is responsible for our perceptions.

Memory is a mental phenomenon that facilitates the functioning of perception, which in turn builds up memory by marking objects. When the same object is repeatedly recognized, perception itself can be understood to be functioning as memory. To this extent only, memory is related to perception.

Memories can be wholesome or unwholesome. Perception, on the other hand, is neither wholesome nor unwholesome. It acquires the ethical quality of the wholesome or unwholesome mental elements that arise with it. Therefore, if we purify the mind of greed, hatred, and delusion, and culture it with non-greed, non-hatred, and non-delusion, we build up a stock of wholesome memories and our perceptions evolve.

Volition *(mental element 4, Vo)*

Volition is the fourth consecutive element to function in the cognitive processes. It is conditioned by sensations, feelings, and perceptions. Volition is the phenomenon of will power or the willingness to take a particular mental action. The organization and coordination of all mental elements in a mental activity comes from volition. In this way, volition gives a particular quality to any mental activity.

Volition itself is ethically neutral (neither wholesome, nor unwholesome), however it serves as a leader of sorts in imparting ethical quality (wholesomeness or unwholesomeness) to any mental action.

Because ethical force (aka volitional force or karmic force) results from ethical mental actions, we can say that volition functions as the most important element in the generation and accumulation of the ethical or volitional force. In other words, volition is the seed of ethics, volitional phenomena, or karma.

As we have previously discussed, volition always results in further volition; thereby it forms the volitional force. This force conditions the arising of present volitional action, and together they lead to the results or fruit of action.

My use of the word "force" is not literal. We cannot quantify volition or the volitional force that it generates because they do not get stored in some ethereal field or in the brain. They are immaterial phenomena (non-things). They should not be considered as "matter" that exists somewhere or as something that belongs to "someone."

If we want to experience good results we must cultivate wholesome volition. We can generally recognize wholesome volition by the good feelings (and good aftereffects) associated with it. When unwholesome volition arises there is always unpleasant feeling associated with it, due to fear, shame, anger, greed, and comparable elements. It is not possible to generate good feeling when there is unwholesome volition.

Volition should not be mistaken as choice making. There is a subtle difference between the two. When a certain choice is made, volition is at the root of it. But due to delusion we misunderstand this volition as being *my* volition. Whenever there is a sense that "I" am *having* volition, the volition becomes a choice and "I" becomes a choice maker. Therefore, even though arousing good volition is important, it is even more important not to arouse it as if one is making a choice. So, let good volitions arise based on the clear understanding of selflessness.

Attention *(mental element 5, At)*

Attention is a crucial element in mental phenomena. Once volition determines the direction of an action, attention takes it in the direction of the final destination. It guides mental elements towards an object like the steering wheel of a car guides the car in a specific direction.

The element of attention is like a driver and the other mental elements together constitute a vehicle.

Sometimes students ask whether attention is the same as mindfulness.

There is a difference between attention and mindfulness, as there is between attention and thinking. Attention is the most preliminary form of thinking or mindfulness. Bare mindfulness can be understood as attention. Paying attention (being attentive) is the first step towards developing either thinking or mindfulness.

Attention generates consciousness out of the flow of the subconscious. When attention is not strong enough, there is no consciousness, meaning no cognitive process or "knowingness" is occurring. For example, when someone is in a coma, the element of attention is extremely weak, and this renders the comatose person subconscious. Similarly, when we do not pay enough attention to what we are doing, we are primarily driven or sustained by subconscious forces. This always leads to suffering.

Mental Life *(mental element 6, Ml)*

All mental elements need sustenance and maintenance so that they can repeatedly occur in mental activity. For example, without sustained volition and attention, you would not be able to read this book for long. During your reading of this book, volition and attention have been sustained and maintained by a unique mental phenomenon having its own intrinsic nature. We call it the element of *mental life* because it is non-material, and also because sustenance and maintenance are functions of "life."

Mental life originates from volitional forces, which also support and foster it. In fact, mental life symbolizes the presence of volitional forces just as light symbolizes the presence of electromagnetic forces.

How the Universal Mind Works

In chapter 1, we discussed how the six essential mental elements function in a typical real life scenario and how together they form the basis for all mental activities. If there were such a thing as a "mother mind" or a "primordial mind," it would be composed of these six elements. The elements of feeling and perception would be its most basic or primitive constituents and the remaining four (as well as the other remaining 46) would be more like mind's derived or "formed" constituents. This is somewhat similar to having hydrogen and helium as the most primitive elements on the periodic table and the remaining elements as formed elements.

Let me remind you that the universal mental elements arise and pass away in extreme rapidity. There is no such thing as a timely or linear succession (one after the other) of elements in a cognitive process. Some elements only perform consequent to each other because they condition each other's occurrence. For example, sensation conditions the occurrence of feeling. Therefore, feelings always occur as a result or consequence of sensations. But this does not mean that feeling actually arises only after a sensation has arisen and passed away. Sensation may continue in consciousness after the feeling is gone.

Following this discussion, I hope it is now apparent that there is no single or fixed entity that performs essential mental functions, but instead that a variety of mental elements do. Does this make you wonder if there really is such a thing as an individual mind (a separate self) that feels, perceives, and wills? Doesn't this reassure you that your existence will continue much the same no matter whether you believe in a separate self or whether you let that belief go?

* * *

Chapter 11

The Special Mind

The seven elements (7–13) that perform extraordinary mental activities are special in that they are not present in all states of consciousness, but only in some. They perform neutral functions of the mind just as the universal mental elements do; however, their functions are exceptional (see figure 11.1).

Thinking *(mental element 7, Tk)*

Thinking is the initial application of thought. Thinking builds on attention by directing and applying attention to an object to unfold and unravel it just as peeling away an orange's thick outer skin begins to reveal its nature.

The phenomenon of thinking is neither unwholesome nor wholesome. It takes on the ethical qualities of other mental elements that arise with it. Conspiracy is unwholesome thinking, because in this case thinking is conjoined with greed and delusion. Contemplating enlightenment is wholesome thinking because in this case thinking is conjoined with mindfulness, non-greed, and non-delusion.

Thinking is considered special since it begins the processes of contemplation and meditation, and also because it removes the hindrance of sloth and torpor (mental dullness). It therefore *commences* the process of the development of higher intelligence.

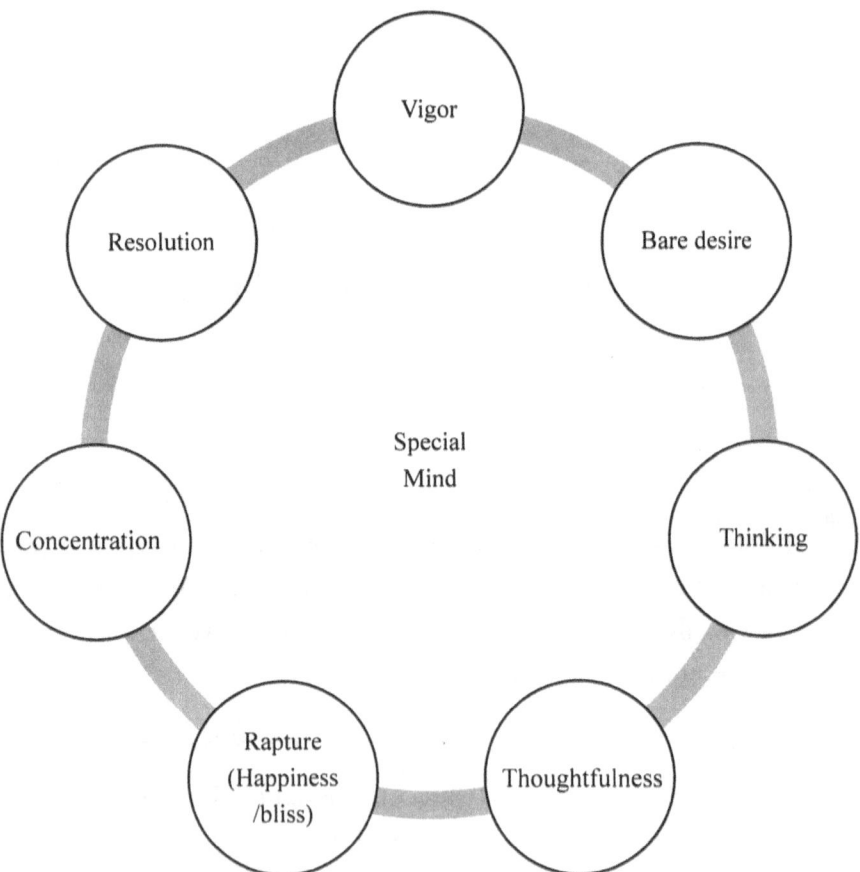

Figure 11.1. The special mind is a group of seven mental elements that perform ethically neutral but extraordinary mental functions.

Thoughtfulness *(mental element 8, Th)*

Thoughtfulness is the sustained application of thought over an object. It examines an object more thoroughly than thinking because it facilitates continuous thought. During meditation, thinking generally

CHAPTER 11 THE SPECIAL MIND

leads to thoughtfulness, just as holding a pen or sitting in front of a computer screen generally leads to actual writing. Like the element of thinking, thoughtfulness is ethically variable. It is special because it deepens the process of contemplation and reduces the hindrance of doubting, skepticism, or suspicion when it arises along with wholesome mental elements. It therefore *anchors* the process of the development of higher intelligence.

A fellow spiritual practitioner once told me that thinking and thoughtfulness were actually not desirable in spiritual practice. In a recent spiritual gathering, the group leader asked participants to get rid of the thinking mind so they could become spiritual. Once I was told that I was born to believe and not to think!

If the purpose of a spiritual practice is simply to relax, feel good, and live pleasantly, then maybe thinking and thoughtfulness are not required. If you simply chant a particular mantra, recite verses, listen to celestial music, or sing melodious prayers there is no thinking or thoughtfulness occurring, at least not wholesome thoughtfulness. But such practices still can bring about a feel-good experience. May I suggest that these experiences—although they are better than mundane worldly pleasures—are more sensual than spiritual in nature? They may soothe or quiet mind temporarily, but they do not purify it. However, such practices can become highly effective in perfecting intelligence if they are combined with wholesome thinking and thoughtfulness.

Unless we think about who we are, why we are the way we are, what is mind, why it is so, why it is not so, how to make it so, and so on, we cannot purify and perfect our minds. We cannot remove superstition and delusion without wholesome thoughtfulness, and wisdom cannot arise without the extinction of delusion. There is absolutely no possibility of attaining perfect intelligence without wisdom. Meditation and contemplation are the tools that we can use to cut through delusion and to develop wisdom. Thinking and thoughtfulness are the raw materials that these tools are made of like a saw is made of a metal blade and a wooden handle.

Rapture (Happiness/Bliss) *(mental element 9, Ra)*

Thinking and thoughtfulness lead to a delightful interest in an object. Such interest eventually leads to the experience of spiritual joy, elation, ecstasy, exultation, and so on. This mental phenomenon is called rapture (or happiness), which is a forerunner to bliss.

A thirsty man naturally thinks about water. As his thirst increases, he starts looking around for water. He starts contemplating finding water. His thinking develops into thoughtfulness. If he finds water while he's in such a state of mind he experiences rapture/happiness. When he actual drinks water and quenches his thirst, he experiences bliss. Similarly, a hungry man feels rapture/happiness when he sees food and he experiences bliss when he actually eats.

Bliss arises whenever there is *refreshment* of the embodiment. Here, the word "embodiment" means soul (body-mind-consciousness) with a predominance of the body.

Unless there is delightful or joyful interest in what we do, we cannot derive happiness from our actions. However, it is important to engage in wholesome actions to become truly happy because happiness can also arise out of unwholesome actions.

Rapture/happiness is not intrinsically wholesome. It becomes wholesome only when it arises with wholesome elements. If a person craves money and wins a jackpot at a casino, he will experience unwholesome happiness, because it arises with greed. If a person ardently contemplates on the separate self and eventually understands the reality behind this illusion, he experiences wholesome happiness because it arises with non-greed and non-delusion.

Unless this is understood clearly, real (wholesome) happiness cannot be experienced. In fact, unreal (unwholesome) happiness becomes an impediment because it binds and imprisons us.

Rapture/happiness is special because it deepens contemplation while restraining the forces of hostility and animosity. It wakes up, stirs up, and stimulates the mind to attain higher states and thus awakens mind's ultimate potential.

CHAPTER 11   THE SPECIAL MIND

I consider rapture/happiness to be the source of mental power. Without it, we cannot develop concentration, which plays a fundamental role in the development of higher intelligence.

Concentration *(mental element 10, Co)*

Concentration unifies and fixes all mental elements on an object. It focuses mind-consciousness on a single object without distraction of any kind. Concentration is the element that facilitates perfection during the process of mental development.

When thinking, thoughtfulness, and rapture (especially) are present, concentration effectively functions to unify all mental phenomena. For concentration to occur, rapture is necessary, because rapture removes the physical and mental afflictions that act as hindrances to the arising of concentration.

Concentration leads to contemplation. And, in fact, it is at the heart of any meditative activity. Even just as a trace, concentration is always present in meditation.

There are increasing levels of concentration, which result in higher and higher states of mental absorption. Ultimately, mental absorption leads to liberation from mental attachments.

Concentration is ethically neutral. It becomes wholesome only when it arises from a wholesome subject or only along with wholesome elements. If a soldier is concentrating on shooting and killing an enemy or if a power-hungry business executive uses concentration to gain the upper hand in an organization, then such concentration is unwholesome because it is rooted in greed, hatred, and delusion. Developing concentration for the purpose of purifying the mind is wholesome.

Concentration is different from mindfulness. Both elements are present in all effective and wholesome meditative activities, but they perform distinct functions. Concentration primarily leads to focus, mental absorption, and calm. Mindfulness primarily results in present-moment awareness and understanding. When mindfulness is present during concentration, it does not allow unwholesome elements to pollute the concentration because it makes you *aware* of their arising. Therefore, in soul meditation, mindfulness and concentration are always combined.

Concentration *decisively* awakens the mind to its ultimate potential. When the mind's wholesome nature is established through ardent and diligent practice, the mind is ready for perfection. Concentration is an important source of mental power.

No amount of intellectual knowledge will unravel the power, beauty, depth, and subtlety of concentration. You have to meditate diligently to witness its wonders.

Resolution *(mental element 11, Re)*

Resolution is the complete settling of mind on an object. The act of resolving a matter (an object) is similar to the act of persuading yourself about it. The expression, "This is it!" is an expression of resolution. It is like liberating the mind from indecisiveness about a specific matter. Resolution is not quite the same as having faith; however, it ultimately results in faith when it arises intensely along with wholesome elements.

Resolution arises in mental activity only when we are certain and convinced about what we are doing. For example, I am certain that the practice of soul meditation is a foolproof path to enlightenment. Therefore resolution arises during my meditation practice and I experience determination and decisiveness about the practice. This ultimately results in clearer and faster realization of the path.

Resolution is ethically neutral. If a person is certain he wants to take revenge or he decides to become a multimillionaire by hook or by crook, such resolution is unwholesome. It is rooted in greed, hatred, and delusion. If a spiritual seeker is certain about the principles of meditation and convinced about its benefits, then the conviction, fervor, and sincerity (collectively known as resolution) that arise during practice are wholesome. Resolution leads to better mindfulness, stronger concentration, higher intelligence, and so on.

Resolution is a special mental element because it provides decisive and unshakable support to a mental action, like a strong spine provides

CHAPTER 11 THE SPECIAL MIND

decisive support to the body. When it arises with wholesome elements it becomes a great mental benefactor. Without great resolution, it is not possible to attain great things.

Vigor *(mental element 12, Vi)*

Vigor is somewhat like the energy of mental states. It reinforces mental phenomena and does not allow them to collapse. When a starving person eats even a small handful of peanuts, he does not fall down due to the *vital* energy coming from eating the small amount of peanuts. Vigor is similar to such vital energy. It is unique in that it arises in an emergency situation or in any situation where we feel a sense of urgency.

Vigor is responsible for taking forceful and vital action. If one's life is threatened, one experiences a burst of energy that helps one cope. This burst of energy is vigor.

Vigor is ethically variable in its quality. It becomes wholesome or unwholesome depending upon what other elements arise with it. If vigor arises along with anger or hatred, as in the case of a soldier fighting a strong and overpowering enemy in the battlefield, it is not wholesome. If it arises along with compassion as in the case of a Red Cross volunteer working in a war zone or in case of a firefighter combating a blaze, it is wholesome. Wholesome vigor always leads to a non-failing and non-ending state of mind that is critical in pursuing and doing extraordinary stuff.

Wholesome vigor is necessary to avoid and overcome temptation. For example, it is indispensable in overcoming addiction. It is also indispensable in developing healthy habits. Without a sense of urgency to avoid cancer, a smoker would not quit smoking. Without a sense of urgency to prevent diabetes, an obese person would not stop overeating. A sense of urgency is the key to arousing vigor.

If we look at our physical and mental imperfections as a disease, or if we contemplate our impending death, we can arouse vigor out of a sense of urgency to purify the embodiment. Vigor can prevent us from going back to the rat race or status quo. It can reinforce spiritual endeavors. It can also eradicate mental sluggishness that would prevent us from taking powerful action. The restraining power of vigor coupled with mindfulness ultimately does not allow bad habits and sensual desires to endure. For example, when we have a desire to get intoxicated, to cheat, to lie, to overpower others with violence, or to satisfy lust, wholesome vigor prevents these desires from persisting and facilitates us in abandoning them. Because sensual desires are so powerful, we often need a burst of super-energy (like vigor) to oppose them.

Many spiritual (and especially religious) practitioners follow ascetic practices, such as celibacy, fasting, and extreme physical workouts, and many live isolated in forests, monasteries, and seminaries with minimal means all in order to learn to overcome their sensual desires. If they could arouse vigor at will (by arousing a sense of urgency for mental purification), then they wouldn't have to follow these practices. From this perspective, arousing vigor at will could be considered the highest ascetic practice for developing virtues, because vigor (when united with mindfulness and so on) can successfully nullify sensual desires. In my opinion, the practice of arousing wholesome vigor (its restraining power) is the most evolved ascetic practice there is, and it is best suited for a contemporary meditator.

Vigor is a great mental power. However, it must be combined with wholesome mental elements. Vigor can arise out of fear. The fight-or-flight response is unwholesome vigor because it is rooted in greed for survival, hatred for the pain of dying or injury, and delusion about the true nature of self. Wholesome vigor, on the other hand, is that which arises out of the fear of imperfection and ethical/karmic accountability (bad actions generating bad results).

Fear is not intrinsically bad. If it weakens or paralyzes us, it is bad. If it awakens us to the reality of our weaknesses and imperfections, and arouses a sense of urgency to get rid of them, it is good. A person who becomes fearful of negative effects of lust, anger, and so on, and therefore begins his spiritual journey, will experience a sense of urgency that arouses wholesome vigor. Because of this vigor, objects of lust won't attract him. He will develop strength to shy away. Because of vigor, he will be able to refrain from anger. Vigor will provide him enough power to pursue the difficult path of mental purification.

Vigor is like "mental energy" that generates power for restraining vices and for reinforcing and upholding virtues. It should be understood as the basis of all achievement. Vigor is responsible for all extraordinary human attainments.

If vigor arises with greed, it becomes overpowering, passionate, agitating, and so on. But if it arises along with the elements of mindfulness and concentration, its power is kept in balance. That's when it becomes a real mental power.

The use of any power is a matter of skill. One should use mindfulness and concentration to balance the power of vigor. Otherwise vigor can result in passion and agitation. Similarly, one should use vigor to balance the calm of mindfulness and concentration, thereby avoiding too much calm, which can result in idleness. In this way, one should skillfully combine mindfulness/ concentration and vigor into spiritual feet so one can walk *steadily* on the path of mental purification and perfection.

Bare Desire (Intention/Inclination) *(mental element 13, Bd)*

Bare desire is simply an inclination or intention, a mental pull towards an object. It can also be understood just as a "wish to do." Bare desire is not same as a desire in the conventional sense. It is not wanting, craving, or lust.

Like other special elements, bare desire is ethically neutral. It becomes unwholesome—a desire—if it combines with unwholesome elements such as greed, hatred, delusion, and so on. Bare desire with greed would be present in the case of a man or a woman pursuing a rich spouse to acquire wealth. Bare desire with hatred would be present in the case of a vendetta.

Bare desire becomes wholesome if it combines with non-greed, non-hatred, non-delusion, and so on. Bare desire with non-greed would be present in the case of a devoted social worker. Bare desire with non-hatred is present in case of a missionary who preaches a message of love. If you are inclined towards meditation, you are experiencing wholesome bare desire. Such inclination always leads to the development of higher intelligence.

In short, a bare desire is an intention. Unwholesome bare desire is a desire, as we commonly know desire. A wholesome bare desire is a strong will (see figure 11.2). Such understanding is vital, especially for those who cleverly hide sensual desires and passions behind the curtain of enthusiasm or activism.

Many people who are energetic and powerful are driven to activism and social service. However, they contribute to the common good not exclusively because of altruistic motives but also because of self-interest, personal attachment, and vanity. Some people are so blinded by enthusiasm and the quest for personal empowerment that they do not realize what is actually driving their actions. To such people, I would like to humbly suggest that they repeatedly crosscheck their intentions.

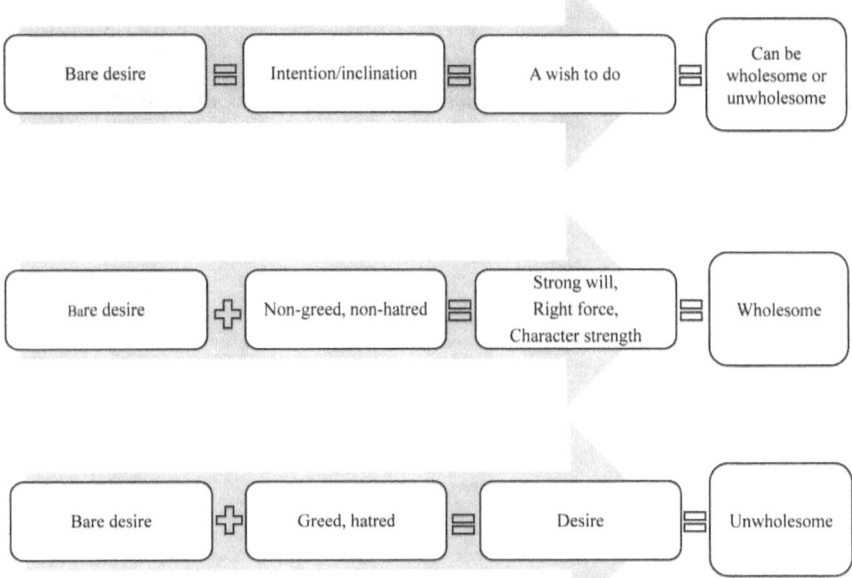

Figure 11.2. What is desire? The difference between bare desire, desire and will. The message is: Employ "will" and fire "desire."

CHAPTER 11   THE SPECIAL MIND

Some people wonder whether we can really do anything without having a desire. For example, why would I write and publish a book if I did not have an intention to sell it and profit?

If I publish a book with an intention to become famous and rich or if a goldsmith makes ornaments with an intention to make ton of money, then such intentions are desires. They are not worth pursuing because they defile the mind with greed. However, if my intention is genuinely to help large numbers of people through a book then my intention is a strong will, not desire. If a goldsmith is genuinely interested in pleasing his customers by adding art and beauty to their lives, then his intention is also a strong will. Strong will is synonymous with self-control, right-force, strength of character, motivation, spirit, and so on. People who are aware and *wise* (rather than clever) can easily determine whether their intentions are desires or the strong will to act.

Bare desire, intention, or whatever you choose to call it is not intrinsically bad for us. We simply have to combine it with wholesome elements. In some spiritual circles, desire is misunderstood. Truthfully these words and definitions don't matter much, as long as the message is clear: Employ "strong will" and fire "desire."

When a sincere meditator employs strong will towards non-greed, non-hatred, non-delusion, the meditator clearly sees the liability in greed, hatred, and delusion. When he employs strong will towards renunciation of physical pleasures, he clearly sees the liability in sensuality. Strong will is the quality that makes the element of bare desire special. Strong will, when it becomes exceptional, leads to accomplishment, as it plays an instrumental role in leading and channeling all our actions towards a target. In this sense, it paves the way for success in any endeavor.

How the Special Mind Works

Let us now see how special mental elements would function in a real life scenario.

Imagine you spot a poor, abandoned child in the streets of New York. From chapter 1, we already know about the functions of universal elements that would first cognize the child. In this cognitive process, attention keeps consciousness in contact with the child. Thinking builds on attention by directing and applying attention to further clarify the condition of the child. If thinking is present, you do not simply watch the child and leave, you watch the child closely. Thinking leads to thoughtfulness. Now you watch the child not only more intensely, but also for a longer period of time. In thinking about the child in this sustained manner, you might soon interpret the child as a poor, abandoned child needing help.

In this progression of observation, if you take joyful interest in the welfare of the child, thoughtfulness next leads to rapture. Due to rapture, concentration soon arises. Now, there is only you, the child, and the process of observation. Depending upon the degree of concentration, nothing else exists at such moments. You will now see and understand the child from more intense or subtler states of mental absorption. You will see his innocent eyes, his helplessness, his inner cries for shelter and love, and so on.

When you do, your mind soon begins to open to the desperate condition of the child. This release happens due to the arising of resolution, a mental element that is conditioned by concentration. If you confirm and decide that the child needs help, this confirmation is resolute. It is unshakable. It liberates the mind from indecisiveness about helping or not helping the child. If you develop sense of urgency, vigor arises and then you do not turn back. You are now able to support and uphold the state of compassionate mind. If wholesome bare desire (strong will) arises, you end up getting out of the car to talk to the child or to call social services or foster care facility, or to take another constructive action.

The end result in this episode was wholesome because, in your consciousness, only wholesome mental elements combined with the special ones. Imagine what would happen if hatred arose at the moment of spotting the child. Instead of thinking about helping, you would be thinking about how irresponsible the child's parents were. Instead of feeling compassionate, you would be feeling angry and sorrowful.

CHAPTER 11 THE SPECIAL MIND

We must understand that any mental power, such as the power of the special elements, is ethically neutral. To make it wholesome, we need not only to metamorphose it with wholesome elements, but also to liberate it from unwholesome ones.

※ ※ ※

Chapter 12

The Unwholesome Mind

The elements 14–27 that we are now going to discuss perform only unwholesome mental functions. At least some of them are always present in every unwholesome mental activity. These elements are inherently unprofitable.

Greed *(mental element 14, Gr)*

Greed is grasping. It functions like glue, in this case one that bonds or attaches the mind to an object. Due to its stickiness, greed primarily manifests as attachment and not letting go. It is synonymous with lust (sensual greed) and craving (trans-sensual greed). Sensual greed is predominantly physical (lust for food, sex, entertainment, and other sensual pleasures). Trans-sensual greed is predominantly mental. Craving existence or non-existence is its manifestation. In its subtlest form, trans-sensual greed is the same as the ego. It exists until the last stages of mental purification because it is extremely strong and resists being removed. A state of egolessness arises only when trans-sensual greed (and not just sensual greed) is eradicated.

THE ELEMENTS OF SOUL

Greed is at the root of all unwholesome mental activities. Because it is an unwholesome root element, greed provides maximum support to unwholesome consciousness and contributes significantly to generalized unwholesomeness. It is present in every kind of ego-related desire, lust, passion, hunger for achievement, wanting more and more, possessiveness, and so on. Greed is the ego's best friend because it supports and protects the ego. In fact, greed is the ego's biggest benefactor. In this sense, greed tops the list of unwholesome elements (see figure 12.1).

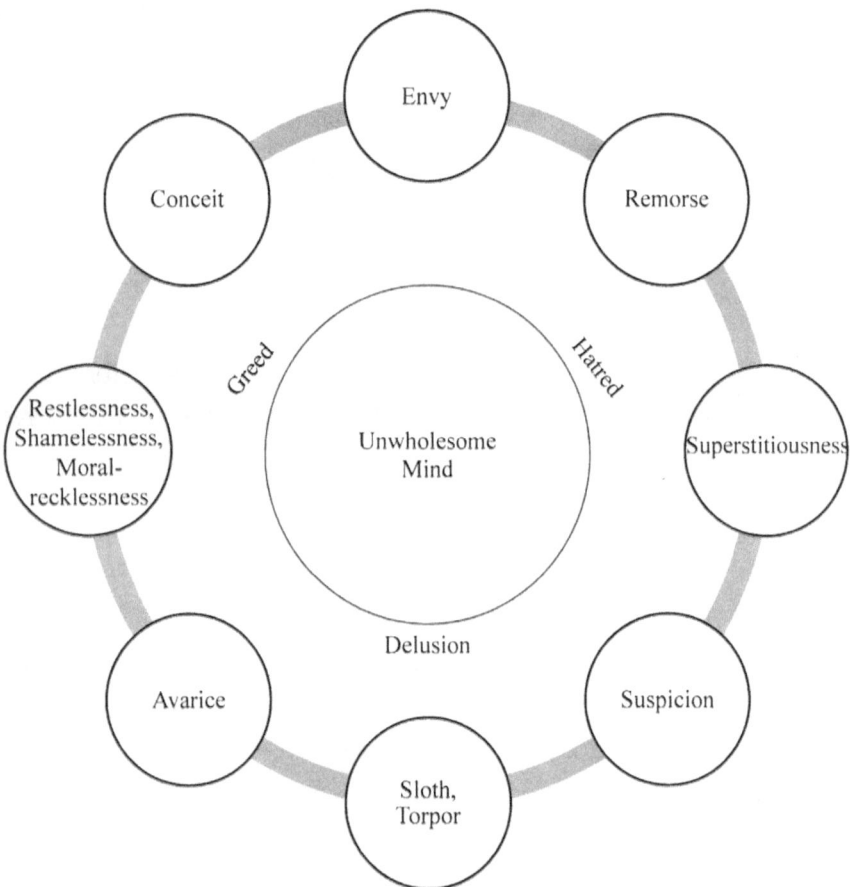

Figure 12.1. The unwholesome mind is a group of 14 mental elements. Greed and hatred are roots and delusion is the ultimate root. Five elements are always present in all unwholesome mental activities: delusion, greed (or hatred), restlessness, shamelessness, and moral recklessness.

CHAPTER 12 THE UNWHOLESOME MIND

In the business of spiritual evolution, there is nothing more *subtly* unprofitable than greed. Why? Because without being obvious as unwholesome it bonds, knots up, clings, ties up, hinders, and defiles the mind. When it arises, it is like a flood that sweeps the mind away from perfection and into an ocean of imperfections. The flood of greed is hard to cross even for a highly trained and developed mind.

Greed is like a yoke that bonds the mind to superstition and ignorance and knots up the mind with covetousness, ill will, and religiousness, because of which strong beliefs are created. It fills the mind with clinging desires because of which dogmas and all kinds of -isms are formed. It hinders the process of mental purification by generating obstacles in the form of laziness, restlessness, remorse, doubt, and delusion. It afflicts and torments the mind by dragging it to immoral, corrupt, evil, and depraved conditions. It ties the mind to cycles of suffering.

We tend to escape greed by suppressing it or fighting it. In truth, it is better if we simply befriend non-greed and thereby see the fault in greed. We must develop will for non-greed in order to deal with greed. In a way, my whole effort is really about sharing with others the way to achieve freedom from unwholesome elements, such as greed.

Meditation is the foremost tool first for becoming aware of greed and its evil functions and causes, and second for developing non-greed to counteract it. In addition, we need to stop engaging ourselves in the activities, relationships, tasks, goals, and so on, which lead to bondage. Whenever we take up a task or enter a relationship, we should try not to get attached to it. As much as possible, when we are dealing with others, we should act with loving-kindness, compassion, and equanimity to eradicate craving, apathy, and indifference.

Each time we sense ourselves getting attached, we should simply let go. We should basically *not cling* to anything, any person, or any feeling even if it is delightful. I am not saying we should not be happy and enjoy ourselves. We should. However, if we cling to anything—even happiness—we eventually suffer, because nothing lasts forever.

We should simply let things, situations, relationships, and experiences come and go. We should let pleasant experiences cheer up the mind and not let them lead us into wanting more. We should not allow them to grow into desires, goals, achievements, and so on. Instead, we should use them to develop the attitude of contentment.

Letting go is not the same as giving up, rather it is the equivalent to going beyond, transcending. It is like graduating from elementary school so you can go to middle school and high school. Unless you let go of the fifth-grade classroom, you cannot enter the sixth grade. This does not mean you abandon or give up what you learned in elementary school. That level of education stays with you forever.

When we let go of happiness and enjoyment, we actually allow the mind to experience higher and higher states, such as ecstasy, joy, and bliss.

Hatred *(mental element 15, Ha)*

If the mind does not hold on to its object, but pushes the object away, the element that is present is hatred. It is synonymous with aversion.

Hatred is like a snake because it stings and is poisonous. When it manifests as anger, it spreads like wild fire and burns up its own support due to its intensity and fierceness. It causes devastation. Hatred is like an enemy that finds an opportunity to persecute.

Like greed, hatred is a strong element. It holds up against resistance or removal. Because it is also an unwholesome root element, it provides maximum support to unwholesome consciousness and contributes significantly to unwholesomeness. It is present in all kinds of ego-driven domineering and in animosity, enmity, ill will, annoyance, irritation, disgust, contempt, displeasure, grief, and resentment.

Hatred is the ego's second best friend because it supports and protects the ego. Besides greed, hatred is the ego's biggest benefactor. In the pursuit of perfect intelligence, hatred is the first monster to be pacified and won over. Until hatred is exterminated, such a pursuit does not catch momentum.

In the business of spiritual evolution, there is nothing more *grossly* unprofitable than hatred. Greed is not always obvious as unwholesome, but hatred always is.

Yes. Greed and hatred are like parents of a child named evil. Greed is craving and hatred is aversion, and together they give birth to all imperfections. Technically speaking, if you abolish greed and hatred you become holy, a saint. Performing miracles or getting an ordination from a religious organization does not make one holy.

On the path of perfect intelligence, we don't suppress or fight hatred. We simply befriend non-hatred. We see the unsightly, unpleasing, and ill-favored effects of hatred, we see the fault in hatred, and then we begin to develop strong will towards non-hatred. As in eliminating greed, meditation is our primary tool. Avoidance of conditions and circumstances that lead to hatred is the secondary tool.

People who easily get angry should avoid conflicts in order to minimize the potential for hatred. They should avoid tasks or relationships that lead to arguments, disagreements, quarrels, clashes, and conflict-of-interest. In addition, they should avoid over-involvement of any kind. If they have to get involved in something, they should engage themselves with equanimity in mind so that aversion, indifference, or apathy does not arise. They should also learn to simply let go whenever unpleasantness, sorrow, or unhappiness is sensed.

I am not saying angry people should abandon the world. What I am saying is that they should minimize the occurrences that lead to developing *distaste* for anything. Angry people should also intensely focus on building two prime qualities of the wholesome mind: patience and forbearance.

Delusion *(mental element 16, De)*

Delusion hides reality by putting a curtain in front of it. It blinds, tricks, and eludes the mind. It is the not knowing of the true nature of things. It is synonymous with ignorance because it prevents us from seeing everything in the world as impermanent, relative, and devoid of a separate self.

Greed and hatred, the twin roots of unwholesomeness, are both, in turn, rooted in delusion. Therefore, the undercurrent of all unwholesome mental activities is delusion. As an ultimate root, delusion is fundamentally responsible for all imperfections. In other words, all our imperfections (and our subsequent human suffering) arise ultimately as a consequence of delusion.

The strongest and most obstinate element is delusion. Its hold on the mind is so incredible that it is capable of resisting its removal until the last stage of enlightenment. Because delusion is the ultimate unwholesome root element, it provides the ultimate support to unwholesome consciousness and contributes most significantly to unwholesomeness. In the business of spiritual evolution, there is nothing more *ultimately* unprofitable than delusion.

Delusion is the grandparent of ego, the evilest of all evils. The ego is primarily rooted in delusion and secondarily rooted in greed and hatred. These three elements manifest as the ego, the ultimate human imperfection (see figure 12.2). Technically speaking, if you abolish not only greed and hatred, but also delusion, you are above and beyond holiness. You are enlightened: perfect.

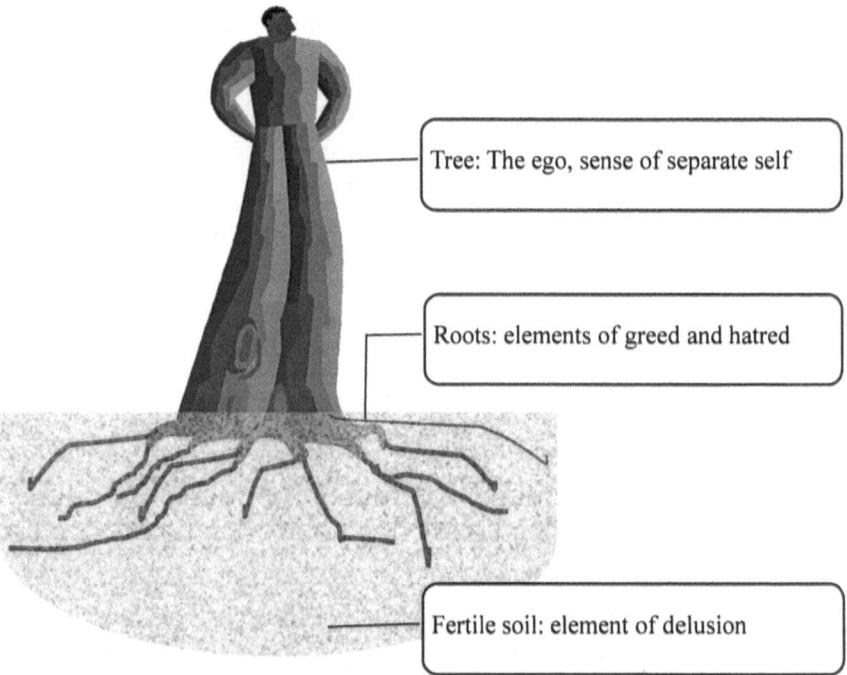

Figure 12.2. The formation of ego: an analogy. The elements of greed and hatred (the roots or parents of ego) are themselves embedded in delusion (the grandparent of ego).

CHAPTER 12 THE UNWHOLESOME MIND

Can we fight delusion (ignorance) to free ourselves from it? No. Just as we don't fight greed or hatred, we don't fight delusion. We simply dedicate ourselves to developing non-delusion (wisdom), which means we spend the rest of our life removing ignorance. We begin to see the fault in our perplexities, superficiality, guessing, superstition, and so on. We see the terror in mental darkness. As we begin to look down upon delusion we start developing a sincere inclination and a sense of urgency (vigor) to attain wisdom. Eventually, we start abiding in each moment, arousing, developing, and perfecting wisdom. In a way, this entire book, *The Elements of Soul,* revolves around the subject of how to accomplish this end.

The root cause of delusion is delusion itself. Delusion in this moment was caused by the delusion of the previous moment. Wise attention in the current moment is the most important activity for the eradication of delusion. A meditation practice that includes the element of wise attention is the foremost tool in the eradication of delusion. Not just any form of meditation is sufficient. Soul meditation, as taught in this book, therefore incorporates wise attention in addition to mindfulness, concentration, and non-reaction.

In addition to meditative practices, we need to stop ignoring, believing blindly, guessing, speculating, and superficially agreeing. We need to seclude ourselves from things that lead to greed and hatred. We need to minimize mental stiffness, sloth, torpor, laziness, and so on. Using the power of wise attention in daily life, we need to let things, situations, relationships, and experiences help us develop the sense of certainty (through understanding of reality) and abandon the sense of uncertainty.

Restlessness *(mental element 17, Rs)*

Restlessness is agitation. It lacks calmness, stillness, peacefulness, and so on. It distracts the consciousness. It is like the water that makes up waves on the surface of ocean that make the surface unsteady. It manifests as turmoil, like dust flung up by a car cruising along a country road.

Like delusion, restlessness is present in all unwholesome mental activities. An obvious mental element, it can be easily noticed as impatience, agitation, irritation, turmoil, and confusion. But its obvious nature can be used for a positive benefit, which is to arouse meditativity. If we notice any amount of restlessness, we should realize that we are in the unwholesome state of mind. Feelings of restlessness can be thus used as wakeup calls to remind us to engage in meditation.

In order to effectively deal with restlessness, the first thing to do is to abandon everything we are doing whenever we feel restless. We literally need to drop everything like a hot potato, give wise attention to our mental disturbances, and meditate for a few minutes until we feel non-distracted and tranquil. The coolness and peacefulness that arise out of tranquility and non-distraction almost always remove restlessness.

Some people think that unless they become restless, they cannot arouse energy for achieving great things. That is not true. People who are restless think they are more energetic because they give *un*wise attention to the state of mind. They mistake restlessness for energy. In fact, it is restlessness that actually overpowers them and makes them aggressive. Just as restlessness is often mistaken as energy, aggression is frequently mistaken as passion.

Whenever there is lack of tranquility and non-distraction, restlessness overpowers the mind. Therefore, energy and passion without the balancing forces of tranquility and non-distraction are unwholesome and eventually lead to suffering. Such understanding is especially important for people who naturally possess lot of active energy (otherwise known as personal power).

It is impossible to achieve truly great things if we become restless. Therefore, we need to constantly keep a tab on our efforts by checking our internal Restless-O-Meter. We should not allow our efforts to result into restlessness or craving. We should skillfully balance our efforts with tranquility and non-distraction so we can maintain a *steady* course of action. Only then can we achieve truly great things. Even a meditator who works too hard at meditation cannot. A spiritual aspirant working too hard for enlightenment can never achieve it because his mind becomes restless.

In truth, only steady balanced efforts can accomplish great things. There are no shortcuts.

Shamelessness *(mental element 18, Shl)*

Shamelessness is non-apprehension about immorality. Its main characteristic is impropriety. It arises due to lack of *respect for others*. Like delusion, a trace of shamelessness is present in all unwholesome mental activities. But it is strong and obvious in people who are corrupt or wicked.

Moral Recklessness *(mental element 19, Mr)*

Moral recklessness is lack of concern (apathy) about immorality. Its' main characteristic is lack of conscience. Moral recklessness has no morality or caution. It is immodesty. It is lack of disgust for misconduct. It arises due to lack of *self-respect*. Like delusion, a trace of moral recklessness is present in all unwholesome consciousness. It is strong and obvious in people who are corrupt or wicked.

Moral recklessness is similar to the element of shamelessness, which precedes it. The characteristic difference between them is lack of apprehension (shamelessness) versus apathy about immorality (moral recklessness). These two elements are predominantly responsible for widespread immorality throughout the world. They are present in cultures wherever there is pornography and disrespect for women, and also in cultures where there is rampant cheating, lying, dishonesty, and corruption.

Conceit *(mental element 20, Cn)*

Conceit has the nature of pride or vanity, or the proclivity "I am." It is characterized by the sense of giving importance to self as superior or inferior, but also as an equal.

In conceit, the sense of being a separate self is present as a subtle feeling of distinctiveness. A superiority complex, an inferiority complex, and an equality complex are various expressions of conceit. They are called "complexes" to signify their psychological underpinnings. The subtlest of all is the equality complex, which is hard for non-meditators to penetrate. In the advanced stages of meditative practice, you will realize that unless you also transcend the sense of being equal to all, you cannot realize the truth of *phenomenal* nature of body-mind-consciousness. Going beyond superiority and inferiority is doing 99 percent of the work. Going beyond equality is the final 1 percent of the work that needs to be accomplished, because only at this stage is the truth of impersonality realized.

It is important to understand that conceit arises only when greed is present. In other words, whenever there is vanity, pride, lack of humility, and so on, there is always greed associated. Depending upon the intensity of the associated greed, conceit can lead to arrogance and to complete loss of modesty. It can even result in madness, such as is present with narcissism or extreme self-centeredness. If unchecked, it is one of those few mental elements that remain until the final stages of mental purification. Therefore, every effort should be made to avoid the arising of this element and to eradicate it whenever it appears.

Let me clarify that conceit is not same as simply having a sense of a separate self. It is much more. Its characteristic is to give *importance* to the self. It manifests as a desire to promote or advertise the self. If there is a subtle sense of self-glorification or self-importance, it is due to conceit.

"I am better," "I am worse," "I am a leader," "I am a follower," "I am a guru," "I am a meditator" are expressions of vanity and pride (if not used only for linguistic purposes). We first have to eradicate these images of superiority and inferiority to understand the equality complex. "I am one with all," "I am Brahman" (meaning, all-pervading consciousness), "I am," are all expressions of the equality complex. If you say, "I am all-pervading consciousness" and think that the sense of a separate self has been eliminated you have not yet attained perfect intelligence.

CHAPTER 12 THE UNWHOLESOME MIND

Many monks, spiritual teachers, and religious leaders reach the level of equality but fail to eradicate the equality complex because they do not thoroughly understand that there are no *entities* to be equal but only the *phenomenon* of body-mind-consciousness. The equality complex is a failure to understand that it is the conceit that says, "I am." Even if they say that the "I" they are declaring is "all-equal, all-pervading, and so on," they do not realize that they are giving importance to the sense of "I-ness." They do not realize that they are glorifying the self. They do not realize that they are expressing the subtlest greed for existence (or non-existence) in the misconception "I am."

At the level of perfect intelligence, it is more appropriate to say, "There is soul," than to say, "I am soul." Abiding in perfect intelligence means going beyond the mystical lure of expressions "I am one with all," "I am Brahman," "I am pure consciousness" and so on.[1]

You may be thinking I am pushing the envelope too much. Maybe I am. But I do so because I must fulfill the purpose of this book, which is to provide you with the complete framework for attaining *perfection*. The equality complex is the last hurdle we have to jump over to reach the finish line.

When you are an advanced meditator, you can penetrate the equality complex by cultivating the understanding of impermanence. Conceit cannot be understood and eliminated until the body-mind-consciousness is *experienced* as a mere bundle of phenomena that are simply arising and passing away.

The real purpose of spiritual practice is to experience and express reality as it is and not to personify it, adorn it, glorify it, identify with it, or get attached to it. While we are training in meditation, wisdom, and especially perfection, it is important to keep watch of our tendency to feel special, distinct, or illuminated, to advertise ourselves, to glorify our spiritual attainments, to publicize our powers, or to develop a spiritual image. The key is to remain aware of greedy tendencies that persist even at very advanced stages of illumination, so we do not cultivate conceit.

Envy *(mental element 21, En)*

Envy has the characteristic of resenting other people's successes. The envious always become sad and unhappy, because it is the function of envy to make them so. Envy works as a fetter that binds us to suffering because it is rooted in aversion towards others' successes. It can create major damage in relationships between family members and friends. If allowed to grow, it can lead to intense jealousy and hatred, and ego-driven competitiveness. Envy can be subdued by developing mental elements of loving-kindness and gladness.

Remorse *(mental element 22, Rm)*

Remorse is the regret that arises after doing wrong or neglecting to do right. It is the repentance related to that. It is the state of worrying about past deeds and inactions. It also manifests as worry or sorrow when we have performed regrettable actions. Despite common belief, remorse is a strictly unwholesome mental phenomenon.

It is not important or necessary to repent if we do something wrong. It is not wholesome to be remorseful or regretful, because such mental states always generate sorrow and worry. States of remorse, regret, repentance, or guilt aren't wholesome because they always distress consciousness and tend to make an already bad situation worse. Moreover, remorse actually enslaves the mind in debate about wrongdoing and right doing. Any meditator can understand this by becoming mindful of unpleasant mental feelings that arise due to remorse.

Instead of remorse, it is better to use meditativity and abstinence to refrain from repeating a bad past action. Instead of becoming remorseful about a mistake you've committed, it is better to evaluate the situation to understand what caused it and what effects came out of it. Instead of feeling guilty, it is better to embrace the understanding of cause and effect so you may learn from the understanding and train yourself to abstain from repeating the mistake.

If we get angry with someone or hurt someone's feelings, it is not wise to feel guilty, because it makes us even angrier (about ourselves). It neither makes us feel good, nor does it alleviate the suffering of

CHAPTER 12 THE UNWHOLESOME MIND

the other person. This does not mean we should not even say we're sorry. What I mean is that instead of feeling guilty, we should not only observe our feelings but also understand other's feelings during and after the incidence. We should aim to realize the unpleasant nature of feelings and understand that they were caused by bad actions. We should then avoid similar bad actions in the present and future. If we develop guilt, it can overpower the mind and may result in us physically harming ourselves. It can also render us helpless at the time when others, those who have been hurt by us, need us most.

A mild version of remorse is worrying. It means worrying about doing something wrong, not doing something, or not finishing. Worrying, in general, is unwholesome, because the inherent nature of worry is to generate more worries.

You may be questioning, "Doesn't worrying help us to get off our butts and do something?" No. Worrying never generates wholesome energy or a useful sense of urgency. Worry is a survival mechanism that causes us to take action in ways that are never profitable because they do not arise out of a happy, tranquil state of mind.

Worrying in any degree must be avoided and eradicated by becoming aware of it, not reacting, and by wisely attending to it. Whenever we feel worried, we must abandon everything we are doing, meditate for a few moments, and become tranquil. Once coolness and peacefulness arise out of tranquility, we should then start dealing with the situation as it is.

Under all circumstances, we should not allow remorse, guilt, and worry to arise in the mind. At a subtle level, they strengthen our sense of separate self and reinforce the ego. We should understand errors, mistakes, blunders, screw-ups, and so on, simply as unwholesome physical-mental phenomena that need to be exterminated.

Superstitiousness *(mental element 23, Su)*

Superstition interprets unjustifiably and wrongly. It is that which looks at something unwisely. It is wrong viewing and wrongly interpreting the nature of things. For example, we often interpret human life as perfect, pleasurable, pious, and sinless, despite obvious human suffering and imperfection. We do so because we are not willing to face the reality, the bitter truth of human imperfection. Many people further solidify their superstitiousness by wrongly interpreting this view of human imperfections as negativity or pessimism. Such people simply do not have a strong inclination for wisdom or for attaining perfection. By evading the reality we run the risk of arousing further superstitiousness.

Some people assume that there are gods and some imagine there are no gods. Some imagine that there is only one. Some speculate that God and self are one, eternal, infinite, permanent being. Some philosophies hold that self and the world are different, eternal and continuous, contracting and expanding ceaselessly. Some think that the world is finite. Others think it is infinite. Some rationalize that body and soul are one. Some say body and soul are different. Some reason that mind or consciousness is the real self or soul.

Some theorize that the self and world came into existence by chance. Some swear by the presumption that the self is nothing but a bundle of matter (created by father and mother), which vanishes after death. Some theorize that the soul is separate from the body and does not die when the body dies. Some interpret that the self is boundless space, infinite consciousness, and so on.

In all these ways, due to superstitiousness, some people speculate about the past, the future, and the nature of things. Such people presume, assume, suppose, believe, imagine, and wrongly interpret. They do so primarily due to lack of inclination for understanding ultimate reality. They do so due to lack of willingness to experientially realize the truth, due to lack of willingness to face reality, which in most cases includes harsh and unpleasant insights because it illuminates our imperfections. This is how the mental element of superstitiousness functions.

Superstitiousness generally manifests as mental rigidity, attachment to religious rites and rituals, conceit, strong beliefs, blind faith, fanaticism, extremism, and martyrdom. We must counteract it by

CHAPTER 12 THE UNWHOLESOME MIND

becoming open-minded, non-resistant, and flexible. We must weaken it by developing the habit of meditation and contemplation, which should involve mindfulness, non-reaction, wise attention, rightful interpretation, and prudent justification. Most importantly, in order to eradicate superstitiousness it is necessary to generate the inclination to go beyond mere thought and *experientially* understand reality. It is also necessary to continuously relinquish spiritual experiences, not to get attached to them, or carried away by them, to continue to penetrate further and further and avoid interpreting limited spiritual experiences as ultimate realities.

Superstitiousness is a monster of unwholesomeness because our inherent tendency to cling to the sense of separate self is directly underlain by it. It is rooted in our greed to exist as a separate entity. Therefore it strengthens delusion and weakens the mental capacity for wisdom. It is by far the most blameworthy element in the generation of mental rust, rigidity, and perversion. It is by far the most reprehensible mental phenomenon, because of which there is endless conceptual proliferation and the consequent generation of rites and rituals, mythology, orthodoxies, philosophies, theories, -isms, and so on. Hence, it should be considered as a giant poisonous weed that has to be rooted out.

Without the eradication of superstitiousness, the process of mental purification cannot really begin. A large portion of this book is dedicated to providing tools for eradicating superstitiousness.

When superstitiousness is absent, it is easy to understand that nothing exists above and beyond phenomenality and conditionality. It is also easy to look at all experiences (including spiritual illuminations, awakenings, birth, death, and so on) as mere phenomena of body-mind-consciousness that arise and cease. It is so because through meditative experience you realize that there is no separate self, no power, no fixed entity that can control, suppress, or change the impermanent nature of all phenomena.

If you no longer vacillate about this impermanent and impersonal nature of reality, you will no longer evade the truth. You won't be shaken any by imperfection, sin, uncertainty, or unknowingness, and thus you will have abandoned superstitiousness.

Suspicion *(mental element 24, Ss)*

The element of suspicion does not diagnose and lacks the will to find an answer. It is uncertain about everything. It does not trust, believe, or accept anything. It lacks the will to think things through, so it does not give wise attention to matters of doubt but simply doubts "negatively." It has the nature of skepticism, agnosticism, non-belief, and non-faith.

If superstitiousness is wrong viewing, we could say that suspicion is "non-viewing." Superstitiousness results in the formation of a wrong theory about the nature of things. Suspicion, on the other hand, results in "no theory" altogether. It results in the lack of decisiveness and lack of definiteness. It makes us waver and vacillate, and causes us to change camps. Because suspicion cannot think through things, it makes the mind uncertain about what is good, bad, wholesome, unwholesome, virtuous, vice-ridden, and so on. It makes the mind wish not for an answer but to remain uncertain and doubtful about everything.

Doubt, as in intellectual curiosity, is necessary for intellectual development. Unless we doubt, how can we evaluate anything critically? But suspicion is not same as mere doubt. Suspicion is *negative* doubt rather mere doubt. In this sense, suspicion is always unwholesome. It literally paralyzes our thinking ability and therefore hinders intellectual development.

Since suspicion is negatively skeptical about everything, it is entirely different from doubting, which involves reasoning and critical analysis. Since suspicion is characterized by the lack of will to think things through, it doesn't encourage reasoning or critical thinking like doubting can. We need to clearly understand the subtle differences between suspicion and doubt so that we can refrain from being suspicious and give the benefit of doubt to any person, situation, or issue that we are dealing with.

People who are superstitious tend to become suspicious. Superstitiousness makes us believe in something without giving it wise attention. So, whenever we are dealing with something that we do not believe in, we become suspicious. In other words, believing in something automatically makes us suspicious of things that we do not believe in.

If you have already developed strong spiritual or religious beliefs, then you may become suspicious about what I am saying in this book. You may not be able to develop confidence in the contents of this book no matter how persuasively I state my case. If you are suspicious, you may never develop enough trust in what I have discussed, no matter how compelling or realistic it may be. If, on the other hand, you give wise attention to this material and remain meditative in your consideration process, then you would not become suspicious. You might remain doubtful and critical, but not suspicious. You might not agree with something, but you would not automatically disagree either. Instead, you would investigate to try to understand and your suspicious nature would transform into investigative nature.

It is better for us to give the benefit of doubt to new ideas than to become suspicious. It is better to remain attentive, investigative, and meditative than to doubt negatively. Otherwise, superstitiousness and suspicion and can pull us down and fetter us to the lowest form of human existence, a life dominated by ignorance and blinded by delusion. As long as superstitiousness and suspicion are present, we cannot develop the special elements of thinking and thoughtfulness, which are raw material for meditative and contemplative practices.

Sloth and Torpor *(mental elements 25 and 26, Sl-To)*

Sloth is mental stiffness and a lack of driving power. It drains your energy and manifests as sluggishness, dullness, and sinking of the mind. Sloth is the sickness of consciousness. When present along with torpor, it literally paralyzes consciousness.

Torpor is lack of cheer, lack of good humor. It is clumsy, unmanageable, and unwieldy. It chokes up the mind and manifests as sleepiness, nodding, laziness, lethargy, and so on. Torpor is the sickness of mind-body.

Sloth and torpor always arise together and basically oppose urgency, vigor, energy, driving power, liveliness, and wakefulness.

The best way to counteract the twin elements of sloth and torpor is to start applying the mind to a wholesome subject of interest, instead of reacting to boredom. A meditator should counteract sloth and torpor by becoming aware of boredom, giving wise attention to it, and arousing energy for self-improvement. In extreme situations, in order to counteract sloth and torpor, it becomes necessary for a meditator to arouse the same inner driving power he would in a do-or-die situation.

If you drift off during meditation, you are reacting because you are not able to deal with boredom, which eventually generates sloth and torpor. This is why many people feel sleepy when they try to meditate. Boredom is actually a subtle form of aversion, and many people have an aversion to silence. That is why they find meditation boring. But boredom should always be handled carefully so as not to allow sloth and torpor to take over and sicken the body-mind-consciousness. For a meditator, the first step is to become aware of any sense of boredom or aversion to silence. The next step is to observe boredom with equanimity as a mere feeling. While maintaining awareness of boredom in this way, the meditator should arouse a sense of urgency for mental development, purification, spiritual growth, and so on, as if it is the most important thing to do.

Literally the sense of urgency you need to arouse is similar to the sense of urgency you would need in a medical emergency where you abandon everything and rush to the hospital. It is like going to a hospital for fixing a dislocated shoulder. If you had a dislocated shoulder, the pain would be so great that going to a hospital would be the most important thing to do.

Arousing a sense of urgency may not be possible all the time, especially for beginners. Even then, in order to counteract sloth and torpor, you should never hit the couch, go to sleep, or take up an activity as a reaction to boredom. You should never take up a task or turn on the TV or radio because you cannot handle boredom or silence. If you cannot arouse a sense of urgency, then the best way to handle

CHAPTER 12 THE UNWHOLESOME MIND

boredom is to end the boring activity with the awareness that the activity is being ended. Then, with the awareness that the boredom has been tackled, you should take up an activity such as contemplating an interesting, wholesome subject, walking in the fresh air in bright sunlight, performing a favorite physical workout, playing outdoors, or doing preferred chores, and so on. That counteracts boredom and stimulates energy. Once boredom is gone, you can then return to the meditation. You should do your best to maintain awareness throughout the transitions from boredom to activity and back again to meditation in order to provide continuity to your meditativity. In this way, you won't allow boredom to generate sloth and torpor.

In spiritual practice, the struggle to counteract sloth and torpor often lasts for a long, long time. It is a formidable task. However, once you have gone through the first few thresholds by means of consistent and steady effort, it becomes easier to penetrate and transcend sloth and torpor.

Some people, especially those who are always busy in worldly activities, believe that it is better to be active than to be sitting quietly and meditating. Worldly-minded people give all kinds of excuses for not being able to meditate. They do not realize that it is mainly an aversion to silence, along with an undercurrent of delusion, which makes them run away from meditation. When they try to deal with silence, sloth and torpor arises in them. They simply react to it by craving activity or thirsting for entertainment. It takes a certain degree of maturity and non-delusion to be able to deal with aversion to silence. Like these worldly-minded people, do not allow the intellect to justify your inability to handle silence in any manner. Realize the sloth and torpor in you (if they exist) and get rid of them by developing vigor for meditation and contemplation.

Avarice *(mental element 27, Av)*

Avarice is meanness. It is being covetous about existing status or fortunes that can be obtained. It makes it hard to share a dwelling, family, gains, knowledge, and fame with others. It has no stomach for sharing. It generates stinginess, greed, fear, and shrinking of consciousness. Avarice literally disfigures the mind. There is always an unpleasant feeling associated with it.

Avarice hides our success and, in a way, basically turns success into failure.

In order to really experience success, we have to rejoice in giving and sharing our fortunes with others. Why? Giving and sharing are necessary conditions for generating non-shrinking (expanding) states of consciousness. Such states can only make us feel genuinely successful.

We must counteract avarice by developing generosity and by taking delight in relinquishing. That's how we can fully and thoroughly appreciate success.

How Unwholesome Mind Works

Let us now see how the 14 unwholesome mental elements would arise and function in the wallet scenario (see page 22). Notice how some of them arise in groups and some don't, with the goal of understanding what that means.

When you spot a lost wallet and if greed arises along with bare desire, it *makes you cling* mentally to the wallet. It does not allow you to let go. It attaches the mind to the wallet and transforms inclination into a desire for acquisition. Because greed is a strong element, it does not allow you to think otherwise about the wallet once it engages your mind. In this way, greed rules mental phenomena and results in you picking up the wallet.

In an advanced stage of understanding, a meditator knows that greed does not and cannot arise by itself. First there is delusion, the ultimate root of unwholesome mental activity. Because of delusion, the source of easy money (the wallet you spot) *blinds* you. You no longer realize that it belongs to someone else. Delusion *hides* this reality. Restlessness then kicks in and makes the mind *unsteady*. You become impatient and lose calmness, get stirred up because you now want that money.

CHAPTER 12   THE UNWHOLESOME MIND

Shamelessness (lack of respect for others) and moral recklessness (lack of self-respect) arise and make the mind apathetic towards the owner who might be suffering due to his loss of the wallet. When this occurs, you neither think about your own morality nor about another's rights or suffering. You end up picking up the wallet. In this way, your unwholesome action of taking away others property is governed by greed but underlain or supported by delusion, restlessness, shamelessness, and moral recklessness: the four universal unwholesome elements that always arise together as a group and combine with other elements to generate unwholesome states.

Here's another example. A corrupt government official steals public funds knowing full well that the money has been earmarked for the purpose of improving road conditions. In this case, greed for money is not the only condition that results in stealing. In addition to greed, the corrupt official has to be deluded by the lure of easy money; he has to be shameless (lacking self-respect), morally reckless (lacking respect for the civic nature of funds), and restless (due to lack of satisfaction or financial instability). If all these conditions were not present, he would not act. What I am trying to say is that, greed does not function by itself. It is always underlain and supported.

Many people take pride in being greedy. They believe that it is not possible to profit or achieve great things without greed or without being attached. They do not know that it is impossible to be greedy without also being deluded, shameless, morally reckless, and restless to some degree. If greedy people were to understand their minds in this way, they would no longer proclaim greed as valuable.

Some people think it is necessary to become angry to achieve certain goals or to get things done. They believe it is not possible to discipline or lead without anger. They do not realize it is impossible to be hateful or angry outside the presence of the four universal unwholesome mental elements. If angry or hateful people were to understand their minds in this way, they would no longer proclaim anger or hatred as useful.

Pride is another one of those wrongly valued elements. Some say, "Take pride in your actions." Some think that without vanity or pride or self-interest, it is not possible to reach the top of the ladder. Some people go to the extent of saying that vanity is benevolence towards oneself! Not knowing that it is a manifestation of conceit, not knowing that it is always underlain by some degree of delusion, shamelessness, moral recklessness, and restlessness, they assume such things and suffer.

The 14 unwholesome elements are *ultimately* responsible for all mental diseases and psychological disorders. Therefore, the process of mental purification relies heavily on their eradication. Mental purification is somewhat like refining gold, a process in which all impurities present in the gold-ore are removed. The only difference is that we do not directly remove unwholesome elements (such as greed), rather we culture mind with wholesome ones (such as non-greed) so that the unwholesome ones are overpowered and eventually fade away from every state and level of consciousness.

* * *

Chapter 13

The Wholesome Mind

The elements (28–46) that we are now going to discuss perform only wholesome mental functions. They are inherently profitable. An interesting aspect of these elements is that they always arise together as a group, although in varying degrees of intensity. So don't pick and choose among them. Work on developing all of them thoroughly.

Non-greed *(mental element 28, NGr)*

Non-greed is like a drop of water on a lotus leaf that does not stick to the leaf. Its main characteristic is non-clinging. It is manifested as real happiness and real wealth.

Non-greed should not be understood merely as the absence of greed. It also should be understood as the opposite of greed and as the means by which we can get rid of greed. It is an active parameter. For example, mere absence of greed does not arouse generosity (the opposite of greed). However, it is due to non-greed that we become generous.

Similarly, mere absence of greed does not arouse non-attachment to sensual pleasures (also the opposite of greed). But it is due to non-greed that we can shake off attachment to sensual pleasures and renounce objects of desire.

Likewise, non-greed is the reason behind the mental ability of reducing self-interest and serving selflessly. In this way, non-greed is the root cause for the arising of wholesome consciousness in which it is present. It has its own intrinsic nature (see figure 13.1).

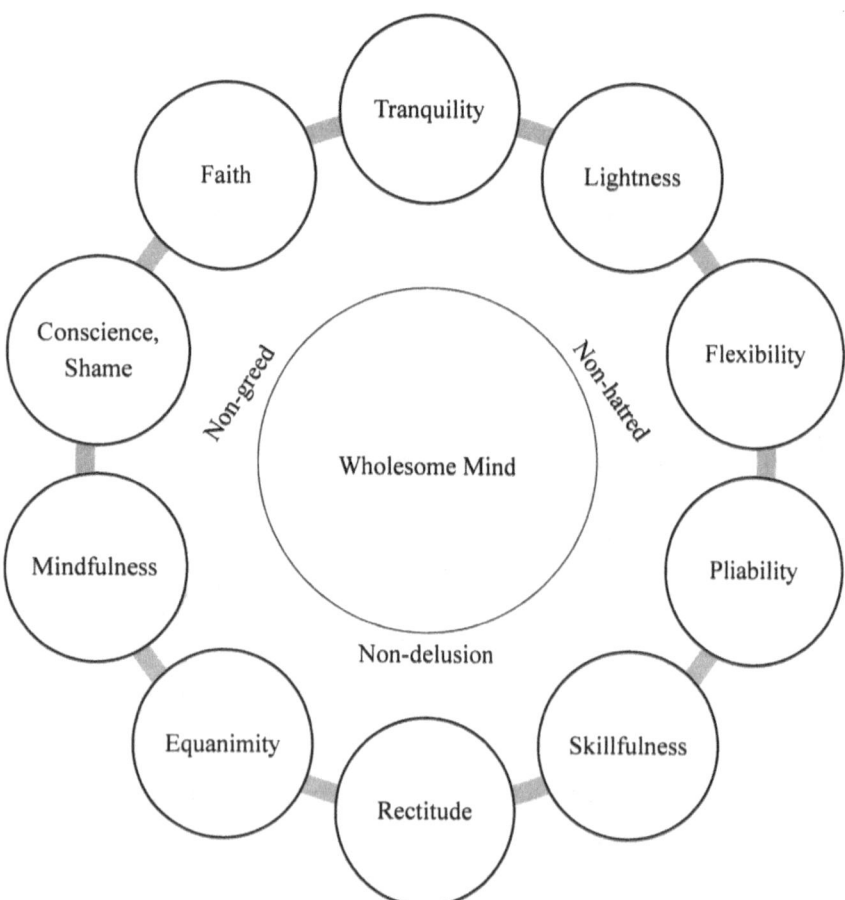

Figure 13.1. The wholesome mind is a group of 19 mental elements. Non-greed and non-hatred are roots and non-delusion is the ultimate root. All 19 elements always arise together as a group and are present to some degree in any wholesome mental activity.

CHAPTER 13 THE WHOLESOME MIND

How can we develop non-greed? The easiest way is to develop disinterest towards worldly and mundane things. This does not mean we should develop aversion for them. If we are greedy about food, for example, we can arouse non-greed by recollecting the impure, organic, earthly, and decaying nature of food. If we are lustful, we can arouse non-greed by recollecting the repulsive qualities of the human body (its excretions, hairiness, disease, and so on).

Another way to develop non-greed is not to take delight in pursuing materialistic goals and not to engage in sensuous activities or in sensuous and egoistic relationships. If you find it hard to develop disinterest in sensual objects due to your temperament, non-greed can be developed through an ascetic practice (deliberate abstinence). Aim to arouse strong will (wholesome desire), resolution, and vigor for this course of action. In advanced stages of practice, you will realize that non-greed is always present in an ascetic state of mind. You will also realize that along with elements of non-hatred and non-delusion, non-greed imparts the distinction of asceticism to any spiritual practice.

A meditator practicing true asceticism soon realizes that he cannot succeed in refraining from sexual activity unless he develops non-greed for sensual pleasure, non-hatred for arisen sensual desire, and non-delusion about what is actually happening. However, if he forces himself to avoid sexual activity by torturing or mortifying his body, he realizes that he cannot succeed in attaining abstinence from sexual activity. The practice of non-greed does not require you to practice sexual abstinence. I am just using this as an example of one way to work on the development of non-greed when you are having difficulty.

Non-greed manifests as happiness *as well as* wealth. This statement may seem contradictory to those who think we can become wealthy only by being greedy. Materialistically speaking, this may be true, but psychologically speaking, a greedy-wealthy man is not truly wealthy. His mind-consciousness is infested with poverty. A greedy-wealthy man hangs onto his money. He clings to it. For him, money simply becomes a number in an account book, which gives him a false sense of security and prosperity. No matter how big the number grows, real security and real prosperity never arise for him because the number itself is a cause of insecurity and fear of loss. Moreover, due to clinging to money, he becomes self-centered, corrupt, and thus poor.

No matter what, if greed is present in matters of wealth, sooner or later poverty consciousness arises and manifests as lack of self-esteem, worry, fear, corruption, cheating, lying, distrust, dishonesty, and so on. This is precisely why many greedy people have amassed considerable wealth and yet are still corrupt. When greed is present, there can never be enough. Many such people are extremely egotistical and live in constant fear of loss.

It is best to become wealthy by being non-greedy. In fact, this is the only way truly to become wealthy. A non-greedy wealthy man is not attached to money, therefore he develops the courage to take risks, invest, create, and expand his wealth. His non-attachment to money generates freedom for the flow of money, due to which it grows and benefits one and all. A non-greedy wealthy man becomes truly wealthy because his consciousness is imbued with courage, creativity, generosity, carefreeness, selflessness, and so on. Such a man becomes truly happy and wealthy because he reaps the fruits of non-greed.

Non-hatred *(mental element 29, NHa)*

Non-hatred is like a fragrance (gentleness, loving-kindness) that removes a disgusting odor (hatred, irritation, anger, and so on). It is like a fresh breeze that cools hot air.

Non-hatred should not be understood as the mere absence of hatred, but also as the opposite of hatred and as the means by which we can get rid of hatred. Mere absence of hatred does not make us loving, kind, gentle, and agreeable. It is non-hatred that makes us so. Similarly, a mere absence of hatred does not eliminate irritation, frustration, anger, and so on. Non-hatred is actually the means to shake off these defilements.

Non-hatred cools the temper. That is its characteristic. The element of non-hatred is the reason that the wholesome consciousness in which

CHAPTER 13 THE WHOLESOME MIND

it is present arises. In this sense, it is a root wholesome element that has its own intrinsic nature.

How can we develop non-hatred? The easiest way is to develop loving-kindness and compassion towards others. If you hate someone who has been unfair to you, for example, you can arouse non-hatred by considering the other person as worthy of loving-kindness. You can also arouse compassion for that individual by contemplating the laws of karma and realizing that the unfair person is bound to suffer from bad karma results.

If you cannot easily develop loving-kindness or compassion due to your temperament, then non-hatred, as in the case of non-greed, can be aroused through deliberate abstinence. Non-hatred is always present in an ascetic state of mind. So, aim to develop strong will and resolution along with non-hatred so you can undertake the ascetic practice. But do not mistake self-sacrifice for asceticism.

The interesting thing about the element of non-hatred is that it plays a significant role in generating pleasant looks. Of course this does not mean that every good-looking person is non-hateful. It means that if we are not hateful we develop an appearance that people find pleasant due to our agreeableness and coolness of consciousness. Angry, hateful people generally don't look good, at least when they are under the spell of anger. It is the very nature of hatred to make things ugly, unattractive, and ill flavored. Even the most adorable children look ugly when they get upset. People who consistently avoid conflict and practice loving-kindness and compassion generally develop a pleasing appearance. We feel at ease in the presence of such people. Their company is enjoyable. These are the people who are actually reaping the fruits of non-hatred.

Mindfulness *(mental element 30, Mi)*

Mindfulness is so intricately associated with meditation that it is difficult to understand it clearly without actually meditating.

Simply stated, mindfulness means being aware or present, or having presence of mind as in awareness. Mindfulness is having awareness of the phenomenon of body, mind, or consciousness occurring at the present moment. It is the opposite of unawareness, forgetfulness, confusion, instability, wandering or drifting away in thoughts, or being carried away by thought. It should not be confused with worldly-minded attentiveness or the ability to focus.

There are various levels of mindfulness, ranging from bare attention to full awareness. Bare attention means simply paying attention to something. Awareness means established mindfulness, which is not just being attentive, perceptive, reflective, or contemplative. It is a combination of all those qualities and many more. Altogether these qualities of mindfulness result in the arising of wisdom about an experience. Established mindfulness can be defined as *minding* an experience in its totality.

In order to arouse, develop, and establish in mindfulness, it is necessary to practice the contemplation of all phenomena related to body-mind-consciousness. It is necessary to observe and contemplate upon everything that we experience: our breath, posture, body parts, feelings, moods, emotions, thoughts, states of consciousness, mental objects, laws of nature, realities of existence, and so on. Meditators especially need to consider these attributes of established mindfulness whenever it is being mulled over.

When a meditator says he is mindful of his breath, he should mean that he is paying attention to his breath, observing it as it moves, reflecting upon its movement, contemplating its changing and impersonal nature, and then becoming aware of it as a bodily phenomenon that is impermanent and impersonal.

Similarly, when a meditator says he is mindful about a feeling, he should mean that he is paying attention to the feeling, observing it as it changes, reflecting upon or perceiving its quality (as painful or pleasant, joy or sorrow), contemplating its changing and impersonal nature, and then becoming aware of it as a mental phenomenon that is impermanent and impersonal.

Likewise, when a meditator says he is mindful about greed, he should mean that he is paying attention to his state of consciousness,

CHAPTER 13 THE WHOLESOME MIND

observing it as it comes and goes, reflecting upon its unwholesome quality (greediness), contemplating its changing and impersonal nature, and then becoming aware of it as a phenomenon of unwholesome consciousness that is impermanent and impersonal.

When a meditator says he is mindful about craving, he should mean that he is paying attention to the presence of craving in consciousness. He should mean that he is observing, reflecting, and contemplating upon its impermanent and impersonal nature, and also upon how it was aroused, how it can be overcome, and how it may not arise in the future. Thereby he becomes aware of the totality of the nature of craving as an unwholesome, impermanent, and impersonal mental formation.

In this way, a meditator should become mindful of everything that is experienced.

Mindfulness, in a way, arises out of the memory of real nature of our existence. It is like remembering who we really are and becoming aware of ourselves. Having understood that, one should not confuse mindfulness with memory. Mindfulness is the mental phenomenon that facilitates the functioning of memory. It awakens memory. Without mindfulness, memory cannot function properly. To this extent, mindfulness and memory are related.

A memory can be wholesome or unwholesome. Mindfulness, on the other hand, is inherently wholesome by its own nature. Its ethical quality is intrinsically good under any circumstances. It always arises with a bunch of other wholesome mental elements. In fact, mindfulness is present in every single wholesome consciousness that arises in our embodiment. It is not limited to spiritual or meditative/absorptive consciousness.

Mindfulness is the foundation of a wholesome mind. Therefore, the practice of mindfulness is meant for developing a wholesome mind and not just awakening the memory. It is meant for making us aware of our true nature.

Now, let us discuss how mindfulness makes us aware of ourselves. First of all, we must understand that mindfulness has to be developed to its full capacity, meaning it has to grow from bare attention to awareness. Table 13.1 (below), "The Stages of Development of Mindfulness Using the Breath as a Meditation Subject," illustrates how this can happen in the case of becoming mindful of the breath during a single meditation experience. While it is possible for any meditator to get to stage 5, most novices do not experience the full development of mindfulness without ardent and consistent practice.

Table 13.1

The Stages of Development of Mindfulness Using Breath as a Meditation Subject

Stage of Development	Meditative Activity
Stage 1: Elementary mindfulness (bare attention)	• Paying attention to breathing
Stage 2: Mindfulness	• Paying attention to the breath as it moves in and out of the nostrils • Feeling the touch of the breath in the nostrils • Bringing the attention back to the breath if mind wanders • Remembering the whole phenomenon as "breath"
Stage 3: Mindfulness with understanding	• Feeling the coolness of the inward breath and the warmth of the outward breath • Realizing that the breath is arising and passing away • Reflecting and contemplating on the changing nature of the breath and understanding its impermanence

Stage 4: Mindfulness as awareness	• Reflecting on the origin of the breath • Understanding that the breath is a bodily phenomenon • Reflecting on the one who is breathing (the breath-taker) and understanding that it is really the body that is breathing, not the self • Understanding that awareness of breathing was mistaken as a breath-taker • Understanding breathing as impersonal
Stage 5: Mindfulness as pure awareness and wisdom (egolessness, mental perfection)	• Experientially understanding the breath as an impermanent and impersonal bodily phenomenon • Just being aware of this to the extent necessary with purified equanimity • Simply abiding in this understanding (pure awareness) without clinging to anything in the world—without a sense of being mindful, being aware, or being a knower

At stage 3 and beyond, there is seeing, wakefulness, vision, and understanding. Here, mindfulness cannot occur without wise attention. The mindfulness faculty "sees" and the wise attention faculty "knows."

Because of mindfulness, a meditator sees the arising and passing away of the breath, and because of wise attention a meditator understands that the arising and passing away of the breath is the nature of impermanence. Seeing and knowing are like spiritual feet, without which walking on the path to self-knowledge is not possible.

Mindfulness vs Concentration

Mindfulness and concentration are different phenomena, even though they are closely related and we use them to denote an activity as a meditation. The following table illustrates a few subtle differences that should help avoid confusion.

Table 13.2

Mindfulness vs. Concentration

Mindfulness	Concentration
Removes forgetfulness, negligence	Removes restlessness, agitation
Reinforces present-moment awareness	Reinforces absorption, focus, calm
Expands consciousness through awareness	Penetrates subtle realities through focus
Serves as a foundation for concentration. Without mindfulness, higher levels of concentration are not possible	Does not serve as a foundation for mindfulness. But without some degree of concentration and purity of mind, mindfulness cannot easily develop into full awareness
Leads primarily to insight, wisdom, and awakening	Leads primarily to purification of mind, supernormal powers, and unity consciousness

If mindfulness were a telescope, concentration would be a microscope. Just as we need telescope and microscope to explore the totality of the material world, we need mindfulness and concentration to explore the totality of the mental world.

It is important to understand that mindfulness and concentration are both necessary for an effective meditation to take place. They play equally important roles. The key is to utilize their uniqueness (as clarified in table 13.2) whenever and wherever necessary. Then meditation practices result in total mental development.

I personally feel that concentration is much harder to practice than mindfulness. Concentration is an active and exclusive meditation, requiring some effort in focusing (activity) and in eliminating distractions (exclusivity). Mindfulness is often effortless because it is inclusive of everything. It only requires being mindful of whatever is happening at the present moment. Notwithstanding, if you are feeling restless and agitated, you should practice concentration meditation, such as focusing on your breath or a mantra. When you are not able to remain present mentally due to rolling thoughts and become negligent, you should practice mindfulness meditation, such as passively observing the arising and passing away of thoughts.

In any meditation, both concentration and mindfulness should be functional. However, one of the two elements should play a dominating role depending upon your mental condition and skill as a meditator. In any case, use mindfulness and concentration to support each other.

Mindfulness and concentration complement each other. But which one is more important for attaining perfect intelligence? In my opinion, mindfulness is more important because it actually begins and guarantees perfection. Concentration alone cannot do that.

Mindfulness: The Foundation for Developing Mental Powers and Eradicating Mental Weaknesses

When mindfulness is established through ardent and diligent practice, it gives rise to a sense of mental mastery. We begin to feel we are in control of the mind. We begin to feel we know our own mind. This sense of mental mastery awakens the mind to its own ultimate potential. We start realizing what our minds can do. We start thinking about extraordinary things. We no longer fall prey to mundane aspects of our existence. Instead, we start pursuing flawlessness, aptness, righteousness, excellence, greatness, and so on. In this way, mindfulness wakes up the mind to attain perfection, meaning, it makes the mind prone to perfection.

Established mindfulness guarantees mental perfection just as entering a river guarantees a one-way journey towards the ocean, the river's final destination. The spiritual path is like a river moving towards the ocean of perfect intelligence. Any spiritual path begun with mindfulness is destined to culminate there. In this sense, established mindfulness is the number one mental power.

Established mindfulness as a mental power assists in awakening six other mental powers: thoughtfulness, vigor, rapture, tranquility, concentration, and equanimity. Mindfulness is the cause and foundation for their arising and development. The spiritual journey does not culminate into perfect intelligence unless mindfulness is combined with these six mental powers (see figure 13.2).

Mindfulness also serves as the cause and foundation for the removal of seven mental weaknesses (greed, superstition, suspicion, sloth and torpor, restlessness, worry, and hatred) that hinder the development of mental powers. Let us see how this happens.

Due to its ability to safeguard and restrain the senses, *mindfulness* naturally leads to the removal of sensual desires (greed). This frees the mind for investigating and discriminating what is wholesome and what is not, what is good and what is not, what is real and what is not, what is the law of nature and what is not. This gives rise to *thoughtfulness*. As the practice of mindfulness matures, the mind develops mental clarity, understanding, faith, and commitment, which leads to the eradication of false beliefs, wrong views, skeptical doubt (superstition and suspicion) about the practice being undertaken and about the supremacy of the laws of nature.

As thoughtfulness matures, it couples with mindfulness about the received benefits and gives rise to *vigor*. This is required for diligence and the continuation of spiritual practice. Vigor coupled with mental clarity, understanding, faith, and commitment eventually leads to the removal of mental sluggishness, dullness, unwieldiness, and mental sickness (sloth and torpor). Absence of sloth and torpor helps combine vigor with mindfulness and *rapture* arises. The natural outcome of rapture is *concentration,* balanced effort, contentment, physical comfort, and so on, which eventually result in peacefulness and coolness: *tranquility*.

CHAPTER 13 THE WHOLESOME MIND

When tranquility matures, it leads to refinement of conduct and deeper knowledge of reality. All these conditions eventually lead to the removal of mental agitation, turmoil, remorse, and regrets (restlessness and worry). Tranquility always leads to improved concentration and contemplation because it makes the mind happier, and frees it from subtle distraction and aversion. When higher levels of concentration develop due to tranquility and when they are coupled with mindfulness, *equanimity*— the ultimate mental power—arises (see figure 13.2).

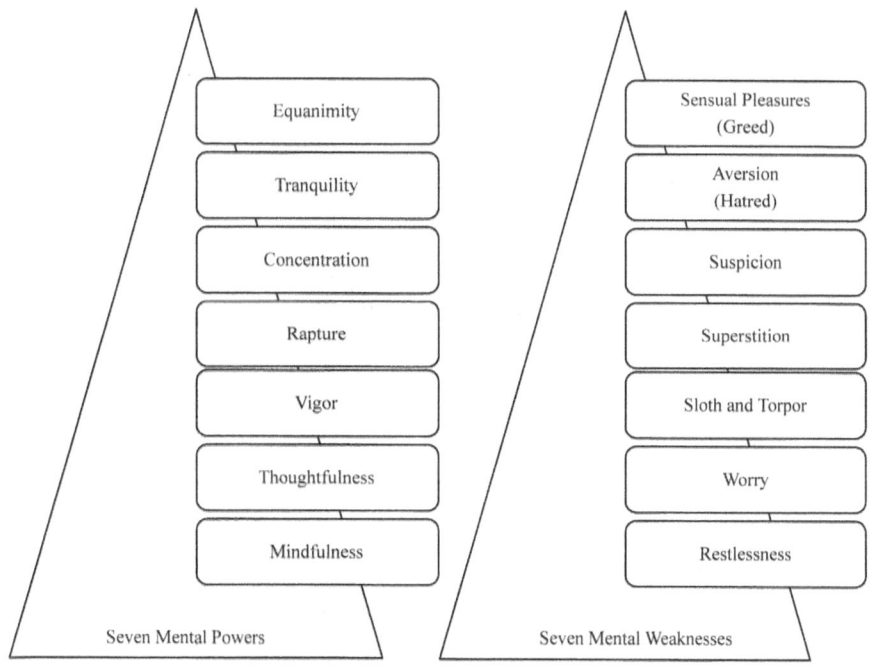

Figure 13.2. Perfect intelligence cannot be attained without the development of seven specific mental powers and the eradication of seven specific mental weaknesses. Mindfulness serves as the cause and foundation for the development of mental powers as well as for the eradication of mental weaknesses.

Mindfulness not only is a powerful spiritual practice, it also is a universal mental remedy. Many mundane mental problems can be solved effectively by its practice. For example, forgetfulness, emotional vulnerability, and addiction to food, drinks, and intoxicants, and high or low self-esteem, among other problems can all be cured by the practice of mindfulness.

221

Mindfulness also serves to balance various mental faculties. If mindfulness is present, faith and vigor do not result in extremism. If mindfulness is present, concentration does not result in idleness or boredom.

Mindfulness is an anchor for spiritual seekers. It becomes their best refuge, island resort, and last home! It protects and restrains the mind and exerts the mind whenever and wherever necessary. It develops the mind wholesomely so that it becomes independent of and unattached to anything in the world. When mindfulness is present, there is no need to search for a safe haven. It itself is the place to rest safely and peacefully.

Conscience and Shame   *(mental elements 31 and 32, Cs-Sh)*

If an individual abandons immoral or unethical action out of *disgust* for immorality, it is due to conscience. Conscience arises out of respect or honor *for oneself.*

Shame is the reason that a person abandons immoral or unethical action out of *apprehension* for immorality. Shame arises out of respect or honor *for others.*

If a playboy gets married or becomes a father and then suddenly stops having extramarital affairs, it is most likely due to the arising of conscience. Now he respects his role as a husband or as a father. If he stops having extramarital affairs to honor his wife, family, society, community, then his chosen course of action is most likely due to the arising of shame. Notice the conditions of self-respect and respect for others.

If a strip club dancer resigns and stops exposing her full body at the club because she gets married or becomes a mother, it is most likely due to conscience. She now respects her role as a wife or a mother. If she stops exposing her full body in public to honor her husband, family, society, community, then her chosen course of action is most likely due to shame.

Because we live in society, in the midst of other people, our actions directly or indirectly impact other people. When we live with conscience and shame, we automatically begin to refine our actions because we start respecting ourselves as well as others. Both conscience and shame are responsible for qualities such as modesty, grace, and reverence.

Conscience and shame are most wholesome when they arise as a pair element. As a pair, these two elements are predominantly responsible for guarding morality and civility in the world. They should be established and practiced in cultures where there is pornography, impropriety, immodesty, and so forth. They should also be practiced and established in cultures where there is rampant corruption, dishonesty, and injustice.

Faith *(mental element 33, Fa)*

Faith is the phenomenon of trusting in something. Faith is that which clarifies the mind, illuminating it to such an extent that the object of trust becomes crystal clear, like a cloudless sky after a thunderstorm. Faith purifies the mind and generates unshakable confidence in the object of trust.

For the arising of faith, the object of trust (a religion, God, views, spiritual tradition, spiritual teachings, and so on) has to be wholesome and pure, and there has to be an experiential understanding of it. Otherwise, faith cannot occur. If the object of trust is not pure, if it is unwholesome, and if there is no experiential understanding, what arises is belief, which is always rooted to some degree in greed, hatred, and delusion. This is the most important aspect of faith to understand.

People who say that it is their faith that if they kill in God's name they will earn a place in heaven are not faithful. The object of trust is not wholesome because it involves killing. Also there is no way to experience heaven, divinity or a godly feeling while killing. It is impossible, because we cannot kill without hatred, and the feeling of hatred is not divine or godly. Killing for religion cannot incorporate the element of faith. It can only demonstrate a *belief* because it is rooted in greed for going to heaven, hatred for others, and delusion about how the mind works.

People who say that according to their faith God will pardon their sins if they surrender to God are mistaking belief for faith. Some say that if they simply chant God's name they will earn favors, fortunes, and a heavenly abode. Some say that if they perform certain rituals they will please God, who will shower them with health and prosperity. All are mistaking belief for faith.[1] They are ignorant of the laws of ethical/volitional accountability (karma), especially of the effect of their attachment to their views and their subtle hatred for other views. Wrong views are simply beliefs, because they arise out of an object that is rooted in greed, hatred, and delusion.

In order to illustrate the differences between faith and belief, let us compare their characteristics, functions, manifestations, proximate causes, and other attributes (see table 13.3).

Table 13.3

Faith vs. Belief

Faith	Belief
Chatacteristics	
• Trusting, confiding	• Believing
Function	
• To clarify • To illuminate • To purify the mind	• To overlook clarification • To hide and suppress illumination • To abandon purification of thought
Manifestations	
• Firm decision • Clarity • Unshakable confidence	• Firm decision • Shaky confidence • Blind devotion, which has no clarity

Proximate Causes	
• The object of faith has to be pure and wholesome • There has to be experiential understanding of the object of faith	• The object of belief is not necessarily pure and wholesome. In most cases, it is unwholesome • There is no experiential understanding of the object of belief
Other Attributes	
• Faith is a wholesome mental element having its own intrinsic nature. Therefore, it does not lead to unwholesome states • Faith is pragmatic and spiritual • Faith leads to the eradication of the ego, the state of mental perfection • Faith leads to wisdom and understanding	• Belief is an unwholesome mental formation structured by superstition, suspicion, greed, delusion, and hatred. Therefore, it may lead to unwholesome states, such as fanaticism, extremism, religiousness, and intolerance • Belief is more religious than spiritual (even when not applied to the institution of a religion). Beliefs are mostly non-pragmatic. Therefore, they actually create a hindrance to spiritual growth • Beliefs lead to the expansion of the ego, due to increased attachment to a personal religion, God, scriptures, or views. Attachments are always rooted in greed, hatred, and delusion • If awareness is created and beliefs are investigated, contemplated, and meditated upon, they can be transformed into faith

Faith only arises out of a pure and wholesome object. For example, when an enlightened master says, "If you observe impermanence and selflessness in all phenomena, you will become wise, happy, and free," one can have faith in this because one can actually experience impermanence and selflessness in all phenomena. Whenever one has that experience, one feels happy and one feels one knows something so deep that it brings a sense of freedom to one's mind.

Faith clarifies and illuminates its own cause. For example, when one develops faith in the enlightened master's statement because one experiences its principles, that faith, in turn, makes it easy for one to understand the statement at deeper levels. It helps one develop confidence in it. It allows one to trust it to such an extent that the trust becomes unshakable.

In the practice of soul meditation, faith generally arises in those who develop insight of the impermanent nature of the phenomenon of matter-mind-consciousness. When this insight matures, it culminates in the arising of freedom from materialism, religiousness, wrong views, beliefs, doubts, superstition, and so on. This may not make sense immediately. However, if you start meditating and develop this understanding from the experiential level, faith will become crystal clear to you. When such a stage emerges, faith becomes a mental faculty. Just as the eye serves as a faculty in the process of seeing, faith serves as a faculty in the process of perfecting the intelligence.

Faith acts like a spiritual hand that assists us in grabbing and establishing wholesome mental states whenever they arise. Faith is also a spiritual wealth. Just as material wealth takes away economic worries of survival and allows us to pursue our core interests, faith removes suspicion and allows us to focus on the core spiritual practices of meditation and contemplation. Faith serves as a decisive support condition when we undertake mental development. In this way, faith is like wholesome resolution. Supported by faith, if spiritual practice or mental development continues, a stage comes when the insight of the "non-self" emerges. At this stage, faith becomes a spiritual power. It is a power in the sense that it can no longer be overcome by anything in the world.

CHAPTER 13 THE WHOLESOME MIND

It succeeds in producing success (or merit) out of spiritual or mental exertion.

Faith is a spiritual treasure in that it not only enables us to embark upon the most elite journey of our life: the soul journey, but also leads us directly to the final destination: the attainment of perfect intelligence and the freedom from all suffering. How? In the presence of faith, there is no suspicion, doubt, and apprehension, turning back, or stopping. The journey becomes like the one-way flow of a river towards the ocean.

Tranquility *(mental elements 34 and 35, Tr1-Tr2)* [2]

Tranquility is the phenomenon that reduces activity. In a way, it makes the mind inactive just as a tranquilizer would make a wild animal inactive. This does not mean the mind becomes slack or dull. It simply indicates the state of mind free of activities such as discursive thinking, agitation, restlessness, worry, distress, stress, and so on. It makes the mind calm and still by crushing these activities. In this sense, tranquility is the opposite of agitation, disturbances, distress, and even stress. It is an essential wholesome element, always present in some degree in all wholesome states of consciousness.

Experienced meditators are aware of the extraordinary delight that results from tranquility of body and mind. This delight is truly superhuman. When tranquility is perfected, delight can also be transcended while in deep concentration, leading to spiritual bliss.

Tranquility is a power element like mindfulness, because it awakens the mind for perfection, assists in bringing mastery to the mind, and makes the mind prone to enlightenment.

Lightness *(mental elements 36 and 37, Li1-Li2)*

Lightness is the phenomenon that crushes the heaviness caused by elements such as sloth and torpor. It makes the mind non-sluggish, just as losing weight makes an obese person lively and nimble. It is like the state of mind-body that is present before a heavy meal, rather than after a heavy meal. Lightness simply indicates a state of mind free of sleepiness, lethargy, boredom, drowsiness, drooping, sinking, and so on. It is an essential wholesome element, meaning it is always present in some degree in all wholesome states of consciousness.

Flexibility *(mental elements No. 38 and 39, Fl1-Fl2)*

Flexibility is the phenomenon that crushes the rigidity that arises from superstition and conceit. It makes the mind supple, like gold becomes after impurities are removed. It does not allow the mind to be influenced by the forces of confrontation or resistance. It is like the state of mind-body that's present after a wholesome workout or after a deep insight. Flexibility simply indicates a state of mind free of stiffness, inflexibility, strictness, hardness, confrontation, resistance, and so on. It is an essential wholesome element, which is always present in some degree in all wholesome states of consciousness.

Pliability *(mental elements 40 and 41, Pl1-Pl2)*

Pliability is the phenomenon that crushes subtle mental impurities or mental hindrances that do not allow *wielding* of the mind. Pliability makes mind maneuverable in wholesome acts like developing faith in things that are worthy or in acts like purifying the mind. Like the wielding of a weapon by an expert martial artist, pliability manifests as efficacy or effectiveness in minding an object. For example, the higher the degree of pliability, the greater is the possibility of success in developing mindfulness of breath. It is an essential wholesome element, which is always present in some degree in all wholesome states of consciousness.

Skillfulness *(mental elements 42 and 43, Sk1-Sk2)*

Skillfulness is the phenomenon that crushes the mental unhealthiness or disability that comes from lack of faith, lack of mindfulness, lack of conscience, lack of shame, lack of equanimity, and so on. It makes mind proficient in removing these mental disabilities. It is an essential wholesome element, which is always present in some degree in all wholesome states of consciousness.

Rectitude (mental elements 44 and 45, Rc1-Rc2)

Rectitude is the phenomenon that crushes the mental indirectness that occurs due to dishonesty, fraud, deceit, swindling, and so on. It develops mental rectitude by removing mental tortuousness. It is an essential wholesome element, which is always present in some degree in all wholesome states of consciousness.

Equanimity (mental element 46, Eq)

Equanimity is neutrality of mind, an ethically wholesome quality related to pure consciousness. It is that phenomenon which keeps mind in the middle between deficiency and excess, between craving and aversion. Here, the word "middle" does not mean a quantitative mid-point (for example, 50 being the mid-point between 0 and 100) but a qualitative core (a center) related to mental balance and impartiality.

Equanimity is not just the absence of craving and aversion; also it is the element that makes the mind balanced and impartial. Mere absence of craving and aversion does not automatically result in a balanced or impartial state of mind. When craving and aversion are eradicated, equanimity arises and makes the mind balanced and impartial. In this sense, equanimity has its own intrinsic functional nature.

Equanimity is degraded to the level of the mundane when people confuse it with the quality of mind control, self-control, pain control, pleasure control, pain-pleasure management, and so on. For example, many spiritual practitioners take pride in being able to tolerate pain, discomfort, and inconvenience because they assume they have more equanimity than those who live in comfort. Only ignorant people think this way. They do not realize that even wild animals are highly capable of tolerating high degrees of discomfort. Does that make wild animals equanimous?

You cannot say you are equanimous just because you are able to tolerate pain. In most cases, it is not equanimity but insensitivity. Moreover, becoming insensitive to pain generally leads to the development of resentment for pleasure. Resentment increases to such a level that you cannot tolerate comfort and become critic of richness and order. Ultimately you feel insecure in a five-star hotel or any other opulent and comfortable environment.

People living in pleasant conditions are neither more, nor less likely to have equanimity than people living in painful conditions. Many spiritual practitioners living in comfort think it is okay to live in comfort as long as they do not get attached to it. Such people become insensitive to pleasure and unknowingly develop resentment for pain. Resentment increases to such a level that they cannot tolerate discomfort and become critics of disorder and poverty. Ultimately they feel insecure in an uncomfortable environment.

Whenever there is any trace of resentment, disapproval or approval, repulsion or attraction there is no real equanimity. A person in a state of equanimity is equally at ease in a royal palace and in a slum. He neither desires, nor chooses comforts or discomforts. He neither approves of affluence, nor disapproves of poverty. He is *disinterested* in these matters because he has transcended the issue of pleasures and pain. He is at peace in all circumstances, because he is desireless. But his desirelessness is rooted in contentment and renunciation, and not abandonment, rejection, or denial.

As you are reading, many questions might have arisen in your mind.

- Should we not desire or choose anything?
- Is it not healthier to choose to live in a clean and pollution-free environment than to live in a slum-like environment? Why should we not approve of something that is good?
- Why should we not disapprove of noise, bad smell, mosquitoes, and whatever that is bad?
- How can we do anything at all, including good such as serving others, if there is no desire or interest?

These are fine questions. They share an answer, which is that you can choose to live in a clean and pollution-free environment as a practice of virtuous living. You can choose to live in comfort as a way to support your meditation practice and minimize waste of energy. You

CHAPTER 13 THE WHOLESOME MIND

can show interest and get involved to serve people, as a practice of loving-kindness, compassion, and so on. But you cannot say you are doing these things in order to develop equanimity. Becoming virtuous, compassionate, loving, and serving all is not the same as equanimity. However, all of these practices eventually lead to equanimity.

Another classic example of confusion about equanimity is assuming that equanimity leads to indifference if practiced while dealing with others. This is not true because in order to deal with others with equanimity you have to first develop the foundation of loving-kindness, compassion, and gladness: the three *divine mental elements,* which we will soon discuss in detail. Without such foundation, yes, you may develop indifference towards others, but not equanimity.

Think of your past. Remember your growth from childhood to adulthood. When you were small, loving-kindness was the predominant quality when your parents dealt with you. When you were sick, compassion was the predominant quality of your parents' attention towards you. When you were young and healthy, gladness was predominant in your parents' mind. When you became an adult, left the house, and were employed, equanimity was the predominant quality of your parents' awareness. Why? They knew you, the adult child, would now be able to take care of himself/herself. Your parents were neither involved in your affairs as they once were, nor did they abandon you in their awareness. Once you became an adult and self-sufficient, you were looked upon without getting involved. This quality of an onlooker without getting involved is similar to equanimity. Lack of involvement is not same as indifference towards the adult child, because in parents' awareness there is always a sense of welfare, compassion, and gladness for their adult child since they graduated through those mental states as their child matured.

The practice of loving-kindness, compassion, and gladness towards other people can only make us equanimous towards them. These practices can only make us impartial, unprejudiced, and neutral towards all beings, including ourselves. These practices can only help us break down the barriers by helping us see all (including ourselves) equally.

When we mature in the practices of loving-kindness, compassion, and gladness, and equanimity arises out of that, we no longer have any friends or enemies. We no longer love one person more than another. Having transcended differences and discrimination, we become neutral. We become like "space," which is impartial towards all beings and formations and yet encompasses all. If space were the body of a person, then equanimity would be that person's mind.

While dealing with others, equanimity is the abiding quality (status quo) of an enlightened master. For example, when an enlightened master sees a drowning child, he knowingly steps out of equanimity, arouses compassion for the child, saves the child, steps back into equanimity of mind, and walks away without rejoicing or expecting a reward. He does not think that "he" has saved the child. Instead, he observes the entire episode as a third person. In this way, an enlightened master abides in the world fully awake, fully active, and supersensitive. The master is able to abide in equanimity only because he practices loving-kindness, compassion, and gladness towards other people.

Equanimity is very subtle. It is hard to understand intellectually and even harder to understand experientially. But, you can get a taste of it during a prolonged meditation practice. Broadly speaking, during a prolonged meditation, equanimity can be somewhat experienced as the *awareness* of the "absence and the opposite" of pleasant or unpleasant feelings. Such awareness is unique. It is an experience of a feeling of "neither pleasure nor pain," which is not only the mere absence of pleasant and unpleasant feelings, but also the opposite of both. This awareness is critical in differentiating equanimity from the worldly attitude of indifference, apathy, coldness, and so on. In apathy, for example, there may be the absence of pleasant or unpleasant feeling but there is no awareness of it. And obviously in apathy there is no possibility of even being aware of such a thing as neither pleasure nor pain.

If you meditate to develop mindfulness, non-reaction, wise attention, and concentration, and then establish yourself in the transcendental and passive states of mind, equanimity arises as a result of that. In other words, equanimity arises only through passive and transcendental actions. In meditation, simply practice observing body-mind-consciousness phenomena passively, transcend higher and higher levels of mental absorption and insight, and let equanimity arise by itself. Later chapters will provide specific instructions on how this is done.

Types of Equanimity

A way of minimizing the confusion about equanimity is to view it as a spectrum: A hierarchy ranging from materialistic equanimity (lowest level 1) to spiritual equanimity (highest level 4) (see table 13.4).

Table 13.4

Levels of Equanimity

Manifestation	Notes of Caution
Level 1: Materialistic Equanimity	
• Not reacting to conditions of poverty or prosperity • Not getting attached to discomforts or comforts • Being at ease with heat or cold, summer or winter, beauty or ugliness, material successes or losses, and so on	• Control, masochism, pain management, power tactics, and so on • Can lead to a false sense of equanimity
Level 2: Physical Equanimity	
• Not reacting to sensations of pleasure or pain caused by bodily conditions • Observing pleasure or pain as physical sensations without developing a craving for pleasant sensations or an aversion for painful sensations	• If practiced as a meditation technique for developing equanimity, this can lead to deep attachment to the technique, ignorance about body-mind phenomena, breeding of meditator ego • a false sense of equanimity

Table 13.4
Levels of Equanimity (Continued)

Level 3: Mental Equanimity	
• Not reacting to feelings of pleasure or pain and joy or sorrow, but observing them as mental phenomena without developing cravings or aversions • Neither becoming glad nor sad • Neither feeling resentful nor seeking approval • Maintaining mental composure • Not being attached to any thought, feeling, or emotion • Perfecting non-greed and non-hatred • Maintaining peace of mind at any cost	• No caution required • Leads to mental purification and the dawn of real equanimity if coupled with the practices of loving-kindness, compassion, and gladness towards all beings, including oneself.
Level 4: Spiritual Equanimity	
• Experiencing neutral feelings of neither pleasure nor pain • Experiencing states of neither perception nor non-perception • Experiencing states of being neither free nor bound • Having a sense of selflessness, serving without thinking, "It is me who is serving" (inaction in action) • Being disinterested in worldly matters while also being fully established in loving-kindness, compassion, and gladness	• No caution required • Realizing that neither perception nor non-perception is a state of awareness rather than a physical feeling • Such mental states result *only* from mental equanimity and consistent practice of mindfulness and wholesome concentration

CHAPTER 13 THE WHOLESOME MIND

As made clear by the notes of caution in table 13.4, in order to arouse equanimity it is best to practice virtue, abstinence, mindfulness, concentration, non-reaction, giving wise attention, loving-kindness, compassion, gladness, and so on and to let equanimity arise by itself as a result. In addition to these specific spiritual practices, in daily life one should avoid the company of prejudiced people. One should avoid over enthusiasm. One should neutralize one's perception and cognition. One should neither agree nor disagree. One should become non-opinionating. One should seclude oneself from worldly mundane matters as much as possible, and consistently incline the mind towards neutrality. Above all, one should develop the mental habit of letting go.

Do not practice equanimity directly—even in meditation. Instead, practice everything that leads to equanimity. Let it arise. Equanimity is highly illusive. It is like the Earth's horizon. If you try to achieve it or reach it, you can never succeed.

Direct practices can lead to confusion, frustration, abandonment, inactivity, indifference, apathy, and coldness. In fact, it is almost certain that unwholesome qualities will develop in worldly-minded people or even in experienced meditators who try to practice equanimity directly in meditation or in daily life. Developing a false sense of equanimity hinders spiritual growth.

The easiest way to know whether or not you are developing equanimity is to become aware of its nearest allies: blissfulness, peacefulness, ease, non-reaction, contentment, lack of expectation for gifts and rewards, renunciation, sense of seclusion, and non-attachment, sense of being space-like (overlooking the world of formations), and so on. If you experience any of these states, then you can be sure that you are approaching the state of equanimity.

As I am saying fantastic things about equanimity, it may sound as if equanimity is perfect intelligence itself. That is not the case. Equanimity itself is an ultimate mental power. However, that is not sufficient. Equanimity has to be conjoined with the other six mental powers (which we have previously discussed) to attain perfect intelligence. However, equanimity is definitely a near-final signpost showing the way to such attainment.

How Wholesome Mind Works

In order *really* to understand all the wholesome elements, it is necessary to contemplate and meditate on their defining criteria. It is important to identify them correctly so they can be effectively cultured into the consciousness. This is like thoroughly understanding the properties of chemicals that make up a medical pill so that the pill can be used to eradicate disease without causing adverse side effects.

Here is a plausible scenario, which briefly illuminates the defining criteria of all the wholesome elements.

You are walking in a park and you spot the most beautiful flower you have ever seen. A desire arises to pluck the flower, although a sign nearby reads, "Public Property."

If non-greed arises, it helps you to overcome the desire because non-greed does not allow you to cling to the flower. Mentally non-greed helps you to let go and detach your mind from objects around it. Non-greed transforms experience into desireless appreciation, of beauty, fragrance, and whatever else has attracted your attention. Because non-greed is strong, you are not drawn to think otherwise about the flower than appreciatively. As a result, you do not choose to pluck the flower.

Let us say that while you are deeply enjoying the flower someone else interrupts and rushes to pluck the flower. If this happens and the element of non-hatred arises, it cools things down and averts the aggravation or irritation that otherwise could have arisen. When non-hatred is present, you do not experience burning sensations or unpleasant feelings. Instead of anger, there is sociability and agreeableness. You are spared the misery of anger.

When non-greed and non-hatred are there, other wholesome elements arise with them. Mindfulness generates and maintains presence of mind and a passive, receptive, and deepening observation of the flower. It stabilizes attention on the flower, not letting it drift away.

CHAPTER 13 THE WHOLESOME MIND

This keeps you in the moment because of which there is a deep experience.

Out of respect for yourself and others, conscience and shame helps your mind refrain from the unethical act of stealing public property (which, let's agree for the sake of argument, plucking the flower would be). It manifests in this case as shying away from greed.

Faith helps you maintain clarity of mind and confidence about the rightfulness of your actions. Tranquility quiets any mental disturbance that arises while observing the flower. It does not allow restlessness to arise. It dissolves stress and brings stillness, coolness of mind, peacefulness, quietness, and serenity to experience. Due to tranquility, the simple observation of flower becomes a heavenly delight.

Lightness, flexibility, pliability, skillfulness, and rectitude perform their unique functions, as discussed previously, and wholesomely intensify the experience. Equanimity neutralizes the mind and completely liberates it from craving the flower. Thus, it manifests as balance of mind in the midst of incredible beauty of the flower and makes the whole experience deeply peaceful.

This concludes our discussion of the wholesome elements. Among them, non-greed and non-hatred stand out as the wholesome *root elements* because all wholesome states are rooted in them. Just as roots provide firmness to a tree, these two elements provide firmness and stability to wholesome consciousness.

Together, the wholesome elements bring grace, beauty, and radiance to consciousness. Even a trace of them has the power to generate favorable conditions for experiencing the divine.

* * *

Chapter 14

The Divine Mind

The mental elements of loving-kindness, compassion, gladness, and equanimity predominantly arise in the consciousness of highly-evolved (divine) beings such as Jesus, Buddha, and other enlightened masters of their like. In light of this, psychologically and phenomenologically speaking, being *divine* means being established in these four elements. Divinity is the exquisiteness of consciousness, a quality of elegance, and not at all related only to godly beings or the supernatural.[1]

When the four divine elements combine with wholesome elements, they form a group which I like to call *the divine mind*.

Philosophically and phenomenologically speaking, love is none other than the direct manifestation of the divine mind (see figure 14.1).

Loving-kindness *(mental element Lk)*

Loving-kindness is a highly-evolved form of the element of nonhatred, which we have already discussed, so there is no element number assigned to it. However, it needs to be further explained to exemplify its divine nature, especially its part in the phenomenon of love.

Cultivating the element of loving-kindness means considering all living creatures as worthy of your love and kindness. Pragmatically speaking, it means becoming friendly, and choosing welfare over harm. The element of loving-kindness actually serves as a reason or root cause for the arising of love consciousness.

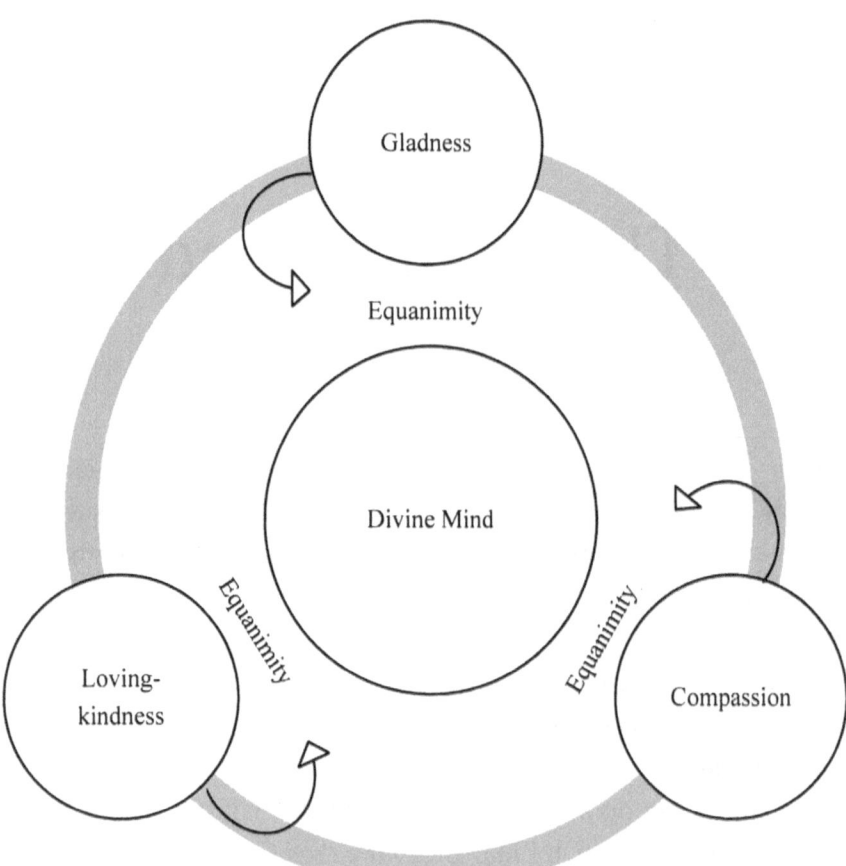

Figure 14.1. The divine mind is a group of four elements, which are present in divine beings like Jesus, Buddha, and enlightened masters of their like. Practicing them while dealing with ourselves and others makes us divine here and now. Love is none other than the direct manifestation of the divine mind.

The easiest way to arouse love is to develop loving-kindness towards near and dear ones, as wells as towards those who are hateful

CHAPTER 14 THE DIVINE MIND

and unfair. The moment we genuinely consider any person as worthy of our loving-kindness, love arises and cools down our anger and resentment. You can understand this experientially by applying it while having a heated argument with your spouse or partner.

Many people wonder whether it is really possible to develop loving-kindness towards someone who has hurt us deeply or towards those who are hostile. Many people outright reject the idea of making enemies into friends. To such people, I would like to humbly say that because loving-kindness exists in nature as a distinct mental phenomenon, and because its function is to choose welfare over harm, eventually it will remove all animosity, hostility, enmity, ill feelings, and ill will towards *all* beings if practiced ardently and consistently. It is just like water, which has the natural ability to extinguish fire.

Of course, it is not as easy to develop loving-kindness towards a hostile person as it is to develop it towards our child or a friend. In fact, if we try haphazardly to develop it towards our enemy, it fatigues the mind. Therefore it is necessary to follow a particular order.

Start developing loving-kindness towards yourself first. You are always the dearest person to you, whether you agree or not. Once you develop love for yourself, you will never harm another because you will realize that just as you are dearest to you, others' selves are dearest to them.

You must learn to love yourself before loving another. This is the foundation of loving-kindness. Loving yourself does not mean becoming self-centered. It simply means not harming yourself in any way.

As we mature in loving-kindness, the sense of self begins to dissolve and the sense of love begins to evolve. It begins to expand and naturally extend to those who are dearest to us and then to those beyond. Eventually love evolves to such an extent that we begin to abide in love consciousness. In this way, loving-kindness gradually purifies all relationships beginning with our children, spouses, parents, siblings, and friends, then people we know favorably, people we don't know, and at last our enemies, if they exist.

The divine quality of loving-kindness leaves no barriers. We cannot have hatred for an enemy when we are absorbed in loving-kindness. What arises in mind is only the welfare and happiness of all.

While developing loving-kindness towards a hostile person, feelings of hurt and resentment are bound to arise. In fact, such feelings may arise while developing loving-kindness towards even a spouse or parents. How can we ignore these feelings? Can we really get rid of all the hurt and resentment? The answer is yes, and I'm certain you'll agree after practicing the loving-kindness meditations discussed in later chapters.

Loving-kindness is not fondness or personal affection towards another person, because, those things are contaminated with greed, hatred, and delusion. It is impossible to love and hate someone at the same time. Therefore, loving-kindness is not at all similar to romantic love or other love-hate relationships. Loving-kindness is also not at all similar to fatherly love, motherly love, brotherly love, friendly love, and so on, which are mostly rooted in selfish affection or fondness. In fact, selfish affection, fondness, liking, craving someone, and so on are like masked enemies of loving-kindness because they distract us from cultivating real love. Real love is not about feeling passionate or becoming crazy about somebody, or getting attached and bonding with someone. In order to avoid such failures at loving, we have to combine loving-kindness with equanimity.

Loving-kindness is truly auspicious because it makes our lives free of resentment, anger, hatred, and so on. When we consistently practice and cultivate loving-kindness and establish ourselves in it, we feel blessed. We abide comfortably in this world due to our harmless nature. We become dear to one and all. We win over all enemies. Our expressions become serene. Our presence carries tranquility and calmness wherever we go.

We become holy. We become divine.

Compassion *(mental element 47, Cm)*

Compassion makes it possible to see and feel the suffering in us and others, and to promote the eradication of that suffering. Like loving-kindness, it is a divine phenomenon, although unique.

You can test the power of compassion by arousing it for your worst enemy and noticing how quickly it cools down the fire of hatred and cruelty. While dealing with a hostile person, if we arouse compassion, it makes us look at the hostile person as someone who is suffering from anger, hatred, and ignorance. Because of our compassionate outlook, we feel relaxed and calm (instead of experiencing the burning heat of anger) which results in an intense urge to alleviate the suffering of the other person.

Because compassion makes it possible to see suffering and inclines us to remove the suffering, instead of *reacting* to someone's hostility, we *act* with sympathy, empathy, consideration, and kindness. Compassion not only makes us non-hostile towards other people, it also makes other people non-hostile towards us. Due to compassion, we win the war for both parties!

While established in some degree of loving-kindness, if we see a diseased or destitute person, compassion arises and not disgust. Do not misunderstand compassion as that which generates sorrow, grief, and sadness. In order to avoid such failures of compassion, we have to combine compassion with equanimity.

The divine quality of compassion will become clearer to you when you practice the compassion meditations that we will discuss in later chapters.

If we use loving-kindness and compassion together, we can skillfully handle challenging life situations. In a moment I will give you a tip or two on how, but first, let me highlight the subtle differences between the two.

Table 14.1

Loving-kindness vs. Compassion

Loving-kindness	Compassion
Characteristics	
Generating welfare and goodwill for others	• Making it possible to see suffering in others • Not being able to overlook others' pain
Functions	
• Preferring goodwill over ill-will • Promoting welfare	Removing suffering
Manifestations	
• Removal of hatred, anger and ill-will • Harmlessness and friendliness	• Non-meanness • Peacefulness
Proximate Causes	
Seeing beings as lovable	Seeing beings as those who are suffering (in the ultimate sense)
Order of Practice	
Arouse it for yourself first and for the enemy last	Arouse it for the enemy first and for yourself last
Marks of Failure	
Loving-kindness fails if it generates selfish affection, personal liking, fondness, or craving	Compassion fails if it generates sorrow and grief

As you can see, loving-kindness arises when we see others as lovable. So it is very difficult to arouse it when we deal with an unjust, hostile, or evil person. However, compassion arises when we see others as beings in suffering. So when someone is angry with *you*, arouse compassion for that person first and then let loving-kindness seep in. When *you* are angry with someone, arouse loving-kindness for yourself first and then let compassion seep in. In this way, let compassion and loving-kindness together engulf you and others in all life situations. Let goodwill, welfare, friendliness, non-hatred, non-meanness, and peace prevail at all times and at any cost.

Gladness *(mental element 48, Gl)*

By removing jealousy and envy, gladness makes it possible for us to see and appreciate other people's successes. You can test the power of gladness by arousing it whenever you sense aversion or envy towards anybody. If you arouse gladness while dealing with highly successful friends, family members, or competitors, you begin to appreciate their successes. This results in pleasantness and happiness because gladness does not allow feelings of envy or aversion to take hold. Instead, gladness permeates consciousness with appreciative joy and makes us feel good.

You can also use the power of gladness to deal with boredom or aversion (which is subtle and hard to detect), which can arise when dealing with other people's successes or otherwise. By contemplating the successes of all the people you can think of, you can quickly get rid of boredom or aversion.

Gladness should not be misunderstood as that which simply generates cheerfulness without the removal of aversion. The divine quality of gladness is deep and exquisite, which will become evident if you practice gladness meditations that are discussed in later chapters.

Compassion generally arises out of seeing others' suffering. Gladness generally arises out of appreciating others' successes. These two elements cannot arise at the same time. You either experience compassion or gladness. Therefore, when we are dealing with enemies and unknown people, we should arouse compassion leading to equanimity. When we are dealing with friends and family, we should arouse loving-kindness and gladness. In between, we should skillfully combine loving-kindness and compassion as we discussed earlier. This is the exquisite way of dealing with others, developing love, and becoming divine here and now.

* * *

Chapter 15

The Noble Mind

When wholesome elements mature and develop some strength, and when divine elements begin to sprout and grow, conditions build up due to which three unique mental elements can arise in consciousness: noble action, noble speech, and noble vocation.[1] These form a group called *the noble mind* (see figure 15.1). The main feature of the group is purposeful and unconditional abstinence, which manifests as deliberately shying away from all wrongdoing under all circumstances, including ethically and morally challenging situations and dilemmas. It is not the mere non-occurrence of wrongdoing that is noble, but the purposeful and unconditional abstinence from wrongdoing. Nobility is the highest degree of courageous intention and greatest will.

Not lying because of fear of perjury and imprisonment is not noble. Not lying because lying leads to mental defilement, not lying even at the cost of fortune and even life is noble.

Noble elements are said to have arisen only when we intentionally and unconditionally refrain from speech, bodily action, and vocation that are unwholesome even to the *slightest* degree. Because these abstinences are purposeful and unconditional, they have their own intrinsic nature due to which they are considered mental elements. The bravery of purposeful and unconditional abstinence is a primary force behind the noble pursuit of enlightenment.

The courage required for purposeful abstinence from wrongdoing cannot be matched by any amount of courage required for worldly achievement. That is why noble elements arise only in those having utmost will power: saints, yogis, rishis, monks, modern meditators, great thinkers, and spiritual activists who consistently pursue mental perfection at any cost. These I call the *noble ones*.

It is extremely difficult to become noble, as it requires tremendous faith, firm resolve, distaste for mundane living and wrongdoing, and a sense of urgency underlain by contentment. In Part III, you'll learn the practices and aspects of attitude and lifestyle that will support you in pursuing the path of nobility.

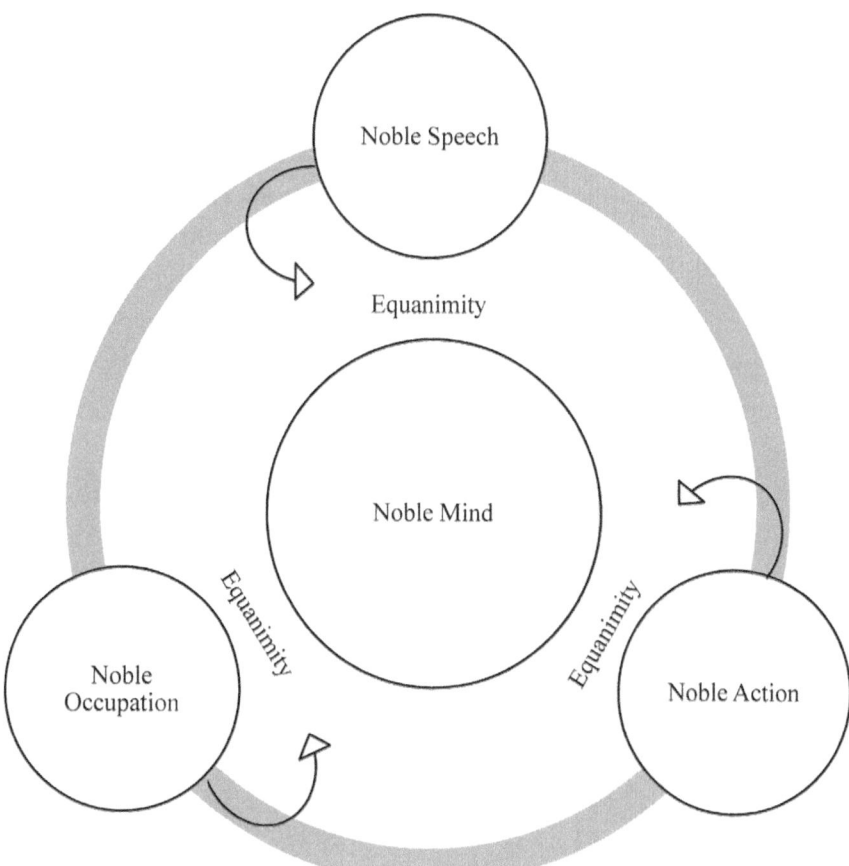

Figure 15.1. The noble mind is a group of three mental elements, which facilitate deliberate and unconditional abstinence from any wrongdoing.

Noble Action *(mental element 49, Na)*

Refraining from fighting for any cause—even the cause of justice—is an example of a noble action. Tremendous bravery and courage is needed. When some people hear this, they usually don't believe it. Many argue that it would actually require bravery and courage to fight for justice. They claim that I am saying the opposite of what is true. Some people make such arguments because they do not clearly understand the mental states that arise during fighting and what it takes to refrain. Here's an explanation.

We cannot fight a cause without bravery and courage. That is true. But the degree of bravery and courage we require to *refrain* from fighting is significantly greater. It is easy to be brave and fight another person who is unjust. Self-defense is even protected by law. However, in most cases fighting is driven by the emotions of anger and fear, which are rooted in ego. A worldly person cannot fight an unjust person without feeling angry or restless. Even if the fight is won from a physical, monetary, or social perspective, it is never won from a spiritual perspective because of the mental impurities caused by the fight. Therefore, for a spiritual seeker such victories are a loss. Whenever the ego is involved, no real victory is possible.

Only a noble person can arouse enough bravery and courage to refrain from fighting, because the ego desperately wants to fight. The ego cannot tolerate injustice. It wants fairness and recognition. By purposefully abstaining from doing what the ego wants, the noble person does not let the ego have its way. Overriding the ego's wishes requires courage. Therefore, refraining from fighting is possible only for the noble ones who, in my opinion, are greater than the greatest warriors.

It is not at all easy to face someone who is inflicting pain without fighting back. It also requires tremendous bravery to endure physical pain without fighting back. It needs nobility to maintain composure and compassion while being mistreated or mishandled by others.

Noble ones do not fight at all. Not even for a good cause. They only serve.

When we fight, it is always us versus another person or us versus some organization. When we serve, this is not the case. We simply serve a cause or a principle. For example, if you are living in a city where the municipality is corrupt and you want to do something about it, instead of fighting directly with the municipality or with corrupt officials, simply serve the cause of anti-corruption by writing articles in the newspaper, conducting seminars, arousing grassroots activism, developing social awareness, taking part in lobbying for anti-corruption legislation, and so on. In this way, you avoid directly fighting with specific individuals and there is much less opportunity for the development of anger, hatred, animosity, and so on. In this way, the ills of the world can be removed: by not directly fighting another person but by serving the cause for one and all.

In order to respond in this manner, first we have to develop loving-kindness, compassion, gladness, and equanimity to some extent. Then we have to arouse the noble elements in situations where we must refrain from wrongdoing. When we combine the divine elements and the noble elements we become fit to serve the world. After we train ourselves in loving-kindness, compassion, gladness, and equanimity and we train ourselves to refrain from wrongdoing by speech, action, and vocation only then we should serve for the deliverance of all beings.

Other examples of noble action, among other things, include, refraining from all degrees of violence, physically hurting oneself or others, generating physical pain unwisely, self-mortification, neglecting physical health, drinking and inhaling intoxicants, mishandling or overdecorating the body, and physical activities done specifically to avoid boredom.

Noble Speech *(mental element, 50 Ns)*

Refraining from lying in any degree under any situation is possible due to the element of noble speech.

A spiritual dilemma that generally comes up while groups are discussing this element is whether or not it is okay to lie if it could save someone's life. My answer is no. When you think it is okay to lie for good reasons, you make mind lazy and it begins to use lying as an easy way out. When you think it is not okay to lie for any reason (as noble mind would), you make mind intuitive, creative, and mind finds a way to save someone's life anyway. Noble mind is rooted in loving-kindness and compassion. So obviously you will not be apathetic towards someone who is in danger.

The point is that when we develop noble elements we become increasingly intuitive, creative, and learn to eradicate artificial difficulties. We begin to understand that in reality there are no dilemmas.

Examples of the manifestation of the noble speech element include, among other things, refraining from all degrees of criticizing, condemning, belittling, ridiculing, accusing, scolding, censuring, blaming, opining, interrupting, slandering, arguing, shouting, speaking unkindly, teasing, chatting frivolously, foolish babbling, backbiting, indirectly speaking, roundabout talking, flattering, influencing, asserting, self-glorifying chatter, cleverly arguing, secretly or vaguely or shrewdly speaking, and using scholarly language to show off one's own knowledge.

Noble Occupation *(mental element 51, No)*

Refraining from doing any work that directly or indirectly develops even the slightest degree of greed, hatred, and delusion is possible due to this element.

Those who manufacture and sell arms passionately believe in possessing a weapon and even in killing for self-defense. They are proud of their profession. Such people do not realize that they are mostly driven by their fear of pain and death, and not actually by self-defense. They do not know that defending against fear (and not another person), and defending against hatred are the true forms of self-defense. Defending mind against defilement instead of simply defending the body is the quality of nobility. This does not mean you should abandon the care of your body or overlook the threat of survival and protection. Here's the challenge I am throwing down: Could we develop a higher response than fight-or-flight? Can we evolve?

Mahatma Gandhi protected his rights and freedom without firing a single shot and his threat was not from another person but from the entire British Empire![2] Martin Luther King, Jr., did something similar.[3] Many spiritual masters and missionaries have traveled to, and lived in unknown hostile places without ever carrying a gun. Fearlessness of pain and death (underlain by loving-kindness and compassion) is the mark of the noble ones.

Pragmatically speaking, the noble ones are more fearful of defiling the mind or generating unwholesome volition than they are fearful

CHAPTER 15   THE NOBLE MIND

of pain or death. They are also less worried about poverty and economic survival than they are about maintaining vigil over vices. So they choose vocations that minimize the chances of developing even the slightest degree of greed, hatred, and delusion.

Many of us do our jobs primarily so that we can pay the bills even though we may not like what we do. Many people choose a particular profession because they are lured by big money. Some do not need income; they stay in the workforce simply to keep themselves busy because they cannot handle boredom. In the first case, there is subtle hatred, in second there is subtle greed, and in the third there is subtle delusion.

To identify a noble vocation, ask yourself this question: Could I do something that I truly love doing 18 hours a day without expecting to get paid for it?

This does not mean you should work without getting paid. It means you should work at something you love.

Another way to determine your noble vocation is to figure out the real purpose of your life and get involved in it (see chapter 4, page 75). In most cases, noble vocation and real purpose are aligned. Those who are courageous are most likely to find such a vocation. This usually happens during a mid-life crisis. Once found, people generally follow their noble vocation for the rest of their lives, which brings them deep satisfaction as well as a high probability of financial riches without developing even the slightest degree of greed, hatred, or delusion.

* * *

Chapter 16

The Wise Mind

Real happiness and spiritual bliss in the world arise due to a combination of the wholesome elements, the divine elements, and the noble elements that we have discussed so far. Mental development reaches near-perfection with their successful development. Consequently they lead to the awakening of the wisdom element: non-delusion (see figure 16.1).

Non-delusion *(mental element 52, NDe)*

Non-delusion is known as the wisdom element, as it removes the subtlest of all impurities (ignorance, ego, I-ness) and thereby makes the mind perfect. Both the subtlest and the most powerful of all the mental elements, it permeates and conditions all beneficial mental activities.

Non-delusion is the *ultimate root cause* of all that is spiritually profitable in the world. Non-delusion illuminates the totality of reality and eradicates illusion. When non-delusion is present, no subject-object separation remains because it illuminates the phenomenological nature of experience. The illusion of a seer separate from the scenery, a thinker separate from the thought, or an experiencer separate from that which is being experienced dissolves.

Non-delusion does not allow consciousness to be deluded by the senses and the unwholesome mind. It is like a light that does not allow darkness to exist. It is like an extremely sharp laser that can penetrate all layers of delusion, such as identity derived from race or ethnicity, nationality, religion, region, social stature, gender or gender preference, parental or familial roles, physical appearance or strength, mental competence and ability, and states of consciousness. Ultimately, the penetrative power of non-delusion exposes the real nature of the self so that nothing remains to be exposed about it. Non-delusion is that by means of which we can expose the ultimate essence of all things. Therefore, it is known as the destroyer of ignorance and the builder of wisdom.

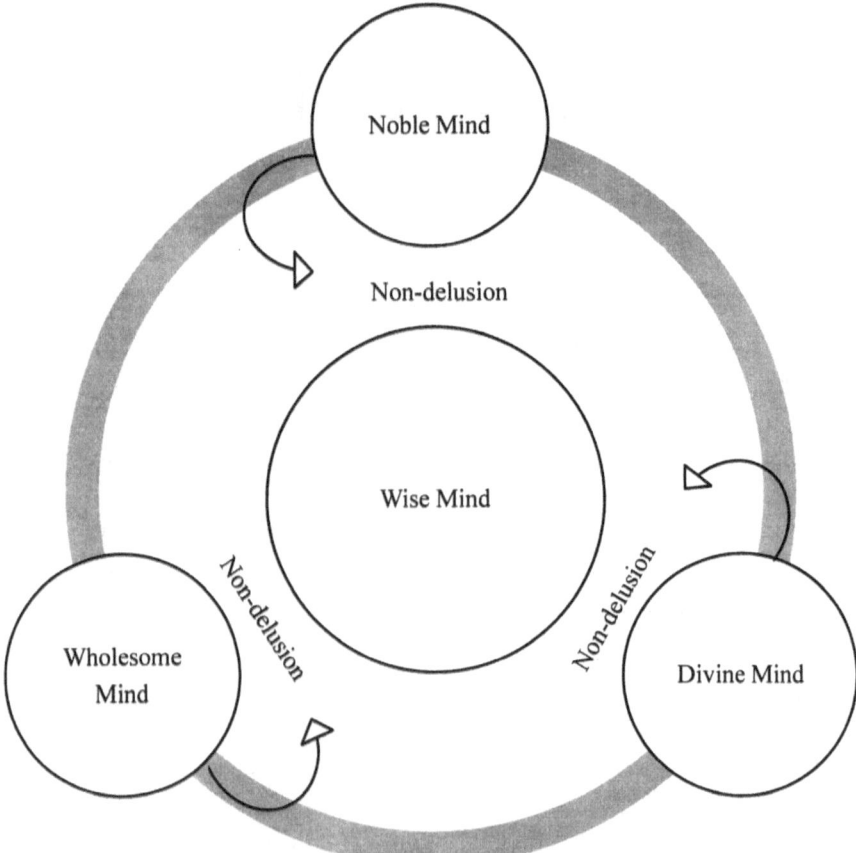

Figure 16.1. The wise mind is made of non-delusion, which results from the development of the wholesome, divine, and noble minds. Known as the wisdom element, non-delusion ultimately brings perfection to the mind.

CHAPTER 16 THE WISE MIND

Non-delusion is the subtlest of mental elements. It can only be arrived at by removing layer after layer of delusion, a task much like peeling an onion to the core. This core, when arrived at, is found to be thoroughly empty. In this sense, non-delusion is the faculty of mind that eliminates mental confusion and bewilderment by guiding us to the core of nothingness, which means *no thing-ness* (such as I-ness), aka selflessness.

Non-delusion should not be understood merely as the absence of delusion. It also is the opposite of delusion, that by means of which we can rid ourselves of delusion. Non-delusion is an active parameter.

The mere absence of delusion does not make one wise. It requires both absence of delusion and presence of non-delusion to become wise. Similarly, mere absence of delusion does not result in the end of ignorance. It is due to the absence of delusion *and* the presence of non-delusion that one can destroy ignorance and attain freedom from all imperfections.

Non-delusion has its own intrinsic nature.

Psychologically, non-delusion means the absence of ego. Non-delusion manifests as knowing the self in terms of the phenomena of body-mind-consciousness or of materiality-mentality. Non-delusion makes you know yourself as you are and not as you appear to be. This knowing is principally different from the manners of perceiving and cognizing. This knowing is *simply knowing,* which is an extremely subtle state beyond mind-consciousness and at the same time not separate from it. This knowing is not always present in mind-consciousness, so it needs to be cultivated.

When we perceive a body, we know it as a male or female, short or tall, beautiful or ugly, and so on. Mere perception cannot know the deeper aspects of the body. When we go further and try to cognize human body, we penetrate the perceptual layer and experientially understand the body as an impermanent and impersonal phenomenon of matter. For cognition to occur, the body has to be experienced as a changing phenomenon of matter that is happening of its own accord without the control of any fixed entity. This happens through meditation and contemplation.

Mere cognition of change and non-self cannot arouse wisdom. Non-delusion arises when, and only when, the cognition of change and non-self manifests as wisdom. The arousal of wisdom is what the element of non-delusion is all about. The subtle difference between cognition and wisdom is that in cognition there is still a hidden cognizer, whereas in wisdom there is only awareness and understanding without a subtle feeling of being a self that is aware. Wisdom is *pure understanding*.

Wisdom is the act of knowing that is rooted in non-delusion. Such knowing is egoless knowing. It completely releases us from the subtlest knots of bondage of all ego-driven concepts, perceptions, and cognitions, and culminates in perfection. Non-delusion is ultimately responsible for the attainment of perfect intelligence.

Imagine that three people are looking at a vintage car: a perceiver, a cognizer, and a wise person. The perceiver simply *perceives* (knows) the car as an old vehicle. The cognizer knows the car as a vintage car—a collector's car—that is a precious vehicle because he has *experienced* its value in the marketplace. The wise (non-deluded) person not only recognizes the car as a precious vehicle but also as a luxury sports vehicle having so much horsepower and so much fuel efficiency, and as being made of such-and-such materials by such-and-such carmaker with a certain reputation. A wise person *understands* the car by extending the penetration so deeply and thoroughly that nothing else remains to be known about the car.

Notwithstanding the preceding description, non-delusion should not be confused with thoroughness or material perfection. The example was a simple way of demonstrating the subtle difference between perceiving, cognizing, and understanding. Let us look at how these distinctions can help us in daily life.

You are driving through busy streets of a metropolis, running late, trying to reach your office on time. Suddenly you are overtaken by a speeding car, which cuts across your path just before the traffic lights turn red, thus forcing you to stop. If you look at this episode from the viewpoint of a perceptive mind, you will most likely feel frustrated

CHAPTER 16 THE WISE MIND

and enraged, and burn with these feelings. If you look at it from the viewpoint of a cognitive mind, you will detect these unpleasant feelings and identify them as a reaction to the event.

If you apply the element of non-delusion to the same situation, you will realize the truth of your reaction and try to figure out what caused it. In addition you'll wonder what prompted the other driver to speed up like that. Non-delusion creates an opportunity to investigate why someone would do such a thing. You might guess that the guy was in a hurry to take someone to the hospital or that he was running late and desperately needed to be somewhere, rather than deciding that the guy is a jerk who was put on Earth to ruin your morning. Due to the application of non-delusion, you will set aside your ego and try to *understand*.

Pragmatically speaking, non-delusion can be appreciated as a mental faculty that enables us to understand others and ourselves. Based on my own practice, I have come to value non-delusion as a force generating empathy and peace within my relationships.

Philosophically, non-delusion is pure knowledge. It can be identified as the purest state of awareness, meaning a state of consciousness that has been purified of all traces of ignorance.

Spiritually, non-delusion is the state of enlightenment. Being non-deluded simply means abiding in pure awareness.

Since non-delusion is the subtlest of all elements, it is the most powerful. The ultimate mental power that arises out of non-delusion is like nuclear power arising out of the ultimate core of matter.[1] The only difference is that the ultimate power of non-delusion does not have any side effects. It is foolproof. It cannot be used for unwholesome purposes. It is thoroughly wholesome under all circumstances and in every situation. It is the prime root element, which is present to some degree in all states of wholesome consciousness.

If you want to set one goal for your entire life, the development of non-delusion would be my suggestion.

* * *

Part III

Soul Realization: The Attainment of Perfect Intelligence

Using the theoretical understanding you developed through studying Parts One and Two of this book as a platform, you are ready to participate in a course of experiential study, which over time leads to soul realization. The scope of experiential study involves undertaking five specific groups of practices, as described in the upcoming five chapters. These practices are designed to help you develop an intelligent attitude, intelligent senses, an intelligent body, an intelligent mind, and an intelligent heart. They will support, train, strengthen, develop, and sharpen your faculties of meditation and understanding, without which the attainment of perfect intelligence is not possible.

The five specific groups of practices are also essential for developing an energetic, virtuous, and contemplative lifestyle. This lifestyle facilitates embarking upon and continuing on a long and arduous (but most gratifying) journey of soul realization.

Begin with a spiritual sentiment. This is the key to undertaking spiritual practices. Spiritual sentiment is a deep, tender, refined feeling of commitment to the purification and perfection of being. I humbly suggest that you do not practice simply for the purpose of moral or personal development, or, train merely for the sake of developing abilities, life strategies, or skills. That could be counterproductive. It could lead to commercializing, self-labeling, self-imaging, and cultism.

In addition, focus on internalizing the practices, which I like to call "pure learning." Without pure learning, transformation won't occur. Pure learning takes place only through *playful,* active-passive self-instruction and not through blind or rigid adherence to a book or a teacher. The various forms of soul meditation and contemplation prescribed in the remaining chapters of this book are examples of pure learning. Modify them as necessary based on your experience, and practice them *lightheartedly* until you are enlightened.

Do not settle for less.

* * *

Chapter 17

Developing an Intelligent Attitude

An *attitude* is a mindset, a mental position or a mental manner that is built by developing mental qualities. An *intelligent attitude* is built by developing wholesome mental qualities (virtues), whereas an *egoistic attitude* is built by developing unwholesome mental qualities (vices).

An intelligent attitude has two parts. The first is related to the mental manners in which we deal with others. The second is related to the mental manners in which we deal with ourselves. In order to develop an intelligent attitude, we need to work on building both parts of our attitude simultaneously. The first part is built by developing five virtues: non-violence, truthfulness, non-stealing, non-indulgence, and sexual piety. The second part is built by developing another five virtues: physical purity, contentment, austerity, self-study, and surrender.

THE ELEMENTS OF SOUL

In this chapter, we will discuss each of these ten virtues in detail.[1] Studying and developing them, you will discover that they are fundamentally rooted in the elements of non-greed, non-hatred, and non-delusion, because of which their development results in the most efficient shakeup of the ego and the subsequent loosening of its grip on the mind. Loosening the ego's grip is the most favorable condition for undertaking the intensive soul meditation practices that are described in subsequent chapters, practices which eventually give rise to higher levels of intelligence.

The opposites of these ten virtues are the vices of lying, killing, stealing, sexual misconduct, overindulgence, impure living, discontentment, lack of austerity, lack of self-study, judgment, fighting, and lack of surrender. These vices contribute *most significantly* to building and strengthening greed, hatred, and delusion, the three roots of the unwholesome mind. They also create huge stockpiles of harmful memories (mental impressions), which generally come to the surface during meditation and adversely impact the ability to remain mindful, non-reactive, and focused. It takes significant and prolonged efforts to eradicate harmful memories. Therefore, the opposites of the ten virtues are the most unprofitable vices from the standpoint of practicing soul meditation (or any activity related to wholesome mental development). They bring about the maximum loss in meditativity and the biggest fall in climbing the intelligence ladder.

Your ability to do soul meditation well will improve as you train in developing the ten virtues. The more often and the more effectively you practice soul meditation, the easier it will be to develop an intelligent attitude.

On an advisory note: Do not turn the virtues into a doctrine of self-discipline, a system of morality, or religious commandments. If the virtues are treated as disciplines or the basis of morality they actually lose their purifying power.

Virtues are more than moral values. The basic element of virtue is the *volition* for mental purification and perfection. A self-disciplined and moral person can be arrogant, self-serving, rigid, and extreme, whereas a virtuous person is composed, blameless, and sagacious. He is calm and cool in all his actions, because he avoids all extremes.

The Virtue of Non-violence

Non-violence means not hurting or harming another living being in any manner, and not violating the peace of others. It means becoming non-resistant. In daily life, if you consider this not as a philosophical view, but as a pragmatic definition, it will be of great benefit to you.

Violence generally results from a strong sense of separation between the world and us. Practicing non-violence slowly removes the sense of separation by loosening the grip of the ego. As we loosen up this grip, we become more inclined towards developing loving-kindness and compassion. Ultimately, these two divine qualities no longer remain a mystery. Due to the practice of non-violence, they start making sense as we experience their power in our life.

The virtue of non-violence can be developed through the following practices.
- Not killing another living being
- Not hurting or harming anyone in any way, either by speech or by physical actions
- Not intentionally disturbing others' peace of mind
- Not encroaching upon others' space, but rather giving space to all to live and evolve
- Not forcing or pushing anyone for anything, even with good intentions
- Accepting circumstances and situations *as they are* without resistance and without losing your ground. Be like a bamboo tree, which neither resists strong winds, nor gives up its ground. A bamboo tree simply bends when the wind is strong and stands upright when the wind abates. It "wins" without fighting

In addition, the virtue of non-violence can be developed through the practice of soul meditation as follows.
- Remaining mindful of all physical and verbal actions

- Not reacting to the fearful, hateful, or unwholesome thoughts that generate violent tendencies
- Giving wise attention to the impermanent and impersonal nature of such tendencies, and allowing them to subside in mind on their own before they gain enough strength and turn into violent physical or verbal actions
- Concentrating on developing the divine qualities of loving-kindness and compassion

Developing the virtue of non-violence is especially useful for those who are aggressive, possessive, passionate, or hateful in temperament.

The Virtue of Truthfulness

Truthfulness simply means being grounded in reality and upholding it. It means not lying. It also means expressing the facts as they are.

People who lie have the tendency to be greedy, fearful, weak, lazy, and worrisome. They are not courageous or patient enough to face the truth. They are not audacious enough to face unfavorable situations. By lying, they find an easy way out. But they harm themselves by lying, because they reinforce in their consciousness unwholesome mental elements, such as greed, hatred, delusion, sloth, torpor, and restlessness. The more people lie the more fearful, greedy, weak, lazy, and worrisome they become, which in turn leads them to lie again.

Lying is a vicious cycle. It's important to break out of this cycle as soon as possible. Otherwise, it soon becomes a disease of consciousness.

Nothing else strains and disturbs the consciousness as much as lying does. Nothing else increases the chances of developing illusion, delusion, or ignorance more than lying does. People who lie fool themselves, because truth actually cannot be hidden. Therefore, lying must be abandoned completely by developing the virtue of truthfulness as follows.

- Doing what you say you will do
- Saying what you mean or intend

CHAPTER 17   DEVELOPING AN INTELLIGENT ATTITUDE

- Neither exaggerating nor understating facts, which means expressing facts *as they are*
- Not speaking cleverly or scholarly or vaguely to intentionally hide the truth
- Not speaking too much
- Speaking only the truth, and standing up for it at all times in all situations

In addition, the virtue of truthfulness can be developed through the practice of soul meditation as follows.

- Remaining mindful of every word of your speech
- Not reacting to the greedy, fearful, or unwholesome thoughts that generate the tendency of lying
- Giving wise attention to the impermanent and impersonal nature of such tendencies, and allowing them to subside in mind on their own before they gain enough strength to turn into the verbal action of lying
- Concentrating on upholding the truth unconditionally, at any cost

The consistent practicing of truthfulness makes us courageous, fearless, decisive, energetic, zestful, intuitive, and carefree. Truthfulness effectively boosts the energy we have available for action. Truthfulness is the fastest way to achieve perfection in our actions, and the easiest and surest way we can feel good about ourselves is to speak the truth. The quickest way to get rid of hatred, envy, avarice, worry, and doubt is to wholeheartedly embrace the truth. When we speak truthfully, we purify our communication. Also, we make many friends since we are perceived as trustworthy.

Developing the virtue of truthfulness is especially useful for those who are lazy, greedy, possessive, weak, and delusive in temperament.

The Virtue of Non-stealing

People steal or exploit others because of fear, envy, greed, conceit, laziness, shamelessness, and boldness. Stealing, exploitation, corruption, and the like are nothing but cowardice in disguise. Every act of stealing, exploitation, and corruption greatly strengthens the

unwholesome mind. Therefore, such acts must be abandoned entirely by developing the virtue of non-stealing as follows.
- Not taking or using anything that belongs to others without permission
- Not charging without working, not overcharging, not manipulating or doing accounting tricks to meet financial expectations and goals
- Not exploiting others, especially those who are weak and needy
- Not being corrupt by virtue of power or authority

In addition, the virtue of non-stealing can be developed through the practice of soul meditation as follows.
- Remaining mindful of greedy desires of acquisition
- Not reacting to the greedy, conceited, fearful, or unwholesome thoughts that generate the tendencies of stealing
- Giving wise attention to the impermanent and impersonal nature of such tendencies, and allowing them to subside in the mind on their own before they gain enough strength to turn into the physical action of stealing
- Concentrating on upholding the qualities of honesty, integrity, fearlessness, and generosity

Whenever we have a desire to *acquire* something, we should first become aware of it and then contemplate its nature to make sure that there is no stealing, exploitation, or corruption involved in our desire. The best way to notice any trace of unwholesome mind in our acquiring actions is to observe how it feels while performing the act. A practitioner of soul meditation can easily notice a feeling of shamelessness and fear during the actions of stealing, exploitation or corruption. In the beginning, this feeling may be overtaken by greed and conceit. However, there always remains an aftereffect of shamelessness. As we become aware of this kind of feeling, we need to use its unpleasant nature to train ourselves not to react to acquiring desires and to let them simply come and go each time they arise. At the same time, we need to recollect, contemplate, and concentrate on the wholesome qualities of honesty, integrity, fearlessness, and generosity.

Developing the virtue of non-stealing is especially useful in eradicating the fear of poverty and loss. All the exploitation, corruption, embezzlement, and appropriation in the world would cease to exist if everyone were to perfect the virtue of non-stealing.

The Virtue of Sexual Piety

Sexual conduct based on conscience and shame (self-respect, respect for others, dignity, and honor) is sexual piety. The virtue of sexual piety is necessary for the removal of greed and lust. In daily life, it can be developed as follows.
- Refraining from all forms of sexual misconduct and shamelessness
- Involvement in sexual relationships that are only based on the partners' faith and devotion for each other
- Performing sexual activities only as a means to experience wholeness and oneness, rather than for satisfying one's lust

In addition, the virtue of sexual piety can be developed through the practice of soul meditation as follows.
- Remaining mindful of all lustful desires
- Not reacting blindly to such desires, but skillfully attending to them
- Giving wise attention to the impermanent and impersonal nature of such desires, and allowing them to subside in mind on their own before they gain enough strength to turn into lustful physical actions
- Concentrating on upholding the qualities of faithfulness, devoutness, wholeness, oneness, and non-greed

Recollect and contemplate on sexual piety prior to entering any sexual relationship. Before entering into physical union with a partner, aim to become aware of any lustful feelings. If you realize that you are being driven by lust, simply freeze and do not proceed with physical union. Step back for a few moments and observe those lustful feelings as they arise and cease. As the lustful feelings start losing strength, begin to recollect and contemplate on the wholesome quality of sexual piety. Only when you begin to feel a sense of faithfulness and devotion towards your partner should you proceed further into physical union. Throughout the physical union, maintain awareness of your feelings so you can experience moments of wholeness and oneness in your sexual activities.

Because it is easy to be carried away by the formidable power of lust, maintaining awareness during sexual conduct is most critical. If you remain meditative, the overall experience and aftereffects of sexual activity will always be blissful. With the sustained practice of sexual piety, the aspect of physical union becomes secondary. You not only start feeling that you are demonstrating love more often towards your partner (rather than simply satisfying lust), but also that your partner loves you.

Do not intentionally perform sexual activity as a means to train yourself in sexual piety, because it is not a means to an end. It simply is an attitudinal restraint to remove lust. Be wise and do not allow mind to justify sexual indulgence by cleverly devising various philosophies and ideologies around sexual piety.[2]

Sexual piety should be used to eliminate sexual misconduct, to minimize sexual indulgence, and to retire eventually from indulging in sexual thoughts in old age. Such retiring is necessary because our bodies are not capable of responding in old age to sexual thoughts, which could cause us to burn in the fire of unfulfilled desires and experience unimaginable suffering.

The Virtue of Non-indulgence

Non-indulgence is an attitudinal restraint for removing delusion, greed, conceit, sloth and torpor. Developing the virtue of non-indulgence means:
- Avoiding all excesses, luxuries, and extravagance.
- Not collecting things for greater and greater comfort.
- Not collecting things for more and more consumption.
- Living in moderation and minimizing liabilities.

CHAPTER 17 DEVELOPING AN INTELLIGENT ATTITUDE

- Clearly knowing our necessities and acquiring things only to fulfill our needs.
- Developing simplicity.
- Conserving resources and supplies.

The virtue of non-indulgence can be developed through the practice of soul meditation as follows.

- Becoming mindful of wants and greedy desires
- Not reacting to wants and greedy desires
- Giving wise attention to the impermanent and impersonal nature of greedy desires, and allowing them to subside in the mind on their own before they gain sufficient strength to turn into the physical action of acquiring more stuff
- Concentrating on non-greed, moderation, simplicity, conservation, and the management of resources

Many of us are self-indulgent because we do not understand the distinction between wanting and needing. We keep reacting to our wants by acquiring more things. One want leads to another until very soon the material things that surround us overwhelm us. Things start ruling our lives. Eventually we are enslaved to them. Therefore, before deciding to buy more, we need to become aware of our thoughts, so we can detect greed. We simply need to remain aware of greedy thoughts as they arise and pass away and not react to them by jumping into the car to go shopping. We need to give wise attention not only to the impermanent and impersonal nature of greedy thoughts, but also to the situation that's triggering greed, so that we can simplify the situation and thereby avoid increasing our liabilities. We need to make a sincere effort to try to find out if we can live without what is being acquired. In most cases, we can eliminate the want by using conservation and management techniques and minimize liabilities.

Developing the virtue of non-indulgence is one of the best ways to free oneself for spiritual practice.

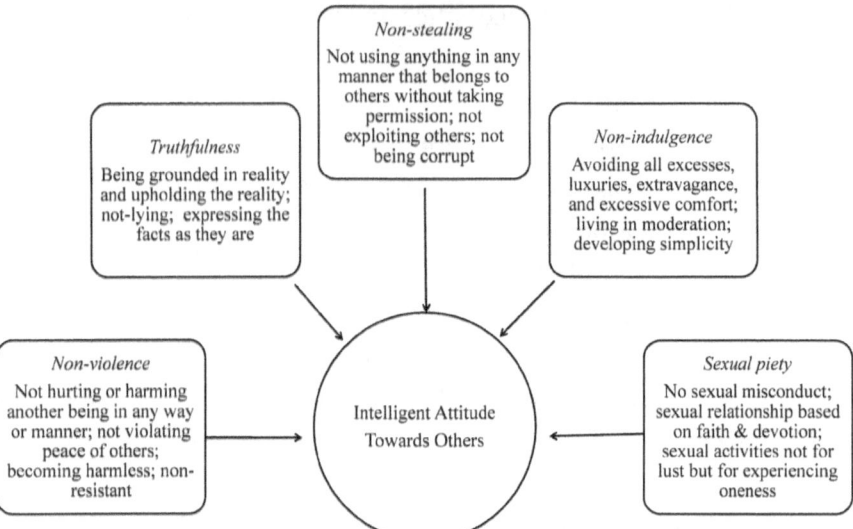

Figure 17.1. Five specific virtues for developing an intelligent attitude towards others.

This concludes our discussion of the five virtues that lead to the development of an intelligent attitude towards others. For my own practice, I use the preceding illustration (figure 17.1) as a reminder card. It is posted on my refrigerator and on the dashboard of my car.

Let us now talk about the five virtues that lead to the development of an intelligent attitude towards oneself. These resemble the five wholesome practices of day-to-day living and serve as a foundation for the possibly long, sometimes arduous upward journey of developing higher and higher levels of intelligence.

The Virtue of Physical Purity

Keeping the body pure and clean, outside *and* inside, comes from:
- Regular bathing and hygienic practices.
- Avoiding intoxicants, such as alcoholic drinks, soda, tea, and coffee, which not only harm the body, but also imbalance the mind.
- Refraining from smoking or chewing tobacco.
- Refraining from drugs, other than necessary medications, as the use of drugs—and especially the abuse of drugs—leads to immense physical, physiological, and mental impurity (*Caution:*

CHAPTER 17 DEVELOPING AN INTELLIGENT ATTITUDE

Before decreasing the dosage or going off of any prescribed medication it is advisable to consult a professional health care practitioner, as there may be risks of stopping medication).
- Avoiding the consumption of oily, fatty, and stale foods, which make the body-mind dull and lethargic.
- Not eating too much meat, as meat typically arouses the lust for food and sex.
- Drinking at least two gallons (about six–eight glasses) of water daily to flush toxins out of the body.
- Eating water-rich, fibrous fruits and vegetables to clean the digestive tract.

The virtue of physical purity can be developed by practicing soul meditation as follows.
- Becoming mindful of gastronomic cravings and other intoxicating desires
- Not reacting to such cravings and desires
- Giving wise attention to the impermanent and impersonal nature of such cravings and desires, and allowing them to subside in mind on their own before they gain sufficient strength to turn into the physical action of consuming unhealthy foods and intoxicants
- Concentrating on the benefits of physical purity and physical well-being

Eating oily, fatty, and stale foods and drinking intoxicants makes it hard to meditate, contemplate, and think deeply. Lightness of body and good physical health are necessary in order to perform challenging mental activities such as meditation and contemplation. Moreover, if one is under the influence of intoxicants, one's attitude will suffer. It is more likely that one will lie, steal, or sexually misbehave.

The virtue of physical purity has a huge potential to release one from harmful habits and addictions, such as smoking and drinking. The probability of incurring this benefit deepens if one is regularly practicing soul meditation for physical purity.

Here's an example. Whenever you feel like drinking alcohol, become aware of the physical sensations that underlie your craving for alcohol, observing them without reacting. The first step is to *become aware* of craving. If you are not aware, then nothing else is possible. Once you become aware of an arisen craving, simply observe it until it passes away so that you avoid grabbing a drink out of reaction. Because no craving or feeling lasts forever, you will soon realize that your cravings arise due to habitual patterns of mind, and they subside on their own when you do not cling to them.

Also give wise attention to your cravings, understanding that the cravings are not only momentary and changing, but also impersonal. Your aim is to understand that no person, being, or self is doing the craving. Craving is simply a physical-mental phenomenon, that's all. As you establish yourselves in giving such wise attention to the craving, you will not feel remorseful if you succumb to the craving and drink. You will simply realize the conditionality behind the craving and you will try again to not react to it. In this way, you will slowly get rid of the addiction without frustration and remorse, especially if you constantly focus on the benefits of physical purity and well-being.

In this way, if you practice soul meditation, you can become free of all addictions. However, do not expect overnight results. Since you are dealing with mind, which is quite stubborn, you must remain patient, as well as training consistently and ardently. (See upcoming chapters for more specific meditations on how to deal with addictions.)

Unless we maintain physical purity, we cannot seriously pursue the spiritual practices that lead to higher levels of intelligence.

The Virtue of Contentment

Contentment means being satisfied with whatever one has. It is developed by:
- Not wanting more.
- Having few wishes.

In addition, the virtue of contentment is developed by practicing soul meditation as follows.
- Becoming mindful of goals, wants, and desires

CHAPTER 17 DEVELOPING AN INTELLIGENT ATTITUDE

- Not reacting to the feelings that arise from goals, wants, and desires
- Giving wise attention to their impermanent and impersonal nature, and allowing them to subside in mind on their own before they gain sufficient strength to turn into cravings and passion
- Concentrating on the benefits of contentment and the attainment of higher states of mind

Not wanting more and having few wishes do not mean *not having goals*. They also do not mean giving up the pursuit of excellence. They simply mean pursuing higher states of mind rather than striving for more and more of the same thing. For instance, if you are a millionaire, become content with that and do not effort to become a multimillionaire. Instead pursue or improve upon your artistic skills, relationships, social involvements, spirituality, and so on. These are higher states of attainment than becoming wealthier and amassing possessions. Unless we are content with the material things and wealth we have, we cannot succeed in attaining higher levels of intelligence.

Having few wishes is paramount in meditation because it is difficult to concentrate if we are constantly thinking about achieving this and achieving that, or becoming this and becoming that. When we are not content, the mind becomes greedy and wanders around like a monkey in search of something to amuse itself. The greedy mind simply cannot remain present in the moment. Moreover, if we are not content because of greed we are more likely to lie and steal, and even to kill. The virtue of contentment thus supports and strengthens other virtues that make up an intelligent attitude.

Practicing soul meditation for developing the virtue of contentment is a means to cultivate a wholesome lifestyle. Whenever there is a desire or a want, become aware of it and contemplate its nature to find out whether it is a desire for more of the same thing (greed) or a desire to excel and improve. If there is an undercurrent of greed, then simply observe the desire without reacting. Give wise attention to it, which means, not only do a check on greed, but also compare how you feel when you are greedy and when you are content. Become specifically aware of how restless greed makes you feel and how peaceful contentment makes you feel. Reinforce this awareness as much as possible, so that you are more likely to effort to become *content* than to *compete* to acquire more.

Ultimately contentment comes only through the purifying effect of meditation—in essence, neither by suppressing desires nor by thinking positively about higher states to temporarily control the desires. Positive thinking is a superficial, cosmetic mental treatment. It just does not go deep enough to transform us. It is superficial because it takes place only at the thinking level and does not reach the depths of consciousness where the roots of greed are embedded. Soul meditation, on the other hand, reaches the depth of consciousness, as it transcends the superficial mental activity of positive thinking and actually eradicates greed, which is the root cause of discontent.

The Virtue of Austerity

Austerity means wholesome rigor. It does not equate with pain or loss, as is sometimes erroneously believed. In fact, it makes the soul journey pleasant and enjoyable. It speeds up the process of climbing the ladder of intelligence. It is spiritually rewarding.

Developing the virtue of austerity means:
- Living upon the minimum resources necessary, so that there is neither physical torture, nor indulgence. This requires a balanced level of convenience and comfort.
- Living in a moderate-sized house—neither cramped, nor overly spacious.
- Neither fasting, nor overeating. Eat so that your stomach always remains 30 percent empty.
- Speaking sparingly, listening frequently, and avoiding frivolous chatting, useless discussions, criticism, and so on.
- Neither being miserly, nor being wasteful.
- Avoiding noisy and crowded places.
- Avoiding excessive or back-to-back entertainment.

CHAPTER 17 DEVELOPING AN INTELLIGENT ATTITUDE

- Spending more time in silence and seclusion than with people.
- Minimizing (rather than suppressing) sexual activities and eventually eliminating sexual thoughts as old age approaches.

Also, the virtue of austerity can be developed by practicing soul meditation as follows.

- Remaining mindful of desires for more: more things, food, talk, entertainment, money, space, power, and so on
- Not reacting to such desires
- Giving wise attention to the impermanent and impersonal nature of such desires, and allowing them to subside in mind on their own before they gain sufficient strength to turn into cravings and struggle for opulence, material abundance, and undue comfort
- Concentrating on the beneficial aftereffects of austerity, which include wakefulness, alertness, energy, and a sense of accomplishment

Whenever you feel like having "more," observe that feeling without reacting, recollect the benefits of austerity, and compare those benefits to the conditions of non-austere living. Such recollection and comparison will arouse the energy for non-reaction and wise attention.

Whenever you succeed in not reacting to the desire for "more," observe how good you feel. The aftereffects are wonderful. In the beginning of being austere, it may be painful or even distasteful. You may find it hard to stop eating when your stomach is 70 percent full, but if you stop anyway later you'll notice that you are more alert and energetic than before. In addition, you will notice a sense of accomplishment and the pleasant feeling of being able to master the mind.

Austerity begets wholesome discipline. It helps minimize the controlling influence of the immediate environment on the body and mind. It helps the body and mind stay awake, alert, and energetic. These qualities are necessary both for having fun and maintaining the stamina while working hard, as well as for making the efforts significant. Without such a combination of "fun, hard work, stamina and results" the extraordinary pursuit of higher intelligence does not last for long.

The Virtue of Self-study

Self-study means wholesome doing, studying, experimenting, and learning through one's life experiences. The virtue of self-study is developed as follows.
- Studying philosophical, psychological, and spiritual literature
- Interacting and spending more time with refined, studious, and industrious people and avoiding the company of unrefined, unintelligent, and lazy people
- Using the senses (watching, reading, or listening) not for entertainment but for the purpose of studying oneself and the surrounding world as it relates to oneself
- Making one's life a laboratory for knowing oneself and the world at ever deeper levels
- Using all experiences to enlighten oneself about the causes of one's actions, the effects of one's reactions, and the inherent nature of actions and reactions
- Accepting the facts about oneself and the world only based on the results of studying, contemplating, experimenting, and reflecting upon the results and the cause-effect relationships. Never accepting anything blindly out of cultural attachment, tradition, emotion, devotion, belief, and so on

In addition, practicing the following soul meditation develops the virtue of self-study.
- Becoming mindful of one's strengths and weaknesses
- Not reacting to strengths and weaknesses, meaning, neither becoming proud or overconfident because of strengths, nor discouraged or dispirited because of weaknesses
- Giving wise attention to the impermanent and impersonal nature of one's strengths and weaknesses
- Concentrating on consistent self-improvement and spiritual evolution

CHAPTER 17 DEVELOPING AN INTELLIGENT ATTITUDE

The virtue of self-study should be used to increase awareness of our actions and reactions so that our strengths and weaknesses can be revealed to us *by us*. When that happens, we are more willing to accept who we are. We also become more able to strategically utilize our strengths to eliminate our weaknesses for our own benefit and for the benefit of others.

Let's say I have the weakness of blowing up when an argument, discussion, or debate does not go my way. In this case, if I were to apply the virtue of self-study, I would first aim to become *aware* of the fact that I am an angry person. Then, I would contemplate the circumstances that led me to anger in the past, so I would know what triggers my temper. Once I am aware of my weakness and the triggers, I enter future debates, during which I observe how unpleasant it feels when temper arises in me, how tiring it feels afterwards, how harmful it is, and how I incur huge losses (if I lose my temper) or benefits (if I don't lose my temper). Once an argument, discussion, or debate is over, through wise attention I find out why I was angry, what caused it, and why and how it ended. What specific strength or quality helped me end it?

In this way, due to the virtue of self-study we can understand ourselves in terms of our strengths and weaknesses, and avoid judging, evaluating, or analyzing other people. In self-study, we only study ourselves and no one else. We also study the world—however, only in relation to ourselves.

Knowing oneself through self-study is a giant initial step towards removing the hindrances of anger, sensual pleasures, gross delusion, and laziness. When such hindrances are removed through self-study, spiritual evolution automatically leads one towards the four divine qualities of loving-kindness, compassion, gladness, and equanimity. Developing these qualities ensures success in the process of attaining perfect intelligence.

Many people never grow or evolve because they never make an effort to know who they are and identify their weaknesses. The virtue of self-study can help such people tremendously.

The Virtue of Surrender

A carefree, peaceful mindset is the result of surrender, a virtue that is developed by:
- Laying down arms and non-resisting.
- Freeing oneself from the burden of judgment.
- Freeing oneself from the burden of fighting for justice.
- Developing trust in the fairness of the laws of karma (soul mechanics, conditionality, and so on).
- Surrendering to the laws of karma as the ultimate authority on delivering justice.

Practicing soul meditation as follows can also develop the virtue of surrender.
- Remaining mindful of the laws of karma and their perfect accounting capability
- Not reacting to feelings of unfairness, injustice, heaviness, and rigidity, or to a tendency for judging, fighting, resisting, and so on
- Giving wise attention to the impermanent and impersonal nature of such unwholesome tendencies, and allowing them to subside in mind on their own before they gain enough strength to turn into the physical and mental actions of judging, fighting, and resisting
- Concentrating on the beauty and power of surrender, and on becoming peaceful and carefree

Whenever there is a feeling of unfairness, injustice, heaviness, or rigidity, become aware of it and observe it in light of the virtue of surrender. Concentrate on the benefits of becoming peaceful and carefree, and then notice how those unwholesome feelings eventually die out. Whenever there is a tendency to be hypocritical, forceful, judging, and so on, become aware of it and observe it as you surrender to the laws of karma that govern the universe. Let the universe handle the task of dispensing justice. When you do that, notice how quickly the unwholesome tendencies of fighting for justice or fairness

CHAPTER 17 DEVELOPING AN INTELLIGENT ATTITUDE

begin to lose strength, and how light and malleable you begin to feel in the body and mind.

Surrendering in this way has a profound effect on one's being. It generates impartiality, lightness, straightforwardness, faithfulness, flexibility, non-resistance, and non-attachment. These qualities facilitate effortlessness in one's actions and eventually, due to surrendering, one becomes peaceful and carefree.

Let's say a colleague deceives you during a business deal. In a situation like this, if you are surrendering, it does not mean you will simply abandon or overlook what your colleague did. Also, you do not say, "Let me not worry and let me not fight for justice because the universe will judge him and he will be punished fairly." This would not be in the spirit of surrender. If you are rightfully surrendering, what you will do is recollect the laws of karma and understand that the unwholesome action of your colleague will generate unwholesome fruit. A sense of compassion will then arise in you for your colleague because you will know for sure that your colleague is going to suffer now or later as a result of his unwholesome action. Due to compassion arising out of surrender, you will feel light, peaceful, and at ease. Notice that it is compassion (and *not* a sense of getting justice or getting even) that has positive results. For this to occur, you will have to firmly establish yourself in surrendering to the ultimate laws of the universe—the laws of karma. Your faith in them should be unshakable.

In many spiritual traditions, the ultimate laws of the universe are misunderstood as God. The practice of surrendering is therefore mistaken as the act of surrendering to God.[3] This is wrong. The act of surrender actually is not something that happens between two entities (you and God). It is absolute, meaning it is non-relative.

If you imagine that you are surrendering to the judgment of an entity, such as God, you are simply shifting the ego and passing on the burden of judgment to that entity. In surrender, there is absolute letting go of everything, including the judge, the one being judged, and the judgment. In surrender, there is no desire or wish for justice. Instead, there is forgiveness. This is the definition of absolute letting go, based on perfect understanding of the accountability of the laws of karma.

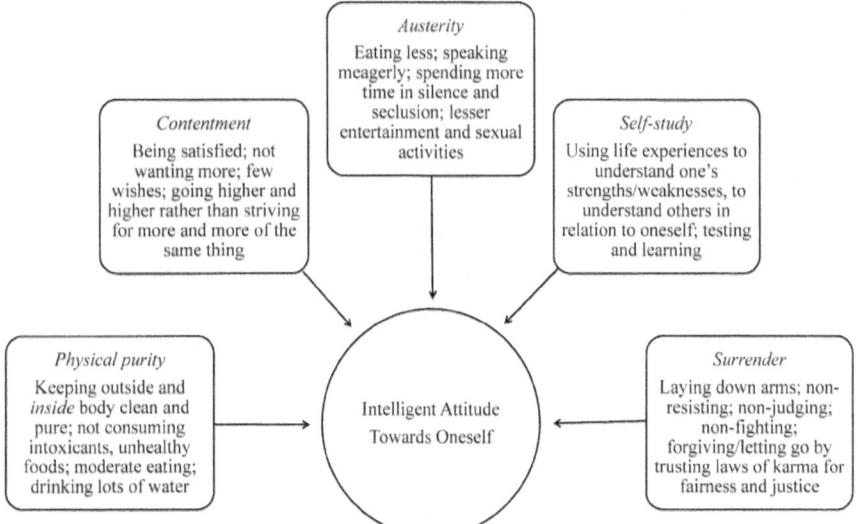

Figure 17.2. Five specific virtues for developing an intelligent attitude towards oneself.

This concludes our discussion of the five virtues that lead to the development of an intelligent attitude towards oneself. The preceding illustration (figure 17.2) is another reminder card that I have stuck on my refrigerator and on the dashboard of my car.

Is It Really Practical?

Often, I've been asked if it is really practical to implement the ten virtues that we have discussed here. Can they be actually applied in the real world, which is fraught with greed, hatred, competition, and the mentality that seeks to win? People wonder whether or not it is really possible to remain non-violent and truthful when their life, fortune, name, or fame is at stake. They wonder whether or not it is possible to let go of their negative feelings towards an unjust person and forgive when it seems extremely unfair or even suicidal to do so.

These are valid questions and concerns. They also arise in me from time to time. When they do, I simply observe them without reacting,

CHAPTER 17   DEVELOPING AN INTELLIGENT ATTITUDE

which allows me to give wise attention to them. First, I recognize them as the products of a mediocre mindset that thinks in terms of mundane parameters, such as fairness, survival, material loss or gain, name, fame, and so on. Second, I concentrate on inspiring myself to go beyond the mediocrity of this mindset and to live an extraordinarily virtuous life in pursuit of excellence. Third, I embrace the ten virtues that make up an intelligent attitude, as the true marks of excellence. And then, due to wise attention, I am able to practice them wholeheartedly.

I invite you to do the same.

* * *

Chapter 18

Developing Intelligent Senses

Our senses can be ordinary or intelligent. They become ordinary when used primarily for the fulfillment of sensual desires through eating, smelling, seeing, hearing, and touching. Sensual desires mostly include physical pleasures, which never bring fulfillment no matter what amount of energy is expended on them.

Why not? The answer is simple. Just as nothing else lasts, moments of physical pleasure don't last. As fast as they come, they pass away. Because we find it hard to let go we try to hold on to them. But that has no effect on their transience. Even harder is the memory of pleasantness created by our moments of pleasure. Our memories make us want more pleasure, and the more we try to fulfill our desire, the more we crave what is gone. Thus we remain dissatisfied.

The senses and sensual pleasures combined are a trap. As you will soon realize, there is no way out of this trap unless we make the senses intelligent.

The ordinary senses become intelligent when we use them not to fulfill sensual desires but to develop higher levels of intelligence. How to do that will be the subject of the following discussion. For now, let me assure you of one thing: If you use your senses to develop higher levels of intelligence you not only will live an extraordinarily fulfilling sensual life but you will also make your senses supersensitive. Moreover, you will experience the expansion of sense consciousness. *Expanded sense consciousness* is a state of sensual awareness and equanimity in which there is thorough knowledge of sensual experience as the phenomenon of body-mind-consciousness, its impermanence, and no feeling of owning the senses—no attachment to the senses as *my* senses. I guarantee you will find this experience profound and liberating.

At present, this definition of expanded sense consciousness may sound a bit esoteric. But if you undertake the following five practices for developing intelligent senses you may agree to what I have said and appreciate its pragmatic value. The five practices consist of guidelines for developing wholesome sensual habits, including specific soul meditation practices to be employed during sensual activities. Do not view these practices as daily rituals, routines, or guided meditations. Simply study them, try to understand their logic, and then practice them at least once a week—and more if you want.

Intelligent Eating

The purpose of this practice is to transform the activity of eating into a portal of delight and contentment. For that to happen, one has to practice the following whenever possible.

- Eating only with the intention of *providing nourishment* to the body. Not eating for the purpose of savoring food. Not eating in reaction to hunger or when the mouth is watering. Not eating to feed cravings

CHAPTER 18   DEVELOPING INTELLIGENT SENSES

- Remaining silent while eating. If necessary, talking only when mouth is entirely empty
- Not eating while watching TV or reading a newspaper
- Practicing the following soul meditation while eating to develop the habit of experiencing *delight and contentment* in all acts of eating

Begin your session by taking a few deep breaths to become aware of the phenomenon of breathing. Then, breathe normally and move your attention to the inside of your mouth. Really feel around (mentally touch) the whole interior. Mentally ready yourself to eat the meal with the sole intention of providing nourishment to the body. When you have established this intention, take your first bite of the meal.

While chewing, first become aware of the act of chewing and then try to sense the taste of food. Now, become mindful of the taste as a *pleasant* or *unpleasant feeling,* which is what the real nature of taste is. Observe taste as a mere feeling and remain non-reactive to the taste in order to avoid a craving or an aversion to that feeling. Simply observe the feeling as a "feeling" and not as good, bad, tasty, or bland.

If you remain non-reactive in this way, sooner or later you will be able to develop neither a craving for pizza (a tasty, but unhealthy food) nor an aversion to green salad (a bland, but healthy food), thus facilitating you in making healthier food choices. Your food choices no longer will be governed by cravings, but by their nutritional value. This does not mean you will become insensitive to flavors. Contrary to what you might think, you actually will become supersensitive to flavors. You will have a deeper, more heightened experience of the taste of the foods you eat due to the presence of mindfulness and non-reaction.

Let's say you took a bite of semi-sweet dark chocolate. If you were a chocolate lover, a craving would arise because you liked the flavor. If you have practiced intelligent eating, you would observe this craving as a result of your attachment to a *pleasant feeling* (of taste) that has arisen. You would then purposefully not smack your lips or make sounds like, "Mmm." You would not describe the taste mentally and label its aspects. You would simply contemplate the taste as a *mere feeling* and try not clinging to it. Due to non-reaction, any arisen cravings would die out. Moreover, because of increased mindfulness you would experience a deeper flavor of chocolate that you had not experienced before. At the same time, because of the absence of craving, you would not overeat!

If you practice intelligent eating at least once a week for several months you most likely will begin to notice a feeling of delight and contentment while eating that continues after the meal is over. If such feelings do not arise naturally, after the meal is over contemplate like this:

"This meditative eating is healthy, delightful, and fulfilling.

"I feel alive, energetic, and content after the meal.

"It is wonderful."

After experiencing delight and contentment while eating, you will neither overeat nor starve yourself ever again. Moreover, due to the application of mindfulness and non-reaction during intelligent eating you not only will have nourished the body, but also mind.

Intelligent Touching

This practice is for transforming the activity of touching into a portal of healing. Our sense of touch has a healing property. Use it to heal yourself and others.

Try walking barefooted on a beach and feeling the healing touch of the sand. Walk on a well-maintained lawn and feel the healing touch of grass or walk on a soft patch of land and feel the healing touch of soil. You could also sit on the bank of a river with your feet immersed in flowing water and feel the healing touch of the water. Sit outdoors early in the morning to feel the healing touch of a cool breeze on a warm summer day or to feel the healing touch of the warm sunshine on a chilly winter day.

In this way, first understand the sense of touch as a portal of healing experientially. Then, practice the following soul meditation to become established in healing through touch.

CHAPTER 18 DEVELOPING INTELLIGENT SENSES

Close your eyes and take a few deep breaths to become aware of your breathing. Then, breathe normally and move your attention to both of your palms. By touching them mentally, try to feel them from the tips of your fingers to the base of your wrists. Once you become aware of your palms in this way, get ready to physically touch your body with the sole intention of *healing*. Once you have set this intention, begin touching yourself.

Move your palms from the top of your head to the bottom of your feet while touching yourself very slowly and gently. Become mindful of touch as a *physiological feeling* and then recollect its healing nature. Anchor your attention on the healing aspect of touch as you move your palms gently to cover the entire body. Notice how a mere touch turns into a *non-sensual, pleasant feeling* due to anchoring your attention on its feeling and healing nature. However, do not react to its pleasantness and develop a craving for it. Developing non-reaction is of utmost importance for experiencing the healing through pleasantness.[1]

If at first you do not experience healing in your touch, silently say the word "heal" as you move your palms over the body. Synchronize your repetitions of this word with the movement of your palms. Always remain aware of the healing aspect of touch and decide to feel it conspicuously.

With practice, your intention for your touch to be healing will grow stronger until it becomes your second nature. At that time, your ordinary act of touching will have become intelligent touching.

You can also practice intelligent touching while giving your children a bath, anointing them with lotion or oils, massaging them, putting them to sleep, and cuddling them while reading a storybook. You can also practice it on a spouse or lover who is suffering from depression, stress, or disease. If you are working in the field of massage therapy, practice the method of intelligent touching religiously so that you provide maximum benefits to your clients.[2]

With the regular practice of intelligent touching, you will develop supersensitivity to touch due to its healing nature. Supersensitivity will help you to reduce stress and to promote physical *and* mental health. Due to supersensitivity, if you are shy in nature you will become less reclusive. If you are aggressive, you will become gentler and more restrained. You will develop a stronger degree of connectivity in relationships as you transfer healing through all kinds of touching from a mere handshake to hugging to physical intimacy. Due to the practice of intelligent touching, you will develop the power to heal both body and mind.

Intelligent Smelling

This practice is for transforming the activity of smelling into a portal for experiencing sanctity, a sense of holiness or sacredness. Similar to the sense of touch, our sense of smell has healing properties. Use it not only to heal yourself of anxiety and stress but also to experience sanctity.

Try walking through a flower garden and smell the flowery aroma and notice how your state of mind changes quickly. Visit a holy place and smell the essence sticks and burning scented candles, and observe how holy thoughts begin to arise. Sit down with a scented flower or a piece of aromatic fruit, such as a ripe peach and meditate. See how easily you settle down and relax. Also, try aromatherapy. In these ways, first understand the healing property of the sense of smell experientially. Then, practice the following soul meditation to develop the habit of experiencing sanctity through smell.

Close your eyes. Take a few deep breaths and become aware of your breathing. Then, breathe normally and move your attention to your nose. By touching it mentally, really feel its interior and exterior.

Now, get ready to smell your scented flower or incense with the sole intention of *experiencing sanctity*. If you cannot develop the intention, silently utter the words "holy" and "sacred" as you smell the scented object. While smelling it, inhale slowly and gently. Do not take individual sniffs. Just become aware of the pervasive smell in the air as you breathe and sense the distinct *non-sensual, pleasant feeling*, which will arise due to the combining of scented smell with the wholesome intention.

CHAPTER 18 DEVELOPING INTELLIGENT SENSES

Always remain aware of the healing aspect of smell and train to experience sanctity. Try to experience it conspicuously whenever you smell the scents and fragrances.

With practice, your intention for experiencing sanctity will grow stronger until it becomes your second nature. At that time, your ordinary act of smelling will become intelligent smelling, because then you won't indulge in fragrances for sensual pleasure.

Intelligent Hearing

The purpose of intelligent hearing is to transform the activity of hearing into a portal of entrainment and peace. Here, *entrainment* means resonating and synchronizing with sound (such as soft music, a mantra, or words spoken in a conversation), becoming one with it, tuning into it. Entrainment gives you a taste of egoless mind (because it temporarily removes separation) and makes you a great listener and a conversationalist. Most importantly, it conserves energy, generates alpha wave rhythms of the human brain, and leads to the experience of peace.[3] For that to happen, one must do the following.

- Avoid noisy places
- Avoid loud music with violent lyrics
- Listen more to educational and spiritual discourses than to entertainment material
- Listen more and speak less during conversations
- Avoid combining activities, such as eating and reading, with listening
- Avoid the urge to turn on a radio or any entertainment device in reaction to silence or boredom
- As much as possible, spend some time in silence every day
- Practice the following soul meditation to transform the activity of hearing into a portal of entrainment and peace

To begin, close your eyes. Take a few deep breaths and become aware of your breathing. Then, breathe normally and move your attention to your ears. By touching them mentally, try to feel their interior and exterior. Now, listen for a continuous, soft humming sound in the ears, which is always present. Anchor your attention in the ears using that sound. Pursue this action for about five minutes and then let go. Do not be concerned if you are not able to hear the continuous, soft humming sound. Simply keep your attention on the ears.

Turn on a chosen piece of slow, relaxing music or a mantra recording with the sole intention of hearing *the gaps of silence* that exist between words or musical notes (rather than the music or the mantra itself). Once you have set this intention, start actively listening for the gaps.

While listening to these gaps of silence, anchor your attention on them and hear everything else in relation to the silence. Make a genuine effort to hear it conspicuously. It is easy to hear the gaps of silence if you were able to experience the constant humming sound in the ear in the beginning of this meditation. If at first you have trouble anchoring your attention on the gaps of silence, mentally say the word "silence" while noticing the gaps.

Now, pay attention to sounds or words in relation to the silence that you experienced in the gaps. Due to the contrast, you will become aware of sounds or words as a vibration in the ears. You will be able to *feel* the sounds or words. The idea here is to become mindful of sounds or words as a feeling (of vibrations).

This practice will help you not to react with craving or aversion to the sounds you hear. This will also help you not to classify what you hear as loud or soft, harmonious or atonal, fair or unfair, praise or criticism. This will help you become equanimous to the screaming of a child or to the sweetness of her laugh, and ultimately it will make you an unconditionally caring person.

If a craving or an aversion arises to words or sounds, become aware of it and immediately take your attention back to the gaps of silence. Understand *experientially* how mindfulness of silence facilitates non-reaction to words and sounds.

Once you have practiced this meditation for several months, try applying it to sounds in your everyday life. Listen to your favorite pop song and remain aware of the gaps of silence between the words as

CHAPTER 18 DEVELOPING INTELLIGENT SENSES

well as between beats. Notice how your awareness helps you not to get carried away by the song's rhythm and the meaning of the lyrics. Notice how you enjoy the music more and resonate better with the singer's emotions.

While listening to someone in a conversation, anchor your attention in the gaps of silence between spoken words and notice how this anchoring automatically results in you not arguing or interrupting to contribute your own comments.

Notice how you neither feel shy nor reclusive in conversation when you listen in this manner. Notice how you become a good listener, how you better understand the other person's point of view, how you transform negativity into positivity, and how you develop higher sociability. While attending a lecture, notice how you are able to remain non-judgmental and detached from the contents of the conversation by anchoring your attention in the gaps of silence between the words. Most importantly, notice how your mindfulness of the gaps of silence and non-reaction to words give rise to concentration and wise attention. Notice how easy it becomes to increase your attention span, enabling you to learn faster and have better comprehension of everything you hear.

As you develop the habit of remaining mindful of gaps of silence, a day will come when the gaps will lead you to the undercurrent of silence. In other words, the gaps will serve as a portal to the "ocean" of silence that is ever-existing, but not experienced due to its subtlety. You will begin to abide in this undercurrent as you listen to whatever comes in contact with your ears. You will begin to notice that all sounds are underlain by perpetual silence. It is somewhat like noticing the all-encompassing space that occupies every object in the universe.

The moments of abiding in the undercurrent of silence will become the moments of your entrainment because in those moments you will resonate, synchronize, and become one with whatever you are hearing. In those moments, your being will vibrate in sync with vibrations of the outer world. A crude way of confirming this is to make point of noticing how your heartbeat or pattern of breathing synchronizes with the rhythms of the music or mantra to which you are listening.

The more entrained you become to silence the less separation you will feel. As a result, you will experience liveliness, serenity, and peace in the midst of the hustle and bustle of life and the raucousness of the modern world.

Intelligent Seeing

This practice is for transforming a visual activity into a portal of wholesome enchantment and peace. *Wholesome enchantment* means experiencing charm, delight, beauty, thrill, wonder, and magic without getting attracted, fascinated, or spellbound. Similar to entrainment, wholesome enchantment gives a taste of egoless mind (because it temporarily removes the illusion of separation) and makes you a great observer and a lover of the world. Most importantly, it boosts energy, generates interest in the extraordinary and wondrous, and leads to the experience of peace. For that to happen, one must do the following.

- Moderate the time you watch TV, DVDs, motion pictures, and cartoons
- Watch quality programs and educational programs only
- Avoid the viewing of pornography and violence entirely
- Avoid watching TV or playing video games continuously for more than one hour
- Blink gently every ten minutes to keep the eyes relaxed
- Avoid combining activities, such as eating, with watching
- Avoid turning on a visual entertainment device in reaction to boredom
- As much as possible, spend some time meditating with closed eyes every day
- Practice the following soul meditation to transform the activity of seeing into a portal of wholesome enchantment and peace

To begin, close your eyes and take a few deep breaths to become aware of your breathing. Then, breathe normally and move your

CHAPTER 18 DEVELOPING INTELLIGENT SENSES

attention to the eyes. Feel them by mentally touching them from the outermost to the innermost edges, from inside out. Then, get ready to see the chosen object with the sole intention of experiencing *emptiness* and the *stillness of space*. Once you have set this intention, open your eyes and start focusing on the chosen object.

While looking at the object directly in front of you, become aware of the space surrounding the object. This will awaken your peripheral vision and help you watch everything *panoramically*. For example, as you are reading this book, look at the space surrounding it without taking your eyes off the book. Simply become aware of the surrounding space. If you choose a desktop globe as the object of your meditation, first look at the globe, then the edges of it, and then the space that surrounds the globe by expanding your vision without moving your eyes off the globe. Simply become aware of all the space that you can see while fixing your eyes on the globe. You are basically using the globe to become visually aware of the space around it by virtue of the contrast between them. If your object of focus is a painting, do not only fix your eyes on the area within the edges of the painting; also expand your vision so you can see the painting as an object situated within an environment of surrounding space.

Once you are established in the ability to panoramically see the objects, meaning you have the ability to see not only the object but also the surrounding space, shift your awareness (not your eyes) to the "emptiness" of the surrounding space. Although your eyes are fixed on the object and you are seeing the surrounding space, your awareness is on the emptiness of space—the *visual quality* of that space. If you are not able to anchor your attention on the emptiness of the space, silently say the word "emptiness." Keep repeating it until your attention is anchored in the emptiness. When that happens, you will be able to *feel* the space. Remain aware of the feeling aspect of your vision. Become mindful of space as "the feeling of emptiness."

Once you are established in the mindfulness of space (the feeling of emptiness), shift your awareness back to the object of focus. Notice how such mindfulness leads to non-reactive or equanimous observation.

For example, while you are looking at horrific pictures of war, disease, or destruction, if you become mindful of the space surrounding the pictures, you are more likely not to react to them with fear, disgust, aversion, pity, or sorrow, but rather with courage, concern, and compassion. You are more likely not to classify what you see as good, bad, beautiful, or ugly, or to get carried away by it. You are likely to pay more attention to visual objects and to use visual clues to your advantage and to the advantage of others.

Similarly, you are more likely to feel wholesomely enchanted by the beauty of a flower or a woman if you observe the object with mindfulness of the space surrounding it (the feeling of emptiness). Note that the feeling of emptiness coupled with non-reaction makes your observation charming, enthralling, and delightful. At the same time, it protects you from getting carried away by beauty or lust.

The preceding meditation is intended for use when looking at stationary objects. If your object of focus is a moving object, then instead of shifting your awareness to the "emptiness" of the surrounding space (as in the case of stationary objects) shift your awareness to the "stillness" of the surrounding space. Follow all other steps as described before.

Test the power of this meditation by practicing it while watching an emotional, dramatic, or fantastical movie. Notice how you become non-reactive to the scenes as soon as you shift your awareness to emptiness and stillness of space surrounding the objects of motion or scenes as they move across the screen. Notice how much more you are able to enjoy the movie *without* getting carried away by the story or the melodrama, without getting spell-bounded by the magic.

Notice how much more sensitivity and appreciation you develop towards the storyline, motions, colors, the beauty and skill of the actors, and so on, *without* developing a craving or an aversion for any of it. Also, notice how you feel energized and inspired by the wonder and the magic of the movie rather than feeling overwhelmed, stunned, or shocked.

CHAPTER 18 DEVELOPING INTELLIGENT SENSES

You can also practice this meditation in daily life situations. For example, observe a screaming boss or client, a crying child, a barking dog, a threatening neighbor, or beautiful houses, bundles of cash, captivating ads, or a dashing sports car in relation to the emptiness and stillness of the surrounding space.

If you become established in the awareness of the emptiness and stillness of space, no ugliness or disorder will disturb your peace of mind. At the same time, the orderly, the extraordinary, and the beautiful will wholesomely enchant you. Sooner or later, due to consistent practice and the experiencing of wholesome enchantment, whenever your eyes are open you will abide neither in fear nor awe, but in peace in the midst of varying scenery of the world.

Why?

The most common questions I face when I discuss intelligent sensing practices are:
- "Why are we making our senses insensitive?"
- "Why can't we just have fun?"
- "Won't your suggestions make life boring?"

I hope it is obvious to you that the five practices don't make the senses insensitive, but instead supersensitive. In other words, they facilitate a sensual experience that is deeper than usual, at the same time developing higher levels of intelligence.

When you eat, touch, and smell intelligently, you experience delight, contentment, healing, and sanctity. These sensual experiences are more profound than the mundane sensual pleasures of flavor, aroma, and bodily contact. When you hear and see intelligently, you experience entrainment, wholesome enchantment, and peace. These sensual experiences are more profound than the mundane sensual pleasures of sight and sound. Delight, contentment, healing, and sanctity generate EQ and SQ, and the experience of entrainment, wholesome enchantment, and peace generates SQ and soul intelligence (see figure 18.1).

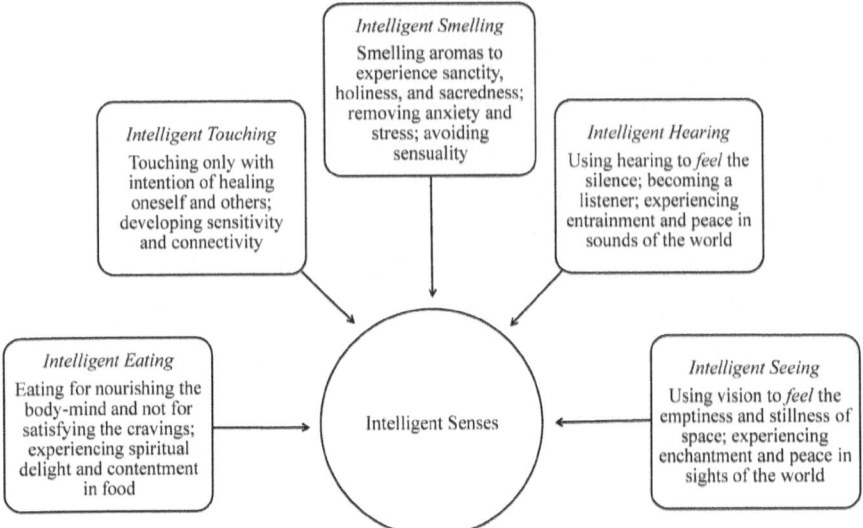

Figure 18.1. Five practices transform the ordinary senses into intelligent ones and lead to the development of higher levels of intelligence.

People who are trapped in the fire of their senses mistakenly assume reacting to the flames of sensual desire is "fun." A cigarette smoker, an alcoholic, an impulsive eater, a movie buff, a music fan, a scent addict, and a sex enthusiast are such people who unfortunately think they are having fun when they are actually suffering. Deeper sensual experiences and the higher intelligence that arises out of the intelligent use of the senses extinguish these flames and bring about mental and emotional coolness. Intelligent sensing makes our lives peaceful, but not boring.

As the senses cool down and we become somewhat peaceful sensually, we begin to give wise attention to sensual experiences. We start realizing that all sensual experiences arise and pass away, that no taste (or smell or sight or sound) lasts forever no matter what we do, and that sensual stimuli are impermanent and cannot satisfy our cravings permanently. Due to such wise attention, we develop equanimity towards sensual experiences.

Due to equanimity, we soon begin to witness that sensual experiences arise only when there is body-mind-consciousness. For example,

CHAPTER 18 DEVELOPING INTELLIGENT SENSES

an experience of taste arises only if there is a mouth, contact with food, and consciousness. The mouth is the body. Contact is the mental element of sensation (the mind), and consciousness is taste consciousness. Similarly, an experience of sight arises only if there is an eye, contact with a visual object, and eye consciousness.

A day eventually dawns when we experience the expansion of sense consciousness: We realize that sensual experiences are conditionally-arisen soul phenomena and there is no "I" in them. Our image of being a sensor and the delusion that "I am the eater, smeller, healer, seer, hearer" completely fades away. Attachment to sensual pleasures also fades away. And thus we attain freedom from the sensual trap.

* * *

Chapter 19

Developing an Intelligent Body

In the previous chapter, we discussed how to transform ordinary senses into intelligent ones. We will now discuss how to do the same for the whole body.

An ordinary body, which is a carrier of the ego, a cause of self-centeredness, a facilitator of conceit and self-image, and, to some people, a burden, can be transformed into a catalyst and an aid to developing higher levels of intelligence. If you use your body for developing higher levels of intelligence, not only you will live an affliction-free, addiction-free, pain-transcendent, happy, healthy, prosperous, and long life, you also will make your mind fit for perfection. Mental perfection will become possible because you will experience a state of physical awareness and equanimity. By this, I mean that you will experience a transcendental feeling of not owning the body—not feeling attached to it as *your* body. You will enjoy this authentic out-of-body experience (rooted in wisdom rather than ignorance or intoxication)[1] and become fond of it due to its liberating power. You will also experience the body as a flow of awareness (rather than a solid entity) that will bring about a profound transformation in you by eradicating the subtlest trace of ego linked with the body.

Although it may sound a bit cryptic right now, if you undertake the following five practices you will soon understand the profundity of the preceding statement. These practices will seem most expedient and profitable if you intelligently pursue them as guidelines, not just as daily exercises or drills. I encourage you to study these practices with the goal of understanding their meditative nature, and then to implement them whenever, wherever, and as often as you can.

Intelligent Work Habits

The purpose of this practice is to transform physical work, including both daily chores and professional employment, into a means of developing physical awareness and equanimity towards the body without losing the material or financial benefits of work activities. As you will soon discover, the purpose is to transform physical engagement into the act of developing intelligence without spending extra time at it and while increasing efficiency and effectiveness.

Pick a chore of any kind (for example, brushing your teeth or hair, showering, washing the dishes, vacuuming the floor, gardening, or cleaning the car)—it's your choice—and start executing the chore with the intention of developing whole-body awareness. When you simply observe your physical movements using outward awareness, as if you were a third person or a fly on the wall looking at your body, whole-body awareness arises. Develop it while working by becoming mindful of every shifting position of your limbs and overall bodily postures. Become aware of all the sequences of your physical movements.

In order to maintain continuity of whole-body awareness, in the beginning you may even silently verbalize your movements like a commentary in your mind.

CHAPTER 19 DEVELOPING AN INTELLIGENT BODY

You might be wondering, "How do I look at my own body without using a mirror?"

In this exercise you are not trying to visually look at the body *per se*. You are simply trying to become aware of it while working. This is easy. Go ahead and try it. Right now, intend to look at yourself as a third person while reading this book. Without taking your eyes off the book shift your attention into the space surrounding the book and you. This simple intention, when it is coupled with attention, brings about body awareness from the perspective of a third person. You are not trying to feel anything; you are simply becoming aware of your body by observing it from the outside.

Here's another example. Without looking into a mirror, while brushing your teeth observe how you are holding the toothbrush, how you are standing, and how you are cleaning your teeth. Count the number of times you move the toothbrush from left to right. Do not try to feel the taste of the toothpaste or any other physical sensations. Simply focus on attending to the body as if you were a third person. If you try to feel the body, then it is very difficult to look at it from this perspective. Simply look at the body through awareness as if you are watching a 3D movie.

While watering the plants in your garden, observe how you are holding the hose, how you are watering, and how you are moving around the garden.

While cleaning the car, observe how you are bending, how you are moving your arms while rubbing the polish, how you are moving in and out of the car and collecting things and organizing, and so forth.

In this way, while taking care of mundane tasks, you can transform your bodily activities into the activity of awareness, which ultimately leads to higher intelligence. You can get the most out of the time spent on taking care of routine tasks of life simply by executing them with awareness. If you do, soon, you'll notice that you enjoy doing chores more than before. You will no longer despise any of them.

Do the same while speaking on the telephone or working at your computer. Pay attention to how you are sitting, how you are holding the phone, how your lips are moving while talking, how your fingers are moving across the keyboard, and so on.

In a meeting, look at the whole group, including yourself, as a third person would and simply observe how you and the others move your bodies and go about doing business. Contrary to what you might think, such an observation will help you focus better on the meeting and on the other people's viewpoints and needs. Body awareness will not hinder your capacity to better listen, analyze, evaluate, and respond. Rather it will facilitate these abilities. But don't believe me. Confirm what I'm saying. Try it for yourself and find out how work can become a play of awareness and how happily you will do all your tasks without preferring one to another.

If you are a weight lifter, a construction worker, a mechanic, or a technocrat using a variety of powerful tools, whole-body awareness practice will help you remain neutral towards the power of your limbs and the tools. Such power has a tendency to increase body-centeredness, which fosters the ego and hinders the development of higher intelligence. So whenever you are handling raw power, keep your attention on your entire body and set a firm intention to develop higher intelligence. This will not only minimize accidents and maximize productivity it will also help you keep a check on the burgeoning ego.

Lastly, try sporting a subtle smile while you are working. The smile should not be forced or unnatural. Just a slight expansion of the lips coupled with an intention of developing body awareness will do the trick. Keep smiling while working in order to ease the task of developing whole-body awareness. What will happen is that smiling consciousness (a unique form of functional consciousness that we discussed in previous chapters) and body consciousness will alternate and make the whole process very pleasing. Moreover, you will train yourself to be truly human. As far as I know, no other mammal knows how to smile.

As you mature in whole-body awareness through daily chores and tasks, you will experience an occasional flash of body-as-body experience. You will feel that the body is simply moving as a body. It is not *your* body, but simply *a* body. You will feel as if you are purely awareness. The body simply will move effortlessly and you will just abide in the awareness of that. This flash of effortlessness, which is rooted in selflessness, is a powerful force. It can bring perfection to your work. Extraordinary artists, athletes, and dancers frequently go through this experience. Familiarize yourself with such an experience and become established in it.

Intelligent Exercising

Exercising has a tendency to make us body-centered if it is not done intelligently. Body-centeredness arises due to the increasing physical strength, flexibility, and beauty resulting from an exercise regimen. The purpose of this practice is to transform exercising (something as simple as walking on a treadmill, as intense as martial arts and weight-lifting, or as fluid as yoga and tai-chi) into a means of developing awareness of the body and equanimity towards the body without losing out on health benefits, without spending extra time, and most importantly, minimizing body-centeredness.

Pick an exercise to do of any kind—it's your choice—and begin a workout with the intention of developing whole-body awareness. Like developing intelligent work habits, while exercising, aim to be mindful of every single movement you make, every shifting position of your limbs, and your overall posture. For example, while running on a treadmill, do not watch TV. Instead watch yourself. Try to observe the pace of the running, its rhythm, and your hands as they move in sync with your feet. If you want, you may count your steps, however only up to ten. At ten, start over. You don't want to get carried away in counting. Your aim is to focus on becoming aware of the body outwardly.

In the same manner, while weight lifting, become aware of the grips and the movement of your limbs as you lift and drop the weights. Observe all your movements and all the sequences of movement you do with open eyes. Again, the key is to not feel bodily sensations but rather to simply look at the body as a third person would. If you do this, especially in a repetitive exercise, such as running or walking on a treadmill, sooner or later you will experience the body as *a* body and not *your* body due to the maturing of whole-body awareness.

In the beginning you may find it hard not to watch TV or not to listen to music while you're working out. Don't force yourself. Simply make a genuine effort to devote all your senses to the workout. Give your 100 percent to this perspective, so that you not only exercise the body but also the mind *without* spending extra time. Developing body awareness is a mental exercise.

Maintaining body awareness during your workouts significantly reduces the chance of physical damage caused by overstretching, overstraining, overworking, or overlooking. It also accelerates gains in physical strength, flexibility, and beauty, and does so without generating pride and vanity about such qualities.

For serious practitioners of soul meditation, in addition to the outward awareness practice we have discussed, I recommend the following inward awareness practice. The main difference between the two is that in the inward awareness practice you train yourself to *feel* the body. The purpose is to become aware of its real makeup and thereby remove subtler bodily attachment.

Begin with the intention of becoming aware of the four essential material elements of which the body is ultimately made: earth, water, fire, and air. If necessary, spend a few moments reviewing and recollecting the characteristics and functions of these elements, as discussed in previous chapters. Then, start a rigorous exercise of your choice.

During the workout, try to feel the heaviness and rigidity of the body. Feel the body's initial resistance to movement. Feel the inertia. Understand the body's heaviness, rigidity, resistance, or inertia as an indirect experience of the element of earth. Likewise, feel body heat and physical pain as indirect experiences of the element of fire.

Then feel the movements involved in your limbs, the contraction and expansion of the chest and the movement of breath. Understand this feeling as an indirect experience of the element of air.

CHAPTER 19 DEVELOPING AN INTELLIGENT BODY

Finally, become aware of how the body *flows* into different postures. Become aware of the body's cohesiveness and the interconnectivity of cartilage, muscles, tendons, and bones. You may not be able to feel this conspicuously. Nevertheless, understand these qualities as an indirect experience of the element of water.

In this way, through actual experience, come to understand how the body is a material phenomenon made up of the four essential elements of matter. Such an experience has profound implications. Knowing pain as the element of fire, rather than as pain, can significantly reduce your reaction to pain. Knowing the body's heaviness and inertia as the element of earth can significantly improve your body's flexibility by reducing your reactivity to sloth and torpor.

With ardent and diligent practicing of such meditation while exercising, a stage will come when you will know with certainty that your body is nothing but a bundle of material elements that come and go based on conditionality. You will also realize that you do not have absolute control over the body. For example, when you feel pain while lifting a heavy weight, try to eradicate the pain by simply commanding the body. Nothing happens, right? When you run out of breath while swimming, try to direct the body to swim anyway. The body does not obey. Pain will go away only if you reduce the weight or train appropriately. The body will swim only if you slow down and catch a breath or condition it properly.

Although so downright obvious, make a note of these things. Provided you have developed a certain degree of meditativity, such noting will give rise to a fundamental question in your mind: "How can I call this body mine when I do not have absolute control over it?" You will then begin to contemplate the autonomous functions of the body (for example, growth, digestion, aging, wound recovery, sleep, and excretion) that occur without you telling the body what to do.

You may begin to wonder, "Who is commanding the body? Where is the 'I' in the body?" If you reach this lucky moment, try to feel the "I" in the body and realize that the only thing you could feel were the four material elements. Basically, through this practice you are trying to understand that your previous feelings, experiences, and awareness of the four material elements have been mistakenly construed as the "I."

Intelligent Pain Management

The body is subjected to physical pain due to aging, disease, environmental conditions, and so on. Every person in the world has experienced physical pain. There is no way to get rid of pain permanently no matter how medically advanced we become. The only way to deal with pain is to manage it and to make the body pain transcendent. A pain-transcendent body is an intelligent body.

We have briefly mentioned how knowing pain as the element of fire can reduce our reaction to it. The purpose of this practice is to further deepen the understanding of pain so we can manage it and make the body pain transcendent.

Pick any physical activity or exercise and, as you perform it, begin to notice how your body is subjected to stretching, straining, and resistance from gravity, because of which unpleasant feelings of discomfort or exertion arise. Become mindful of unpleasant feelings in the body, as they always arise before the advent of pain. Note that unpleasant feelings become pain only when you develop an aversion to them, meaning, only when you react to their unpleasantness. So, in order to distinguish between unpleasant feelings and pain, remain aware of the degree of aversion—in other words, your mood during the practice.

Once you notice unpleasant feelings, observe them without reacting. Do not suppress or fight the unpleasantness. Simply observe it as it arises during a prolonged state of physical activity. Notice how unpleasantness eventually ceases due to mindfulness of unpleasantness and non-reaction to it. Also notice how it aggravates and eventually turns into physical pain if you react or try to resist it. In other words, try to realize that unpleasantness itself is not necessarily pain. It becomes pain *only* when you react, resist, or fight it. Also, realize that when you let go of unpleasantness it ceases to control the mind and does not result into pain.

CHAPTER 19 DEVELOPING AN INTELLIGENT BODY

Now, apply wise attention to your feelings of unpleasantness and try to understand experientially that the degree of unpleasantness and your reaction to it is directly proportional to your attachment to the body—to your attachment to the *memory* of past experiences of *pleasant feelings* in the body. In this way, first understand pain experientially as a reactive state of mind arising from the experiencing of unpleasant *as well as* pleasant feelings in the body. Then, start observing all pleasant bodily feelings without liking them and all unpleasant feelings without disliking them. In this way, start eradicating deep-rooted craving and aversion, and develop equanimity towards bodily feelings.

Also, learn how to increase your tolerance towards unpleasantness. Start any physical activity or an exercise of your choice. Slowly increase your physical efforts or the intensity of your workout only up to the limit where you can maintain equanimity towards unpleasantness. You want the unpleasantness just to begin being aggravated, but not to reach the level of physical pain. In this way, find out your current boundaries of the comfort zone or physical tolerance and expand or increase it intelligently without subjecting yourself to outright pain.

In subsequent workouts, as stamina and strength increases along with equanimity, continue expanding your envelope of physical tolerance by adding the elements of vigor and resolution to your practice. Make sure you review the characteristics and functions of these two special mental elements (as were discussed in previous chapters) prior to beginning your workout. Also, while practicing, concentrate on transcending pain rather than on attaining physical-mastery or pain-control.

This process of slowly and skillfully increasing your tolerance towards unpleasantness, without inflicting pain and without developing the physical ego, is what I like to call *refinement*. Due to refinement, a day will come when you will not experience physical pain. Although you will still experience physical unpleasantness from time to time, because it is the body's nature, with ardent and consistent practice you will attain a pain-transcendent body.

Intelligent Management of Emotions and Addictions

Similar to pain, other emotions, including fear, anger, hunger, passion, and lust, are rooted in the body. The purpose of this practice is to understand these emotions experientially and to manage them wholesomely.

Pick any physical activity. As you perform it, try to feel the pleasure or displeasure while the body is engaged. Become aware of a feeling of displeasure when the body is subjected to contraction, heaviness, burning sensations, imbalance, or numbness. Become aware of a feeling of pleasure when the body is subjected to extension, lightness, or balance. Become aware of the sense of satisfaction (or dissatisfaction) or the sense of achievement (or failure) at the end of a physical activity. It may not be possible to become aware of all of the aforementioned parameters at all times. Therefore, during a particular day, choose a particular set of parameters (balance or imbalance, for example) and work diligently only on it. Another day, change the set of parameters and repeat the process. Keep switching parameters until you have experienced all of the possible parameters. In this way, by conspicuously feeling various mental states triggered by bodily activity, become *mindful* of the body at subtler levels.

Once you have developed mindfulness of the body in this way, start observing specific emotions, such as fear, anger, aversion, remorse, guilt, hunger, lust, passion, and craving, while being engaged physically. Become mindful of the unpleasant or pleasant feeling in the body that is associated with each emotion. For example, become mindful of the emotion of fear as an unpleasant feeling in the body, and the emotion of lust as a pleasant feeling in the body. If you continue such practice, due to increasing mindfulness you will soon begin to notice that these emotions—especially the strong ones or the ones you react to—have a "sting" (a feeling of intoxication) associated with them. The sting of a strong emotion is somewhat like the "kick" of drinking a beer or smoking tobacco.

Start identifying the sting of strong emotions in the body. The more you are able to identify the sting, the more you will become capable

CHAPTER 19 DEVELOPING AN INTELLIGENT BODY

of observing strong emotions without getting intoxicated by them. In other words, you will become able not to react to strong emotions. You will become able to allow them to arise and cease on their own accord, harmlessly. For example, arisen anger will no longer intoxicate you with a sense of power. Passion won't intoxicate you with a sense of heroism or boldness.

"Easier said than done," I hear you whispering.

Many people find it almost impossible to deal with strong emotions. For them, I recommend the following practice. This practice is extremely profitable because it not only eliminates the expression or suppression of strong emotions, but it also facilitates the transmutation of unwholesome emotional power into the will power.

Start a rigorous physical workout, which means maintaining a particular posture for a longer period of time than usual. Stretch, elongate, or contract the body parts further. Hold the body posture in balance longer than usual. Lift heavier weights. Hike an extra mile. Do more pushups and sit-ups. Train under more and more difficult physical conditions. And so forth. Apply the elements of resolution and vigor, and keep increasing the severity of your activity. Train arduously, but remain mindful of the wholesome purpose, do not get attached to the increasing physical strength, give wise attention to the boundaries of pain, and concentrate on developing will power through resolution and vigor. In this way, first strengthen the body and mind.

Once you are equipped with a strong body and mind, keep a vigil on your emotions by keeping an eye on their sting. Whenever you feel you are being overcome by an emotion, identify that feeling as an indication of a sting. Quickly get out of the environment you are in and get into the rigorous workout as described above. The key is to have a strong body and mind so you can promptly engage yourself in a rigorous workout whenever attacked by the sting. For example, while you are in an argument with your spouse, if you identify the sting of anger, simply excuse yourself and get out of the house. Hit the trail or go to the gym, and apply the energy of the sting to fuel the rigorous workout. Do the same if you feel the sting of lust or passion. In this way, burn up strong emotions by facilitating the transmutation of their unwholesome power and avoid harm caused by their suppression or expression.

I like to call this practice a "sting operation." It is not only an effective way to manage strong emotions, but also to overcome addictions.

Generally speaking, addictions are deeply rooted in bodily feelings, especially the sting. It is the sting that an addict is addicted to, and not an external object. For example, when a smoker sees a cigarette, it arouses feelings of pleasure rooted *in the* body. If the smoker is not in touch with his body, meaning he does not have physical awareness, he cannot realize it. Because of unawareness, he clings to pleasantness, allowing the pleasant feelings to gather strength and turn into a craving. Because a habitual smoker neither is aware of the craving, nor does he have the capacity to observe it with equanimity, he reacts and ends up lighting a cigarette to satisfy the craving. This further intensifies the craving and turns it into a sting, which intoxicates the addict.

If a smoker trains himself in body awareness and then begins a daily rigorous physical workout suitable to his physical conditions, he will have a substantial chance of getting rid of his addiction. Due to the practice of body awareness, the smoker will be able to become *mindful* of the craving for tobacco as soon as it surfaces while smoking. He then will be able to notice how his craving is turning into a sting of tobacco. The moment he identifies the sting, if he quickly abandons the cigarette and subjects himself to a physical workout and sweats it out, he will be able to transform the unwholesome energy of addictive mind into the wholesome energy of productive mind. While working out, if he contemplates the ill effects of smoking, such as cancer and asthma, and the benefits of non-smoking, such as better health and substantially reduced medical expenses, he will avoid grabbing another cigarette.

A diehard smoker, if not able to practice as described above, should light a cigarette with complete awareness, knowing that he is lighting the cigarette as a result of succumbing to the craving. He should then smoke the cigarette with awareness and simply observe the pleasant

CHAPTER 19 DEVELOPING AN INTELLIGENT BODY

physical sensations that arise while smoking. He should not take the next puff until the pleasant sensations completely die out on their own. Only then, with awareness, should he take the next puff.

As he takes the next puff, the smoker should inhale the smoke while recollecting and concentrating on the ill effects of smoking. He should repeat this process throughout the episode of smoking. As pleasant sensations are observed while smoking and as ill effects of smoking are recollected with each puff, cravings for cigarettes will significantly reduce.

These methods are a foolproof way of taming the habit of smoking or any other similar habit that is deeply rooted *in the body*. Note that there is no coercion or suppression involved in the approach.

Intelligent Breathing

The purpose of this practice is to make your breath a versatile object of attention by learning to focus on it and to synchronize it with physical activities so that all your bodily engagements are transformed into a breathing workout and a mental workout. Here is an example.

While walking or jogging, place your attention upon your breath. Become aware of each inhalation and exhalation. Then synchronize the movement of your breath with the movement of your body (your steps, in this case). Purposefully breathe in deeply, as you take, let's say, four steps. Then breathe out thoroughly as you take the next four steps, thus synchronizing your breathing with walking.

If you walk like this for a few minutes you will get a physical workout (due to walking or jogging), a breathing workout (due to deep and thorough breathing), and a mental workout (due to paying attention to the body and the breath). You will triple the gains without investing additional resources or time! You will not only walk or jog longer, but you will also feel accomplished and happier at the end.

After having experienced the benefits a few times, you will never carry an iPod or entertain yourself while walking or jogging (or while doing anything for that matter), because you will no longer consider any activity—especially regular exercise—boring or burdensome.

After having developed breath awareness through synchronizing your physical movements with your breath movements during your daily activities, start giving more attention to the exhalation and observing the state of your mind during exhalation. You will notice that the mind is more flexible and more willing to let go during exhalation than during inhalation. You will also discover that during exhalation, like the body rids itself of physical toxins such as carbon dioxide, the mind also rids itself of mental toxins, such as anger, fear, lust, sloth, and torpor, provided you have trained the mind for that. This happens because the movement of breath is linked to your state of mind.

An easy way to confirm the linkage of breath and mind is to notice how the movement of your breath mirrors the movement of your thoughts. For example, your breath is hard and fast when you are fearful or lustful. It is shallow and dull when you laze out.

Knowing this, intelligently start using your exhalation whenever you are experiencing unwholesome states of mind. Expel unwholesome states through your exhalations by using the power of intention and the power of the movement of the breath. If necessary, arouse *resolution* and *vigor* to augment your intention of expelling mental toxins.

For example, if you are feeling lazy, first become aware of the shallow and dull breath, then quickly change it to a deep and forceful breath, and intentionally breathe out sloth and torpor with each exhalation. Feel the expulsion of sloth and torpor as you exhale forcefully. If you cannot feel it, you may run a mental commentary while exhaling. For example, something like: "I am breathing out sloth and torpor. I am expelling them out of my mind. Yes!"

Similarly, if you are feeling fearful or lustful, first become aware of the shortness and hardness of your breath, then quickly change it to deep and soft breathing, and intentionally breathe out fear or lust with each exhalation. Feel the expulsion of greed (in the case of lust) or hatred (in the case of fear) as you exhale deeply and softly.

You can also use this technique to deal with physical pain. If there is pain in a localized area of the body, take your attention there, mentally

CHAPTER 19 DEVELOPING AN INTELLIGENT BODY

confine your exhalation to that area and expel the aversion (to pain) with each exhalation while silently saying the word "heal."

In this manner, by combining a strong intention with attention on the exhalation, you might be able to clean your mind of various toxic emotions. The key is to quickly adapt the breath movement that is exactly opposite to what it is during the influence of the toxic emotion, and then to employ the exhalation intelligently.

Last, but not least, try the following seated meditation. The purpose of this meditation is to experience wholesome mental states simply by thinking about them while intentionally exhaling.

Sit erect in a comfortable posture, close your eyes, and gently take your attention to the triangular nose area (the nostrils). Take a couple of long in-breaths and release a couple of long out-breaths with the intention of developing concentration.

Start observing your breath by feeling the touch of the breath in the entire nostril area. In other words, become aware of the breath by *feeling* it and not by mere attention.

Continue breathing in and out deeply until you become aware of the inhalation and exhalation by feeling their touch in the nostrils. This awareness should be so distinct that the in-breath is felt as a cool sensation in the nostrils, the out-breath is felt as a warm sensation in the nostrils, and the gap between the two is experienced as a separate event.

Notice how you feel differently when you inhale and when you exhale. Notice how sublime exhalation is compared to inhalation. At this stage, you will have developed the required level of concentration.

Now, move your attention to the area below the nostrils and above the upper lip. Just feel the light touch of the breath there. Maintain your awareness at this location for some time until the touch of the breath is obvious. Then, let go of inhalation and simply focus on exhalation by feeling its warm touch in the chosen area of focus. With sustained awareness, you will start feeling tingling sensations at this location with each exhalation.

Stay focused on the exhalation. Move your attention to different small areas of the body, maintaining your attention in each area and *intentionally* exhaling in that confined area until you feel the same tingling sensations. Begin with your lips. Feel the lips thoroughly.

Next move your attention to your left cheek. Intentionally exhale there and feel.

Then move your attention to your right cheek. Intentionally exhale there and feel.

Keep shifting your attention and intentionally exhaling until you have covered all areas of your body. Do not move your attention continuously. Make sure you maintain your attention in a small confined area of the body for some time before moving to the next area. Simply feel the chosen area. Do not label it as "ear" or "nose" or "kneecap." Your task is simply to feel it by confinement (meaning mentally touching it through exhalation), so that eventually your entire body has been felt.

It is important not to move your attention rapidly from part to part because speed works against the development of concentration. Maintain awareness on one small, confined area until you feel it to some extent (at least for a minute) and only then move further.

If you mindfully scan your body in this manner for an extended period of time you will eventually become *aware* of the whole body, meaning you actually will *feel* the whole body as you exhale while moving your attention in a flash from the top of your head to the bottom of your feet. You will feel as if the whole body is alive. With practice, you will effortlessly feel the whole body with each exhalation. The distinction in this experience is "feeling a subtle breath passing through the middle of your being and not through your nose." It feels as if the whole body is breathing and not you.

Now, let go of all intentional breathing, breathe normally (meaning, let the body breathe by itself) and start thinking about rapture. Mentally recollect the characteristics and function of this mental element (as discussed in previous chapters) while being aware of the subtle breath passing through the middle of your being. You may want to mentally repeat, "I shall breathe in to experience rapture. I shall breathe out to experience rapture."

As you continue thinking about rapture in this way, it will give rise to the element of thoughtfulness and, eventually, due to sustained application of thought, moments of rapture will arise. The distinction in this experience is "feeling exhilaration and lightness in your body." It may even feel as if the body is momentarily uplifted.

Do not get attached to this experience. Just observe it as it comes and goes. Let it simply gladden the mind, as you remain non-reactive. Provided you do that, sooner or later, due to increased concentration and non-reaction, your thinking and thoughtfulness will fade away and you will start experiencing bliss—a bodily experience even subtler than rapture.

The distinction in this experience is "feeling emptiness in the body, as if there is only space and no solidity." It may even feel as if the body has been pervaded with happiness, but without a sense of having physical boundaries. If equanimity is well established you will feel as if you are liberated from the body, that you are not the body, that there is only awareness. This is bliss as experienced *in the body*.

Once you experience bliss, even if momentarily, you will stop craving bodily pleasures. This happens because the experience of bliss dwarfs physical and sensual pleasures. Once sensual pleasures feel ordinary and mundane, they will no longer drive you. Through experiencing bliss, you will remove subtler physical attachments and develop physical equanimity.

A Word of Encouragement

I hope it has become obvious to you that the five practices we've just discussed can basically transform your general physical activities into means of developing higher levels of intelligence, *without* investing extra time or resources (except in the case of sitting meditation). Who would not want to reap more benefits for the same cost?

THE ELEMENTS OF SOUL

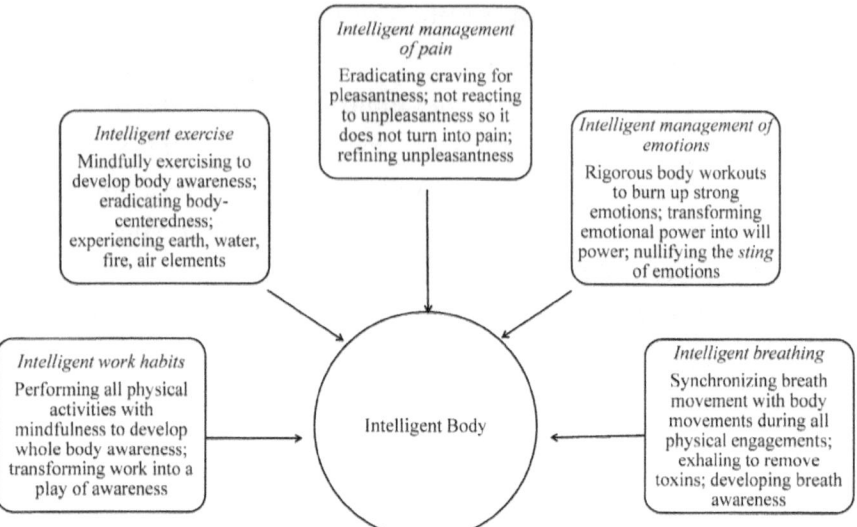

Figure 19.1. Five practices for developing an intelligent body.

Use figure 19.1 (above) to remind yourself of the five principles of developing an intelligent body. It is so easy to get involved in our daily activity that having a quick reminder is helpful.

As you apply these principles in daily life and as you experience higher and higher levels of physical awareness and equanimity, you will begin to dis-identify with the body. Your body-image, the delusion that "I am the doer" will eventually fade away and thus you will be liberated.

* * *

Chapter 20

Developing Intelligent Mind

All the practices that we have discussed so far for developing an intelligent attitude, intelligent senses, and an intelligent body are meant to create a solid spiritual foundation for the development of an intelligent mind. An intelligent mind is a purely equanimous state of mind in which there is thorough knowledge of the functioning of mind but no sense of owning the mind. There is no attachment to the mind as *my* mind, there is only awareness and understanding that *mind is mind*. It is the mind established in the highest level of intelligence.

Here are four practices that one can undertake to develop such a state of mind.[1]

Transcending

Transcending means experiencing the cessation of a phenomenon (as it fades away) by virtue of realizing its gross nature, and going beyond it. For example, transcending thoughts means going beyond thinking (such as reasoning or logic) by *realizing* its coarseness (lack of depth), which is all it takes for thinking to fade away and for thoughtfulness to arise.

Thinking generally involves a quick and perfunctory application of thought, as we customarily do it during our daily activities. Because of this habit, most of us live a superficial mental life. Thoughtfulness, on the other hand, generally involves a *sustained* application of thought. It is a focused state of mind, which makes mental activity more enjoyable, as you will soon find out.

If you were to go further and realize the coarse nature of thoughtfulness, you will develop the habit of *contemplation*, a subtler mental activity than thoughtfulness. As you will soon find out, contemplating is subtler because it is rooted in equanimity, a state of mind that is free of personal views, prejudices, and past conditioning.

While reading this book, if you realize that, simply reading it while in bed did not reveal its depth, you might attempt to study it thoughtfully sitting in a chair, which then might lead you to contemplate its contents. In other words, due to transcending, you might be able to apply higher states of mind to experiencing this book and benefit much more from it than you would by abandoning it the moment you were unable to understand a sentence or two.

Similarly, due to transcending sensual pleasures, meaning, realizing their coarse (mundane) nature, you might be able to experience happiness, delight, and joy—experiences that are subtler than sensual pleasures. By transcending further, you might be able to experience rapture, ecstasy, and bliss.

Transcending is the way to attain extraordinary and empowered states of mind such as contentment, equanimity, non-attachment, blissfulness, and peacefulness. It is so because the inherent nature of transcendence is to surmount, overcome, and effectively still the consciousness and to facilitate the penetration of subtler and subtler realities.

CHAPTER 20 DEVELOPING INTELLIGENT MIND

In daily life, transcending can be practiced as:

- *Graduating from sensual pleasures:* To try to graduate from sensual pleasures does not mean to forget sensuality and become a vegetable. Simply make a consistent effort to realize the mundane nature of sensual experiences, such as feasting, entertainment, too much sex, so you can transcend them and experience higher mental states.
- *Neutralizing the mind:* To try to neutralize mind does not mean to become inactive and ineffective. Simply make a consistent effort to transcend excess and deficit in order to attain balance and moderation in your daily activities.
- *Non-reacting to life conditions:* To try to non-react to life conditions (life situations and circumstances) does not mean to become insensitive to what occurs in your life. Simply make a consistent effort to transcend liking, disliking, craving, and aversion so you can develop calmness, composure, and equanimity—the sublime qualities that facilitate deeper contemplation and spiritual growth.
- *Letting go of plans, goals, and passions:* To try to let go of your plans, goals, and passions does not mean to give up your dreams. Simply make a consistent effort to transcend your attachment to the outcome so you can better focus on the process and accomplish whatever you dream of without stress and striving.
- *Becoming desireless:* To try to become desireless does not mean have no aspirations or wishes. Simply make a consistent effort to transcend self-interest and live a purpose driven life.
- *Going beyond family so you can serve others:* To try to go beyond family and serve others does not mean to abandon your family. Simply make a consistent effort to transcend the sense of exclusive responsibility and duty towards your family, which is largely rooted in family attachments, and expand your love.
- *Non-differentiating people or circumstances:* To try to non-differentiate people or circumstances does not mean to become indiscriminate. Simply make a consistent effort to transcend preferences, differences, prejudices, and partiality so you can develop the qualities of discernment and wise judgment.

- *Becoming disinterested in any particular person or thing:* To try to become disinterested in any particular person or thing does not mean to become indifferent and apathetic towards someone or something. Simply make a consistent effort to transcend all barriers and cultivate oneness.
- *Renouncing the world:* To try to renounce the world does not mean to leave, reject, or abandon it. Simply make a consistent and diligent effort to transcend all worldly attachments so you can abide here and now with a sense of relinquishment and surrender.

If you try genuinely, you will mature in transcendence. As you mature in transcendence you are certain to experience a sense of contentment, a sense of renunciation, a sense of blissfulness, a sense of equanimity, a sense of non-attachment, and ultimately peacefulness, in that order of increasing subtlety (see figure 20.1).

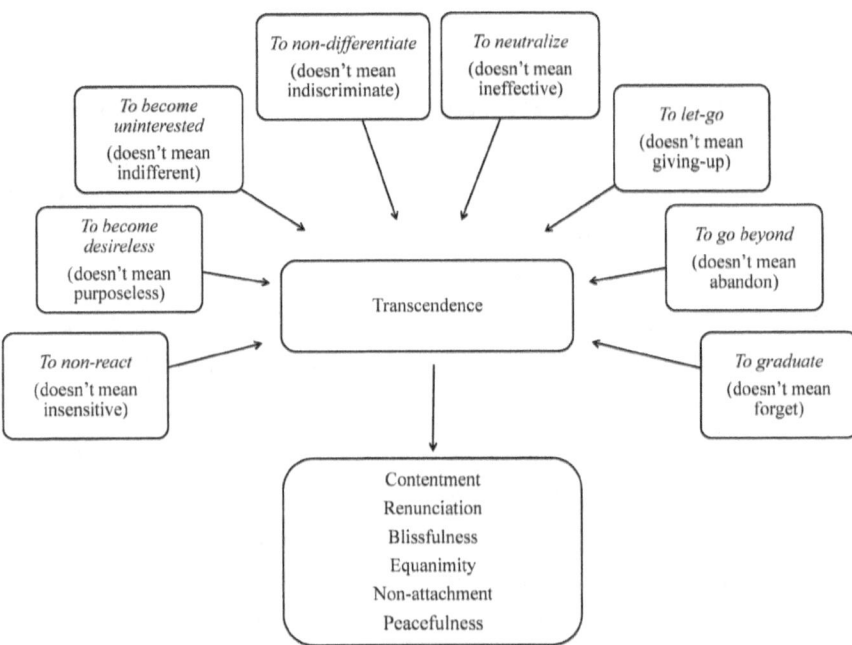

Figure 20.1. Daily practices for experiencing transcendence and realizing subtler states of mind.

CHAPTER 20   DEVELOPING INTELLIGENT MIND

Concentrating the Mind: Experiencing "Zero"

Transcending is not easy, especially for non-meditators and those who cannot concentrate well. The purpose of this practice is to facilitate increasing levels of concentration so you can understand transcendence experientially and develop an ability to apply it in daily life. You can train yourself to live a transcendental life through concentration practice.

The following concentration practice requires dedication and sustained effort. Therefore, I recommend practicing it on a weekend so that you are not pressed for time. Or better yet, take an entire weekend off from everything and go on a self-retreat once every six months and practice in seclusion.

First, study all the steps to develop an idea of the purpose and the flow of meditation. Then, practice steps 1–3 in one sitting that lasts about one hour. Take a break of about 10 minutes to relax your feet and lower back, and then practice steps 4–6 in another sitting of about an hour. Take another break, and then continue again using the same alternating time frames until all thirteen steps of the meditation have been covered.

Please consider the given timing, as well as the steps, as guidelines only. Depending upon your meditative preferences, come up with your own practice that encompasses the guidelines. Your personally designed practice might reflect only the key aspects of the suggested meditation. The key aspects are breath awareness, non-reaction, concentration, transcendence, and contemplation.

Step 1: Develop breath awareness: Sit in a comfortable posture, close your eyes, and practice intelligent breathing (as described in the preceding chapter, see page 315) so you can become aware of the touch of the breath below the tip of the nostrils.

Step 2: Understand thinking as the outcome of coarseness of mind: Once you have developed a certain level of breath awareness, let go of the breath and take your attention to whatever thoughts might be arising in the background of your mind. After some practice, you will begin to notice those thoughts primarily consisting of emotional roller coasters, recollection of past events, future planning, mental lists of things to do, worrying, and so on. Recognize the random and discursive nature of the thoughts. Understand their occurrence as a result of the coarseness of mind (lack of adequate concentration).

Step 3: Understand thoughtfulness as the outcome of concentrated mind: Let go of the thoughts and take your attention back to the touch of the breath. Let thoughts come and go without reacting to them. If you maintain your attention on the touch of the breath continuously, even for a minute, you will notice that the breath becomes softer and subtler. Understand this softness of breath as the outcome of increased concentration on the breath and the absence of discursive thinking. Increased concentration is a sustained application of thought (thoughtfulness). Become aware of the fact that due to increased concentration you were able to transcend discursive thinking and experience thoughtfulness.

Step 4: Transcend thoughtfulness and experience rapture: Continue observing the breath until it becomes soft and subtle to such an extent that it will generate a feeling of silky touch, a feeling of a subtle vibration in the confined area of focus below the nostrils. This feeling will be somewhat rapturous. Understand the silkiness of the breath and the associated rapture as the outcome of increased concentration on breath. Become aware of the fact that due to increased concentration you were able to transcend thoughtfulness and experience rapture.

Step 5: Transcend rapture and experience momentary bliss: As subtle breath is replaced by the subtle vibration, silky touch, or tingle of the warmth of life, observe the feeling ardently and consistently without reacting to any thoughts that may arise. Then move your attention to an area other than the small area below the nose tip. For instance, move it to your cheek and maintain it there until you experience the subtle vibration there. Then move it to other parts of the body, one by one, by moving the awareness gently from part to part.

In this way, cover the entire body from top of head to the tip of toes.

Repeat this process by going back and forth from top to bottom of the body. You should neither stop at any one place for a long time, nor move your awareness in a continuous manner. Just stay at one confined area of focus for about a minute and move on. The subtle vibrations will arise and pass away on their own accord.

CHAPTER 20 DEVELOPING INTELLIGENT MIND

Do not strive to feel the vibrations or the subtle touch. Do not develop a craving for them. Your task is not to strive for any feeling of subtle vibrations. The main task is to develop higher and higher levels of awareness and concentration. This is an important warning because, if you are not aware of it, your practice may become a means for the enjoyment of rapture that arise out of the feeling of subtle vibrations. Develop equanimity towards the pleasant, subtle vibrations by simply observing them as they come and go. This is the first big challenge the meditator should confront successfully.

While moving the attention over the body, you may pass through soft areas of subtle vibrations and hard areas of pain and stiffness. Do not develop a liking for soft areas and an aversion for hard areas. Do not classify then as pain or pleasure. Simply observe them as they are without stopping for longer time in soft areas and without avoiding hard areas. With intentional equanimity, continue to move the attention throughout the body.

A stage will come when you will feel subtle vibrations throughout the body as you move your awareness from part to part. At this stage, take a long in-breath and expel a long out-breath with an intention of feeling subtle vibrations in the entire body in one in-breath or one out-breath. Continue the practice until you can experience the whole body by feeling the subtle vibrations throughout the body in one long breath.

Then, practice until you can experience the whole body by feeling subtle vibrations throughout the body in one short in-breath and out-breath. Alternate the short and long breath and feel the entire body as a bundle of subtle vibrations in one breath without developing any craving. Soon, you will begin to experience lightness in the body.

Now, breathe normally. There should be no intentionally long or short breaths. Experience the whole body by feeling subtle vibrations throughout the body during your normal in-breaths and out-breaths. The experience of subtle vibrations throughout the body will be blissful, although momentary. Understand this experience as momentary bliss, an outcome of increased concentration and awareness. Become aware of the fact that due to increased concentration you were able to transcend rapture and experience momentary bliss.

Step 6: Transcend momentary bliss and experience showering bliss: Suspend the breath after each exhalation and, with mere intention, move your awareness from top to bottom of the body experiencing the whole body as a flow of awareness. Then move your awareness from bottom to the top experiencing the same flow. Do this only while the breath is in a suspension. Do not hold your breath. Simply suspend the breath after each exhalation for a brief moment.

As you move your awareness through the whole body effortlessly, you will experience the body as a flow of awareness. Understand this experience as showering bliss, an outcome of increased concentration and awareness. Become aware of the fact that, due to increased concentration, you were able to transcend momentary bliss and experience showering bliss.

Step 7: Transcend showering bliss and experience uplifting bliss: Soon, due to increasing concentration and showering bliss, you will feel as if the body is being uplifted. It is a subtle feeling of weightlessness (not emptiness). Understand this experience as uplifting bliss, an outcome of increased concentration and awareness. Become aware of the fact that due to increased concentration you were able to transcend showering bliss and experience uplifting bliss.

Step 8: Transcend uplifting bliss and experience pervading bliss: Suspend your breath for a couple of moments between in-breaths and out-breaths. Use the gap generated by the suspension of the breath for stilling the breath. While the breath is suspended, move your awareness from the top to the bottom and from the bottom to the top of body with a strong intention of stilling and transcending the body.

As the duration of the gap and suspension increase and your awareness flows effortlessly throughout the body, you will feel as if the body is completely weightless, hollow, and empty. You will feel as if there is no body, only the flow of awareness. The body is now simply experienced as a flow of awareness, *without boundaries.* In this state, there is no thinking of body except an understanding that there is an experience of body as a flow of awareness and nothing else. Mathematically speaking, it is somewhat like experiencing zero.

CHAPTER 20   DEVELOPING INTELLIGENT MIND

Understand this experience as pervading bliss, an outcome of increased concentration and awareness. Become aware of the fact that due to increased concentration you were able to transcend uplifting bliss and experience pervading bliss.

When this awareness and understanding is established beyond doubt, there is a unique transcendental experience, which has a pervading quality. In these moments of transcendence, there is a feeling of renunciation, contentment, lack of desire, and satisfaction.

Step 9: Transcend pervading bliss and reflect upon the meditative experience: Let pervading bliss come and go as you reflect upon the entire meditative experience. Through reflection, become established in the understanding that due to increasing levels of concentration you were able to transcend from coarser states of mind to subtler states of mind, and how profoundly more blissful those subtler mental states were compared to coarser mental states (see figure 20.2).

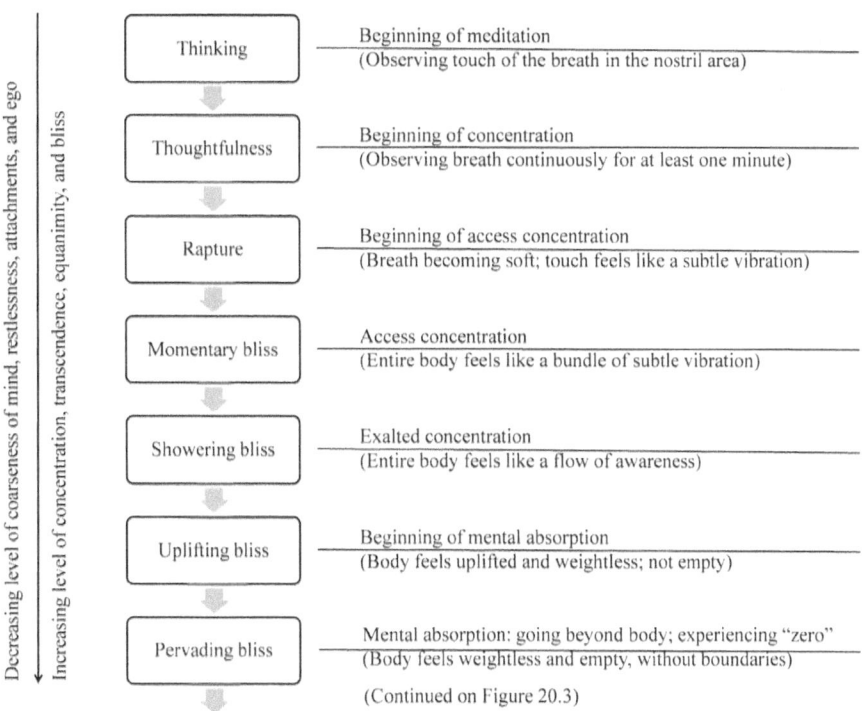

Figure 20.2. A meditative practice for concentrating the mind. This practice facilitates transcending coarser mental states and experiencing higher levels of bliss. (Also see figure 20.3.)

329

Also, through wise attention, understand how rapture and bliss support higher levels of concentration and vice versa. The understanding you are trying to develop is that higher levels of rapture and bliss are necessary for living a transcendental life, not only concentration. Such an understanding will help you abandon mundane sensual activities. You will take on activities that give rise to rapture and bliss. Due to meditative experience, you also will know which activities generate pleasures and which activities generate rapture and bliss. You will then start leaning towards participating in the latter types of activity.

Expanding Mind: Experiencing "Infinity" and Soul

The purpose of the next three steps of our meditation practice is to expand your mind so that mind can be experienced as empty, just as the body was experienced in the preceding practice. Mathematically speaking, if the experience of the emptiness of the body is like experiencing zero, the experience of the emptiness of mind is like experiencing infinity.

Practice the following meditation as a continuation of the preceding practice. You have the option to run quickly through steps 1–9 to reach this point.

Step 10: Transcend pervading bliss and experience spaceness: While abiding in pervading bliss (review step 9), become aware of the "empty space" within the nostrils through which the breath moves. Awareness of empty space should result from the *removal of the awareness* of the breath. It is as if you remove the breath and become aware of what remains: empty space.

Remain aware of this empty space by constantly regarding the awareness as "space." Contemplate the awareness as space until *spaceness* is established. This is awareness rooted in space rather than in the breath as it was before. Expand this awareness beyond the nostrils in stages to such an extent that there remains only spaceness through in and throughout.

Spaceness is literal. With this awareness, in a sense you *become* space. When that happens, you have not only transcended the body and

CHAPTER 20 DEVELOPING INTELLIGENT MIND

the senses you have also extinguished *bodyness* and *sensuality*. This does not mean you die. It simply means that while you are absorbed in the awareness of spaceness you do not hear any sound, you do not feel any touch, you do not see anything, you do not smell anything, and you do not taste anything. There remains no feeling or perception of matter anymore. Matter no longer generates any contact because no senses are arising. Also, spaceness is literal in the sense that you do not perceive any differences or varieties that arise due to materiality. Space is uniform and unbounded. Thus, spaceness brings about non-material, non-sensual, and non-variant unbounded awareness.

Step 11: Transcend spaceness and experience consciousness: While abiding in spaceness, shift your awareness to the consciousness that pervades it. Understand that this consciousness arose when space was made the object of awareness. Contemplate like this:

"This spaceness is really the consciousness that pervades it.

"The consciousness is unbounded because there is now only awareness of consciousness and not the awareness of space.

"Thus the subject of meditation, space, has been transcended by the arisen consciousness.

"This consciousness now abides in consciousness itself! It is thus unbounded consciousness and nothing else."

Step 12: Transcend consciousness and experience infinity: While abiding in boundless consciousness, shift your awareness to the *emptiness* and *nothingness* of space. Shift your awareness to its *voidness* and "not-ness." The awareness of emptiness, nothingness, voidness, and not-ness should result from the *removal of the awareness* of space. It is as if you remove the space and become aware of what remains.

Remain aware by constantly regarding the awareness as "emptiness, nothingness, voidness, and not-ness." Contemplate the awareness as such until *non-existence* is established. This is nothing but the arising of awareness that is *rooted* in emptiness and nothingness rather than space as it was before.

The awareness of emptiness and nothingness reaches such an extent that there remains no feeling even of non-matter (such as mind-consciousness) anymore. Matter and non-matter no longer generate any contact because neither matter nor mind is arising. In this way, when you *transcend* the unbounded consciousness and abide in emptiness and nothingness, you experience emptiness of the mind. It is somewhat like experiencing infinity.

The emptiness and nothingness is literal in the sense that you become empty or you *un-become*. Now, you have not only transcended the body and senses (steps 8 and 9) and extinguished the bodyness and sensuality (step 10), you also have extinguished feeling (steps 11 and 12). This does not mean you vanish. It simply means that while you are absorbed in this way, you do not perceive you as you because you do not *feel* that there is a "you."

This is what emptiness or nothingness is. It is *non-clinging* of any kind. It is *non-attachment* of even awareness due to *non-feeling*. It is the *non-existence* of owner, doer, thinker, feeler, and experiencer. What really remains now is just a perception of emptiness and nothingness.

Step 13: Transcend infinity and experience the soul: While abiding in the perception of emptiness and nothingness, contemplate as follows.

"There is a perception of emptiness and nothingness.

"It is not absolute nothingness because there is still a perception of it.

"This abiding is imperfect. It is not peaceful because perception still exists. It is not final liberation."

By contemplating in this way, develop dispassion for the perception of emptiness and nothingness and shift your awareness to the peacefulness of *non-perception*. Direct the awareness to peacefulness of non-perception again and again until awareness arises with neither perception nor non-perception. In this way, when you *transcend* the emptiness and nothingness and abide in neither perception nor non-perception, you enter the realm beyond infinity.

The awareness of neither perception nor non-perception is neither gross awareness in which there is perception, nor so subtle awareness that there is no perception. It is so extremely subtle that there is only the *residue* of perception, which is incapable of performing the

CHAPTER 20 DEVELOPING INTELLIGENT MIND

function of perception decisively. However, it is not completely absent. It is like moist soil, which does not contain enough quantity of water for drinking, but still the soil cannot technically be called dry due to residual moisture.

Soon, a stage will come when the faculties of awareness and concentration will be perfected to such an extent that there will be not even perception of any kind left. This is born out of the cessation of feeling (step 12) and the cessation of the awareness of neither perception nor non-perception due to transcendence and due to the complete eradication of hidden traces of the ego. In this way, when you *transcend* the stage of neither perception nor non-perception and abide (or non-abide) in the cessation of feeling *and* perception, you enter the realm of soul.

The realm of soul is the attainment of *cessation* born out of being-ness *without* perception of body-mind-consciousness. What then remains is *being-ness without*. You could also call this *being-less-ness* (see figure 20.3).

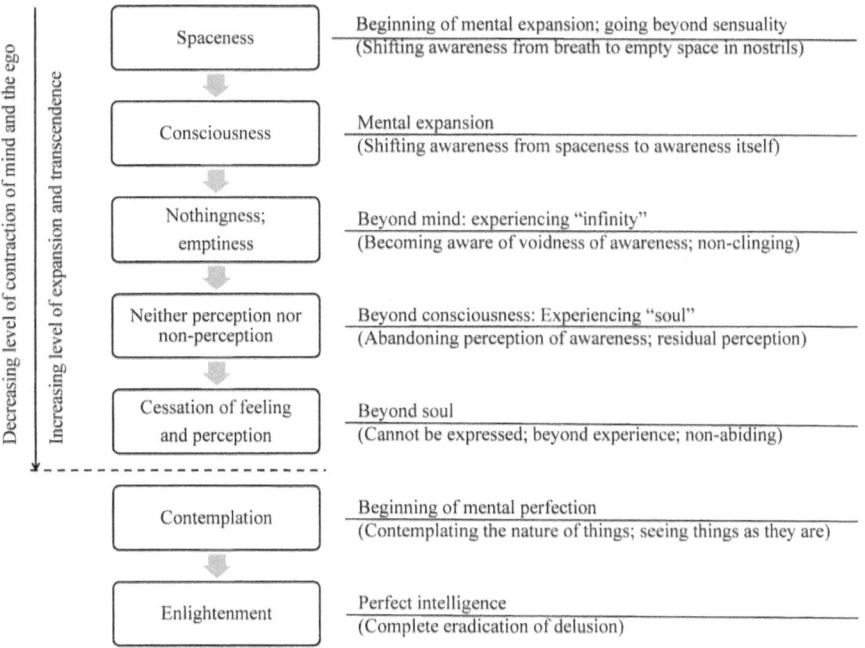

Figure 20.3. A meditative practice for expanding the mind. This practice facilitates experiencing infinity and soul.

In this state, the body, mind, and consciousness exist as they are. However, there is *neither feeling nor perception* of them. Body, mind, and consciousness do not exist belonging to someone. There is no more a person or an entity because the *subtlest* impurities of such ignorance are completely rooted out. Even though the meditator still exists *relative* to the world, no being, no person enters the realm of soul.

Such moments of abiding in soul give one a taste of *nirvanic* peace. Nirvanic peace, at least momentarily, brings about complete release from the clutches of ignorance (the ego). In these moments, equanimity arises in its purest form. It is this equanimity that facilitates the complete removal of the ego (including its latent tendencies) and establishes perfect intelligence, provided one learns and practices the way of contemplating that I shall soon describe.

While the practices of transcending, concentrating, and expanding of mind facilitate experiencing soul, the practice of contemplating facilitates the establishing of perfect intelligence. It is, however, not necessary to wait until you have experienced soul to undertake the following practice.

Contemplating: Seeing Things as They Are

Although contemplation sounds like thinking, it is not so. Thinking and thoughtfulness can be contaminated with delusion, conceit, superstition, personal views, dogmas, philosophical attachments, and so on. Contemplation, on the other hand, is free from these mental defilements because it is rooted in equanimity, the neutrality of mind. Therefore, I like to call contemplation the mental activity of *seeing things as they are.*

Contemplation is the activity of a wholesome purified mind, not just any mind. Wholesome contemplation is what ultimately leads to the developing and establishing of perfect intelligence.

The following is an example of the practice of contemplating for seeing the mind as it is. (Here I am using the word mind as a collectively term for mind-consciousness.) Note that it is simply an example

CHAPTER 20   DEVELOPING INTELLIGENT MIND

based on my own practice. After you have understood the nature of the practice, you may want to come up with your own.

Begin by sitting in a comfortable posture and going through the practice of concentrating and expanding the mind as best as you can. As you are experiencing some kind of bliss, set a strong intention to see the mind as it is. Use the following series of statements or make up your own.

"I will now discern the true nature of the mind.

"I will see the mind as it is and not as it appears to be."

Now, take your attention to your body and try to feel the characteristics of the material elements. For feeling the earth element, physically touch and feel the hardness of your bones, teeth, and nails. Feel the pressure (or hardness) of floor or cushion on which you are sitting. Then, physically touch and feel the softness of your skin, cheeks, and lips.

For feeling the fire element, notice the warmth of your out-breath and the coolness of your in-breath as your breath moves in and out of the nostrils. Try to feel the burning sensation (heat) inside the stomach, and physically touch and feel the coolness of fingers and the palms.

For feeling the air element, become aware of the heartbeats—the movement of your heart—and the movement of the stomach as you breathe.

After you have experienced all four elements, continue your contemplation by asking series of questions. For example:

"I was able to discern the earth element due to feeling the hardness and the softness of the body, the fire element due to feeling the heat or the coolness of the body, and the air element due to the feeling of motion in the body. Thus, the phenomena of materiality became evident to me because of *feeling*.

"Who is the one that is feeling the body?

"To whom do these feelings belong?"

Let go, observe silence for a few moments, and then continue contemplating.

"It feels unpleasant when there is pain and sorrow. I do not like that unpleasantness. I want it to end immediately. But, does it?

"It feels pleasant when there is happiness and joy. I like that pleasantness. I want it to last forever. But, does it?

"Why I cannot change the nature of feelings the way I want?

"Why I cannot change their impermanent nature?

"Why I do not have absolute control over the feelings?"

Contemplate to find the answers or raise more questions.

"Does it mean that feelings are not mine?

"Does it mean that it is not me who is feeling?"

Contemplate to find the answers or raise more questions.

"If these feelings come and go on their own, is it possible that it is not me but it is mind itself that feels?"

Let go, observe silence for a few moments, and then again ask another series of questions.

"When there is anger, grief, sorrow, why do I feel unpleasant and not pleasant?

"When there is joy or happiness, why do I feel pleasant and not unpleasant?

"Can I make myself feel pleasant while I am angry?

"Can I make myself feel unpleasant when there is joy?

"Why do anger, grief, and sorrow generate only unpleasant feeling?

"Why does joy or happiness generate only pleasant feeling?"

Contemplate to find the answers and then continue questioning.

"Does this mean there is a law or a phenomenon of feeling?

"Can I change this law or phenomenon of feeling?

"Can I have absolute control over the law or phenomenon of feeling?"

Contemplate to find the answers and then continue questioning.

"If I cannot, then does that mean that feeling is a unique mental phenomenon that occurs by itself without a controller or a feeler behind it?

"Is it possible that feeling is an element of mind that generates the mental ability to feel?

CHAPTER 20 DEVELOPING INTELLIGENT MIND

"Is it possible that mind feels due to the element of feeling and not due to me?

"Is it possible that mind is mind, not my mind, because there is no 'I' in it?"

Contemplate to find the answers and then immerse yourself in the spiritual delight that will arise out of the answers. Spiritual delight is guaranteed because the answers will be derived from the neutrality of mind.

After few moments, continue contemplating in a similar fashion to explore all the other mental elements, including perception, volition, attention, and so forth.

Now contemplate by arousing the following type of questions.

"Is it possible that mind is just a name given to a bundle of various mental elements that perform various mental activities, such as feeling, perceiving, giving attention, and so on?

"Is it possible that mind is not something that exists as a single, fixed entity?

"Is it possible that mind is just a bundle of mental phenomena that come and go of their own accord depending upon conditionality?

As you find the answers, immerse yourself in the spiritual delight that will arise out of them.

Now, contemplate further by asking the following type of questions.

"What is the *awareness* and understanding that remain at the end of each contemplation that I have gone through so far?

"Maybe this awareness, this understanding, is who I really am?

"This awareness has always been there, right from the beginning of this contemplation until now. So, maybe it is the 'I' who is aware?"

Now simply let go of contemplating and let everything be as it is. Let it just be. After a while, if you are in a state of relinquishment, you might notice some questions arising automatically. Here is a sample.

"Is it possible that 'I' is not aware but awareness itself is aware?

"Then, what is the 'I'?

"But why there has to be an 'I'?

"Am I somehow trying to cling to something?

"Am I trying to identify with something somehow because I cannot let go of the 'I'?

"Am I attached to the 'I'?

"This tendency of clinging, this tendency of identifying with something, is this *itself* what the 'I' might be?

"Are these tendencies arising because consciousness is deluded?

"Is it deluded consciousness that perceives itself as 'I,' because it is deluded?

"Is this what the ego is?

"Is the ego simply deluded consciousness?

"But then, who is the one that is aware that the ego is deluded consciousness?

"Is it me who is aware?

"But why does it have to be me?

"Is it not possible that awareness itself is aware?

"Is such awareness what non-deluded consciousness is?

"Is non-deluded consciousness what pure awareness is?

"Is it pure awareness that is simply aware without the need for a being to be aware?

"Is it then possible that even pure awareness is not who I am?

"Is pure awareness simply consciousness that is conscious that it is pure consciousness?

"Is there really any need or reason to understand pure awareness or pure consciousness as my 'self'?

"Would that be wise or unwise?"

Due to the neutrality of mind and increasing degree of relinquishment arising out of this contemplation, answers to these questions will spontaneously manifest and enlighten your mind. You will experience *liberating bliss*. Enjoy it and become absorbed in it.

A few moments of such abiding and absorption can have a profound effect on you because such abiding does three things:

CHAPTER 20   DEVELOPING INTELLIGENT MIND

1. It makes you infinitely more aware and wakeful than before. Awareness or wakefulness is the fundamental quality of a truly happy, enlightened, and liberated mind.
2. It purifies mind-consciousness by removing the roots of craving and aversion, which are "I," "me," and "mine." Therefore, you eventually become peaceful in the truest sense.
3. It makes you wise—also in the truest sense—because it establishes perfect intelligence. In this life your ultimate reward is perfect intelligence. *Only* perfect intelligence can eradicate ignorance (the ego), which is the root cause of all human suffering. Ignorance is the ultimate disease and perfect intelligence is the ultimate remedy.

* * *

Chapter 21

Developing an Intelligent Heart

Once a child asked an angel, "What is heaven?"
The angel replied, "My dear one, heaven is none other than the heart full of love."
The child then asked, "What is hell?"
The angel replied, "My dear one, hell is none other than the heart empty of love."
Metaphorically speaking, the heart full of love is an intelligent heart. Here, the word "heart" symbolizes the mind and the word "love" symbolizes the presence of the four divine mental elements. In other words, an intelligent heart is mind predominantly made of loving-kindness, compassion, gladness, and oneness/equanimity (see figure 21.1).

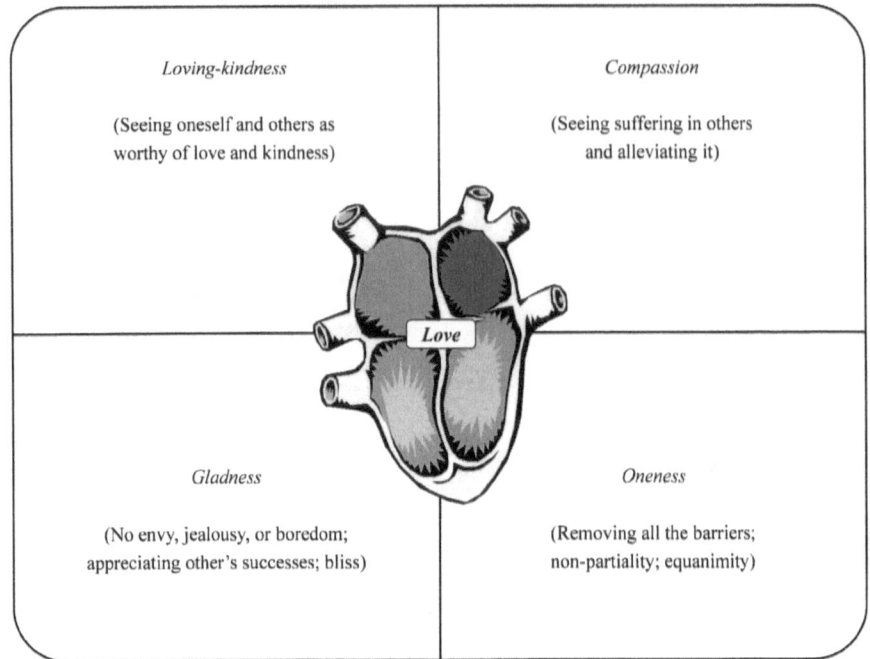

Figure 21.1. The four elements of an intelligent heart—of love—are loving-kindness, compassion, gladness, and oneness (equanimity).

When the four elements of an intelligent heart interact with wholesome mental elements, they generate higher levels of intelligence, especially SQ and soul intelligence. Thereby they make possible an excellent, extraordinary, and immaculate way of dealing with all beings. They provide the best means for abiding exquisitely, elegantly, and gracefully in the world among other beings. Ultimately, they lay the groundwork for living a perfect life here and now.

The following four practices are the means to accomplishing that end.[1]

Cultivating Loving-kindness

The purpose of this practice is to develop the ability to see oneself and others as worthy of unconditional love and kindness. Loving-kindness can be cultivated through contemplation, which conditions the mind for non-hatred.

CHAPTER 21 DEVELOPING AN INTELLIGENT HEART

Sit in a comfortable posture in a pleasing environment. Gently close your eyes and practice intelligent breathing (as previously discussed on page 315) for five minutes to develop a basic level of concentration. Then, open your eyes and study the following narrative.

Once you understand the nature of this sample contemplation, come up with a narrative in your own voice. Write it down in a similar format to the sample narrative and then read it, reflect upon it, or meditate on it as frequently as you like, especially when you are feeling dejected or irritated.

Always begin your contemplation by acknowledging your shortcomings and realizing the need for cultivating loving-kindness. An example:

"I love my spouse, my children, my father, my mother, my teacher, my countrymen.

"I have loving relationships with many people.

"But I still don't feel there is real love in my life.

"I feel so because I often get irritated and angry. I kind of feel that I am not satisfied with life.

"Also, when I do something for family or friends I expect something in return.

"Why do I have these expectations?

"I sometimes even hate the same people I love so dearly.

"Why?

"Do I really love them or do I just have selfish affection for them?

"My love seems impure.

"It must be so because hate, anger, aversion, and resentment still arise in me.

"When they arise, I feel miserable and tired.

"Hate, anger, aversion, and resentment are truly evil things. They bring pain and suffering not only to me, but also to those who are near and dear to me.

"There is a great danger in hate, anger, aversion, and resentment. This danger must be removed so that I may develop real love.

"For that, I must cultivate loving-kindness.

"I know that when I am established in loving-kindness I will be able to see all beings worthy of my love and kindness, unconditionally.

"The contemplation that I am going to do now is the way to develop loving-kindness because it will generate the volitional force along with mindfulness of loving-kindness, and eventually this will reflect in my physical, verbal, and mental actions.

"Let me now begin the contemplation."

Observe silence for a minute, allow yourself to feel the enthusiasm that has arisen, and then begin contemplating as follows.

"May I be free from hate, anger, aversion, and resentment.

"May I seclude myself from all sorts of aggravation, irritation, annoyance, and anxiety.

"May I become more agreeable with others so I can develop real friendship.

"May I become gentle and amiable towards all those with whom I come in contact.

"May I help others and participate in their welfare.

"May I become so loving and kind that no trace of ill will remains in my heart.

"May this loving-kindness pervade my entire being.

"May I thus become happy and healthy.

"May I become free from pain and suffering.

"May I live in safety and joy.

"May I live an auspicious and prosperous life.

"May I live in peace."

Repeat the entire contemplation from top to bottom as many times as you can in a five-minute period. Then remain silent and feel the pleasantness that arises due to continuous remembrance of the states of loving-kindness directed towards you.

Do not react to any thoughts of doubt, suspicion, low self-esteem, guilt, remorse, and worry that arise during the period of contemplation. The ego might say, "Don't be stupid. Don't be crazy. Don't fool yourself," and so on. Don't give in to such thoughts. Keep going

CHAPTER 21   DEVELOPING AN INTELLIGENT HEART

back to your repetitions. Continue until you begin to feel good about yourself. In the beginning, you may need to continue longer than five minutes to generate a pleasant feeling. In any case, give wise attention to the pleasantness of the feeling as the emergence of loving-kindness. Concentrate on that pleasant feeling, become familiar with it, and let it energize your state of mind.

Then, through contemplation, start extending loving-kindness to your children, spouse, parents, friends, and so on, in that order (or follow another order that reflects your liking). It is important to start with someone you love deeply. You may want to start with your children.

"May the arisen loving-kindness in me extend to my children.
"May they become happy and healthy.
"May they become free from pain and suffering.
"May they live in safety and joy.
"May they live an auspicious and prosperous life.
"May they live in peace."

After repeating the above six lines for about five minutes, remain silent and give wise attention to how pleasant you feel towards your children. Concentrate on that pleasant feeling and become familiar with it. After a few moments, repeat the same six lines for your spouse until you begin to feel good about him or her. Repeat longer than five minutes if needed. The key is to generate a good feeling about your spouse. Then, repeat the process for your brothers and sisters, and so forth. At the end, contemplate as follows:

"May the loving-kindness in me extend to those I know and to those I do not know.
"May the loving-kindness in me extend to my enemies if they exist.
"May the loving-kindness in me pervade the entire universe.
"May all living beings become happy and healthy.
"May all living beings become free from pain and suffering.
"May all living beings live in safety and joy.
"May all living beings live an auspicious and prosperous life.
"May all living beings live in peace."

Remember to develop loving-kindness towards yourself first, then towards those who are near and dear to you, and then towards others. This is the easiest and the most natural way.

Feelings of resentment may arise while developing loving-kindness towards your wife or parents, or towards someone who has hurt you in the past. Observe such feelings non-reactively. They will soon lose strength and cease. If you react (meaning, if you get carried away by them) your mind will go on an emotional roller-coaster ride. Eventually, due to sustained practice, mindfulness will arise again.

For beginners, it is not always possible to remain mindful if thoughts of hurt and resentment arise. If this happens to you, immediately change the person to whom you are extending your loving-kindness. For some time, extend your loving-kindness to a person who is very dear to you or whom you admire and respect and for whom there is no resentment, such as a child or a venerable teacher. When you shift your subject of loving-kindness in this way, feelings of hurt and resentment will subside and feelings of love, admiration, respect, and honor will take over. With that wholesome state of mind, again go back to the previous subject and start extending or showering your loving kindness. If this technique does not help much, then contemplate deeper to remove the hurt and resentment as demonstrated by the following sample.

"I was only hurt emotionally. I am resentful because my feelings were hurt. I am resentful because I was not treated fairly and justly.

"Is it really that bad?

"Is it so bad that I cannot forgive him (or her, or them)?

"Let me forgive him for whatever he did and not bother about fairness and justice.

"Let me surrender to the laws of karma, the ultimate judge."

Remain silent for a few moments and then contemplate further, as follows:

"May he not suffer.

"May he become wise.

CHAPTER 21 DEVELOPING AN INTELLIGENT HEART

"May he become kind, fair, and just so he does not generate bad karma.

"May he begin his spiritual evolution like I have begun mine.

"May he purify his mind, as I am purifying mine.

"May he become happy, as I am now becoming happy."

Check your feelings. If the resentment still hasn't gone, continue contemplating, as follows:

"Was Jesus treated fairly?

"Can there be anything more unfair and unjust than how Jesus was executed? Even then, he asked for the forgiveness for his executors.

"How wonderful it is to be merciful!

"How wonderful it is to forgive!"

Feel the pleasantness of these thoughts for few moments, and then continue.

"I forgive all those who have hurt me and who have been unfair and unjust to me.

"I forgive myself for being resentful.

"Let all beings be forgiven for their deeds.

"Let the law of karma take its course.

"Let all beings understand the law.

"In this way, let all beings free themselves from hurt, resentment, pain, and suffering."

If you contemplate in this way, ardently and consistently, you will certainly get rid of all the emotional baggage you have been carrying, provided you are patient with the practice. Any mental development activity takes a long time to bear fruits. So, please be patient. Wholesome results are bound to follow.

Notwithstanding, getting rid of anger is the toughest challenge. So, if you are hoarding anger against someone, augment your cultivation of loving-kindness by applying wise attention during your contemplation. Here is an example.

"I feel angry whenever things don't go my way. Can I really control the environment so nothing goes against my wish? Is it really possible?

"There are so many people, so many conditions, and so many variables behind every circumstance. I cannot possibly control all circumstances or cause people to fulfill my wishes. So, is it really wise to become angry at anybody or at any situation when things don't go my way?

"Whenever I feel angry about somebody, I just don't feel good. There is an unpleasant burning sensation in my body. I feel so weak after the anger is over.

"Also, when I am angry I look very ugly! Other people look ugly when they are angry. It must also be true for me.

"Anger is not going to make me friends. Instead, I will have more enemies.

"Anger is so unprofitable. It is definitely not worth getting angry. It is such a loss, such a pain, such a failure."

Now, recall an incidence of anger (for example, an argument with your spouse) and reflect upon it. An example:

"Despite knowing all this, why do I still feel angry about my wife (or husband or boss or son or father or a friend, whatever the case may be)?

"It must be due to lack of loving-kindness, for anger cannot exist where there is loving-kindness.

"I am not good enough as a lover. I do not have enough loving-kindness to defeat anger towards this person. I must now develop it urgently. I must strengthen and improve my practice of loving-kindness at any cost."

Now, check your feelings and see if you are still feeling angry. If you do then continue:

"I am still feeling angry about my wife (or husband, or boss, or son, or father, or friend), maybe because I am focusing too much on her bad qualities and ignoring her good qualities.

"I must try to recollect and focus on all her good qualities."

Now, start recollecting every bit of other person's goodness, every possible incidence you can think of. Do not react to ego-driven

CHAPTER 21   DEVELOPING AN INTELLIGENT HEART

thoughts that will try to sway you away from your focus on the good. Give wise attention to the pleasant feelings that arise when you think about every bit of goodness in others. Once you come up with a few examples of goodness, say it mentally to become mindful of it. For example:

"My wife is hard working. She is running around taking care of kids and other affairs day in and day out. It must be so difficult to handle kids. She is also handling her career so well. She must be getting tired now and then, and maybe she just wants me to give her some attention, to hear her out."

Here, recollect as many good qualities as possible before continuing. If you do, you are bound to feel more appreciative and less angry. Mentally verbalize what you feel. An example:

"Wow! She is really not such a bad person. She has so many good qualities that I never paid attention to.

"I feel like I am now developing confidence about her as a good person by admiring her goodness. I am now, in fact, feeling good about her!

"It is so interesting.

"It is so wonderful.

"It feels so good to think good about others.

"It feels so good not to have anger towards another person!"

Once you start experiencing pleasantness, increase your mindfulness of the person you are thinking about by visualizing that person. If you notice that you are smiling, keep the smile going for as long as you can while contemplating as follows.

"May the arisen loving-kindness in me engulf my wife (or husband, or boss, or son, or father, or friend).

"May she become happy and healthy.

"May she become free from pain and suffering.

"May she live in safety and joy.

"May she live an auspicious and prosperous life.

"May she live in peace."

If you feel angry with someone who is simply a bad character, meaning a person who does not have any goodness inside at all, then you need to deepen your contemplation. Here is a sample:

"My boss is such a jerk! There is simply nothing good in him. I cannot think of any good qualities in him.

"But after all, he is another human being and I must consider him worthy of my kindness.

"He may not be good now, but he may become good in the future.

"May he become fair and just.

"May he become wise.

"May he begin his spiritual evolution, as I have begun mine.

"May he purify his mind, as I am purifying mine, and may his badness be reduced.

"May he become happy, as I am now becoming happy."

As you contemplate, you will start feeling a bit better about the person. Your mind will open up and allow you to give wise attention. This is a good time to direct your contemplation towards yourself. The following are some examples:

"I feel angry about my boss because he has hurt me. He has been unfair to me.

"But is it really possible for him to hurt me unless I allow him to? After all, it is my mind. It is my domain.

"I should not allow him to influence my mind. That would be his victory.

"Let me just abandon this anger towards him and gain a victory.

"After all, this anger itself is the cause of unhappiness and *not* him."

Be silent for a few moments and absorb the mind in such understanding. Then continue:

"This anger is the biggest hindrance on the path of virtue. Why should I let it grow?

"It is foolish to grow or hold something that is so harmful, detrimental, and poisonous!

CHAPTER 21   DEVELOPING AN INTELLIGENT HEART

"If he has hurt me already, why should I multiply the suffering by feeling angry towards him? Why should I hurt myself as he has hurt me?

"I am, in a way, copying his unwholesome deeds, because I am hurting myself by feeling angry just as he has hurt me."

Many times, as you are contemplating in this way to develop loving-kindness towards the "bad guys" in your life, the ego will arise in an attempt to thwart the practice. The following contemplation is an example of what you can do when this happens. It is important not to give up or react, but to keep training by strengthening wise attention. This is the only way to neither suppress your emotions nor express them, but to nullify their unwholesome power through wisdom.

"Maybe I should just express my anger towards him and get even. (*Voice of the ego.*)

"No! It is not wise to express anger back at someone to get even. That would be even worse than his anger. (*Your response.*)

"Because of my anger, he may feel unpleasant or he may not, but I will definitely experience those unpleasant burning sensations, that ugly look, that post-anger weakness. Because of expressing anger I will actually multiply my own misery.

"Responding to anger with anger is like trying to hit him with a hot iron rod. It would burn my hands first.

"Responding to anger with anger is like throwing red chili powder against the wind. It would get in my eyes and hurt me first.

"There is no way to win the battle by responding to anger with anger. The battle can only be won by forgiving and by remaining peaceful in response to anger.

"I must win this battle against anger.

"Let me forgive him for his mistakes.

"Let me also forgive myself for my mistakes."

Now, check and see if you are still feeling angry. If yes, then your anger is deep rooted. You must continue your contemplation to allow for further wise attention and to purge and eradicate deep-rooted unwholesome memories. Here's an example:

"It looks like my forgiveness is not enough. I am still feeling angry.

"The boss is not here and nothing is happening that should arouse anger in me at this very moment.

"What am I angry at right now? Why am I angry right now?

"I guess it is all in the mind. My anger is due to deep-rooted memories, which are coming to the surface.

"Why do I hold on to them and react?

"I am holding on to them because I am neither mindful of, nor giving enough wise attention to the emotion of anger that is arising at this very moment. After all, anger (an emotion) is only a mental phenomenon. It lasts for just a few moments. It comes and goes.

"Let me just observe it as it comes and goes and not cling to it.

"Let me not get angry at anger itself.

"Let me not become resentful towards resentment itself.

"Let it just come and go and let me maintain equanimity towards all of it."

The moment you start thinking about equanimity, everything will change for the better. You will first start feeling deeply pleasant, almost peaceful. Become mindful of that and mentally iterate what you are experiencing. Here's an example:

"Wow! This equanimity is so wonderful.

"I feel so peaceful now because I see everything so clearly.

"I see who is the one getting angry.

"I see that it is the ego, the sense of separate self (ignorance).

"It is delusion, the lack of wisdom, which is at the root of it all.

"This understanding is so sublime.

"It is so uplifting.

"It is so auspicious.

"It is divine!"

After the contemplation ends, remain silent and enjoy the bliss of understanding.

CHAPTER 21   DEVELOPING AN INTELLIGENT HEART

Cultivating Compassion

In your life, you may have encountered evildoers so bad that you simply cannot develop loving-kindness towards them. For such people, cultivate compassion because it is easier to do so. Why? Because compassion makes you see the evildoer as someone who is diseased and suffering, thereby removing your anger and resentment of the highest degree.

Let us say you simply detest your competitor who sued you unfairly and brought tremendous harm to your business, you, and your family. You cannot even stand the sight of him and you feel that there is no possibility of ever cultivating loving-kindness towards him. Now, let us say, one day you find out that your competitor has been diagnosed with an extremely painful fatal disease. How will you then feel about him? Most likely, your anger and resentment towards him will reduce, because you will now see the same person as someone who is diseased and suffering. In other words, a bit of compassion will arise in you.

When we notice physical diseases, extreme poverty, and any other such physical conditions in others, we generally feel compassionate. What if we were to notice another's stupidity, meanness, unjust and unfair behavior, and animosity as that person's disease (although mental)? We will stop *reacting* with anger and resentment and *start* acting with compassion.

The purpose of the following contemplation is to cultivate the habit of seeing suffering (or disease) in others so that compassion can arise. These sample statements are derived from my personal practice. After you understand their nature, you must come up with your own voice.

Begin by thinking about someone who is evil, someone you simply cannot stand. As unpleasant feelings start to arise, begin contemplating as follows.

"This person is suffering from mental diseases.

"He is suffering from greed, hatred, delusion, moral recklessness, restlessness, and shamelessness. But unfortunately he is not aware of it.

"He does not know he is generating unwholesome karma that will certainly bear unwholesome fruits.

"No one escapes the grip of karma.

"Although already suffering, this person is going to suffer even more pain and agony due to fruition of the evil karma.

"Even though looking happy and powerful right now, he is making grounds for his own suffering.

"Just as a thief looks happy, healthy, and powerful before his arrest, not knowing that one day an arrest will happen and result in his painful imprisonment, this person, even though he is looking happy and powerful right now, will certainly bear pain and suffering.

"He is destined for untold misery.

"His evil deeds will only create evil destiny.

"He is unaware that his actions are the mark of suffering.

"His current victory and his powers are worthless. They are, in fact, taking him closer to a painful future, which is certain.

"It is unfortunate but it is unavoidable."

You will now begin to notice the subsidence of unpleasant feelings and the arising of peaceful feelings due to compassion. Your heart will open up. At that time, start contemplating (as in a prayer) as follows.

"May this person become aware of his evil actions.

"May he realize the evil nature of his deeds.

"May he realize the harm he is doing to himself and others.

"May he become wise.

"May he not generate more evil karma and may his pain and suffering be reduced.

"May he become truly happy and not suffer.

"May he live in peace."

As you contemplate like this, compassion will take root in you. It will manifest as non-meanness and hold you back from resorting to force, anger, violence, and revenge towards the evildoer. Due to this non-meanness, your sorrow or fear will significantly vanish and you will become peaceful.

CHAPTER 21 DEVELOPING AN INTELLIGENT HEART

If after such contemplation perfect compassion still does not arise, then recollect the greatness of compassionate masters, like Jesus or Buddha. For example:

"Jesus was such a compassionate master. He showered compassion on his own persecutors, who crucified him. No one could take away his peace. No one could make him fearful. He proved, how magnificent, how excellent compassion is.

"Buddha was the epitome of compassion. His compassion permeated everything and subdued his opponents, hostile cousin, hostile pundits, a murderer who attacked him, and the wild beasts that lived by his side in the deep forests. Because of such compassion, there was no possibility for the arising of meanness in his presence.

"Compassion is so powerful, so peaceful.

"May I be inspired by these great masters.

"May I become compassionate towards the evildoer."

At the end of contemplation, remain silent for a while as you enjoy the feelings of peace.

Having discussed how to cultivate loving-kindness and compassion through contemplation, we can now talk about their combined application in daily life. But first, note the fact that loving-kindness arises when you see others as lovable. So, it is very easy to arouse it for yourself and dear ones, and very difficult to arouse it for a hostile or evil person. Compassion arises when you see others as being diseased and suffering. So, it is very difficult to arouse it for yourself (because you generally don't want to see yourself as suffering or diseased) and very easy, almost natural to arouse it for a hostile or evil person.

Knowing this, when someone is angry at you arouse compassion for that person first and then let loving-kindness seep in. On the other hand, when *you* are angry at someone you don't like, arouse loving-kindness for yourself first and then let compassion seep in. In this way, together, let compassion and loving-kindness engulf you and others in all life situations. Let goodwill, welfare, friendliness, non-hatred, non-meanness, and peace prevail at all times and at any cost.

Cultivating Gladness

When it comes to eradicating hatred, anger, resentment, meanness, and so on, the elements of loving-kindness and compassion can do wonders. But when it comes to eradicating jealousy and envy, you need to add the third element of love to your arsenal: gladness.

You can cultivate gladness by simply remembering and contemplating other people's successes. Start with a person who is very dear to you and who is always glad and very accomplished, or by remembering someone who is always cheerful and brings smiles to you. This person could be your sweet little child, your accomplished adult son, your spiritual teacher, or your best friend. Then, follow up with other successful people who may not be near to you, but who are glad and successful. Finally, remember successful people of whom you are jealous or envious. In that order, remember and contemplate other's successes. Here is a sample:

"This person is really a happy being.

"He is always smiling, always so cheerful.

"He is, indeed, glad.

"I feel so happy when I think about his successes.

"I feel so happy for him. I feel such a joy."

Become mindful of pleasant (joyous) feelings that will arise due to wise remembrance. Then mentally iterate what you are feeling. For example:

"Oh! This joy is so wonderful! It is so excellent!"

Now, contemplate as follows:

"Just as I feel happy about this person's success, may I also feel happy and glad about Mr. Jones (a person you envy).

"May I appreciate his success and accomplishment.

"May I feel joy in that.

"May I become glad."

Repeat this contemplation for all other people, one by one, in the order specified earlier. Once you are developed and established in gladness, extend your gladness and let it extend out and permeate your world by contemplating like this:

CHAPTER 21   DEVELOPING AN INTELLIGENT HEART

"Just as I am now feeling glad, may all human beings become glad.

"May there be no envy, jealousy, discontent, or boredom among beings.

"May they all derive joy from others success.

"In this way, may all beings be gladdened in their heart."

At the end of contemplation, remain silent for a while as you enjoy the feelings of appreciative joy.

Cultivating Oneness

Once you start cultivating loving-kindness, compassion, and gladness, you will begin to *rise* in love and never again *fall* in love. Eventually, equanimity (the aptitude of oneness) will arise of its own accord. It will then help you break down all the barriers and make you impartial, unprejudiced, and neutral towards all beings, including yourself. You will no longer have any friends or enemies. You will no longer love someone more than the other. You will no longer have expectations of any kind. You will care less for gifts and rewards. You will simply become neutralized due to transcending all differences and discriminations. Your heart will expand immeasurably and become space-like. You will be impartial towards all beings and all formations and yet all encompassing. You will experience blissfulness, peacefulness, ease, contentment, and a sense of accomplishment.

Although oneness arises naturally out of the other three elements of love, you can also cultivate it through contemplation and expedite its development. So, if you want to attain oneness (especially all those fantastic mental states that come out of oneness) sooner rather than later this is a practice that will accelerate your progress.

Remember one of your acquaintances whom you neither like nor dislike, or someone about whom you have a neutral opinion. Then, remember other acquaintances, your friends, and your dear ones. Think about yourself at the end. As you remember each one in that order, contemplate as demonstrated here.

"This person is performing the karmic acts that will bear him fruit.

"His wholesome karma will bear wholesome fruits.
"His unwholesome karma will bear unwholesome fruits.
"The law of karma is the ultimate ruler."

Then, remember the next person on your list according to the prescribed order. Repeat the preceding contemplation for this individual and each one who follows. At the end, contemplate:

"The rule of karma is the same for all of us.
"It has no barriers.
"It is just and fair.
"In view of this law, there is really no difference between the acquaintances, the friends, the dear ones, and myself.
"In a way, all are equal."

Remain silent for about a minute, absorb the mind in reflection, and then resume your contemplation.

"Let karma rule.
"Why should I like and dislike people based on their deeds?
"Why should I be prejudiced about people?
"Why should I become interested in some and resent some?
"Why should I be craving to make some people happy and some people miserable?
"That is not wise."

Remain silent for about a minute, absorb your mind in reflection, and then resume contemplating as follows.

"All beings are ruled by their karma and they all are bearer of its fruit.
"This is now certain.
"It is now my understanding.
"It is now my wisdom."

Remain silent for about a minute, become mindful of peaceful feelings, and then resume contemplating by mentally iterating what you are feeling. Here's an example:

"This wisdom is so peaceful.
"I feel such stillness inside now.
"I am neither feeling a craving nor resentment towards anyone.

CHAPTER 21   DEVELOPING AN INTELLIGENT HEART

"There is neither a painful feeling, nor a pleasant one.
"There is neither joy nor sorrow.
"There is just this sublimity and bliss.
"This feeling is really extraordinary.
"This must be the experience of equanimity.
"This equanimity is most excellent.
"May I become established in equanimity and thereby abide in peace.
"May all beings establish themselves in equanimity and thereby abide in peace."

At the end of contemplation, remain silent for a while as you enjoy the feelings of serenity and peace.

The Evolution of Love

Even though all four elements of love cannot be developed equally at the same time, they should be all practiced *together* to develop various aspects of perfect living among other beings. First, the aspect of non-hatred, goodwill, and friendliness should be developed, because without the removal of hatred, ill will, and selfish affection love really cannot occur. In other words, unless the element of loving-kindness is well developed we cannot even enter the realm of love.

Once loving-kindness is developed, the aspect of human suffering becomes evident, which means compassion has arisen. Compassion promotes the removal of human suffering. Once loving-kindness and compassion are developed, gladness arises by being able to see successes of beings and by not having envy, jealousy, and aversion (boredom) towards others. Once all three aspects are developed, equanimity arises due to balance, detachment, impartiality, and neutrality towards all beings. In this way, even though all four elements are practiced together, loving-kindness is prominent first, then compassion, then gladness, and finally the equanimity, in that order of significance.

The significance of each element reduces as higher and higher aspects of love are developed. The significance of loving-kindness reduces as compassion is developed, and it further reduces as gladness is developed, and it becomes insignificant as equanimity is developed. This reducing scale of significance is similar to transcendence and *not* to irrelevance.

Now let me briefly explain how exactly these four elements of love evolve and lead us to perfect way of living here and now.

When we are thoroughly established in loving-kindness, we become the beauty of the world. How? By becoming adorable, lovable, and non-repulsive just as a beautiful thing is.

While we are abiding in loving-kindness, we appreciate the beauty of the world and, in return, the world appreciates the beauty of our being.

If we do not get stuck in our own beauty or in the glory it brings to us, our love continues to evolve. Soon, with the base of loving-kindness, we begin to clearly see the suffering of others and it moves our heart. Our love now matures to such an extent that we now only think of alleviating others suffering, because, at this stage, we look through and beyond people and things, and notice the common underlying phenomena of human suffering. It is like expanding our awareness and noticing not just the beautiful lotus but also the non-beautiful mud that it is rooted in. It is also like seeing the space that surrounds the lotus as more beautiful than the lotus, because space is devoid of decaying and perishing, and because space is not rooted in anything non-beautiful. At this stage, we transcend the beauty of the world and its grasping. The world of beautiful feelings and things, the world of pleasures no longer grips our consciousness. Our love (that was dominated by loving-kindness) now becomes predominantly *compassionate*.

Once we are thoroughly established in compassion, it makes it possible, through contemplative practice, to not envy anything or become jealous of anybody. We begin to feel glad when others succeed. We begin to rejoice more when others are happy, because, we see others' underlying suffering due to our purified and penetrative vision. It is like becoming glad when a terminally ill child gives us a smile. This gladness is infinitely more blissful than the happiness that arises out

CHAPTER 21 DEVELOPING AN INTELLIGENT HEART

of the physical beauty of a healthy child's smile. It is so because this gladness is based on compassion, which is generated by realizing the terminal condition (the suffering) of the ill child. This gladness is supported by compassion and not by pity or sorrow.

The arising of gladness is like realizing that the happiness or bliss is the quality of consciousness and not the quality of materiality. The experience of gladness is like connecting with others at the level of consciousness and not at the level of matter. It is like penetrating space (that surrounds the lotus) and apprehending the underlying nonmaterial reality of consciousness that sees the lotus. At this stage, we completely transcend the materiality aspects of the world. The world of matter no longer grips our consciousness. Our love now becomes predominantly *blissful*.

Once we are thoroughly established in gladness (bliss), we abide in this world at the level of consciousness. We perceive everything in terms of consciousness. Consciousness becomes our point of reference. When we deal with a hostile person, we don't look at a person being hostile. We look at person's hostility as *hostile consciousness*. Similarly, an angry man is not seen as a man with anger, but as *anger consciousness*. A kind man is not seen as a man with kindness, but as *kind consciousness*. The entire world is seen as the play of consciousness. Our own actions are seen as the arising and cessation of various states of consciousness.

In light of such purified and penetrative vision, we do not react, of course, to unwholesome situations. But neither do we react to wholesome situations. We are no longer moved by pain or pleasure, sorrow or joy. At this stage, we transcend the karmic (mental) aspects of the world. The world of karmic mind no longer grips our consciousness. In this way, our gladness leads us to oneness. Our love now enters the state of *equanimity*.

Once we are thoroughly established in equanimity, it is impossible to react to anything—good or bad. There is neither reaction nor karmic action. We become peaceful. The peace of equanimity is infinitely more sublime than bliss. It is so because this equanimity is based on gladness, which is generated by *blissfully conscious consciousness*. This equanimity is supported by gladness, not by indifference, apathy, or coldness. This sublime equanimity and the worldly equanimity (mind-control, self-restraint, material tolerance) of ignorant, worldly-minded people are like the opposite ends of the line of infinity. The understanding of sublime equanimity is beyond the reach of non-meditators.

The arising of sublime equanimity is like realizing that there is truly nothing else beyond consciousness. It is a realization that there is no being, no personality, and no fixed entity behind consciousness. It is a realization that consciousness does not belong to anyone. Consciousness is empty. Consciousness is just a phenomenon.

The experience of equanimity is like connecting with others at the level of emptiness or nothingness and not at the level of mind or self-consciousness. It is like seeing all as a bundle of consciousness that is empty of separate selves and of ego. It is also like penetrating consciousness itself and apprehending the underlying non-self reality of all beings: soul. This state of egolessness, of perfect love is worthy of our pursuit. It is perfect because nothing else remains to be perfected. Nothing else remains to be done.

At this stage, we completely transcend the material aspects of the world *as well as* the mental aspects. The world of mind and matter no longer grips consciousness because consciousness now is totally purified. Our body continues to exist in the human realm because it was born there, but consciousness simply abides in the heavenly realm. And we begin to live as if *we are in this world but not of it*.

* * *

Epilogue

Enlightened? Now What?

Kindly go back to the mirror you looked into when you began reading this book.
Look again and find out what you see.
If you see your*self*, then know that you are not enlightened.
If you do not see yourself but you are scared, then know that you are not enlightened.
If you do not see yourself *and* you are smiling, then . . .
The truth of the matter is that there are no enlightened people, only enlightened *moments*.[1] To be more precise, there is only enlightenment, an unconditional *phenomenon*. Our job is to continue to tap into this phenomenon, no matter what. Even Buddha did that. After enlightenment, he continued his daily meditation practice until death.[2] There is practice before enlightenment and after. That is the way.

On a more down-to-earth note, here is what we need to do post-enlightenment.
- Reexamine and cross-examine the realized truth carefully by contemplating on it for several weeks following the enlightenment
- Remain awake (as in awareness) 24/7, which means, witness the body as the *body,* mind as *mind,* consciousness as *consciousness* (and none as *your* body, mind, or consciousness). Witness everything from moment to moment as a phenomenon
- Live in an accomplished way. Live as if you have attained the highest peak and there is no more climbing to do—simply look up and admire the heavens
- Live selflessly, unconditionally, and carefree. Live as if your abode is the highest peak and your vision is space overlooking the world of formations
- Enjoy the freedom and peace of enlightenment by reflecting upon it daily without clinging to it
- Share your enlightenment with others in your own way using your unique talents so that others might be inspired by it, pursue it, and become enlightened, too
- And as usual, do your laundry!

Is It the End of Knowing?

Enlightenment is not the end of the quest for knowledge. It is a gateway to new horizons of wisdom.

If you are enlightened, you will know the elemental (ultimate) nature of everything. You will have the knowledge and vision of the fundamental laws of suffering, impermanence, and non-self. But you will not necessarily know the myriads of cause-effect relations and the conditionality that underlies those laws. For example, knowing that the speed of light is constant and that it is the universal speed limit is one thing; knowing the countless applications of modern physics derived from that fundamental law is another.

With an enlightened mind, you will begin to explore the specific details of what you have discovered and continue to bathe in the bliss

EPILOGUE ENLIGHTENED? NOW WHAT?

that will arise from the newfound wisdom. You will, however, never become omniscient. No one ever will. Buddha was enlightened, but still he did not know what we know today about the brain, genetics, and atoms.[3]

Just as the universe, the sphere of knowledge, is constantly expanding, the domain of knowledge will always remain inexhaustible. Post-enlightenment, you will always have the work of discovery to do. This does not mean enlightenment is incomplete. It is simply unlimited—without an end.

Enlightenment is unconditional.

* * *

Appendix A

The Material Elements in Terms of Their Characteristics, Functions, Manifestations, and Proximate Causes

THE ELEMENTS OF SOUL

No.	Elements	Characteristics	Functions	Manifestations	Proximate Causes
1	Earth	• Hardness • Rigidity • Stiffness • Harshness	To provide foundation or support for other material elements	Receiving	Water, fire, and air elements
2	Water	• Fluidity • Trickling • Oozing	To intensify coexisting material states	• Cohesion • Holding together	Earth, fire, and air elements
3	Fire	• Temperature (heat/coldness) • Maintenance • Digestion	To mature or ripen coexisting material states	Continuous supply of softness	Earth, water, and air elements
4	Air	• Distention • Conveyance • Movement	To cause motion in other material elements	Conveyance to other places	Earth, water, and fire elements
5	Nutriment	• Nutritive essence • Nutritional substance	To uphold physical body	• Fortifying the body • Consolidating the body	Gross edible food
6	Taste	Impinging on the tongue	To become the object of tongue consciousness	Resort of the respective sense consciousness	Earth, water, fire, and air elements
7	Form/color	Impinging on the eyes	To become the object of eye consciousness	Resort of the respective sense consciousness	Earth, water, fire, and air elements
8	Smell	Impinging on the nose	To become the object of nose consciousness	Resort of the respective sense consciousness	Earth, water, fire, and air elements
9	Eye sensitivity (subtle eye matter)	Sensitivity springing from desire to see	To pick up visible datum or forms as an object	Material base for eye consciousness	Earth, water, fire, and air elements born out of karma (desire to see)

APPENDIX A

10	Ear sensitivity (subtle ear matter)	Sensitivity springing from desire to hear	To pick up sound or audible datum or forms as an object	Material base for ear consciousness	Earth, water, fire, and air elements born out of karma (desire to hear)
11	Nose sensitivity (subtle nose matter)	Sensitivity springing from desire to smell	To pick up smell or odor as an object	Material base for nose consciousness	Earth, water, fire, and air elements born out of karma (desire to smell)
12	Tongue sensitivity (subtle eye matter)	Sensitivity springing from desire to taste	To pick up taste or flavor as an object	Material base for tongue consciousness	Earth, water, fire, air elements born out of karma (desire to taste)
13	Body sensitivity (subtle body matter)	Sensitivity springing from desire to touch	To pick up tactile sensations as an object	Material base for body consciousness	Earth, water, fire, air elements born out of karma (desire to touch)
14	Male sexuality	Masculinity	To show masculinity	Sexual structure of the body, male features or occupations, reason for the mark, sign, work, and ways of male	Earth, water, fire, air elements born out of karma (desire to propagate the species)
15	Female sexuality	Femininity	To show femininity	Sexual structure of the body, female features or occupations, reason for the mark, sign, work, and ways of female	Earth, water, fire, air elements born out of karma (desire to propagate the species)
16	Material life	Maintaining coexisting matter at the moment of their presence	To make matter occur	Establishment of the presence of matter	Earth, water, fire, and air elements that are to be maintained or sustained
17	Mind sensitivity (subtle heart matter)	Sensitivity springing from desire to think and know	To support and uphold mind or mind consciousness elements	Material base for mind consciousness (all types of consciousness except the five sense types)	Earth, water, fire, and air elements born out of karma (desire to think and know)
18	Sound	Impinging on the ears	To become the object of ear consciousness	Resort of the respective sense consciousness	Earth, water, fire, and air elements

369

THE ELEMENTS OF SOUL

19	Bodily intimation	Communication of ideas and feelings	To display intention	Cause of bodily movements	Earth, water, fire, and air elements born out of consciousness
20	Vocal intimation	Communication of ideas and feelings	To display intention	Cause of verbal expressions or voice	Earth, water, fire, and air elements born out of consciousness
21	Continuity	Occurrence of matter	To anchor matter	Non-interruption in arising of matter	Matter to be anchored
22	Lightness	• Diminishing of material heaviness • Non-sluggishness	To crush heaviness in matter	Light transformability	Light (non-heavy) matter
23	Flexibility	Diminishing of mental rigidity	To crush rigidity in matter	Non- resistance to any action	Flexible matter
24	Pliability	Calming and diminishing of unwieldiness in bodily action	To crush and to quiet down unwieldiness in matter	Non-weakness	Pliable, workable matter
25	Production	Launching or arising or setting up of matter	To make matter arise for the first time	• Arisen matter • Completed state of matter	Matter produced
26	Decay	Aging or decaying of matter	To lead matter towards termination	Loss of newness without loss of individual essence	Decaying matter
27	Impermanence	Complete breaking up of matter	To make matter subside	• Destruction of matter • Falling away of matter	Matter that is completely breaking up
28	Space	• Delimiting of matter • Voidness	• To display boundaries of matter • To enable perceiving of various types of matter as distinct from each other	• Confines of matter • State of gaps and apertures	Matter delimited

Appendix B

The 121 Types of Consciousness

The following list is organized to exhibit the hierarchy of consciousness from unwholesome to wholesome and beyond.

THE ELEMENTS OF SOUL

Type I. Unwholesome Consciousness

No.	Composition of Mental Elements	Description
1	1–14, 16–19, 23	Predominantly rooted in greed • Habitually engrossed in sensual pleasures • Justifying attachments with a belief that it is the right way to live • The adage "Ignorance is bliss" describes it
2	1–14, 16–19, 23, 25–26	Predominantly rooted in greed • Willfully engrossed in sensual pleasures • Justifying attachments with a belief that it is the right way to live • There is a lack of mental energy for understanding right from wrong
3	1–14, 16–19, 20	Predominantly rooted in greed • Habitually engrossed in sensual pleasures due to madness arising from the ego • No justification for attachments
4	1–14, 16–19, 20, 25–26	Predominantly rooted in greed • Willfully engrossed in sensual pleasures due to madness arising from the ego • No justification for attachments • There is a lack of mental energy for understanding right from wrong
5	1–8, 10–14, 16–19, 23	Predominantly rooted in greed • Habitually engrossed in self-centered activities, not necessarily sensual pleasures • Justifying attachments with a belief that it is the right way to live • Being insensitive
6	1–8, 10–14, 16–19, 23, 25, 26	Predominantly rooted in greed • Willfully engrossed in self-centered activities, not necessarily sensual pleasures • Justifying attachments with a belief that it is the right way to live • Being insensitive • There is a lack of mental energy for understanding right from wrong
7	1–8, 10–14, 16–19, 20	Predominantly rooted in greed • Habitually engrossed in self-centered activities due to madness arising from ego • No justification for attachments

APPENDIX B

8	1–8, 10–14, 16–19, 20, 25, 26	Predominantly rooted in greed • Willfully engrossed in self-centered activities due to madness arising from the ego • No justification for attachments • There is a lack of mental energy for understanding right from wrong
9	1–8, 10–13, 15–19, 21, 22, 27	Predominantly rooted in hatred • Habitual acts of displeasure and aversion
10	1–8, 10–13, 15–19, 21, 22, 25–27	Predominantly rooted in hatred • Willful acts of displeasure and aversion • There is a lack of mental energy for understanding right from wrong
11	1–8, 10, 16–19, 24	Predominantly rooted in delusion • Sheer delusion, as in insensitivity and perplexed thinking • Predominantly suspicious • There is a lack of knowledge in general
12	1–8, 10–12, 16–19	Predominantly rooted in delusion • Sheer delusion, as in insensitivity and perplexed thinking • Predominantly restless • There is a lack of knowledge in general
		Type II: Wholesome Consciousness
13	1–13, 28–51	Predominantly rooted in non-greed and non-hatred • Habitual
14	1–13, 28–51	Predominantly rooted in non-greed and non-hatred • Willful
15	1–8, 10–13, 28–51	Predominantly rooted in non-greed and non-hatred • Habitual • Non-rapturous
16	1–8, 10–13, 28–51	Predominantly rooted in non-greed and non-hatred • Willful • Non-rapturous

THE ELEMENTS OF SOUL

17	1–13, 28–52	Rooted in non-greed, non-hatred, and non-delusion • Habitual
18	1–13, 28–52	Rooted in non-greed, non-hatred, and non-delusion • Willful
19	1–8, 10–13, 28–52	Rooted in non-greed, non-hatred, and non-delusion • Habitual • Non-rapturous
20	1–8, 10–13, 28–52	Rooted in non-greed, non-hatred, and non-delusion • Willful • Non-rapturous
21	1–13, 28–48, 52	First level of mental absorption during meditation • Presence of thinking, thoughtfulness, rapture, and divine elements
22	1–6, 8–13, 28–48, 52	Second level of mental absorption during meditation • Transcending thinking
23	1–6, 9–13, 28–48, 52	Third level of mental absorption during meditation • Transcending thinking and thoughtfulness
24	1–6, 10–13, 28–48, 52	Fourth level of mental absorption during meditation • Transcending thinking, thoughtfulness, and rapture
25	1–6, 10–13, 28–46, 52	Fifth level of mental absorption during meditation • Transcending thinking, thoughtfulness, rapture, and divine elements • Entering spaceness
26	1–6, 10–13, 28–46, 52	Sixth level of mental absorption during meditation • Experiencing spaceness (zero)
27	1–6, 10–13, 28–46, 52	Seventh level of mental absorption during meditation • Transcending spaceness • Entering and experiencing consciousness

APPENDIX B

28	1–6, 10–13, 28–46, 52	Eighth level of mental absorption during meditation • Transcending consciousness • Entering and experiencing nothingness (infinity)
29	1–6, 10–13, 28–46, 52	Ninth level of mental absorption during meditation • Transcending infinity • Entering the soul (beyond experience)
30	1–13, 28–46, 49-52	Contemplation and purification stage 1: level 1
31	1–6, 8–13, 28–46, 49-52	Contemplation and purification stage 1: level 2
32	1–6, 9–13, 28–46, 49-52	Contemplation and purification stage 1: level 3
33	1–6, 10–13, 28–46, 49-52	Contemplation and purification stage 1: level 4
34	1–6, 10–13, 28–46, 49-52	Contemplation and purification stage 1: level 5
35	1–13, 28–46, 49-52	Contemplation and purification stage 2: level 1
36	1–6, 8–13, 28–46, 49-52	Contemplation and purification stage 2: level 2
37	1–6, 9–13, 28–46, 49-52	Contemplation and purification stage 2: level 3
38	1–6, 10–13, 28–46, 49-52	Contemplation and purification stage 2: level 4
39	1–6, 10–13, 28–46, 49-52	Contemplation and purification stage 2: level 5
40	1–13, 28–46, 49-52	Contemplation and purification stage 3: level 1
41	1–6, 8–13, 28–46, 49-52	Contemplation and purification stage 3: level 2
42	1–6, 9–13, 28–46, 49-52	Contemplation and purification stage 3: level 3
43	1–6, 10–13, 28–46, 49-52	Contemplation and purification stage 3: level 4
44	1–6, 10–13, 28–46, 49-52	Contemplation and purification stage 3: level 5

45	1–13, 28–46, 49-52	Contemplation and purification stage 4: level 1
46	1–6, 8–13, 28–46, 49-52	Contemplation and purification stage 4: level 2
47	1–6, 9–13, 28–46, 49-52	Contemplation and purification stage 4: level 3
48	1–6, 10–13, 28–46, 49-52	Contemplation and purification stage 4: level 4
49	1–6, 10–13, 28–46, 49-52	Contemplation and purification stage 4: level 5
		Type III: Resultant Consciousness
50	1–6	Eye consciousness • Sense consciousness resulting from unwholesome volitional actions of the past
51	1–6	Ear consciousness • Sense consciousness resulting from unwholesome volitional actions of the past
52	1–6	Nose consciousness • Sense consciousness resulting from unwholesome volitional actions of the past
53	1–6	Tongue consciousness • Sense consciousness resulting from unwholesome volitional actions of the past
54	1–6	Body consciousness accompanied by pain • Sense consciousness resulting from unwholesome volitional actions of the past
55	1–8, 10–11	Receiving consciousness resulting from unwholesome volitional actions of the past
56	1–8, 10–11	Investigating consciousness resulting from unwholesome volitional actions of the past
57	1–6	Eye consciousness • Sense consciousness resulting from wholesome volitional actions of the past
58	1–6	Ear consciousness • Sense consciousness resulting from wholesome volitional actions of the past

APPENDIX B

59	1–6	Nose consciousness • Sense consciousness resulting from wholesome volitional actions of the past
60	1–6	Tongue consciousness • Sense consciousness resulting from wholesome volitional actions of the past
61	1–6	Body consciousness accompanied by pleasure • Sense consciousness resulting from wholesome volitional actions of the past
62	1–8, 10–11	Receiving consciousness resulting from wholesome volitional actions of the past
63	1–8, 10–11	Investigating consciousness resulting from wholesome volitional actions of the past
64	1–11	Investigating consciousness resulting from wholesome volitional actions of the past • Rapturous
65	1–13, 28–46, 52	Birth or death consciousness rooted in non-greed, non-hatred, and non-delusion • Spontaneous
66	1–13, 28–46, 52	Birth or death consciousness rooted in non-greed, non-hatred, and non-delusion • Willful
67	1–13, 28–46	Birth or death consciousness rooted in non-greed and non-hatred • Spontaneous
68	1–13, 28–46	Birth or death consciousness rooted in non-greed and non-hatred • Willful
69	1–8, 10–13, 28–46, 52	Birth or death consciousness rooted in non-greed, non-hatred, and non-delusion • Spontaneous with equanimity
70	1–8, 10–13, 28–46, 52	Birth or death consciousness rooted in non-greed, non-hatred, non-delusion • Willful with equanimity
71	1–8, 10–13, 28–46	Birth or death consciousness rooted in non-greed and non-hatred • Spontaneous with equanimity

THE ELEMENTS OF SOUL

72	Birth or death consciousness rooted in non-greed and non-hatred • Willful with equanimity	1–8, 10–13, 28–46
73	Resultant of wholesome consciousness no. 21 • Fruition of the first level of mental absorption	1–13, 28–48, 52
74	Resultant of wholesome consciousness no. 22 • Fruition of the second level of mental absorption	1–6, 8–13, 28–48, 52
75	Resultant of wholesome consciousness no. 23 • Fruition of the third level of mental absorption	1–6, 9–13, 28–48, 52
76	Resultant of wholesome consciousness no. 24 • Fruition of the fourth level of mental absorption	1–6, 10–13, 28–48, 52
77	Resultant of wholesome consciousness no. 25 • Fruition of the fifth level of mental absorption	1–6, 10–13, 28–48, 52
78	Resultant of wholesome consciousness no. 26 • Fruition of the sixth level of mental absorption	1–6, 10–13, 28–46, 52
79	Resultant of wholesome consciousness no. 27 • Fruition of the seventh level of mental absorption	1–6, 10–13, 28–46, 52
80	Resultant of wholesome consciousness no. 28 • Fruition of the eighth level of mental absorption	1–6, 10–13, 28–46, 52
81	Resultant of wholesome consciousness no. 29 • Fruition of the ninth level of mental absorption	1–6, 10–13, 28–46, 52
82	Enlightenment stage 1 • Resultant of wholesome consciousness no. 30 • Fruition of contemplation and purification stage 1 : level 1	1–13, 28–46, 49–52
83	Enlightenment stage 1 • Resultant of wholesome consciousness no. 31 • Fruition of contemplation and purification stage 1 : level 2	1–6, 8–13, 28–46, 49–52

APPENDIX B

84	1–6, 9–13, 28–46, 49-52	Enlightenment stage 1 • Resultant of wholesome consciousness no. 32 • Fruition of contemplation and purification stage 1: level 3	
85	1–6, 10–13, 28–46, 49-52	Enlightenment stage 1 • Resultant of wholesome consciousness no. 33 • Fruition of contemplation and purification stage 1: level 4	
86	1–6, 10–13, 28–46, 49-52	Enlightenment stage 1 • Resultant of wholesome consciousness no. 34 • Fruition of contemplation and purification stage 1: level 5	
87	1–13, 28–46, 49-52	Enlightenment stage 2 • Resultant of wholesome consciousness no. 35 • Fruition of contemplation and purification stage 2: level 1	
88	1–6, 8–13, 28–46, 49-52	Enlightenment stage 2 • Resultant of wholesome consciousness no. 36 • Fruition of contemplation and purification stage 2: level 2	
89	1–6, 9–13, 28–46, 49-52	Enlightenment stage 2 • Resultant of wholesome consciousness no. 37 • Fruition of contemplation and purification stage 2: level 3	
90	1–6, 10–13, 28–46, 49-52	Enlightenment stage 2 • Resultant of wholesome consciousness no. 38 • Fruition of contemplation and purification stage 2: level 4	
91	1–6, 10–13, 28–46, 49-52	Enlightenment stage 2 • Resultant of wholesome consciousness no. 39 • Fruition of contemplation and purification stage 2: level 5	
92	1–13, 28–46, 49-52	Enlightenment stage 3 • Resultant of wholesome consciousness no. 40 • Fruition of contemplation and purification stage 3: level 1	

93	1–6, 8–13, 28–46, 49-52	Enlightenment stage 3 • Resultant of wholesome consciousness no. 41 • Fruition of contemplation and purification stage 3: level 2
94	1–6, 9–13, 28–46, 49-52	Enlightenment stage 3 • Resultant of wholesome consciousness no. 42 • Fruition of contemplation and purification stage 3: level 3
95	1–6, 10–13, 28–46, 49-52	Enlightenment stage 3 • Resultant of wholesome consciousness no. 43 • Fruition of contemplation and purification stage 3: level 4
96	1–6, 10–13, 28–46, 49-52	Enlightenment stage 3 • Resultant of wholesome consciousness no. 44 • Fruition of contemplation and purification stage 3: level 5
97	1–13, 28–46, 49-52	Enlightenment stage 4 • Resultant of wholesome consciousness no. 45 • Fruition of contemplation and purification stage 4: level 1
98	1–6, 8–13, 28–46, 49-52	Enlightenment stage 4 • Resultant of wholesome consciousness no. 46 • Fruition of contemplation and purification stage 4: level 2
99	1–6, 9–13, 28–46, 49-52	Enlightenment stage 4 • Resultant of wholesome consciousness no. 47 • Fruition of contemplation and purification stage 4: level 3
100	1–6, 10–13, 28–46, 49-52	Enlightenment stage 4 • Resultant of wholesome consciousness no. 48 • Fruition of contemplation and purification stage 4: level 4
101	1–6, 10–13, 28–46, 49-52	Enlightenment stage 4 (fully enlightened) • Resultant of wholesome consciousness no. 49 • Fruition of contemplation and purification stage 4: level 5

APPENDIX B

		Type IV: Functional Consciousness
102	1–8, 10–11	Five sense-enabling consciousness
103	1–8, 10–12	Mind-enabling consciousness (also determining consciousness)
104	1–12	Smile-producing consciousness
105	1–13, 28–48, 52	Divine consciousness rooted in non-greed, non-hatred, and non-delusion • Spontaneous
106	1–13, 28–48, 52	Divine consciousness rooted in non-greed, non-hatred, and non-delusion • Willful
107	1–13, 28–48	Divine consciousness rooted in non-greed, non-hatred • Spontaneous
108	1–13, 28–48	Divine consciousness rooted in non-greed, non-hatred • Willful
109	1–8, 10–13, 28–48, 52	Divine consciousness rooted in non-greed, non-hatred, and non-delusion • Spontaneous with equanimity
110	1–8, 10–13, 28–48, 52	Divine consciousness rooted in non-greed, non-hatred, and non-delusion • Willful with equanimity
111	1–8,10–13, 28–48	Divine consciousness rooted in non-greed and non-hatred • Spontaneous with equanimity
112	1–8, 10–13, 28–48	Divine consciousness rooted in non-greed and non-hatred • Willful with equanimity
113	1–13, 28–48, 52	Enlightened master in meditation during post-enlightenment routine practice • First level of mental absorption
114	1–6, 8–13, 28–48, 52	Enlightened master in meditation during post-enlightenment routine practice • Second level of mental absorption

115	1–6, 9–13, 28–48, 52	Enlightened master in meditation during post-enlightenment routine practice • Third level of mental absorption
116	1–6, 10–13, 28–48, 52	Enlightened master in meditation during post-enlightenment routine practice • Fourth level of mental absorption
117	1–6, 10–13, 28–46, 52	Enlightened master in meditation during post-enlightenment routine practice • Fifth level of mental absorption
118	1–6, 10–13, 28–46, 52	Enlightened master in meditation during post-enlightenment routine practice • Sixth level of mental absorption
119	1–6, 10–13, 28–46, 52	Enlightened master in meditation during post-enlightenment routine practice • Seventh level of mental absorption
120	1–6, 10–13, 28–46, 52	Enlightened master in meditation during post-enlightenment routine practice • Eighth level of mental absorption
121	1–6, 10–13, 28–46, 52	Enlightened master in meditation during post-enlightenment routine practice • Ninth level of mental absorption

Appendix C

Mental Elements in Terms of Their Characteristics, Functions, Manifestations, and Proximate Causes

THE ELEMENTS OF SOUL

No.	Element	Characteristics	Functions	Manifestations	Proximate Causes
1	Sensation	• Touch of an object • Initiation of the cognitive process	Making consciousness and its object impinge upon each other	Meeting of consciousness, sense faculty (matter), and an object	An external object that has come in contact with mind
2	Feeling	• Affective feeling of an object • Initiation of experience	Making consciousness experience an object directly and thoroughly	Pleasure, pain, joy, sorrow, equanimity, and so on	Sensation (and tranquility for subtle feelings of equanimity)
3	Perception	Perception of the qualities of an object	• Making the mark or memory of an object • Recognizing an object in future based on the mark or memory	Interpretation of an object based on mark or memory	Appearance of an object due to sensation and feeling
4	Volition	• Willingness for mental action • Acting as will power	• Deciding further course of mental action following perception • Determining the ethical quality (wholesome or unwholesome) of mental action	Bringing together and leading all the other mental elements (present in a particular mental activity) to work on the decided course of action	Mental elements present in a particular mental activity
5	Attention	Guiding of all mental elements towards an object	Bonding all mental elements with an object Steering the mind towards a destination	Facing an object and confronting it	An object of attention
6	Mental life	Vitalization, maintenance, and sustenance of mental phenomena	Facilitating the arising of mind with consciousness	Presence of mind	Mental elements to be vitalized, maintained, and sustained
7	Thinking	Initial application of mind to an object	Attacking to unfold, open up, or unravel an object	Guiding or leading of consciousness to an object	An object of thinking
8	Thoughtfulness	Sustained application of thought	Examining an object through sustained thinking	Anchoring of consciousness to an object	An object of examination

APPENDIX C

9	Rapture (happiness/bliss)	Delight or joyful interest in an object of examination	Pervading the mind-body with ecstasy	• Exultation of consciousness • Elation • Uplifting or lightness of the body	The embodiment (body-mind-consciousness with predominance of the body) Rapture, happiness, bliss
10	Concentration	• Non-distraction • One-pointedness of mind	• Unifying all mental phenomena • Contemplating on an object • Meditating on an object	• Peacefulness of consciousness • Mental absorption	
11	Resolution	• Conviction and fervor • Sincerity	• Confirming • Non-groping	• Determination • Unshakability • Decision	Being certain or convinced about something
12	Vigor	• Energetic efforts • Vigorous, vital action	• Not turning back • Reinforcing • Supporting • Consolidating • Restraining the mind	• Non-failing of mental state • Non-ending of mental state	• Sense of urgency • Anything that arouses energetic effort
13	Bare-desire (inclination/intention)	An inclination for action or performance	Looking for an object to work on	Requiring an object	An object in need
14	Greed	Grasping of an object	• Creating attachment • Bonding through sticky/glue-like conditions	• Not letting go • Craving and clinging • Passion and lust • Selfishness • Ego	• Taking delight in things, activities, relationships, tasks, and goals that lead to bondage
15	Hatred	• Intensity, fierceness • Viciousness	• Putting things on fire • Spreading like fire • Burning up or devastating its own support	• Persecution • Aversion, anger • Disgust • Displeasure • Ego	• Conditions for aggravation or irritation

THE ELEMENTS OF SOUL

16	Delusion	• Ignorance • Not-knowing the reality of phenomena • Mental-blindness	• Creating illusion • Hiding the truth • Covering up the reality of phenomena	• Lack of understanding • Stupidity • Ego	• Delusion itself • Lack of wise attention	
17	Restlessness	• Mental anxiety • Lack of calmness • Lack of stillness • Disquiet	• Making the mind unsteady and wavering like wind generating waves on the surface of an ocean	• Impatience • Agitation • Irritation • Turmoil • Confusion, indecision	• Giving unwise attention to mental disturbances	
18	Shamelessness	• Non-apprehension about doing bad things • Immorality	• Making the mind do sinful, wicked, or immoral acts	• Lack of dread or anxiety about immorality • Wildness • Unruliness	• Lack of respect, honor, or reverence for oneself	
19	Moral recklessness	• Apathy for misconduct • Apathy for doing bad things	• Making the mind do sinful, wicked, or immoral acts	• No moral caution • Not caring about or not shying away from unwholesomeness	• Lack of respect, honor, or reverence for oneself	
20	Conceit	• Self-importance • Pride, haughtiness	• Glorifying or praising the self • Making arrogant	• Vanity • Intoxication • A desire to advertise oneself	• Greed without justification • Delusion	
21	Envy	• Resentment about others' successes, achievements, and progress	• Making the mind dissatisfied and unhappy	• Disliking or distaste • Boredom or aversion due to others' successes	• Others' upper hand, achievements, victories, successes, progress, growth, or attainments	
22	Remorse	• Regret about doing something wrong • Neglecting	• Making the mind sorrowful and mournful	• Repentance or guilt • Worry • Feeling of sorrow about doing wrong	• Not doing what ought to be done or doing what ought not to be done • Regrettable actions	

APPENDIX C

23	Superstitiousness	• Wrong Views • Unjustifiable interpretation of things and phenomena	• Presuming, assuming, or supposing • Believing	• Beliefs • Unwise interpretations • Assumptions • Unhealthy religiousness • Personalized philosophies and -isms	• Lack of willingness to experience the truth or face reality • Lack of inclination towards wisdom • Evading reality
24	Suspicion	• Uncertainty • Inability to trust • Lack of desire to think through	• Wavering or vacillating • Making uncertain	• Lack of firmness • Indecisiveness • Changing camps	• Not giving wise attention to matters of doubt • Deciding without proper understanding
25	Sloth	• Stiffness • Lack of driving energy	• Removing mental energy	• Subsiding of mind • Lack of urgency and lack of energy when combined with torpor	• Lack of thinking • Giving unwise attention to boredom, monotony, and loneliness
26	Torpor	• Unwieldiness • Morbidity	• Choking the mind	• Sleepiness, laziness, and lethargy • Lack of urgency and lack of energy when combined with sloth	• Lack of thinking • Giving unwise attention to boredom, monotony, and loneliness
27	Avarice	• Hiding • Not sharing one's fortunes and successes with others	• Making sharing with others hard to stomach	• Stinginess, lack of generosity • Covetousness	• One's fortunes and successes
28	Non-greed	• Non-grasping • Non-sticking • Desirelessness	• Not attaching to an object • Non-clinging	• Letting go • Non-craving • Non-clinging • Non-attachment • Generosity • Unselfishness • Renunciation	• Not taking delight in things, activities, relationships, tasks, and goals that lead to greed

THE ELEMENTS OF SOUL

29	Non-hatred	• Lack of fierceness • Lack of resistance • Lack of opposition	Removing all types of irritation, frustration, annoyance, anger, and over-enthusiasm	• Loving-kindness • Sociability • Agreeableness • Amity • Gentleness • Friendliness • Calmness, softness, coolness, and pleasant appearance	• Seeing others as worthy of kindness and compassion • Recollecting the perfect accountability of the laws of karma
30	Mindfulness	• Presence of mind • Present-moment awareness • Steadiness and fullness of attention • Passive, relaxed, impartial, silent, receptive, and deepening observation	• Eliminating forgetfulness of the present moment • Remembering • Awakening • Stabilizing attention on an object by not drifting away from it • Minding an object of attention	• Facing and guarding an object of attention • Meditation • Awareness	• Strong, stable perception • Mindful contemplation of the phenomena of body-mind-consciousness
31	Conscience	• Disgust for misconduct • A sense of morality • Scrupulousness • Being principle-driven • Being ethical	Making mind not do sinful, immoral, or unethical things	• Modesty • Caring about or shying away from unwholesomeness • Moral caution • Civilized and cultured nature • Grace and reverence	Respect, honor, reverence for the self
32	Shame	• Apprehension for misconduct • A sense of morality • Scrupulousness • Being principle-driven • Being ethical	Making mind not do sinful, immoral, or unethical things	• Modesty • Caring about or shying away from unwholesomeness • Moral caution • Civilized and cultured nature	Respect, honor, reverence for others

APPENDIX C

33	Faith	• Trust • Confidence	• Clarifying • Illuminating • Purifying the belief	• Firm decision • Clarity • Unshakable confidence	Experiential understanding of the 'subject or object' of faith
34 & 35	Tranquility of mind-body	Calming of disturbances and agitation	• Crushing and quieting disturbances • Destroying stress and distress • Removing restlessness and worry	• Stillness • Coolness • Peacefulness, quietness • Serenity • Heavenly delight • Dawning of bliss	• Uplifting happiness • Concentration • Insight related to body-mind-consciousness
36 & 37	Lightness of mind-body	Diminishing of heaviness	• Crushing heaviness • Removing sloth and torpor	• Nimbleness • Non-sluggishness	• Concentration • Insight related to body-mind-consciousness
38 & 39	Flexibility of mind-body	Diminishing of rigidity	• Crushing rigidity • Removing superstitiousness and conceit	• Non-resistance • Lack of stubbornness and obstinacy • Suppleness	• Concentration • Insight related to body-mind-consciousness
40 & 41	Pliability of mind-body	Diminishing of unworkability of mind	Crushing and quieting unworkability of mind	• Success in making something an object of mind • Profitable application of mind	• Concentration • Insight related to body-mind-consciousness
42 & 43	Skillfulness of mind-body	• Proficiency • Healthiness • Fitness	Crushing unhealthiness and disability	Absence of disability	• Concentration • Insight related to body-mind-consciousness
44 & 45	Rectitude of mind-body	• Directness • Uprightness	Crushing indirectness	Absence of impurities such as dishonesty, evasiveness, cleverness, smartness, and roundabout-ness, crookedness	• Concentration • Insight related to body-mind-consciousness

THE ELEMENTS OF SOUL

46	Equanimity	• Neutrality of mind • Being in the middle • Non-reaction	• Neutralizing • Liberating from craving and aversion • Transcending pleasure and pain, joy and sorrow • Seeing all beings as equal including oneself	• Balance of mind • Disinterestedness of mind (not indifference) • Lack of greed, hatred • Absence of craving and aversion • Non-attachment • Middle-ness • Egolessness	• Mindfulness, concentration, and non-reaction • Maturing of loving-kindness, compassion, and gladness • Recollection of the laws of karma • Not taking delight in anything that lead to greed or hatred
47	Compassion	Inclination for removing others' suffering	• Making it possible to see suffering in others • Not being able to overlook others' suffering	• Non-meanness • Absence of cruelty • Making oneself peaceful	Seeing others as beings who are suffering (in the ultimate sense)
48	Gladness	Feelings of happiness, joy, and cheerfulness about the success of others	Eradicating jealousy and envy towards others' success	• Absence of irritation • Absence of aversion	Noticing and appreciating others' successes
49	Noble action	Unconditional non-wrongdoing by action	Shying away from or minimizing the generation of bad karma	Deliberate abstinence from wrong action	• Noble faith • Resolution • A sense of urgency for attaining mental perfection • A sense of contentment • Distaste for mundane living or wrongdoing
50	Noble speech	Unconditional non-wrongdoing by speech	Shying away from or minimizing the generation of bad karma	Deliberate abstinence from wrong speech	• Noble faith • Resolution • A sense of urgency for attaining mental perfection • Distaste for mundane living or wrongdoing

APPENDIX C

51	Noble occupation	Unconditional non-wrongdoing by occupation	Shying away from or minimizing the generation of bad karma	Deliberate abstinence from wrong occupation	• Noble faith in spiritual practices • Resolution • A sense of urgency for attaining mental perfection • A sense of contentment • Distaste for mundane living or wrongdoing
52	Non-delusion	• Penetration of the intrinsic nature of reality • Mental illumination • Knowledge of ultimate reality • Complete absence of ignorance	• Illuminating an object of investigation to the ultimate depth by piercing it • Exposing the truth as it is • Shaking off delusion • Eliminating superstition and religiousness • Enlightening mind	• Non-confusion • Wisdom • Egolessness • Pure understanding • Pure knowledge • Clear comprehension • Purification of views • Mental perfection • Enlightenment	• Giving wise-attention • Penetrating insight • Established mindfulness

Notes

This book is primarily based on my study of the following five sources and the realization of the various teachings that they describe. If paragraphs in *The Elements of Soul* should have been annotated, but were missed, in such cases the reader should refer to these five main sources, which alphabetically include:
- Access to Insight website: accesstoinsight.org.
- Analayo. *Satipatthana: The Direct Path to Realization.* Birmingham, UK: Windhorse Publications, 2004.
- Bodhi, Bhikkhu. *A Comprehensive Manual of Abhidhamma.* Onalaska, WA: Pariyatti Publications, 1999.
- Nanamoli, Bhikkhu. *Visuddhimagga: The Path of Purification.* Onalaska, WA: Pariyatti Publications, 1999.
- Rainbow Body Network website: rainbowbody.net/HeartMind/Yogasutra.htm.

I am solely responsible for all interpretations and extrapolations presented in my own work. Any faults, misrepresentations, or inadequacies should be considered the outcome of my limited understanding of these sources.

Preface

1. Roughly 2,500 years ago, Buddha was born as Gautama, a royal Indian prince in northern India. As a young prince, he grew disenchanted with leading a life of luxury and at age 29 he renounced royalty and became a wandering ascetic. He practiced extreme austerities in the forest for six years, defied fear, and surpassed the accomplishments of his spiritual teachers, but he wasn't enlightened until he abandoned austerity and adopted the so-called "middle way" (the way of moderation). Soon after (about one year later), he was enlightened to the truth of suffering, impermanence, and non-self. After enlightenment, he preached for roughly 45 years until his death. His disciples included people from all walks of life, including kings and members of his renounced family. His teachings were pragmatic and mainly consisted of developing virtuous conduct, the four noble truths, and the eightfold path. These teachings were systematically preserved in the form of more than 1,000 discourses in the Pali Canon (the Tipitaka). For further reading, visit accesstoinsight.org/ptf/buddha.html. Also see Nanamoli, 2001.

   Roughly 2000 years ago, an India sage named Patanjali (not to be confused with the inventor of yoga), wrote a compendium of ancient, pre-existing oral yoga teachings, which became known as *The Yoga Sutras*. These are a collection of 195 spiritual aphorisms divided into four *padas* (chapters) that describe the path of yoga for the attainment of mental perfection. *The Yoga Sutras* are the oldest written form describing the yogic practices of non-grasping and meditation. For further reading, see Roche and McNally. Also visit rainbowbody.net/HeartMind/Yogasutra.htm.

Chapter 1: What Is Soul?

1. The number of material elements, mental elements, and types of consciousness are derived from Abhidhamma Pitaka, a division of the Pali Canon, which is widely known as the collection of the Buddha's higher teachings. Although Abhidhamma does not

talk about soul, like this book it is concerned with understanding reality through experience in a phenomenological and psychological way. For further reading, see Bodhi.
2. If you look at consciousness as that which has the single characteristic of cognizing an object, then you would not want to classify it into various types. However, if you want to signify the fact that there are momentary acts of cognition performed by a series of consciousnesses and not by a single consciousness, then it becomes necessary to look at consciousness as a stream of various types. It also facilitates understanding consciousness as a transient phenomenon. Depending upon the method of delineation, there can be 89 or 121 types. Bodhi: p. 29.
3. There are 24 conditional relations between various ultimate realities, which give rise to various experiences. How this happens will be explained in the sequel to this book, *Soul Mechanics*.
4. Here, intrinsic nature means the recurring (periodic) chemical properties, or atomic number, or patterns or trends in atomic radius, ionization energy, and electronegativity of the elements, or the electron configurations in the valence shell of an element.
5. Bodhi: p. 78.
6. These four criteria have been proposed by Buddhist commentators to reveal the nature of any ultimate reality. Bodhi: p. 29.
7. Bodhi: p. 136 and p. 144.
8. Bodhi: pp. 144–5.
9. Bodhi: pp. 235–6 and pp. 246–250.

Chapter 2: What Is Not Soul?

1. According to Abhidhamma philosophy, the four ultimate realities are: consciousness, mental factors, matter, and nirvana (enlightenment). Mental factors are similar to the mental elements that are known collectively as mind in *The Elements of Soul*. Source: Bodhi: p. 27.

Chapter 3: What Is Beyond Soul?

1. According to the glossary of Pali terms on the Access to Insight website, parinirvana means total unbinding, the complete cessation of five aggregates (matter, feeling, perception, mental formations, and consciousness) that occurs upon the death of a fully enlightened person (*arahant*). The main difference between nirvana and parinirvana is the respective presence or absence of the live body of a fully enlightened master. Source website: accesstoinsight.org/glossary.html#pq. Also see Buddha's discourse Parinibbana Sutta 6.15. Website: accesstoinsight.org/tipitaka/sn/sn06/sn06.015.than.html.

Chapter 4: How Soul Works

1. *Classical (Newtonian) mechanics tell us about the behavior of macroscopic physical objects, ranging from pebbles to planets . . .* The term "classical mechanics" was introduced in the scientific world in the 20th century. It is used to refer collectively to mathematical physics, developed by Isaac Newton and other 17th–20th century scientists; Lagrangian mechanics; Hamiltonian mechanics; and Albert Einstein's mechanics. For further reading, see Sussman and Wisdom with Mayer.

Quantum mechanics tell us about the behavior of microscopic physical objects, ranging from molecules and atoms, to electrons and strings . . . Quantum mechanics differs from classical mechanics in that it considers not only the point particle of very small size (such as an electron), but also the spin of particles. Quantum mechanics was developed in the first half of 20th century by scientists like Albert Einstein, Werner Heisenberg, Max Planck, Erwin Schrödinger, Niels Bohr, Paul Dirac, and the likes. It goes beyond classical mechanics by describing the workings of physical systems at the atomic level and beyond. The most important aspect of quantum mechanics is its ability to address the dual nature of matter, which is both particle-like and wave-like. In classical mechanics, Newton's second law of motion can be used to obtain the determinate position of a particle. According to quantum mechanics, there is no such thing as a determinate or certain position of a particle, but only the wave function of the particle. A wave function provides only the statistical likelihood of the position of a particle in space. This is also known as the uncertainty principle, which states that there is no way to know the position and velocity of an electron at the same time. See Griffiths, 1987: pp. 1–5.

Popularly they are searching for a theory of everything (TOE) ... There are four known fundamental forces in nature: gravity, electromagnetism, strong nuclear force, and weak nuclear force. Classical mechanics (and general relativity) can describe the workings of gravity and quantum mechanics can describe the workings of other three forces. But neither can describe the workings of all the forces. Scientists are searching for a new theory that will unify all the forces. This theory is known as the theory of everything. Sources: Griffiths, 2004: pp. 46–8; and Weinberg: pp. 200–5.
2. Kaku: p. 236.
3. Here, the word "conserve" is used in a technical sense (the law of conservation of energy) and not in a vernacular sense, as in avoiding waste.
4. *Even great physicists like Isaac Newton and Albert Einstein firmly believed that the universe ran like a clock* ... Kaku: pp. 242, 292–3. Einstein's statement, *"God does not throw dice,"* is cited in Kaku: p. 58.
5. Niels Bohr's statement, "Don't tell God what to do!" is cited in Rae: p. 22. Some doubt the historical accuracy of this statement. Walter Isaccson quotes Einstein, "I have earned the right to be wrong," in *Einstein: His Life and Universe*: p. 515. Elsewhere there are slightly different versions of this utterance.
6. See note 2.

Chapter 5: Soul Intelligence

1. See Bibliography for details on the books of evolutionary biologist Richard Dawkins, D.Phil., child psychiatrist Jim Tucker,

M.D., molecular biologist A.G. Cairns-Smith, Ph.D., physicist Michio Kaku, Ph.D., zoologist and journalist Matt Ridley, D. Phil., astrobiologist and astrophysicist David Darling, Ph.D., and futurist Ray Kurzweil.

2. Definitions of intelligence used here were derived from the works of psychologist Alfred Binet, Ph.D., inventor of the IQ test; educational psychologist Sir Cyril Burt; educational psychologist Linda Gottfredson; psychologist and psychometrician Robert Sternberg; psychologist David Weshler, the creator of intelligence scales; and educator Howard Gardner, Ph.D. For further reading, see Neisser et al: pp. 77–101; and Acton. Website: personalityresearch.org/intelligence.html.

3. *The most widely known method is based on psychometrics...* Gardner, 2000: pp. 11–3. For further reading, see Furr and Bacharach.

Howard Gardner, a well-known intelligence theorist from Harvard University, believes that there is no such thing as "general" intelligence (g) or IQ that can fully describe cognitive ability ... Gardner: pp. 13 and 22.

4. Sources: Kaku: p. 112 and Kurzweil, 1999: p. 69.

5. Sources: Kaku: pp. 24 and 123; Kurzweil, 1999: pp. 20–5 and 33; and Kurzweil, 2005: p. 25.

6. *Concepts of emotional intelligence (which is popularly known as EQ) were introduced, developed, and...* Goleman: pp. 34–6; Payne; and Greenspan, 1990.

In fact, seeds of EQ were planted... Bradberry and Greaves: pp. 24–5.

Edward Thorndike, who conceived of the idea...Bradberry: p. 24. Also, see Plucker.

Howard Gardner introduced the model of multiple ... Gardner: pp. 33–5.

However it wasn't until Daniel Goleman ... Goleman: pp. ix-x, and Gardner: p. 10.

NOTES

7. *Some of the models, such as the competency-based model proposed by Goleman, are criticized as being pop psychology* ... Mayer, Roberts, and Barsade: pp. 507–36.
8. Locke: pp. 425-31. Also see Eysenck.
9. *The term itself was reportedly coined by Danah Zohar...* See Zohar and Marshall.

    Other thinkers, among them... See Buzan. Also see Noble: pp. 1–29, and King.

    oward Gardner excluded SQ from his theory... Gardner: pp. 60 and 65–6.
10. *However, these laws break down beyond* ... For further details, see Imamura.
11. Earth is surrounded by magnetic field that makes a compass needle move in a particular direction. Earth's gravitational field gives rise to gravitational force at a particular location. In this sense, I am suggesting that we are permeated by the field of intelligence, due to which we experience volitional forces that are responsible for our mental actions.
12. Sources: Kaku: p. 104; Searle: pp. 88–91; Kurzweil, 1999: p. 69; Kurzweil, 2005: pp. 8–9, 25–6; and Penrose, 1989: pp. 526–31.
13. Hydrogen is thought to have formed due to big bang nucleogenesis. Hydrogen is by far the most abundant element in the universe, accounting for about 90 percent of atoms and 75 percent of mass in the universe. It is the dominant constituent of the most abundant matter in the universe, plasma. Its molecule, H_2, is also the most abundant molecule in the universe. The four most abundant elements in human body are hydrogen, oxygen, carbon, and nitrogen. These elements exist because of hydrogen and various types of nucleosynthesis (thermonuclear fusion and fission) that created them. Clayton: pp. 11–2.
14. See Russell. Also see Barras.
15. Kaku: p. 104 and Penrose, 1989: p. 526.
16. Details on the death of Ludwig Boltzmann come from Kaku: p. 265.

Biographical details on Hans Berger are drawn from the website: chem.ch.huji.ac.il/history/berger.html.

Details on the death of Edwin Armstrong come from the obituary column "Milestones" in *Time* (February 8, 1954).

Biographical details on George Eastman come from The NNDB Tracker website: nndb.com/people/980/000086722/#FN1.

17. Kaku: pp. 106–7.
18. Kaku: p. 198.

Chapter 6: Soul Meditation

1. Derived from Nanamoli, 1999: p. 261.
2. Derived from vipassana meditation practice, as taught by S.N. Goenka. For further reading, visit the Vipassana Meditation website: dhamma.org.

Chapter 7: Exploring the Ultimate Building Blocks of Matter

1. According to the molecular or kinetic theory of matter, matter is simply made of molecules that are constantly moving and bouncing off each other. According to the atomic theory of matter, matter is made of atoms, which in turn are made of electrons, protons, and neutrons. According to the modern universal theory of matter, matter is made of quarks and gluons, and thus it is essentially "matter fields" or "scalar fields." According to string theory, matter is not really made of any particles at all, but of vibrating strings. The Bureau International defines matter as "substance."
2. Here the word "entropy' is used to indicate the amount of disorder or randomness, or wasted energy for attaining equilibrium in an isolated system. An in-depth study of entropy is recommended to avoid misunderstanding.
3. A basic understanding of the four essential material elements can arise by studying some of their salient features, which include the following:

NOTES

A) Earth, water, fire, and air are distinct elements because they bear their own characteristics. However, they cannot be separated from each other. None can be discovered or demonstrated as an individual element. They always arise together and serve as a common base for the occurrence of matter such as a rock or a human body.

B) Taken together, the four essential elements are supported by earth, held together by water, maintained by fire, and distended by air. Earth is held together by water, maintained by fire, and distended by air, so that matter is neither scattered nor dissipated, but manifests as small, big, tall, short, rough, rigid, hard, and so on. Water is founded on earth, maintained by fire, and distended by air, so it does neither trickles nor flows away, but provides cohesion, continuity, and flow. Fire is established on earth, held together by water element, and distended by air, so it provides warmth and maintains the body. Fire prevents the animate body from rotting. Air is founded on earth element, held together by water, and maintained by fire, so it does not allow the body to collapse, but makes it stand erect, walk, wiggle, and sit, and otherwise moves the body parts.

C) Although they do not exist without each other, the four essential elements are found neither inside nor outside of each other. They mutually condition each other and assist each other in fulfilling their functions.

D) The differences in material things are not due to differences in the characteristics of the essential elements, but to a difference in the capability and quality of the essential material elements that have arisen. Mt. Fuji and the Colorado River are different not because there is a greater quantity of earth in soil and rock or because there is a lesser quantity of earth in rapidly flowing water. Mt. Fuji has an excess of earth element in capability and in quality.

Similarly, hot water does not have fire in excess quantity. Nor does cold water lack fire. Hot water is hot because of excessive capability or quality of fire. Cold water is cold because of less capability or quality of fire. In brief, various material things exist because of differences in the capability or quality of four elements and not in their quantity.

4. See "On Nature," the poetic work of Empedocles describing his teachings. Stanford Encyclopedia of Philosophy website: plato.stanford.edu/entries/empedocles/#1.
5. See "Plato's Timaeus: Physics," Stanford Encyclopedia of Philosophy website: plato.stanford.edu/entries/plato-timaeus/#8.
6. Arikha: pp. 3–6. Also see Garrison.
7. "Kayagata-sati Sutta: Mindfulness Immersed in the Body," MN 119, translated by Thanissaro Bhikkhu. Website: accesstoinsight.org/tipitaka/mn/mn.119.than.html.
8. See Miyamoto.
9. Svoboda: pp. 29–39.
10. Popular modern examples of the four elements include the comic book series *The Fantastic Four* (Marvel Comics, written by Stan Lee and illustrated by Jack Kirby) and the movie *Fantastic Four* (Fox 2005, directed by Tim Story); the Harry Potter book series written by J.K. Rowling (*Harry Potter and the Sorcerer's Stone*, Scholastic 1998) and movie series (Warner Brothers). Also see Heslewood.
11. The standard model is a theory of elementary particles that make up all the matter in the universe. More precisely, it is a theory about the interaction between particles of matter—a means to describe all the known forces in nature as one common force (aka the super force). At present, this theory is considered incomplete because it does not include gravity. For further reading on this topic, see Griffiths, 1987: pp. 46–8.
12. Kaku: pp. 234–5; Greene, 2003: pp. 13–20; Greene, 2004: pp. 328–75; and Penrose, 2005: pp. 884–900. For additional information on string theory, see "The Elegant Universe," *Nova*. Public Broadcasting System website: pbs.org/wgbh/nova/elegant; and The Official String Theory website: superstringtheory.com.

13. See Capra.
14. Kaku: p. 236. Also see "The Elegant Universe" and The Official String Theory website.
15. Kaku: p. 302.
16–17. Kaku: pp. 264–5 and pp. 296–7.
18. Kaku: p. 287–90.
19. See "What Is a Cell?" National Center for Biotechnology Information website: ncbi.nlm.nih.gov/About/primer/genetics_cell.html.
20. See Weiss. Also see Wright.
21. See O'Reilly.
22. Kaku: p. 270.
23. Ibid.
24. Derived from Bodhi: p. 246.
25. Iannone: p. 30. Also see Potter.
26. For detailed reading, explore *Space and Time: Inertial Frames at* plato.stanford.edu/entries/spacetime-iframes.
27. Based on Kaku: pp. 247, 250–2, and 282. For further reading, see Greene, 2004.
28. The term "non-concrete matter" is derived from Bodhi: pp. 240–1.
29. See "General Relativity," *Einstein Online*. Website: einstein-online.info/en/spotlights/gr/index.html.
30. Derived from Bodhi: pp. 236–42.

Chapter 8: Exploring Consciousness

1. In the past, René Descartes (16–17th century), who is sometimes called the father of modern philosophy, defined consciousness as ideas, imaginings, and perceptions in space and time. Philosophers from the 18th–20th century generally related consciousness to relations, processes, and thoughts. Modern philosophers attribute consciousness to thoughts, moods, sensations, perceptions, dreams, self-awareness, and being awake and responsive to the environment. Some psychologists attribute

consciousness to that which arises due to the language of high complexity.

For most of the 20th century, although the research related to consciousness was banned in the scientific psychology circles, consciousness was studied as a topic of "attention." (source: susanblackmore.co.uk/books/consciousness/cons.htm) Evolutionary biologists approach consciousness as the subject of "adaptation." Theoretical neurobiologists define consciousness as "supremely functional adaptation." Some philosophers from the field of cognitive sciences define consciousness as that which passes the Turing test (Searle: pp. 70–4) or the mirror test (source: sciencedaily.com/articles/m/mirror_test.htm). Some modern physicists consider consciousness to be the subject of quantum entanglement and superposition. Physicist Roger Penrose explains consciousness in his orchestrated objective reduction theory through mathematics, physics, and anesthesia as a non-algorithmic and non-computable function of the brain. It appears that he relates wave function collapse in microtubes of neurons to consciousness. For further reading, see Penrose, 1994: pp. 161 and 350–377, Penrose, 1989: pp. 521–5, Blackmore, 1989.

2. Due to its vastness and complexity, the rationale behind the composition of mental elements for each type of consciousness will be discussed in *Soul Mechanics,* the upcoming sequel to this book.

3. Due to its wide scope and implications, the phenomena of birth and death consciousness (and the boundary conditions of the human lifespan) will be discussed in detail in *Soul Mechanics*, the upcoming sequel to this book.

4–5. Derived from Bodhi: pp. 151–6.

Chapter 9: Exploring the Ultimate Building Blocks of Mind

1. Neuroscientists believe that mind is same as the brain, which thinks, perceives, wills, and feels. Philosophers believe that mind is a non-material entity separate from the body and it is that

which permits a person to think, love, hate, and so forth. Neurophysiologists consider mind as a functional entity related only to the existence of the brain and to the brain's reception of sensory inputs. Cognitive neuroscientists attribute mind to the activity of neural cells. Some philosophers, mystics, and theological thinkers define mind as the essence of a person, as spirit or soul. For further reading, see Searle.
2. How memory is stored and retrieved, why the brain sleeps and dreams, what is time (as perceived by the brain), what the baseline activity of the brain is, how to develop an artificial brain (AI), what consciousness is, what an emotion is, where we (and our thoughts) come from, what the beginning of evolution is, creation vs. evolution, nature vs. nurture, and what the secrete of life is—these are some of our current scientific mysteries.
3. This description of all the mental elements is derived from my studies of Visuddhimagga (source: Nanamoli, 1999) and the Abhidhamma treatises (source: Bodhi), and from my own insights.
4. Derived from Bodhi: pp. 78–90.

Chapter 10: The Universal Mind

1. Derived from Analayo: p. 158.
2. In Jainism, Judaism, some forms of Orthodox Christianity and Catholicism, Buddhism, and Zen Buddhism, as well as in the religious yoga tradition, painful ascetic practices are undertaken, such as no personal ownership, extreme fasting, self-denial, extreme physical exercises, and forced celibacy, under the assumption that they will burn up the effects of unwholesome past deeds and bring about salvation, purification, and retribution.

Chapter 12: The Unwholesome Mind

1. Although mysticism can take a practitioner beyond religious doctrine by facilitating exploration of the esoteric aspects of spirituality, mysticism can become a hindrance to enlightenment—especially if the equality complex is not understood clearly.

I humbly urge practitioners of various mystical traditions, such as Vedanta Hinduism, Kabbalism, and Sufism, as well as Christian mysticism, to go beyond the final threshold of the equality complex and attain perfection.

Chapter 13: The Wholesome Mind

1. By far, confusing belief with faith is the biggest mistake that the majority of religious practitioners make. In fact, many of them go to the extent of equating faith with religion. This is also the costliest mistake made by human beings. It would not be very difficult to prove that human beings have fought more wars due to *belief* (racial, social, cultural, or religious) than due to any other reason.
2. Note that tranquility Tr1 (element 34) refers to tranquility of body, however, it is not necessarily related to the physical body, but to the entire group (a body) of 19 wholesome elements. Tranquility Tr2 (element 35) refers to tranquility of mind which means tranquility is a distinct mental element. So is the case with the other five pairs. Together, the 12 mental elements 34–45 form six pairs, which always arise together as a group.

Chapter 14: The Divine Mind

1. Many theological thinkers believe that divinity is an attribute only of a godly figure having supernatural powers. They also believe divinity is an entity, such as a godhead, a deity, or a supreme being (aka the Almighty) that resides beyond the human realm. Some theological thinkers also use this word in terms of divine intervention.

Chapter 15: The Noble Mind

1. These three elements are specifically derived from three elements of abstinence listed in Bodhi: p. 79.
2. Derived from Fischer.
3. Frady: pp. 102–3 and pp. 123–4.

Chapter 16: The Perfect Mind

1. As made obvious by Einstein's famous equation, $E=MC^2$ (where M equals the mass of a particle and C equals the speed of light), a tremendous amount of energy can be released by an atom (the core) of uranium when it is subjected to a nuclear fission reaction.

Chapter 17: Developing an Intelligent Attitude

1. The ten virtues are derived from Patanjali's Yoga Sutras. For further study, visit rainbowbody.net/HeartMind/Yogasutra.htm.
2. Acharya Rajnish was an Indian mystic who preached sexual liberation and sexual *tantras* (techniques) as a means of spiritual growth. His teachings may have adversely impacted the spiritual quest of many innocent followers. There are many tantric and yogic practices (such as yama marga, maithuna, Shiva-Shaktism, and yogic sexual union) that ignorantly assume sexual activity as a means of liberation, thereby encouraging sexual overindulgence.
3. In religious yoga traditions, such as Darshan Yoga and Om Yoga Sansthan, among others, Ishwar pranidhana, the *niyama* (lifestyle/virtue) mentioned in Patanjali's Yoga Sutras (which is written in Sanskrit), is misunderstood as surrendering to God or finding shelter in God. This misunderstanding has occurred because the ancient Sanskrit word "Ishwar" means "God." Similar misunderstanding is present in almost all religious traditions that follow religious texts written in ancient languages.

Chapter 18: Developing Intelligent Senses

1. If you are a beginner, you must avoid touching the genitals while practicing this meditation so that you can maintain non-reaction throughout the session.
2. Here, the word "religiously" is used to convey the seriousness of practice. Massage therapists must also practice the other meditations given in this book so that they can maintain purity of thought and purity of action while working with their clients.

3. For information on entrainment, as it is generally thought of, visit Jonathan Goldman's Healing Sounds website: healingsounds.com/articles/sonic-entrainment.asp. In this book, the idea of entrainment is taken further and deeper by instructing the practitioner to focus on gaps of silence embedded in the sound track.

Chapter 19: Developing an Intelligent Body

1. Out-of-body experiences (OBE) derived from taking psychedelic drugs or experiencing traumatic near-death experiences, extreme dehydration, dreams, and such are generally rooted in ignorance or intoxication. An authentic OBE is the spiritual experience of transcending the body—meaning, going beyond bodily attachments.

Chapter 20: Developing an Intelligent Mind

1. These four practices are derived from my realization of the teachings described in Abhidhamma (see Bodhi) and Visuddhimagga (see Nanamoli).

Chapter 21: Developing an Intelligent Heart

1. These four practices are derived from my realization of the teachings described in Visuddhimagga (see Nanamoli).

Epilogue

1. This statement is attributed to Joko Charlotte Beck, a Zen Buddhist teacher. Some people wonder why terms such as "enlightened master," "the Buddha," and so on are used. They are used for the sake of communication, just as we use the words "I" and "you" even though we may know that there is no such thing. In reality, there is no "person" attaining enlightenment. Impersonality is, in fact, the mark of enlightenment.

2. Buddha's daily routine was extraordinary. He spent most of his time teaching and meditating. He would meditate during the very early hours of the morning (2 a.m. to 6 a.m.) either while sitting, walking, or by contemplating enlightenment. He slept no more

NOTES

than two hours each night. According to some accounts, he slept just one hour a day. See Nanamoli.

3. According to Merriam-Webster's Online Dictionary, the word "omniscient" means "having infinite understanding or complete knowledge." Considering this meaning, it is obvious that a person (who is finite) cannot become omniscient. Buddha himself never explicitly stated that he was omniscient. He, in fact, considered the idea of omniscience to be irrelevant and taught his disciples instead to focus on the conditionality of all phenomena. He also stated that it is not possible to know everything simultaneously. See Majjhima Nikaya, Sutta 90. Website: accesstoinsight.org/tipitaka/mn/mn.090.than.html. Also see Thomas: p. 213.

* * *

Bibliography

Acton, G. Scott, Ph.D. "Intelligence," online article (updated January 1999). Great Ideas in Personality Website: personalityresearch.org/intelligence.html.

Analayo. *Satipatthana: The Direct Path to Realization.* Birmingham, UK: Windhorse Publications, 2003.

Arikha, Noga. *Passions and Tempers: A History of the Humours.* New York, NY: Ecco Press, 2007.

Bar-On, Reuven, Maree, J.G., and Maurice, Jesse E., editors. *Educating People to Be Emotionally Intelligent.* Westport, CT: Praeger Publishers, 2007.

Barras, Colin. "Smart Amoebas Reveal Origins of Primitive Intelligence," *New Scientist*, vol. 16, no. 11 (October 2008). Website: newscientist.com/article/dn15068.

Blackmore, Susan. Website: susanblackmore.co.uk.

Blackmore, Susan. *Consciousness: An Introduction:* New York, NY: Oxford University Press, 2004

Bodhi, Bhikkhu. *A Comprehensive Manual of Abhidhamma.* Onalaska, WA: Pariyatti Publications, 1999.

Bradberry, Travis and Greaves Jean. *Emotional Intelligence Quickbook: Everything You Need to Know.* San Diego, CA: TalentSmart, 2003.

Buzan, Tony. *The Power of Spiritual Intelligence: Ten Ways to Tap into Your Spiritual Genius.* London, UK: Thorsons, 2001.

Cairns-Smith, A.G. *Evolving the Mind: On the Nature of Matter and the Origin of Consciousness.* Cambridge, UK: Cambridge University Press, 1998.

Capra, Fritjof. *The Turning Point: Science, Society, and the Rising Culture.* New York, NY: Bantam, 1984.

Chopra, Ananda S. "Ayurveda," from *Medicine Across Cultures: History and Practice of Medicine in Non-western Cultures*, edited by Helaine Selin and Hugh Shapiro. Norwell, MA: Kluwer Academic Publishers, 2003.

Clayton, Donald. *Handbook of Isotopes in the Cosmos: Hydrogen to Gallium.* Cambridge, UK: Cambridge University Press, 2003.

Darling, David. *Life Everywhere: The Maverick Science of Astrobiology.* New York, NY: Basic Books, 2002.

Darling, David. *Zen Physics: The Science of Death, The Logic of Reincarnation.* New York, NY: HarperCollins Publishers, 1996.

Dawkins, Richard. *The Extended Phenotype: The Long Reach of the Gene.* Revised edition. New York, NY: Oxford University Press, 1999.

Dawkins, Richard. *The Ancestor's Tale: A Pilgrimage to the Dawn of Evolution.* New York, NY: Houghton Mifflin, 2004.

Diggha Nikaya, Sutta 16. *Mahaparinibbana Sutta.* Website: accesstoinsight.org.

DiSalle, Robert. "Space and Time: Inertial Frames," *Stanford Encyclopedia of Philosophy.* Posted online March 2002. Website: plato.stanford.edu/entries/spacetime-iframes.

Empedocles. "On Nature," *Stanford Encyclopedia of Philosophy.* Website: plato.stanford.edu/entries/empedocles/#1.

Eysenck, Hans J. *Intelligence: A New Look.* New Brunswick, NJ: Transaction Publishers, 1998.

Fischer, Louis. *Gandhi: His Life and Message for the World.* Denver, CO: Mentor Books, 1954.

Frady, Marshall. *Martin Luther King, Jr.: A Life.* New York, NY: Viking Penguin, 2002.

Furr, R. Michael and Bacharach, Verne R. *Psychometrics: An Introduction.* Thousand Oaks, CA: Sage Publications, 2008.

Gardner, Howard. *Intelligence Reframed: Multiple Intelligences for the 21st Century.* New York, NY: Basic Books, 2000.

Garrison, Fielding H. *An Introduction to the History of Medicine: With Medical Chronology, Suggestions for Study, and Bibliographic Data.* Fourth edition. Philadelphia, PA: W.B. Saunders and Company, 1967.

Goldman, Jonathan. The Healing Sounds website: healingsounds.com.

Goleman, Daniel. *Emotional Intelligence: Why It Can Matter More Than IQ.* New York, NY: Bantam Books, 1995.

Greene, Brian. *The Elegant Universe: Superstrings, Hidden Dimensions, and the Quest for the Ultimate Theory.* New York, NY: W.W. Norton & Company, 2003.

Greene, Brian. *The Fabric of the Cosmos: Space, Time, and the Texture of Reality.* New York, NY: Alfred A. Knopf, 2004.

Greenspan, Stanley I. *The Development of the Ego: Implications for Personality Theory, Psychopathology, and the Psychotherapeutic Process.* Madison, CT: International Universities Press, 1990.

Greenspan, Stanley I. *The Essential Partnership: How Parents and Children Can Meet the Emotional Challenges of Infancy and Childhood.* New York, NY: Viking, 1989.

Griffiths, David J. *Introduction to Elementary Particles.* New York, NY: John Wiley & Sons, 1987.

Griffiths, David J. *Introduction to Quantum Mechanics.* Second edition. Upper Saddle River, NJ: Benjamin Cummings, 2004.

Heslewood, Juliet. *Earth, Air, Fire, and Water.* New York, NY: Oxford University Press, 1989.

Hertzig, Margaret E., M.D., and Farber, Ellen A., Ph.D., editors. *Annual Progress in Child Psychiatry and Child Development 1997*. New York, NY: Routledge, 1998.
Iannone, A. Pablo. *Dictionary of World Philosophy*. New York, NY: Routledge, 2001.
Imamura, James N. "Newton and Einstein," online article (accessed December 2008). University of Oregon Website: zebu.uoregon.edu/~imamura/talks/gravity_waves/newton.html.
Isaccson, Walter. *Einstein: His Life and Universe*. New York, NY: Simon and Schuster, 2007.
Kaku, Michio. *Physics of the Impossible: A Scientific Exploration into the World of Phasers, Force Fields, Teleportation, and Time Travel*. New York, NY: Doubleday, 2008.
King, David B. The Spiritual Intelligence Project Website: dbking.net/spiritualintelligence.
Kurzweil, Ray. *The Age of Spiritual Machines: When Computers Exceed Human Intelligence*. New York, NY: Viking, 1999.
Kurzweil, Ray. *The Singularity Is Near: When Humans Transcend Biology*. New York, NY: Viking Penguin, 2005.
Locke, Edwin A. "Why Emotional Intelligence Is an Invalid Concept," *Journal of Organizational Behavior*, vol. 26, no. 4 (April 2005): pp. 425-31.
Majjhima Nikaya, Sutta 90. *Kannakatthala Sutta*. Website: accesstoinsight.org.
Mayer, John D., Roberts, Richard D., and Barsade, Sigal G. "Human Abilities: Emotional Intelligence," *Annual Reviews of Psychology*, vol. 59 (January 2008): pp. 507-536.
Merriam-Webster Online Dictionary. Website: merriam-webster.com.
Miyamoto, Musashi, *A Book of Five Rings*. Website: miyamotomusashi.com/gorin.htm.
Nanamoli, Bhikkhu, *The Life of the Buddha: According to the Pali Canon*. Onaslaska, WA: Pariyatti Publishing, 2001.
Nanamoli, Bhikkhu. *Visuddhimagga: The Path of Purification*. Onaslaska, WA: Pariyatti Publications, 1999.

Neisser, Ulric, Boodoo, Gwyneth, Bouchard, Thomas J., Jr., Boykin, A. Wade, Brody, Nathan, Ceci, Stephen J., Halpern, Diane F., Loehlin, John C., Perloff, Robert, Sternberg, Robert J., Urbina, Susana. "Intelligence: Knowns and Unknowns," *American Psychologist*, vol. 51, no. 2 (February 1996): pp. 77-101.

Noble, Kathleen D. "Spiritual Intelligence: A New Frame of Mind," *Advanced Development Journal*, vol. 9 (2000): pp. 1-29.

Noble, Kathleen D. "Spiritual Intelligence: Global Perspectives," Consciousness Research Abstracts, *Journal of Consciousness Studies*, vol. 376 (2000).

Noble, Kathleen D. *Riding the Windhorse: Spiritual Intelligence and the Growth of the Self.* Cresskill, N.J.: Hampton Press, 2001.

O'Reilly, Deirdre, M.D. "Fetal Development," *MedlinePlus Medical Encyclopedia* (updated October 2007). U.S. National Library of Medicine and Public Health Website: www.nlm.nih.gov/medlineplus/ency/article/002398.htm.

Payne, Wayne L. "A Study of Emotion: Developing Emotional Intelligence," a 1985 doctoral thesis, The Union Institute. Website: eqi.org/payne.htm.

Penrose, Roger. *The Emperor's New Mind: Concerning Computers, Minds, and the Laws of Physics.* New York, NY: Oxford University Press, 1989.

Penrose, Roger. *Shadows of the Mind: A Search for the Missing Science of Consciousness.* New York, NY: Oxford University Press, 1994.

Penrose, Roger. *The Road to Reality: A Complete Guide to the Laws of the Universe.* New York, NY: Alfred A. Knopf, 2005.

Plucker, J. A. (Ed.). "Human Intelligence: Historical Influences, Current Controversies, Teaching Resources" (2003). Retrieved October 2008 from indiana.edu/~intell/.

Potter, Karl H., editor. *Indian Metaphysics and Epistemology: The Tradition of Nyaya-Vaisesika Up to Gangesa.* Princeton, NJ: Princeton University Press 1978.

Rae, Alastair. *Quantum Physics: Illusion or Reality?* Cambridge, UK: Cambridge University Press, 1984.

Ridley, Matt. *Genome: The Autobiography of Species in 23 Chapters.* New York, NY: HarperCollins Publishers, 2000.

Roche, Geshe Michael and McNally, Christie. *The Essential Yoga Sutra: Ancient Wisdom for Your Yoga.* New York, NY: Three Leaves Press, 2005.

Russell, Dale A. "Speculations on the Evolution of Intelligence in Multicellular Organisms," a paper presented at the Life in the Universe Conference held at National Ames Research Center in Moffet Field, California (June 19–20, 1979). Website: history.nasa.gov/CP-2156/ch4.3.htm.

Schwarz, Patricia. The Official String Theory Website: superstringtheory.com.

Searle, John R. *Mind: A Brief Introduction.* New York, NY: Oxford University Press, 2004.

Sussman, Gerald Jay and Wisdom, Jack with Mayer, Meinhard E. *Structures and Interpretation of Classical Mechanics.* Cambridge, MA: The MIT Press, 2001.

Sukys, Paul. *Lifting the Scientific Veil: Science Appreciation for the Nonscientist.* Lanham, MD: Ardsley House Publishers, 1999.

Svoboda, Robert. *Ayurveda: Life, Health, and Longevity.* Albuquerque, NM: The
Ayurvedic Press, 2004.

Thomas, Edward J. *The Life of Buddha as Legend and History.* New Delhi, India: Motilal Banarsidass Publishers, 1993.

Thorndike, R.K. "Intelligence and Its Uses," *Harper's Magazine*, vol. 140 (1920): pp.227-335.

Tucker, Jim B. *Life Before Life: A Scientific Investigation of Children's Memories of Previous Lives.* New York, NY: St. Martin's Press, 2005.

The Vipassana Meditation Website: dhamma.org.

Weinberg, Steven. *Dreams of a Final Theory: The Scientist's Search for the Ultimate Laws of Nature.* New York, NY: Pantheon, 1993.

BIBLIOGRAPHY

Weiss, Achim. "Big Bang Nucleosynthesis: Cooking up the First Light Elements," online article (updated April 2006). Einstein Online Website: einstein-online.info/en/spotlights/BBN/index.html

Wright, Edward L. "Big Bang Nucleosynthesis," online article (2002–2004). Website: astro.ucla.edu/~wright/BBNS.html.

Zohar, Danah and Marshall, Ian. *Spiritual Intelligence: the Ultimate Intelligence.* London, UK: Bloomsbury Publishing, 1999.

Zohar, Danah and Marshall, Ian. *Spiritual Capital: Wealth We Can Live By.* San Francisco, CA: Berrett-Koehler Publishers, 2004.

* * *

Index

absolute, 49, 50, 85, 135-36, 152, 283-84
absorption, 56, 106, 147, 177
abstinence, 198, 211, 247-49
addiction, 179, 221, 275-76, 314
addiction-free, 303
affliction-free, 303
aggression, 194
agnosticism, 202
air, 34-35, 43, 108, 111, 121-23, 148, 292, 308, 335, 401
Akash, 136
alpha wave rhythm, 293
AM modulation, 33
AM/FM receiver, 33
Ancient Greeks, 123-24
anger, 40, 73, 92, 94, 107, 156, 165, 190, 207, 212-13, 241-44, 250-51, 312-13, 336, 343-44, 347-54, 356, 361
animosity, 176, 190, 241, 251, 353
anti-corruption, 250
anti-materialism, 120, 139
apathy, 189, 191, 195, 232, 235, 362
appreciative joy, 245, 357
Aristotle, 124
aromatherapy, 292
artificial intelligence (AI), 87
asceticism, 211, 213
Atma, 147
atom, 121, 125-26, 131-32, 407
attachment, 13-14, 50, 89, 138, 161, 182, 187, 200, 210, 224-25, 233, 311, 321
attention span, 295

austerity, 265-66, 278-79, 394
autonomous functions, 309
avarice, 205-06, 269
aversion, 45-6, 65, 109-10, 113-14, 163-66, 190-91, 198, 204-05, 221, 229, 245, 310, 343-44, 359
awareness, 4, 6, 19, 50, 56, 102, 110-11, 162, 204-05, 213-14, 216-18, 234, 325-33, 337-39
Ayurveda, 124
balance, 181, 194, 222, 229, 312, 323
bare desire, 181-84, 206
being, 19, 50, 71, 85, 152, 200, 276, 406
belief, 50-51, 223-25, 406
benevolence, 208
Berger, Hans, 93, 400
Big Bang Observer, 129
Big Bang, 87, 134, 136-37, 399, 417
biofeedback, 97-98
birth, 81, 144, 147, 404
blind devotion, 224
blind faith, 200
bliss, 176, 319, 330, 359, 361, 364
  liberating, 338
  momentary, 326-28
  pervading, 328-30
  showering, 328
  uplifting, 328-29
blood, 33, 130, 132-33
bodily-intimation, 36-37, 138

body, 11-14, 16, 61, 89, 111, 119-20, 124, 130, 132-33, 139, 146, 167, 211, 217, 257, 274-75, 288-91, 303-20, 327-28, 330
Bohr, Niels, 78, 396
Boltzmann, Ludwig, 93, 399
bones, 34, 130, 309, 335
boredom, 110, 204-05, 222, 228, 245, 253
boundless space, 200
Brahman, 196-97
brain, 32-35, 61, 83, 87-88, 133, 148, 404-05
breath, 34, 106-13, 216-17, 315-18, 325-28, 330, 335
breath awareness, 107-12, 316, 325
breathing, 61, 106, 111, 289, 296, 315, 325
breath-taker, 111, 217
British empire, 252
Buddha, 5, 24, 124, 240, 355, 363, 365, 396, 408, 414, 416
Buzan, Tony, 84, 399, 412
calm, 177, 181, 218, 227
cancer, 92, 179, 314
carbohydrates, 130
carbon, 24, 64, 130-31, 316, 399
carbon dioxide, 64, 316
carefreeness, 212
catalyst, 303
cause, 14, 19, 49, 134-36
cause-effect, 102, 280, 364

INDEX

celibacy, 180, 405
cell, 121, 133, 403
chance, 78-80
chemistry, 153-54
choice, 72-74, 80, 150, 169
choice maker, 72, 74, 80, 150, 169
classical mechanics, 58, 78-9, 396-97
clear comprehension, 111-12, 143
coarseness of mind, 325-26
cognitive process, 28-29, 148-51
color, 124-25
coma, 29, 146, 170
comfort zone, 311
compassion, 243-46, 283, 342, 353-61
competitiveness, 198
computational agents, 83
computer, 33, 44, 61, 83, 93, 175, 305
conceit, 195-97, 200
concentration, 99, 177-78, 184, 218-19, 220-22, 325-30
concept, 41, 43, 48, 50
conception, 32, 144, 147
conceptual proliferation, 201
concrete matter, 137, 403
conditionality, 71, 85, 102-03, 135, 201, 309
consciousness, 11-30, 49, 85-86, 132-33, 141-43, 151-52, 301, 331-32, 360-62
  all-pervading, 196
  ballet of, 152
  birth, 144
  blissful conscious, 362
  body, 143
  classification of, 146
  death, 144
  definition of, 11-30
  deluded, 142
  determining, 145
  dynamics of, 148
  ear, 15, 31, 143
  eternal, 21
  eye, 19, 143
  father, 21
  functional, 19, 31, 144
  greedy, 142
  hateful, 142
  investigating, 144
  love, 240-41
  mind, 120, 128
  mind-enabling, 144
  mother, 21
  non-deluded, 143
  non-greedy, 143
  non-hateful, 143
  nose, 143, 148
  pure, 54-55, 91, 197, 229
  receiving, 143
  registering, 144
  resultant, 19, 143
  sense-enabling, 31, 144
  source of, 33
  tongue, 31, 143
  types of, 20-21, 141

the ultimate reality, 17
universal, 21
unwholesome, 19-20, 65, 142
wholesome, 19-20, 65, 142
conservation, 273, 397
contact, 157-58, 184, 331-32
contemplation, 162, 174-77, 214, 275, 334-37
contentment, 143, 190, 276-78, 288-89, 324
control, 110, 167, 183, 229, 233, 309, 336
core of nothingness, 257
corruption, 195, 212, 223, 250, 269-71
craving, 46, 68, 110, 160, 164, 166, 181, 187-191, 191, 215, 229, 233, 244, 275, 339
creation, 81, 133-135, 150, 405
cultism, 263
dark energy, 134
Darwin, Charles, 83
death, 55, 71, 81, 139, 144, 147, 179, 201, 252, 363, 396, 404
Deep Blue, 83, 88
delusion, 21, 23, 44, 46-47, 68-69, 72-74, 142, 175, 188, 191-93, 206-208, 255, 352
denial, 230, 405
desire, 56, 74, 75, 181-83, 300, 329
destiny, 78-80
digestion, 132, 309

disability, 228
divine, 25, 231, 237, 239-46, 267, 281, 341, 352, 406
DNA, 133, 154
doshas, 124
doubt, 202-03, 220
ear sensitivity, 31, 132, 148
earth, 34-36, 43, 121-23, 136-37, 308-09, 335, 401
Eastman, George, 93, 400
ecstasy, 176, 190, 322
EEG machine, 93
effectiveness, 228, 304
efficacy, 63, 71, 228
effortlessness, 69, 283, 307
ego, 13-14, 18-19, 40, 46-47, 51, 55, 69, 72, 80, 94, 99, 187-88, 190, 233, 250, 255, 259, 266-67, 283, 303, 311, 333-34
Einstein, Albert, 50, 58, 78, 93, 396-97, 403
elation, 176
electricity, 16
electromagnetic force, 61
electrons, 34, 58, 120-21, 125-26, 139, 396
elements, 9, 13-14, 25, 30, 86, 100, 137
  abstract material, 138
  classification of mental, 24
  concrete material, 138
  divine mental, 231, 241
  material, 20, 24, 33-37, 94, 120-39, 367

INDEX

mental, 20-29, 86, 141-45, 153-56, 383
noble mental, 247-53
of soul, 13-14, 16, 18, 40
root, 188, 190, 192, 237
special mental, 178, 183
ultimate root, 188, 191, 206, 210, 255
ultimate wholesome root, 237
universal mental, 28, 171
universal unwholesome, 207
unwholesome mental, 187, 207
unwholesome root, 192
wholesome mental, 209-10
wholesome root, 237
wise mental, 255-58
embezzlement, 271
embodiment, 176, 179, 215
emotion, 165-67, 312-13, 317, 352
emotional power, 313
Empedocles, 123, 402
emptiness, 54, 70, 297-98, 319, 328, 330-332
empty space, 137, 330
enchantment, 296, 299
energy, 61-64, 121, 180, 194, 199, 293, 407
enlightened master, 5, 55, 147, 163, 226, 232, 396, 408
enlightenment, 6, 9, 40, 49, 53-56, 178, 192, 195, 227, 248, 259, 363-65, 394, 408
entertainment, 45, 205, 278-79, 293, 295, 323
enthusiasm, 182, 235, 344
entity, 17, 19, 23, 30, 44, 49-50, 70-71, 362
entrainment, 295-96, 408
entropy, 119, 400
envy, 198, 245, 356-57
EQ (see intelligence)
equality complex, 196-97, 406
equanimity, 90, 92-94, 100, 103, 110, 159, 161, 217, 228-33, 235, 242-43, 251, 281, 300, 303, 311, 314, 319-20, 323, 334, 341, 352, 357
eternal, 21, 71, 147, 151, 200
ether, 136
ethical force, 60, 88, 169
ethics, 169
evil, 189, 191, 343, 353
evolution, 61, 68, 81, 83, 87-88, 99, 189, 359
exhalation, 107, 315-18, 328
existence, 13, 17, 42, 46, 55, 71, 125, 146
experiential physics, 58
experiential reality, 123
extravagance, 272
extremism, 200, 222, 225
eye, 15, 31, 143, 148
Eysenck, Hans, 84, 412
faculty, 226
faith, 51-52, 222-23, 283, 406
fanaticism, 200, 225

fasting, 180, 278, 405
fate, 78-80
fear, 66, 107, 155, 180, 312, 354
feeling, 21-23, 28, 87-92, 98,
    158-65, 171, 335-36, 396
  neither pleasant nor
    unpleasant, 159, 161-62
  neutral, 159, 161-62, 234
  physiological, 160-61, 163,
    274, 291
  psychological, 160-61
  pleasant, 289, 291-92, 311, 345
  unpleasant, 28, 92, 159, 163,
    206, 232
fetus, 32
fight-or-flight response, 252
fire, 23, 34, 40, 123, 138, 148,
    401
first cause, 49, 135-36
five sense types, 143, 149
flavors, 31, 289
flexibility, 228, 237, 283, 308
flow, 17, 19, 21, 71, 146-47, 170,
    212, 304
flux, 17, 120, 138
FM modulation, 33
focus, 103, 177, 218
fondness, 242, 244
forbearance, 143, 191
force, 58-68, 70-71, 86, 132,
    147, 169, 397, 399
forgiveness, 99, 284, 347, 352
frames of mind, 113
future, 48, 71

galaxy, 129
Gandhi, Mahatma, 252, 413
Gardner, Howard, 82-84,
    398-99
general intelligence factor, 82
general relativity, 137, 397, 403
generosity, 59, 65, 143, 206, 209,
    212, 270
genetics, 133, 365, 403
gladness, 231-32, 245-46,
    356-57, 359-60
glory, 360
god, 49-51, 99, 129, 135, 200,
    223-25, 283
godly beings, 239
Goleman, Daniel, 83, 398
grace, 223, 237
grand unifying force, 62
gravity, 60, 85, 127-29, 137, 147,
    397, 402
greed, 21-23, 28-29, 65, 67, 100,
    103, 107, 142, 160, 166,
    187-97, 206-08, 266
Greenspan, Stanley, 83, 398
gurus, 101
happiness, 160, 176-77, 211,
    322, 361
Harvard University, 82-84, 398
hatred, 21-23, 28, 40, 47, 64, 67,
    100, 103, 155, 160, 168,
    188, 190-91, 193, 212-13,
    342, 353
healing, 77, 290-93, 299, 408
health, 6, 275, 292, 307

heart, 31-34, 56, 132-33, 147, 149, 341, 354, 408
heat, 40, 48, 70, 103, 105, 123, 233, 243, 335
heaven, 51, 223, 341
helium, 131, 171
hell, 341
Himalayas, 124
Hindu, 44, 124, 147
Hippocrates, 124
Hitler, Adolph, 42
holocaust, 42
holy, 191, 242
holy grail, 81
humors, 124
hydrocarbon, 131
hydrogen, 13, 24, 39, 87, 126, 130-32, 134, 171, 399
I-atom, 130-33
ignorance, 14, 17, 35, 40, 47, 189, 191, 193, 255-57
ill will, 189-90, 244, 344
illusion, 13, 17, 48, 71, 94, 136, 176, 255
imbalance, 124, 274, 312
immodesty, 195, 223
immorality, 195, 222
impartiality, 225, 283, 359
impatience, 142, 194
imperfection, 14, 180, 192, 200, 202
impermanence, 48, 90, 103, 138-39, 197, 216-17, 226, 288, 364, 394
impersonality, 138-39, 196, 408
imprisonment, 44, 67-68, 247, 354
impropriety, 195, 223
impulse, 73, 150
inclination, 181-82, 206
indifference, 142, 162, 231-32, 235, 362
Indus valley, 124
inertia, 308-09
inferiority complex, 196
infinity, 330-33
inhalation, 315-17
injustice, 250, 282
intellect, 14, 44, 50-52, 55, 86, 93, 205
intelligence, 14, 19, 82-86, 98-100, 114, 128
  artificial, 87
  definition of, 284
  emotional (EQ), 6, 83, 88, 398
  existential, 84
  general (IQ), 82
  higher levels of, 88, 100, 105, 266, 342
  ladder of, 94, 113, 278
  perfect, 6, 14, 47, 50, 56, 95, 139, 162, 175, 190-91, 196-97, 219-20, 235, 258, 282, 334, 339
  primitive element of, 87
  redefining, 85
  social, 83

soul, 6, 81-82, 84-86, 89-90,
    92-94, 98, 100, 104, 112,
    299, 342, 397
  spiritual (SQ), 6, 81, 83-85,
    91, 342
  types of, 86, 88-91
  what is, 82-86
intelligent
  attitude, 263
  breathing, 315
  eating, 288
  exercising, 307
  hearing, 293
  heart, 341
  seeing, 296
  smelling, 292
  touching, 290
intention, 181-82, 288, 291-94,
    304-05, 308, 317, 335
intoxicants, 221, 251, 274-75
introspection, 98
intuition, 84
IQ test, 82-83, 93, 398
jealousy, 198, 245, 356-57,
    359
Jesus, 99, 239-40, 347, 355
joy, 12, 48, 78, 143, 162-63, 176,
    190, 214, 234, 245, 322,
    336, 345, 356
Kalapa, 124
karma, 59-79, 213, 224,
    282-84, 346-47, 358
karmic force, 169
karmic retribution, 164

Kasparov, Gary, 83
kindness, 59, 66, 239-40, 341, 357
King, David, 84
knowingness, 156, 170
knowledge, 17-18, 34, 56, 89,
    91, 94, 142, 162, 217,
    364-65
Laser Interferometer (LIGO), 129
laws of karma, 65-72, 282-84
lethargy, 155, 203, 228
life, 29, 61, 81, 132, 146, 170,
    322, 339
life continuum, 146
light, 17, 47, 147, 170, 256, 407
lightness, 138, 227, 283, 312,
    319, 327
lipids, 130
living matter, 130-34
Locke, Edwin, 84
logic, 83, 87, 93, 288, 322
love, 59, 88, 94, 240-46,
    341-46, 348, 356-57,
    359-62
  consciousness, 239-40
  fall in, 357
  four elements of, 342, 359-60
  heart full of, 341
  rise in, 357
  romantic, 242
loving-kindness, 239-45
luck, 78-80
lust, 73, 94, 107, 165, 180-81,
    187-88, 271-72, 298,
    312-13, 316

INDEX

lying, 195, 212, 247, 251, 268-69
madness, 196
magic, 296, 298
Mahabhutas, 124
male, 132
mango, 18, 65-66
King, Martin Luther, Jr., 252
martyrdom, 200
masked enemies, 242
mass, 34, 119-20, 123, 137, 399, 407
material, 11-12, 15, 31, 361, 404
  base, 31-32, 145
  elements, 20, 33-37, 130-34, 308, 367
  life, 130
  phenomenon, 12, 21, 120, 123, 130
  universe, 282
  voidness, 137
materialism, 84, 120, 139, 226
materiality-mentality, 257
matrix, 44-45
matter, 12-13, 15-17, 24, 30-35, 40, 51, 62, 119-128, 130-38, 146, 160, 169, 331-32, 361-62
  abstract, 136, 138
  attributes of, 138
  concrete, 137
  non-concrete, 137
  inorganic, 15, 153
  living matter, 130-34
  non-organic, 15-16, 31
  organic, 15-16, 31
  origin of, 133, 135
  smallest recognizable unit of, 124, 130
  subtle, 31
  subtle-heart, 132
  types of, 15
  ultimate building blocks of, 33, 119
maturity, 205
maya, 43-47
Mcginn, Colin, 88
meanness, 205, 244-45, 353-56
mechanics, 20, 57-58
meditation, 24, 65, 74, 98, 175, 189, 204-05, 219, 226, 230, 257, 266, 278, 325
  definition of, 98
  for cultivating compassion, 353-55
  for cultivating gladness, 356-57
  for cultivating loving-kindness, 342-52
  for cultivating oneness, 357-59
  for developing breath awareness, 108-12
  for developing austerity, 279
  for developing contentment, 277
  for developing non-indulgence, 273
  for developing non-stealing, 270
  for developing non-violence, 267

for developing physical purity, 275
for developing self-study, 280
for developing sexual piety, 271
for developing surrender, 282
for developing truthfulness, 269
for experiencing infinity and soul, 330, 339
for experiencing zero, 325-330
for intelligent breathing, 315-19
for intelligent eating, 288-90
for intelligent exercising, 307-310
for intelligent hearing, 293-96
for intelligent seeing, 296-99
for intelligent smelling, 292-93
for intelligent touching, 290-92
for intelligent work habits, 304-07
for managing emotions and addictions, 312-315
for pain management, 310-11
for transcending, 321-24
lifestyle of, 104
object of, 107, 110
soul, 97-102, 104
meditativity, 73-74, 77, 104, 108, 194, 198, 205, 266, 309
memory, 18, 82, 89, 147, 168, 215, 311
mental phenomenon, 12, 21, 26-27, 65, 85
absorption, 184
energy, 181
force, 60-61
life, 28-29, 170, 322
power, 177-78, 180-81, 185, 219-21
refinement, 155
rigidity, 200-01
rust, 201
unhealthiness, 228
weaknesses, 220-21
metabolism, 132
microscope, 15, 31, 82, 121, 218
middle way, 78, 229, 394
mid-life crisis, 77, 253
mind, 11-17, 19, 21, 24, 30, 33, 47, 49, 55, 64-66, 86, 99, 113, 120, 136-37, 146, 148, 153-56, 156, 189, 209, 211-13, 218-24, 227, 229, 232, 235, 256-57, 266, 277, 279, 316-17, 319, 321-26, 329-30, 332-39
divine, 25, 239-40, 242-43, 406
noble, 25, 247-51
primordial, 171
special, 173-76, 178, 180-85
sensitivity, 31-33, 132, 148
ultimate building blocks of, 21, 25, 153
universal, 25, 90, 157, 170, 405
unwholesome, 25, 90-91, 187-88, 206

wholesome, 25, 90, 191, 209-10, 215
wise, 25, 255-56
mindfulness, 73, 77, 99-104, 112, 161, 163-64, 170, 177-78, 181, 213-22, 294-95, 297-98, 310, 312, 344, 349, 402
MIT, 84
moderation, 105, 272-73, 323, 394
moods, 110, 214, 230
Moore's Law, 83
moral recklessness, 23, 188, 195, 207-08
morality, 195, 207, 223, 266
motion, 34, 59, 61, 63, 85, 123, 128, 133
motivation, 183
multiple intelligences, 83-84
mythology, 201
narcissism, 196
natural breath, 107, 109-10
negativity, 142, 200, 295
neither perception nor non-perception, 234, 332-33
neither pleasure nor pain, 232, 234
nervous system, 133
Newton, Isaac, 78, 136, 396-97
Newtonian mechanics, 58, 84, 396
nirvana, 6, 55, 395-96
nirvanic peace, 334

nitrogen, 130, 399
Nobel Prize, 93
nobility, 247-48, 250, 252
noble action, 249, 251
Noble, Kathleen, 84
noble ones, 248, 250, 252
noble speech, 247, 251-52
noble vocation, 252-53
non-attachment, 162, 210, 212, 235, 283, 322, 324
non-being, 55
non-belief, 202
non-believer, 50
non-concrete matter, 137
non-delusion, 73, 91, 103, 141, 181, 193, 210-11, 255-59, 266
non-distraction, 194
non-existence, 55, 187, 197, 331-32
non-faith, 202
non-greed, 74, 90, 154, 174, 181, 209-213, 234, 236, 266, 271, 273
non-hatred, 23, 74, 90, 142
non-indulgence, 265, 272-73
non-matter, 331
non-meanness, 244-45, 354
non-perception, 234, 332-33
non-reaction, 73, 99-101, 103, 112, 114, 163-65, 291, 295, 298, 319, 407
non-reality, 40-43, 46-51
  definition of, 41
  test of, 43

non-relative, 283
non-resistance, 283
non-self, 94, 103, 139, 226, 258, 362, 364
non-stealing, 265, 270-71
non-striving, 69
non-violence, 267-68
nose sensitivity, 31, 132, 148
nostrils, 108-09, 216, 317, 325-26, 330
nothingness, 257, 331-32, 362
not-ness, 331
nourishment, 73, 288-89
nuclear fusion, 131
nuclear power, 259
nucleic acids, 130
nucleogenesis, 131, 399
nucleosynthesis, 131, 399
nutriment, 125, 132-35
OM, 98, 129, 407
oneness, 54, 84, 143, 271-72, 324, 341-42, 357, 361
out-breath, 111, 317, 327, 335
out-of-body experience (OBE), 408
oxygen, 13, 24, 39, 126, 130-31, 399
pain, 14, 109, 138-39, 158-63, 180, 229-30, 278, 303, 344-45, 354
pain control, 229, 311
pain management, 233, 310
pain-pleasure management, 229
pain-transcendent, 303, 310

parinirvana, 55, 396
particle accelerators, 123, 134
past, 48, 71, 89, 102, 150
patience, 143, 191
Payne, Wayne, 83, 398
peace, 5, 51, 65, 143, 230, 234, 245, 259, 267, 293, 296, 299, 334, 344-45, 354-55
Penrose, Roger, 88, 404
perception, 14, 18, 22, 28, 167-68, 171, 235, 257, 331-34, 396
perfect accounting system, 66, 80
perfect intelligence (see intelligence)
perfect life, 342
perfection, 6, 14, 39, 56, 69-70, 74, 91, 177-78, 189, 197, 219-20, 227, 256, 258, 266, 269, 303, 406
periodic table, 24, 39, 87, 120, 131, 153, 171
personal affection, 242
personal power, 194
perversion, 201
pessimism, 93, 200
phenomenality, 201
phenomenon, 12, 14, 19, 30
philosophy, 120, 124, 395, 402-03, 412
physics, 58, 62, 78, 88, 129, 134, 153, 364

INDEX

pity, 298, 361
planets, 58, 61, 396
Plato, 124, 402-03, 412
pleasant looks, 213
pleasantness, 103, 109, 143,
    161-63, 245, 287
pleasure control, 229
pliability, 138, 228
portal of healing, 290
potentiality, 62, 64, 146
poverty, 211-12, 230, 271
prayer, 99, 101, 130, 354
presence of mind, 17, 102, 213
present-moment awareness, 177,
    218
peer pressure, 45
pride, 42, 65, 195-96, 207-08,
    229, 308
probability, 64, 78-79, 83
process of cognition, 21, 23,
    28-29, 150
production, 138
proteins, 130
providence, 78
psychometrics, 82, 398
pure awareness, 6, 50, 90, 112,
    217, 259, 338
pure learning, 263
pure understanding, 54-55, 77,
    85, 143, 258
purification, 99, 201, 263
purpose of life, 75, 78
quantum mechanics, 9, 57-58,
    78-79, 85, 125, 128, 396

quarks, 120, 126, 139, 400
radio waves, 31-33
rapture, 162, 176-77, 184, 220,
    318-19, 322, 326
reality, 13, 17, 39-46, 49, 85,
    127, 191, 395
    conditional, 40, 146
    definition of, 39-40
    test of, 42-43
    ultimate, 17-18, 23, 34, 40, 47,
        50, 120, 122, 156, 200
    unconditional, 53-55
realization, 11, 46, 62, 77, 362
receiver, 31-33
recognition, 250
rectitude, 229, 237
refinement, 165, 221, 311
refinement of pain, 163
reflection, 98, 329, 358
refreshment, 176
regrets, 221
reincarnation, 81
relaxation, 97-98
religious rites, 200
relinquishment, 324, 337-38
remorse, 198-99, 221, 344
renunciation, 143, 183, 230, 235,
    324, 329
resentment, 190, 229-30, 241-42,
    343-44
resolution, 178-79, 184, 211,
    213, 311, 313
restlessness, 188, 193-94, 207,
    218, 220-21

Restless-O-Meter, 194
revenge, 178, 354
reverence, 65, 223
right doing, 66, 198
right-force, 183
Rishis, 248
rituals, 76, 200-01, 224, 288
RNA, 130, 154
robots, 83, 88
Rutgers University, 88
sacredness, 292
sadness, 12, 110, 243
safe haven, 107, 222
safety, 344-45, 349
saint, 191
sainthood, 143
saliva, 148
sanctity, 292, 299
sand, 101-02
Searle, John, 88, 399, 404
self, 4, 14, 40, 47-48, 55-56, 68-69, 71, 84-85, 89-90, 94, 103, 142, 167, 171, 176, 180, 191, 195-97, 199-203, 241, 256-58, 276, 338, 352
self-annihilation, 68
self-centered, 74, 212, 241
self-centeredness, 196
self-control, 183, 229
self-defense, 250, 252
self-esteem, 212, 221, 344
self-glorification, 196
self-identity, 78
self-importance, 196

self-improvement, 77, 204, 280
self-interest, 75, 182, 208, 210, 323
selfishness, 68, 142-43
selfless, 68-69, 91
self-mastery, 101
self-mortification, 251
self-realization, 77
self-respect, 195, 207, 222, 271
self-retreat, 325
self-sacrifice, 68, 213
self-study, 3, 265-66, 280-81
semantics, 88
sensitivity, 15, 31-33, 132-33, 148-49, 165, 298
sensual greed, 187
sensual matter, 132
sensuality, 183, 323, 331-32
sex, 187, 275, 300, 323
sexual matter, 132
sexual piety, 265, 271-72
sexual relationship, 271
shame, 169, 222-23, 228, 237, 271
shamelessness, 23, 188, 195, 207-08, 269-71
silence, 54, 77, 129, 204-05, 279, 293-94, 335-36, 408
simplicity, 273
sine frequencies, 33
sixth sense, 133
skepticism, 142, 175, 202
skillfulness, 228, 237
sloth, 155, 174, 193, 203-05, 220, 227, 272, 316

INDEX

slum, 230
smallest recognizable unit of matter, 121-25
smell, 31, 121, 125, 132, 148, 230, 292-93, 299
smile, 4, 111, 306, 349, 360
smoking, 179, 274-75, 312, 314-15
sociability, 143, 236, 295
social service, 182
Socrates, 124
soil, 34, 66, 123, 290, 401
Soul
   beyond, 9, 40, 53, 56, 396
   cognitive process of, 148
   elements of (see elements)
   first element of, 14
   genesis, 132
   individual, 59, 90
   intelligence (see intelligence)
   introduction, 7
   mechanics, 58, 60, 63-80, 88, 125, 127
   meditation (see meditation)
   model, 86
   realization, 6, 263
   second element of, 21
   third element of, 30
   what is, 11, 394
   what is not, 39, 395
soul mechanics, 58-79, 104, 125, 127-28, 282, 395, 404
   first law of, 65
   fourth law of, 70
   new scientific frontier, 58
   second law of, 66-67
   third law of, 68
Soul-atom, 124-30
sound element, 129-30
space, 49, 54, 69, 134, 136-37, 148, 200, 232, 235, 295-97, 305, 319, 330-31, 357, 361, 364, 403
space element, 137
spaceness, 330-31
space-time, 59, 61, 85, 136
spectrum, 112, 233
spirit, 84, 151, 183, 283, 407
spiritual, 19, 24, 33, 49-50, 52, 59, 94, 161, 175, 180, 195
   equanimity, 233-34
   evolution, 189-90, 192, 280, 347
   feet, 181, 217
   hands, 226
   image, 197
   intelligence (see intelligence)
   joy, 12, 111, 162-63, 176
   matter, 120
   sentiment, 263
   treasure, 227
   vehicle, 99
   vision, 30, 91-92
SQ (see Intelligence)
Standard Model, 125, 127, 402
stillness, 193, 237, 297-99
sting, 312-14

stinginess, 206
strength of character, 183
stress, 14, 45, 227, 237, 291-92, 323
String Theory, 126-27, 129, 400, 402
stupidity, 65, 353
subatomic particles, 61, 120-21, 125-26, 134
subconscious, 144, 146-50, 170
subtle-heart matter (see matter)
suffering, 14, 44, 46, 73, 100, 138, 142, 167, 170, 189, 192, 194, 243-45, 300, 339, 343-45, 353-55, 359, 364
superiority complex, 196
supersensitive, 232, 288-89, 299
superstition, 175, 189, 193, 199, 220, 225-26, 228, 334
suppression, 110, 313-14
surrender, 223, 265-66, 282-83, 324, 346
suspicion, 202-03, 220, 225-26, 344
syntax, 88
tai chi, 307
taste, 31, 121, 125, 132, 148, 232, 289, 300-01
telescope, 82, 218
temperature, 40, 128, 132-36
temptation, 179
Theory of Everything (TOE), 58, 127, 397

thinking, 15, 18, 21, 82, 88, 90, 99, 145, 170, 173-177, 183-84, 202, 318-19, 322, 325, 334
third eye, 82, 91
Thorndike, Edward, 83, 398
thoughtfulness, 174-77, 184, 203, 220, 319, 322, 326, 334
time, 48-49, 55, 71, 405
timelessness, 70
TOE (see Theory of Everything)
tongue sensitivity, 31, 132, 148
torpor, 155, 174, 193, 203-05, 220, 268, 309, 316
toxins, 275, 316
tranquility, 65, 106, 194, 199, 220-21, 227, 237, 242, 406
tranquilizer, 227
transcendence, 84, 165, 322, 324-25, 333
transience, 287
transmitter, 33
trans-sensual greed, 187
truthfulness, 268-69
Turing, Alan, 93, 404
ultimate, 14, 17-18, 23, 40, 47, 55, 91, 94
  beginning, 48-49
  being, 50
  building blocks, 6, 21, 25-27, 33-34, 36
  end, 48-49
uncertainty, 193, 202, 397

unconditional abstinence, 247-49
undercurrent of silence, 295
understanding, 91-92, 100, 167, 177, 258
universality, 43
universe, 58, 61-62, 78, 80, 122, 129, 134-36, 282, 295, 365, 399, 402
University of California at Berkley, 88
University of Oxford, 88
unmanifest, 64
unpleasantness, 102, 109, 159-66, 191, 310, 336
uranium, 119, 407
vacuum, 134
vanity, 65, 182, 195-96, 208, 308
vibrating string, 126-27, 129
vigor, 179-81, 184, 193, 204-05, 211, 220, 313
vision, 19, 30, 82, 91-92, 111-12, 217, 297, 364
vital energy, 179
vocal intimation, 138
voidness, 137, 331
volition, 15-16, 28-29, 59-70, 72-74, 148, 168, 266
volitional action, 59-62, 64, 70, 73, 150, 169
volitional energy, 61-64, 86, 133-36

volitional force, 60-66, 70-71, 73, 79, 86, 127-28, 130, 132, 147, 149-50, 169-170, 344
volitional formation, 64
volitional universe, 62
wakefulness, 111-12, 204, 217, 279, 339
water, 12-13, 17, 19, 23, 34-35, 41, 59, 62-63, 122-23, 126-27, 130-≈31, 148, 176, 209, 241, 275, 288, 305, 308, 333, 401-02
weightlessness, 328
whole-body awareness, 304, 306-08
will power, 168, 248, 313
wisdom, 47, 85, 91-92, 139, 143, 152, 162, 193, 214, 255-56, 351-52, 358, 364
wise attention, 73, 99-101, 103, 110-13, 193, 217, 232
wonder, 296, 298
worry, 198-99, 212, 220, 227, 269, 283, 344
wrongdoing, 66, 77, 198, 247-49, 251
yoga, 5, 307, 394, 405, 407
yogi, 99, 128
zero, 126, 136, 325, 328, 330
Zohar, Danah, 84, 399
zygote, 133

About the Author

Sam Adettiwar is a master's graduate of engineering from Auburn University, a successful entrepreneur, a practitioner of yoga and martial arts, a devout meditator, and a spiritual scientist. As the founder and director of Soul Research Institute, he is engaged in spiritual research, writing, and teaching. He currently lives in the foothills of the Rocky Mountains in Colorado with his wife and two children. For information on his awakening experience, research themes, cutting edge meditation techniques, and retreats, please visit soulresearchinstitute.org.

www.ingramcontent.com/pod-product-compliance
Lightning Source LLC
Chambersburg PA
CBHW022045160426
43198CB00008B/134